INTERNATIONAL LAW

Crimes Against Humanity

INTERNATIONAL LAW

CRIMES AGAINST HUMANITY

The Limits of Universal Jurisdiction in the Global South

NERGIS CANEFE

UNIVERSITY OF WALES PRESS
2021

www.uwp.co.uk

British Library CIP Data
A catalogue record for this book is available from the British Library.

ISBN 978-1-78683-702-8
eISBN 978-1-78683-703-5

Typeset by Marie Doherty
Printed by CPI Antony Rowe, Melksham, United Kingdom

This work is dedicated to Howard Adelman, an untiring mind with valour and a conscience with patience and wisdom – a mentor, friend, guide and pathfinder: 'hic manebimus optime!'

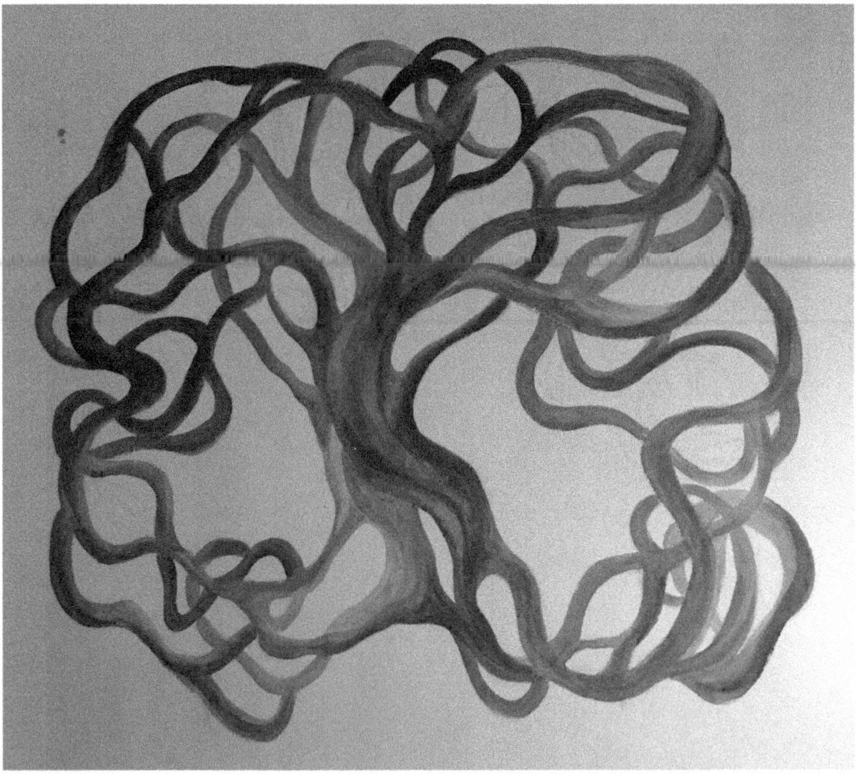

Tree of Life, by Nergis Canefe

Series Preface

The International Law series aims to give a platform to dynamic and cutting-edge research in international law, with a strong focus on legal theory in international law.

Nergis Canefe's *Crimes Against Humanity* is an ambitious scholarly project, which builds on an impressively broad range of scholarship to propose a fundamental rethinking of the role of universal jurisdiction in securing justice and accountability for the victims of egregious and systematic mass human rights violations. Firmly situated in the rich tradition of critical legal scholarship, Canefe's work is notable for its seamless fusion of theoretical and practical considerations.

This outstanding book is a very welcome addition to the International Law series. We continue to welcome proposals for books that bring new and exciting perspectives on diverse areas of international law.

Professor Diane Marie Amann
University of Georgia
Professor Yvonne McDermott
Swansea University

Contents

Acknowledgements

This work's completion spanned over a decade. At Osgoode Hall Law School, Toronto, Canada, I am truly indebted to Craig Scott, Leora Salter, Ruth Buchanan, the late Michael Mandel, Les Jacobs, Allan Hutchinson, Leslie Green, Sharry Aiken, Harry Arthurs, Amar Bhathia, Peer Zumbansen and Sonia Lawrence for their critical stance, superb guidance and scholarly advice.

At the non-Osgoode part of York University, I owe special thanks to colleagues and friends who encouraged me not to give up the 'project' despite illnesses and deaths in the family and my own trials and tribulations with cancer and all that comes with it. I am especially marked by the gentle and yet assuring hand of Brenda Spotton, Lorne Foster, Soren Frederiksen, David Mutimer, Elizabeth Dauphinee, Anna Agathangelou, Margo Baretto and Carolyn Cross. They became the pillars of strength and calm in an ever-changing tide of life circumstances, steadying my racing mind and bringing back focus and concentration whence memory and sense left me adrift.

I also benefited immensely from the scholarship and friendship of Ranabir Samaddar, Paula Banerjee and Nasreen Chowdhory in Calcutta, India; Galya Ben-Arieh in Evanston, USA; Roberto Lopez and Beatriz Sanchaz Mojica in Bogotà, Colombia; Loren Landau in South Africa; Chris Dolan in Kampala, Uganda; and Susan McGrath, Jennifer Hyndman and Michele Millard in Toronto, Canada, all of whom shared their wisdom and insights with me on state criminality and dimensions of human suffering gone unacknowledged. We worked together on various projects pertaining to ethical, socio-political and legal dimensions of transitional justice in the Global South throughout the past decade.

In Istanbul, Turkey, I would like to thank Galma Akdeniz, Seda Kalem, Seda Peker, Gökçe Çataloluk and Bilgi University Law School faculty and students at large for being a most welcoming and yet engagingly critical audience for many of my ideas at their reception. In particular, Turgut Tarhanlı has been both an inspiration and a true beacon of light despite many an unforgivable and unforgettable development in the region. As the long-standing Dean of Bilgi University Law School, he encouraged and actively supported me to mount my own courses on international criminal law, transitional justice, state criminality and comparative administrative law in Turkey. During my several short stays in Istanbul, teaching international law, I had a chance to share some of my findings with extremely courageous and well-read human rights lawyers who were doing their graduate degrees and I also owe them all such gratitude for thinking together, identifying key problem areas concerning the applications of international criminal law in the Global South, and on the rare occasion solving very difficult legal puzzles, at least for future purposes when they will be able to openly engage with these issues despite a genuine threat of incarceration. In particular, I would like to thank Zülfiye Yılmaz, Can Turgut, Özge Demir and Ezgi Çetiner.

As a special note in closing, I owe so much more than thanks to one particular person. I do not know where this work would have been today without the stern but always thoughtful and thorough interventions and, ultimately, guidance of Obiora Okafor. I could only hope that I succeeded in developing a deeper understanding of his commitment to TWAIL scholarship under his tutelage. I am ever so grateful that he took this mammoth project in his able hands and pushed it in the direction of taking the shape of a finite manuscript with inner coherence and contemporary applicability. All the failings and shortcomings of this work are no doubt mine.

While my Osgoode years robbed me of one big ideal and dream concerning mass human suffering, that is the possibility of reaching out to international criminal law as a panacea for deep-seated ills, it allowed me the space and tenacity to start thinking about what is really possible and workable on the ground while aspiring for a whole new sense of 'humanity'. This work allowed me to fulfil a vital demand on my own conscience: to develop an 'insider's' understanding how law works when all else fails, and the limits of what one could expect from it thereof. On that note, I sincerely hope my sons Josef Derya Canefe Wolanczyk and Ezra Witold Canefe Wolanczyk would continue this journey and establish new paths. It is to them and their generation that the onus falls for developing a much stronger sense of global responsibility, something our generation and the one before us tried but succeeded at only minimally. Finally, I owe a very special thanks to my colleague, writer and musician Jonathan Adjemian, who rendered such a layered and at times convoluted work accessible to the reader through his pristine sense of the totality of a work in its original version. I also wish to thank Hammna Iftikhar for the superb editing help she provided.

List of Acronyms

AFRC	Armed Forces Revolutionary Council
AUC	African Union Commission
BIAs	Bilateral Immunity Agreements
CAH	Crimes Against Humanity
CAHWCA	Crimes Against Humanity and War Crimes Act
CDF	Civil Defence Forces
CNDP	Congrès National pour la Défense du Peuple
DRC	Democratic Republic of Congo
EAC	Extraordinary African Chambers
ECCC	Extraordinary Chambers in the Courts of Cambodia
ECHR	European Court of Human Rights
FADRC	National Army of the DRC
FNI	Front National Intégrationiste
FRPI	Force de Résistance Patriotique en Ituri
FRY	Federal Republic of Yugoslavia
GoU	Government of Uganda
HRC	Human Rights Council
ICC	International Criminal Court
ICCPR	International Covenant on Civil and Political Rights
ICCT	International Criminal Courts and Tribunals
ICD	International Criminal Database
ICJ	International Court of Justice
ICL	International Criminal Law
ICTR	International Criminal Tribunal for Rwanda
ICTY	International Criminal Tribunal for the former Yugoslavia
IGAD	Intergovernmental Authority on Development
IHL	International Humanitarian Law
IHRL	International Human Rights Law

ILC	International Law Commission
IMT	International Military Tribunal
IR	International Relations
LRA	Lord's Resistance Army
MLC	Mouvement de Libération du Congo
MoU	Memorandum of Understanding
NGO	Non-Governmental Organizations
NHS	New Haven School
RUF	Revolutionary United Front
SCSL	Special Court for Sierra Leone
SNHR	Syrian Network for Human Rights
TWAIL	Third World Approaches to International Law
UN	United Nations
UNHCR	United Nations Refugee Agency
UPC	Union des Patriotes Congolais
WTO	World Trade Organization

Introduction

This work is an attempt to achieve an informed interpolation between ethics, politics and legal scholarship on the workings of international law, with specific reference to universal jurisdiction as it pertains to crimes against humanity. It posits that critical perspectives from the Global South, combined with a transnational understanding of international law and a committed inclusion of political judgment and collective responsibility for mass crimes, is needed to create a radically different framework for furthering the debate on both the normative underpinnings and procedural qualities of universal jurisdiction.

In this vein, the manuscript brings together three seemingly distinct areas of scholarly endeavour: jurisprudential debates on international criminal law, international law scholarship on the limits of state sovereignty, and applied political philosophy as it pertains to questions of responsibility and accountability in the context of mass political crimes and state criminality. This unique combination offers a compelling view of legal reasoning concerning accountability regimes in the Global South. Furthermore, it purports a critical analysis of the prescriptive norms and institutional maxims of modern international criminal law in the area of universal jurisdiction. It proposes, with courage and yet caution, that crimes against humanity jurisprudence could indeed advance values concerning the sanctity of human life at a global scale, as long as it is not regarded as a closed and rigid system leading to perpetual victimization of states and societies in the Global South.

There are sound reasons behind the current fascination with and heightened expectations from regimes of international legal accountability for state criminality since the end of the Cold War. We are faced with a steady increase in the volume of egregious crimes committed, condoned or initiated by states and state-heads, high-ranking officials, bureaucrats and soldiers, as well as non-state entities such as transnational corporations, though this latter category also owes its protected status to state action/inaction. The multiplication and spread of mass crimes committed by states or via states against their own citizens challenge our faith in domestic jurisprudence and clearly reveal its limited applicability to categories of crimes such as crimes against humanity. International jurisprudence on such crimes is increasingly seen as a panacea for the grave ills of the recalcitrant nation-state system by some, though not by all. The question remains as to whether we could curtail mass and orchestrated assaults on human dignity through international courts and dissemination of international criminal jurisprudence alone.

The ultimate aim of adjudicating the most egregious infractions of international human rights regime as well as humanitarian law is the dictum of 'never again'. And yet, this is not simply a matter of coming up with the most efficient strategies of codification to punish the protagonists of organized political violence. International criminal law strives to develop a shared understanding of, and golden standards for, acceptable behaviour for states and governments, their agencies and institutions. In the following pages, whether these efforts suffer from a dangerous institutional idealism harboured by traditional readings of public international law is carefully examined. A truthful appraisal of the complex amalgam of international criminal law and the dynamic processes of its globalization requires attention to be paid to the critical relations between core and periphery, the Global South and the centres of traditional international law, post-colonial societies and neocolonial powers. This is especially so concerning doctrinal developments in international criminal law pertaining to universal jurisdiction.

To this end, Chapter 1 attends to the emergence of a transnational regime of accountability in international law and re-evaluates the claim that, at least in principle, universal jurisdiction overrides private legal norms as far as certain types of state criminality are concerned. In this chapter, debates on legal pluralism and Third World Approaches to International Law (TWAIL) are utilized to redefine the concept of international law as transnational law within the context of globalization, with particular emphasis on the situational qualities of states and societies in the Global South. Subsequently, distinguishing features of current international accountability regimes and the mechanisms used by institutions such as the International Criminal Court (ICC) for the production of jurisdictional certainty under diverse circumstances are examined. The chapter concludes with a critical evaluation of universal jurisdiction both as a norm and as a practice. Using the premises of the third wave of legal pluralism and purporting a theory of reflexive transnational law, universal jurisdiction is recontextualized.

In Chapter 2, universal jurisdiction is analysed with reference to debates on the State as a privileged legal actor, and, alternative approaches to the static perception of the state in international law are canvassed. Providing an inlet for universal jurisdiction in applicable cases of state criminality while identifying a framework that is not of dubious normative or legal validity is the challenge here. Reformulating universal jurisdiction anew emerges as a necessary shift of focus given the contested history of the very enterprise of international law in the Global South. To this end, TWAIL scholarship and other contesting voices emanating from the Global South as they relate to international criminal law are revisited.

Chapter 3 narrows down the focus and examines historical and political underpinnings of the legal definition of crimes against humanity as the prime category of crimes falling under the purview of universal jurisdiction. Crimes against humanity are supposed to have a collective legal dimension with respect to both the victims and the perpetrators. They take place only in the context of a widespread, orchestrated, planned or systematic attack, and in a societal setting that either condones or supports their committal. Instead of a doctrinaire interpretation of these crimes, this chapter offers a historicized conception and proposes a wider justification for their prosecution through locally adapted universal jurisdiction measures. This has important implications as to which crimes could be justifiably prosecuted and punished by domestic, hybrid or international courts, an issue discussed in detail in Chapter 5 (on hybrid courts).

Chapter 4 deals with a very cumbersome subject, that of collective responsibility. It posits the necessity to question the legalized content of the notion and, in its stead, invites the reader to consider societal wrongdoing as the basis upon which we could revisit the notion of blameworthiness in a political sense. Introducing the Arendt/Jaspers opposition concerning the notion of collective guilt, the chapter concludes with pertinent questions concerning the impossibility of mass violence being committed without societal condonement and endorsement and the long-term consequences of historical injustices left unaddressed. The final chapter, Chapter 5, considers hybrid courts and tribunals. The chapter examines the promise of these third-generation international courts and their potential for domestic appropriations of crimes against humanity jurisprudence and the fundamental features of the universal jurisdiction norm. It also posits that the scope of international criminal justice measures dealing with basic human rights violations should be wider than is currently acknowledged, in that it should include violations that have a collective dimension. These arguments correspond with the proposition developed in Chapter 4 on collective responsibility. They also provide factual grounds for facing the challenges posed by the political and doctrinal limitations of applications of universal jurisdiction in the Global South.

Overall, this treatise invites its readers to consider the following assessment: based on the examination of cases pertaining to transitional justice settings resorting to local interpretations of crimes against humanity jurisprudence, fragmentation of international law and circumscribed applications of universal jurisdiction are necessary aspects of the grand enterprise of overcoming the impasse of international criminal law's tainted legacy in the Global South. Crimes against humanity jurisprudence and the universal jurisdiction dictum pertaining to their adjudication constitute prime examples for evaluation in this regard. If we are to proceed with adjudication of the most egregious and heinous crimes involving state criminality without facing the charge of neocolonialist plotting, we must reckon with localized and domesticated interpretations of international criminal law rather than pursuing strict forms of legislative dictation by international institutions such as the ICC. As such, observed limitations concerning the application of universal jurisdiction lead us to a much-needed reformulation of accountability as a centripetal practice in international criminal law. They also allow for the introduction of the possibility of assuming collective responsibility for societal wrongs above and beyond the grid of criminal jurisprudence, an issue long overlooked in the context of crimes against humanity and yet essential in their proper address.

Key Questions

Notable international law scholars approved of the 1999 bombing of Serbia by the members of the North Atlantic Treaty Organization, despite the fact that some felt it was not compatible with a strict reading of the UN Charter on matters of concern regarding the principle of state sovereignty.[1] The techniques through which these scholars tried to abide by their 'moral intuitions' despite the obvious legal incoherence pertaining to the case of intervention in Yugoslav wars are symptomatic of a general turn to ethics in legal theory, especially in the field of international criminal law. If we are to avoid the danger of international criminal law becoming a behemoth of an oppressive instrument, put to the service of the foreign policy choices of states marked by power and privilege, it must assume the prowess of deliberation and must be historically grounded. Relying entirely on heavy-handed and institutionalized codification of state criminality, its forced applications at politically opportune moments does not appear at all 'universal' in the Global South.

Hence, the first question addressed in this manuscript is, in the absence of widespread consent, why sovereign states are expected to obey international criminal law. However, rather than why they *should*, I venture to ask why states *choose to* embrace certain core principles of it, given the damning history of international law as seen from the Global South. The prevailing legal realist view holds that states act simply out of self-interest, and that if and when they consent to international law, they only consent to those norms and principles to regulate matters of common interest in which they are involved. Here, the emphasis remains squarely on the state as the ultimate unit of international law. This work is written against such a presumption. Instead, it purports to understand international criminal law as a transnational phenomenon shaped by multiple legal actors, the Westphalian state being only one of them. Secondly, I posit that international courts such as the International Criminal Court (ICC) are not to be made into modern-day messiahs of international criminal law. This debate is a very difficult one, more so than questioning the sanctity of the state in international law, particularly in an area such as crimes against humanity given their heinous nature. And yet, these two debates – namely, criticism of the state-centric view of international law, and considerations of the limits of universal jurisdiction in international criminal law – inform each other. The theoretical contribution of this work thus lies in the challenges it poses to the received wisdom concerning the very foundations of international criminal law, and its critique of the ambitions of the regime of accountability addressing state criminality established since the Second World War.

In this vein, in the first half of the work, the principle of state sovereignty and its derivatives in international law are unpacked along with a thorough analysis of the emergence of universal jurisdiction as a supreme norm. The second half is then allocated to the history of the codification and adjudication of crimes against humanity in the post-ICC era. Here, an attempt is made for the normative architecture of crimes against humanity jurisprudence in international law to be linked with a somewhat unusual debate on collective responsibility and societal wrongdoing. Finally, this work takes issue with existing models pertaining to the applications of international criminal law, namely, both the dualist and monist renditions of how international law works. Briefly, the dualist perspective claims international law to be primarily alien to domestic law.[2] It characterizes international law as imposing and undemocratic, and only appropriations of it through internal deliberation are deemed acceptable, otherwise known as the ratification process. This approach is clearly present in the dominant trends of American and German jurisprudential thought, as well as some of the emergent critiques from the Global South, particularly among the Muslim-majority countries and East Asia, and increasingly so in Africa. The monist perspective, on the other hand, is the darling of international law scholars with an institutionalist bent, particularly regarding the issue of universal jurisdiction. Monism advocates 'universal principles', applicable in all contexts due to their claimed normative superiority. In this regard, the ICC's embrace of crimes against humanity is often used as a prime example, as this specific category of crimes enlisted in the Court's enabling statute is indeed a colossal affront to the whole of humanity. And yet, there are significant problems regarding the path followed for their adjudication. According to the monist perspective, particularly in international criminal law, no caveat should be accepted or even proposed, and the standards set by institutions such as the ICC concerning their adjudication are to be accepted as non-negotiable. Exceptions are to be made only due to procedural issues, and even so these are not to question the normative and legal certainties of the jurisprudence itself.

Ultimately, this work poses the question of whether a third perspective is possible – not as an in-between, but one based on a more dynamic and historicized understanding of international (criminal) law. The discussions presented in the following pages indicate that, especially in the Global South, if international criminal law's adjudication mechanisms and procedural aspects are imposed universally using the justification of the unsurmountable validity of its core foundational premises, the whole enterprise runs the risk of becoming suspect. As a counter discourse, this work is constructed around two methodological investigations. The first one addresses the normative framework within which international law is commonly perceived. The presumed alignment of international and domestic law in the area of universal jurisdiction constitutes the key example for this inquiry. The second methodological investigation is built upon the Arendtian notion of political judgment, as opposed to the procedure-oriented understanding of international criminal law. Here, the aim is to shed light on how different interpretations of crimes against humanity jurisprudence could be reconciled without excessive dependency on an overarching institution such as the ICC. A case in point to that end is the multiple reiterations of crimes against humanity at the level of *ad hoc*, regional and hybrid courts in addition to its codification in the Rome Statute. The reader is thus first acclimatized to the severe methodological criticism of international law emanating from the

Global South, and then left with the question of what to do with undeniably egregious instances of state criminality experienced in the very geographies that this critique hails from. The answer comes in the form of re-examining the merits of using a very rigid form of international criminal law in the case of crimes against humanity jurisprudence. An attempt is made to consider the role to be played by societal authorship of the way forward in such instances, which relies upon the inner logic of universal jurisdiction concerning crimes against humanity. In this context, the reader is invited to attend to the merits of an ongoing engagement with the act of judging as defined by Hannah Arendt for developing localized understandings of mass political crimes, societal wrongdoing and implications of historical injustices left unaddressed.

It is true that all of the chapters of this work deal with concerns about the larger debate on international law and problems of incongruity between domestic and international law. However, the case at hand is that of egregious and unforgivable crimes committed by states against their own people. To this end, the chapters on universal jurisdiction and hybrid courts present findings from criminal law trials in order to showcase the interaction and fluidity connecting these two spheres of juridical action. Vis-à-vis the domestic sphere, one is forced to acknowledge the importance of national norms about the constitution of criminality, due to their socio-political effectiveness and long-term legitimacy. Meanwhile, when the frame of analysis is shifted to international (criminal) law, one has to deal with an uncomfortable reality that marks the field: it does *not* have a history of egalitarian decision-making, equal participation, or always transparent relations.[3] Secondly, there appears to be a problem concerning the unaddressed divide separating international humanitarian and human rights law in international criminal law. Thus far, the question of whether jurisprudence pertaining to international criminal law could be legitimately relativized – just as states negotiate trade or labor laws, for instance – has largely been avoided due to the nature of the violence embodied by these acts. There are certain absolutes in this area, and, on these issues, international criminal law avoids the notion of political deliberation for fear of allowing future reversals or tempering of crimes against humanity jurisprudence. What we are faced with on the ground, however, reveals a rather different reality of the adjudication of these egregious crimes: the operationalization of state criminality is context-bound.

Hannah Arendt's work on judgment is introduced precisely for addressing this dilemma. In Arendt's analysis of crimes against humanity, the Aristotelian notion of politics as engagement and the Kantian notion of reflectiveness of judgment are brought together to make sense of how to put the unforgivable to trial. Though Arendt's work on political judgment was left unfinished, as she was writing it at the time of her death, she left us enough to proceed with, especially when her work is read alongside that of Karl Jaspers's and others in the context of the notion of collective responsibility for societal and political crimes. The inquiry that is proposed here is whether adherence to a jurisprudential framework, while remaining open to pluralistic interpretation of the procedural aspects of it at the domestic and regional levels, is possible. Specifically, this work posits that the Arendtian notion of political judgment allows for engagement, deliberation and involvement, and thus offers us a democratic promise for the global application of international criminal law. Nonetheless, a serious complication exists. According to the politics of persuasion, judgment would not allow for absolutes. In cases such as crimes against humanity, however, one is obliged to consider certain absolutes in order to establish criminality and thresholds of admissibility for evidence. The only way to solve this dilemma is to claim that taking an absolute stance against such crimes is morally defendable. In other words, everyone must agree that certain acts constitute egregious crimes.

Meanwhile, another difficulty emerges here: how to reconcile the jurisprudential approach that accepts differences in political judgments pertaining to the adjudication of crimes against humanity with the aforementioned monist defence of universal jurisdiction to be uniformly applied to crimes against humanity. This is the critical junction that the debate on universal jurisdiction has arrived at in the post-ICC era. As argued in the following pages, formations such as hybrid courts in the Global South attending to war crimes and crimes against humanity point to possible new directions that could be taken. The main practical concern fuelling all of these inquiries is the following: one cannot force jurisprudential maxims of international bodies such as the ICC upon societies that are violating the basic principles framing crimes against humanity jurisprudence unless there is a degree of value convergence in place. The issue then becomes how to find a normative common ground upon which domestic courts would willingly incorporate international law such as the ICC jurisprudence if and when the need arises without such cooperation being seen as yet another hegemonic intervention.[4]

Instead of appearing as a stable set of normative demands, across the Global South, international law is largely seen as an important aspect of hegemony-building and maintenance. But as the TWAIL scholarship suggests, it could also be used as a technique for making political claims in terms of legal rights and duties against the powers that be. Accordingly, the looming controversies in international law concerning the use of force, the law of peace, human rights, trade and globalization in effect reflect strategies through which political actors confront the universality claims of others. Unless one is open to institutional and dialogical interventions, building up normative commitments from the bottom up, how could international criminal law provide a genuinely common language of jurisprudence even for the most egregious acts exemplified by crimes against humanity?

Context

International law in general, and international criminal law in particular, is facing new challenges in the post-9/11 era, though only some of these are related to the emergence of the 'new terrorism' discourse in international politics. Reservations about the role and function of international law in domestic affairs are on the rise. These range from marked scepticism about the authority and utility of international law vis-à-vis local conditions, to cautioning about undermining the foundations of the legal systems at the local level. The European Union is a case in point, showing how even the most elaborate regional efforts for juridical unification can backfire in unforeseen directions.[5] Across

Europe, the debate about the relevance of international law is being conducted in such pointed language that the motif of the dangers and limits of constitutional adjustments to 'foreign law' has become the tenor of the most powerful domestic contestations.[6] Law that falls beyond the purview of domestic jurisprudence is characterized as fundamentally anti-democratic and top-down. This point of view leads to a highly negative perception of the legitimacy of international law, as it is reduced to a mechanism that obligates states to justify their local/national practices if they deviate from a supposedly universally coded but relatively alien set of standards. National protectionism thus readily propagates the already mentioned monism/dualism dichotomy, portraying international law either as an external body of law capable of penetrating the national legal order without democratic consent, or as a corpus of alien jurisprudence that must be rigorously filtered through the prism of national constitutional law if it is to accrue any benefit for local constituencies.[7]

According to the traditional dualist perspective, the ultimate legitimate source of legal norms is the democratic process itself. Accordingly, international norms – even those concerning human rights – are domestically enforceable only to the extent that they are incorporated into existing legal orders through statutory endorsement.[8] As such, the relationship between public international law and domestic law is constructed as a tenuous interaction between two separate realms. When such interventions are allowed to take place, the argument goes, they will lead to the emergence of an unaccountable judiciary answering only to its own professional norms of conduct at the expense of domestic legal and political prerogatives. Hence, we witness the equation of international law with the abdication and delegation of [national] sovereignty. This objection, often expressed in terms of the cultural or institutional incompatibility of international jurisprudence with local settings, assumes that norms of public international law inherently clash with local democratic commitments. This viewpoint inherently clouds the horizons of international human rights activism by challenging the local legitimacy of their demands and claims. Equally worrisome is the questioning of the status of the normative principles and jurisprudential reasoning of international criminal law.[9] The deep-rooted suspicion of international criminal law is commonly justified by means of a contractarian view of democratic legitimacy of law, vehemently defended both in the North and the Global South in the name of state sovereignty. Accordingly, the domain of constitutional law has an epistemological priority based on the assumption that there is social and political convergence in the domestic sphere providing a unique moral texture to domestic law.

In summary, the dualists insist that within a heterogeneous and morally divided society – whether defined in domestic or international terms – law should assume the function of establishing a stable framework of rules of interaction, and nothing more. In other words, law is to reveal itself *qua* law. Consequently, judicial discretion built into the process of adjudication is limited to clarifying the antecedent meaning of law and monitoring compliance. Though the argument merits attention, it also hides the essentially hegemonic nature of legal systems in the domestic realm. This issue is particularly critical for developing a deeper understanding of state criminality, both within the domestic sphere and from a transnational point of view.[10] At this point, the plot thickens. It is true that the origins of international law are not based on consensus. The whole enterprise owes its existence to laws of war, treaty obligations, customary practices and unequal and yet binding contracts, always protecting the sanctity of the Westphalian state system and attempting to further the interests of a select group of states within it. And yet, the resultant historical fragmentation of international law is a testimony to law's intimate relationship with power, politics, hegemony, discontent, indeterminacy and change.[11] If so, international law could be portrayed, in opposition to the presumed purism of the domestic legal system reflecting a solid political contract among citizens and the state, as a complex platform harbouring conflicts, negotiations and a multitude of regime-building strategies. These issues are discussed in detail in Chapter 1 at Section II titled 'Transnational Character of Accountability Regimes in International Law and Multicentricity of Legal Practices' where I examine transnational law and fragmented regimes of accountability in international criminal law.

Indeed, from international law's inception in the Grotian legal tradition onwards, international legal discourse has been shaped by a constitutive tension between a view of law as having a contractual genesis, and a view of law as reflecting conflictual moral claims dictated by specific demands of contending parties.[12] This tension in turn feeds into two competing accounts not only of legitimation but also adjudication. The state-centric account, which relies upon private law metaphors such as delegation and trusteeship, emphasizes the necessity of deference to the will of states as representatives of political communities. Its alternative, on the other hand, prioritizes the emergence of common normative principles in the conduct of legal reasoning and delivery of justice.[13] The latter account also proposes the possibility of a global legal enterprise of adjudication based on the juxtaposition of constitutional and international legal systems in select areas. In situations where legal standards differ, and where an international body might interpret an act in a way that runs counter to settled features of domestic law, international law then suggests adjustments to be made to the domestic realm. This could yield both positive and negative results for domestic constituencies, as is deliberated upon in critical debates on public international law. Ultimately, however, this scenario substantiates the dualists' ultimate fear: the weakening of the domestic legal order and its supposedly self-standing adjudicative *acquis*. As the present work suggests, international criminal law needs to rise to the challenge of surpassing these two opposing accounts of adjudication and come up with a normatively oriented model for the realization of an alignment between international and domestic legal spheres. Obsession with adjudicative process brings forward further animosities that dilute the substantive premise of precious developments such as crimes against humanity jurisprudence.

Another key dimension of this debate on law's legitimacy pertains to voluntary compliance.[14] Institutional and third-party enforcement cannot be identified as the only reasons for why such compliance occurs. In democratic constitutional regimes, the absence of morally reprehensible means for ensuring compliance to law implies (at least in principle) that members of the constituent political community are bound by a common ideal of justice, above and beyond particularistic factors such as ethnic, religious, historical and cultural identities. Could there not be a similar, underlying agreement concerning a common ideal of state conduct in international criminal law? As already stated, the difficulty about international law is that a contractual ideal of justice cannot be claimed due to the chequered origin of existing legal systems encapsulated by it.[15] Consequently, legal institutional practices such as the adjudication of crimes against humanity are considered to have incomplete legitimacy. Their adoption requires an agreement about their normative framing, which is presented in the form of the universal jurisdiction norm. However, since they are triggered at the behest of aggrieved individuals and as *ex post facto* developments in de-nationalized or hybrid settings, involved states tend to detest adjudication of crimes against humanity jurisprudence. Contrary to the assertions of contractarian or universalist models of international law, rights and rulings that are defined above and beyond the state and in effect targeting its sanctity are intrinsically political rather than procedural. In other words, international law cannot seek nor depend on the full adoption of its codes by constitutional regimes, otherwise known as the expectation of law's working itself pure.[16] The Hayekian values of certainty, stability and efficiency are no doubt as important for the workings of international law as they are for domestic law. However, conflation of values espoused by political communities purportedly represented by contemporary states with grand ethical prerogatives of international law is a dangerous fiction. Similarly, conception of an institutionally closed, historically self-referential and normatively sealed system of domestic law as a self-reliant legal edifice is an oppressive tale. Theoretically, the present work seeks an alternative beyond this either/or opposition.

If international criminal law is to be re-imagined as an engaged practice of aligned adjudication and, in *tandem*, as a persuasion-based strategy of new norm production rather than criminalization of select states based on universal prerogatives dictated by *erga omnes* obligations, its potential for re-contextualizing international law and introducing a new dynamism to local understandings of justice may be more readily realized. International criminal law is normative by necessity, and it requires the active use of political judgment. Insisting that it must be otherwise only leads to disastrous results, as seen in the widespread reactions to ICC indictments across the Global South. Normative conduct with legal legitimacy is not limited to the domestic constitutional realm. However, for systemic adjudication of state criminality, the ideal of justice endorsed by international criminal law would have to operate as a competing template that reveals the limitations of domestic intuitions and legal systems. No matter how the ideal of justice is perceived – in the case of international criminal law, reference is made to the Eurocentric historical background of the emergent legal regimes, thus tainting the claim of its universality – moral commitments alone cannot be presented as the cornerstone of a normative architecture of criminal jurisprudence within which judgments concerning state criminality are to be produced. And yet, states and other legals actors who have committed crimes against humanity cannot justify their actions based on the perceived needs of a given constitutional order, whether European, postcolonial, or otherwise, either. In other words, vis-à-vis crimes against humanity jurisprudence, their normative legitimacy cannot be addressed within the confines of how political communities govern themselves. In this regard, this work posits that salvation for international criminal law in this particular area would come from a 'thin' rather than a 'thick' universalism. Ultimately, a substantive theory of judgment is required to combat the excesses of universalism, institutionalism, legal realism, legal positivism, contextualism and relativism. Understanding *the role of genuine politics* in the formation of legal judgment is an essential part of this endeavour. The world of international criminal law outside the confines of The Hague calls for genuine exploration as a normative project as well as a jurisprudential imperative.

Methodology

This work uses critical legal theory and comparative approaches to international law as its two prime methodological tools concerning global applications of crimes against humanity jurisprudence. Its chronological focus is the post-Second World War period of adjudication of international crimes, with a particular emphasis on post-2002 developments following the entering into force of the Rome Statute. The overall theoretical framework guiding the present debate on universal jurisdiction and crimes against humanity is indebted to the approach to international law developed and articulated by third generation debates on legal pluralism and TWAIL (Third World Approaches to International Law) scholarship. The debate presented here on collective responsibility, on the other hand, engages with applied political and legal philosophy. The examples referenced throughout the text are drawn from international criminal law jurisprudence. However, case material related to state criminality is primarily related to the Global South, and, unfortunately, that is not by choice. In response, the critical lens used to analyse overall developments in international criminal law and accountability regimes pertaining to state criminality prioritizes the experiences of societies in the Global South.

International law's discontents and excesses have always been exhibited at their starkest in its periphery, a realm that has come to be known as the Global South.[17] The relationship between the peripheries and the core has already been adequately captured by TWAIL scholarship. However, as TWAIL scholars readily attest, the Global South is not solely defined by victimhood but by hegemonic as well as counter-hegemonic relations, shifting and changing class alliances, and regional rather than state-based hubs of power and accumulation. The complexity and endemic tensions within the Global South are in turn symptomatic of the general state of affairs in late capitalism. This is not simply a case of the periphery mirroring what happens at the core. There are voices, forces and opportunities that emanate from the Global South that take issue with, challenge and alter the very enterprise of international law as it is shrouded on a pedestal at the core.

In response to the growth of international law's involvement in the global management of resources, movements of goods and people, and sustaining and embellishing accumulation regimes across the Global South, there emerged a strong call against some of its key tenets since the 1990s. For instance, alter-globalization activists found their voice in alternative governance models built upon North–South and red–green alliances, bringing together organized labour, migrant, environmental, women's and indigenous rights movements. Similarly, different genres of protests began to propose alternative frames of reference for seeking justice and challenging traditional forms of adjudication in areas devastated by organized violence, both political and economic. These distinct, albeit overlapping, responses to international law, echoed in the work of legal scholars and in particular human rights lawyers linked with the Global South, are indicative of a new conceptual model for how we work with, translate, undo and redo international law.

Why TWAIL?

In this work, I apply the rich and layered conceptual framework inherited from TWAIL scholarship, combined with the activism and scholarship nexus in the Global South, to a specific area of international criminal law, that of universal jurisdiction as it pertains to crimes against humanity.[18] I strive to elucidate the limitations of this particular legal construct's applicability according to a rigid and ahistorical frame of reference dictated by centralized institutions such as international courts. Against this absolutist take, I argue that normative strategies centred on the twin concepts of culpability/collective responsibility and human dignity could offer a conceptually coherent and politically buoyant alternative. Furthermore, I argue that there is an urgent need for a new frame of reference concerning *erga omnes* obligations and *jus cogens* norms for international criminal law to speak directly to the realities of societies in the Global South. This cannot be achieved through procedural reiterations of crimes against humanity jurisprudence, or the threat of universal jurisdiction pointing to trials at any court in any constituency as they see fit.

Indeed, there is an impasse concerning applications of international criminal law, but in particular concerning crimes against humanity jurisprudence in the Global South. And yet, critiquing state-centric notions of sovereign power or underlining the hegemonic role played by international law in calcifying inherent power relations across the globe only provides the beginnings of a critical conversation. In the following pages, I argue that we need to go much further and dare to imagine a different path, leading to the adjudication of crimes against humanity much closer to where these crimes are committed. I also suggest that, on the normative plane, the dictum of universal jurisdiction must be domesticated through acceptance of collective responsibility for mass crimes and composite ways of addressing state criminality from within.

A major consequence of the global restructuring of economies, societies and states in the Global South has been the twin processes of further market integration and privatization of what were once common or public goods, on the one hand, and unprecedented waves of social exclusion, precariousness and dispossession on the other.[19] These processes resulted in further growth of the marginalized, displaced and deinstitutionalized subaltern classes, who often became the natural targets for mass political violence at times of societal crises linked with internal or regional conflicts. Standard international law debates on post-conflict legal regimes and transitional justice measures barely touch base with this reality of structural inequalities that preceded mass political violence.[20] In contradistinction, this work seeks to understand and transform the way in which legal regimes of accountability affecting the Global South are studied in international criminal law. The emphasis is on the larger historical context surrounding these legal regimes and the limitations faced when 'imported' or 'imposed' criminal law is used as the only or supreme tool for the identification and remedy of injustices.

Ultimately, I am concerned with institutional formalization of ideals such as universal jurisdiction for societal and political mass crimes in international criminal law. Similarly, the emergence of set forms of punishment for crimes falling under the purview of crimes against humanity jurisprudence, as enshrined by the Rome Statute of the International Criminal Court (ICC), deserves critical questioning. In this vein, this work strives to provide an account of interpretations of crimes against humanity jurisprudence by way of proposing a genuine political engagement with the past in the Global South. In this regard, it is written against apocalyptic and dystopian narratives detailing the usurping and hegemonic monstrosity of international law as much as against the universalistic preaching of it. This constitutes a degree of challenge to critical legal scholarship, as well. After all, there are inherent limits to the standard readings of legal pluralism as the saviour for all ills of international law.

Conceptually speaking, the Global South is one of the many 'grey spaces' positioned between the 'whiteness' of legality/certainty, and the 'blackness' of irregularity/destruction/death. The vast expansion of such grey spaces in contemporary geographies of conflict reflects the emergence of new types of power relations, which are often facilitated and managed by regimes in the Global South themselves. Traditional uses of international law have been a lynchpin of this order, providing tools and methodologies to classify, contain and manage deeply unequal societies. Overall, in this work I propose two kinds of upheaval. First and foremost, I insist that the story about post-Nuremberg juridification of crimes against humanity should no longer be told as one where the states and societies in the Global South are striving hard to establish or operationalize accountability regimes, yet with only a few 'success stories'. Nor should the accent remain on the universalistic analysis of international criminal law with its focus on the core legal institutions, since their authoritative and heavily procedural take on crimes against humanity has proven to be inadequate, inappropriate or incomplete. My findings imply that, as the new generation of TWAIL scholars, we must identify the limits of external impositions of international criminal law without serious contextualization in both historical and normative terms. Crimes against humanity jurisprudence, and its domestication, is sorely needed by the societies in the Global South – but not in the format in which it has been offered thus far.

Searching for the Global South

How is the concept of the Global South to be understood in the context of international (criminal) law? Though this is not the main focus of the present work, it is a very important part of the methodological framework utilized throughout. This question is also very relevant for dealing with egregious crimes committed in the Global South, especially ones that cannot currently be addressed within the domestic legal setting in which they were committed. Application of the dominant conceptual framework of international law to such cases only produces more of the same.[21] As a counterpoint to neutralized universalization, and as an activist strategy towards rights protection and a demand for accountability, there is a need for greater conceptual precision in the analysis of international criminal law. An essential part of this endeavour is paying attention to 'naming practices'.

The term 'Global South' began to be used to overcome the hierarchical and ideological implications of designations such as the Third World.[22] It is also preferred if one refuses to attach epistemological privileges to adjectives such as 'developing' or 'developed' as both are commonly applied to the Global South. In the context of international law, the term owes its legitimacy mainly to TWAIL scholarship. This poses the risk, then, of the Global South becoming a name for people who engage in 'alternative approaches' to international law. In other words, just as revolutions eat their own children, the very coinage of the term Global South introduced the risk of marginalizing the political and intellectual niche it demarcates. Still, it is not only TWAIL scholars who hold onto it, and persistently so. Marxist and post-Marxist critics of contemporary international legal regimes have long pointed out that the grid of international law is determined by the distribution of political and economic power, which in turn created the phenomenon of Global South in the first place.[23] Accordingly, contrary to what the term 'international' implies, there is not and never has been substantive equality across the contemporary canvas of nation-states. Nor is there a reason to believe that a global regime of universal justice could be built upon or sustained within the existing system, due to the multiple layers of historical injustice that have been perpetuated, left unattended or unresolved for centuries. The Global South thus emerges as a domain which is already tainted by the zealous plans for its recuperation and neocolonial re-incorporation via the laws, politics, economies and cultures of the North, or the First World.

The kind of nihilism concerning the reach and potency of international law witnessed in this line of argument is not exhausted by the debates on the North–South divide. The issue assumes even darker tones and more complicated dimensions in terms of South–South relations. Since the present work's focus is on problems and concerns to be addressed by the states and societies in the Global South, this is of utmost significance here. Unequal relations within the Global South are again often left unattended, and only touched upon in terms of the common resistance to the hegemonic nature of North–South relations. Despite this tendency, and if ruminations on neo-imperialist/post-colonial law can be set aside momentarily, another perspective on international law emerges as it relates to the Global South. This new vista relates to adaptations and reiterations of international law in the Global South, without removing the necessary emphasis on power relations or historical contingencies.

Across the Global South, there exist patterns of injustice and abuse that do not only stem from the historic or current interventions of the North. Equally important is the admission that there is indeed law and need for justice in the Global South, rather than its being a lawless place, or its legalities assumed to be a simulacrum of 'Western Law' (Chayes, *The New Sovereignty*). The key issue in this changed context is to decipher variant forms of legality above and beyond the classic legal pluralism debate. Taking into consideration tensions endemic to fragmented and overlapping legal regimes is a good starting point for the task at hand.[24] Secondly, the Global South encompasses a rich canopy of political entities including not just post-colonial nation-states, but also autonomous regional governance structures, federal frameworks, judicial and quasi-judicial bodies such as regional courts and regulatory institutions, civil society organizations, and transnational actors such as INGOs.[25] In other words, it is not a mass of ex-colonial semi-states on the brink of collapse, or a sea of non-descript societies subservient to the interests of the North.[26] Societies in the Global South are not replicas of a post-colonial or post-imperial master model. They harbour their own histories of social and political identities, variant patterns and regimes of capital accumulation and labour control, and different strategies of extraction and amassing of wealth. They also exhibit a wide range of regional alliance-building mechanisms and a canopy of jurisdictional arrangements regulating the relations among themselves.

Consequently, it is apt to suggest that the Global South possesses a multitude of 'unique characteristics' as an object of international law, rather than being a derivative of realities emanating elsewhere, in the proverbial North.

The term Global South contains all the necessary references for histories of colonization, de-colonization and post-coloniality, as well as structurally conditioned material and political inequalities cozily coupled up with state-induced injustices.[27] However, these factors by themselves do not explain how international criminal law works or how it could work from the vantage point of a North imposing law and order onto the Global South. There are emergent hybrid regimes of accountability within the Global South itself.[28] The over-used dichotomies of North/South, developed/developing and First World/Third World offer no new clues here. Urgent questions persist, but we must look for answers elsewhere. For instance, how could we think through, rather than simply think about, unequal distributions of material wealth and political power at a global scale, vis-à-vis their effects on the Global South and emergent forms of state criminality in post-colonial states? Could specific needs of criminal justice, as they pertain to universal jurisdiction of crimes against humanity, be served within existing domestic legal frameworks? Are there novel forms of jurisprudential collaboration facilitated through hybrid mechanisms – through which the societies in the Global South can use international criminal law jurisprudence for their own purposes?

Ultimately, once all is said and done in some criminal court, the work of creating a more just society has only begun. The greatest impediment to reaching a substantive understanding of the legitimacy, efficacy or even possibility of the adjudication of international criminal law in both the Global North and the Global South is the ascription to democratic constitutionalism, which owes its crowned position to the persistence of the statist paradigm in international law. Accordingly, legal practices emerging under the UN Charter, or courts such as the International Criminal Court (ICC), the European Court of Human Rights (ECHR), or general customary international law, are declared to be troubled by unique problems of coherence, efficacy and legitimacy, problems which domestic law supposedly does not suffer from. Statist constitutional thinking exaggerates the value of domestic practices, to the point of casting a dark shadow of suspicion over any form of legal normativity beyond state-made law.

To summarize, the statist paradigm of constitutionalism, and its ideological distortions leading to the presumption of absolute legitimacy of state-made law (and, *faux* realism of rejecting all other normative claims within or beyond its borders), imprisons international law. The efficacy of domestic constitutionalism is so exaggerated that, especially in the area of human rights law, it reaches dangerous proportions of naming human rights lawyers as spies and terrorists targeting the very sanctity of the state. The standard reason given is the quotidian argument about the lack of domestic constitutional provisions for international human rights law, often fortified with the enactment of emergency measures at times of 'breakdown of civil order' and open or covert civil war. Meanwhile, law as a discourse is vulnerable and open to social and political influences both inside and outside the domestic sphere. In addition, domestic law is conditioned by and dependent upon the political context in which it takes shape. Legal scholars of the TWAIL persuasion know this all too well. Perhaps one may go so far as to argue that the statist framing of international law, in the form of a renewed devotion to democratic constitutionalism, is just another Westphalian fantasy *par excellence*, albeit replaying itself some 400 years later and in a distinctly post-colonial context.

At this point, a cautionary note is necessary. The limited scope of universal jurisdiction for select crimes such as crimes against humanity, and its circumscribed application through institutions such as hybrid courts as discussed in the upcoming pages of this work, do not constitute proof that international law is inherently legitimate. An ethically cloaked international legalism suggesting that we have an innate disposition to appreciate law in select areas of criminality and violence, otherwise known as the commonsense approach to law, is not a requirement for endorsing hybrid courts, either. Nonetheless, it is apt to insist that the statist paradigm falsely suggests that jurisprudence concerning restorative justice for political violence and mass crimes involving state criminality must develop solely from within. The presumption that there is a fundamental difference or an unsurpassable separation between state-made law and law beyond the state is itself not only false but also anathema to the very history of rights struggles. In this vein, this work purports that horizontal connections among burgeoning international, regional and hybrid adjudication mechanisms, as well as vertical relations between international and domestic jurisprudence targeting state criminality, are the axes upon which universal jurisdiction must be scrutinized in its applications in the Global South.

Since the foundation of the ICC, there have been substantial changes in the ethos as well as the methods underlying the operationalization of international criminal law. Whereas the norm that once informed international adjudication was the top-town imposition of legal precepts, there is now a growing body of hybrid jurisprudence, as well as an emergent class of domestic jurisprudence conversant with international criminal law. Indeed, a close look at the contemporary international judicial landscape quickly draws our attention to the role of national courts in applying international law, *despite* the myriad jurisdictional and normative conflicts and compliance problems pertaining to universal jurisdiction in select areas such as crimes against humanity. This seems to be the way south for top-down approaches to international law, a predicament that I intend to stand by throughout this work.

1

Topographies of Universal Jurisdiction in International Law, Legal Pluralism and the Curious Case of the International Criminal Court

Introduction

Legal theory has long accentuated the institutional distinctiveness of law from other areas of society, portraying law as discrete, internally coherent and thus self-referential and almost autonomous.[1] In contrast, an immediate way in which law's multidimensionality, complexity, and lack of unity is easily identified is to look at law beyond state boundaries. In this sense, looking at the contemporary legal landscape at the age of late capitalism and globalization is both challenging and rewarding. Meanwhile, the historical fact of the coexistence of multiple legal orders says nothing about their capacity for delivering justice. Recognition of the complexity and plurality of contemporary legal regimes is only the starting point for a theoretical analysis of international law.

In this opening chapter, I endeavour to answer the question of why we should care about the contemporary multiplicity of legal regimes in the specific context of accountability for state criminality. If state interests and domestic judiciary interpretations of international law are by and large coincident with preferences of national political leadership and local legislative concerns, what would be the point in searching for a theory of international law that is not fixated on the Westphalian order of things? How are we to appreciate the consolidation of customary law and regulatory regimes that go above and beyond the direct mandate of the executive powers of states? State-centric accounts of international law entertain a rather rigid view of the field and of the actors who occupy it. In contradistinction, alternative accounts discussed in this chapter provide a depiction of international law as transnational law and, as a result, present us with a different topography of accountability regimes. In this changed context, international-cum-transnational law is seen as a complex and often conflict-laden deliberative process. Similarly, law is seen as a battleground for multifarious interests and actors, only one of which is the state, each trying to determine legal or semi-legal outcomes and judicial processes to their benefit.[2] This alternate take on international law acknowledges the inherently plural (though not necessarily pluralist) composition of law, and engages with the multiple processes involved in the making and utilization of it. This determination, in turn, is crucial for fostering a systemic understanding of *jurispathic* and *jurisgenerative* dimensions of international law, which could lead to a fruitful expansion of theories of jurisprudence concerning state criminality.[3]

The key concern that guides this discussion of the fragmented, plural and transnational nature of contemporary international law is whether the *nomos* (normative universe) of Robert Cover's jurisprudential account of law, when applied to a global context, is substantively different from what we are accustomed to dealing with in national, domestic contexts. This line of questioning also lends itself to addressing the tension between ideas of monism and pluralism in legal scholarship. Legal monism signifies a pervasive positivist understanding of law as a unified structure of valid rules and principles contained within a solid institutional framework.[4] Legal pluralism, on the other hand, emphasizes the multiplicity of legal practices and the hybridity of socio-political platforms upon which legal edifices are built in the form of institutions, rule-based structures and regimes. At least for the last two decades, legal pluralism has already become common currency in contemporary debates on law and globalization, its main claim being that a form of global legal pluralism represents both the most accurate description of law vis-à-vis globalization and the best normative option. At the descriptive level, globally applied legal pluralism is considered more reliable than state-based accounts of how international law works. At the normative level, legal pluralism is understood to provide a platform for opening up the legal realm to previously unheard voices.[5]

The conservative take on legal theory insisting on the singularity, uniformity, harmonization and totality of legal systems could be relaxed both empirically and normatively through the *ethos* of legal pluralism combined with a re-inscription of international law as transnational law.[6] As such, the study of international law would no longer be circumscribed by inquiries about how to maintain the integrity of it as a system.[7] Instead, attention should be paid to injustices and discontent as much as to harmonization and consent. Quasi-legal decision-making bodies (such as hybrid courts and regulatory bodies), internal governance systems of large organizations, alternative modes of dispute resolution and arbitration, regulative systems with a global reach, and myriad other forms and settings that produce legal or law-like effects clearly indicate the multiplicity of legal regimes at the transnational level, encompassing the domestic, the regional, the international, and a fourth dimension, the global.[8] The critical issue is how to read this complexity within a historical context that includes domestic jurisprudence without prioritizing it at the expense of all else.

There is a persistent focus on the singularity of legal discourse as an internally coherent system and on the institutional qualities of legal regimes, including the more recent debate on novel forms of constitutionalism.[9] State law continues to be paraded as a superior enterprise, characterized by its coherence and internal consistency, and by its presumed autonomy from other normative domains. In this context, the first question I will attempt to answer is whether legal pluralism, when applied to international law, could produce the desired change of optics and allow for a genuine discussion on multiplicity, diversity and conflict.[10] The next question is to what extent a legal pluralistic frame of reference would enhance our understanding of the inner dynamics of fragmented and sometimes overlapping accountability regimes in international law, particularly in relation to state criminality.

I. Applications of Legal Pluralism in International Law

There has long been a tenuous relationship between international law and theories of jurisprudence. At the very least, international law was posited as lacking the second order rules and regulations defined by H. L. A. Hart and thus devoid of substantive tenets of a genuine legal system.[11] In the nexus of international law and international politics, on the other hand, this relationship appears to be somewhat less troublesome. International relations scholars look for three elements in order to determine the existence of a legal system: a legal concept, a structure or framework capable of supporting its operationalization as law, and the political consensus to legitimize and recognize it as law.[12] This mode of thinking promises to look beyond the debate over 'legal norm creation' in international law. Rather, it dwells on international law's effectiveness and target constituencies. From this perspective, international law is not seen as a coherent collection of rules, prescriptions and aspirations governing the conduct of states and other international actors through legal processes and jurisdictional negotiations; it is described as a complex structure composed of norms, actors, processes and institutions. Interventions by international relations scholarship has also cut short the somewhat stale conversation on treaty implementation and compliance. In its place, their work invites us to turn our attention to institutional and system-wide normative characteristics of international law, as well as to the authority and governance structures endemic to its operations.

In order to achieve such an insight from within legal scholarship, and not only with reference to international relations theories pertaining to international law, a broader frame of analysis is needed concerning the nature of law and its internal and external meanings. In the following, I will provide a brief account of select debates in legal pluralist scholarship and their applications to international law to this end. I will then proceed with a specific branch of international law scholarship, TWAIL (Third World Approaches to International Law) and its effects on our thinking in terms of contextualizing international law. I will conclude with contemporary interjections made by legal theorists who strive to bridge the gap between jurisprudential scholarship and studies of international law from a radical, reflexive and critical legal pluralist perspective, otherwise known as third-generation legal pluralist scholarship. Although this very modest attempt at creating a map of critical approaches to international law could no doubt include the rich and layered debates exemplified by the work of critical legal studies scholars, feminist legal theorists, critical race theorists, post-colonial debates on justice, and other very important schools of thought, these are not explicitly included here. This is due to the limitations posed by my choice of focus, what legal pluralism can and cannot offer for rethinking accountability regimes in international law.

Until recently, legal pluralist scholarship was divided into two main debates. 'Classical' legal pluralism refers to anthropological and socio-historical analyses of legal systems of ex-colonial or post-colonial societies. These had dual or multiple legal systems derived from indigenous pre-colonial folk, communal or customary law on the one hand and imperial law on the other. In contrast, 'second wave' legal pluralism entertained the insight that all societies, formerly colonized or not, are composed of multiple 'semi-autonomous' fields of normative control and legal discourse. This later position purported the coexistence of many forms of law, the majority of which are non-territorial, non-state, local, or international, and horizontal rather than hierarchical. Both schools of legal pluralism concentrate on legal plurality, and challenge the presumption that state law is singular or indeed a superior source for legal meaning or conduct. However, scant attention was paid to the jurisprudential characteristics of the plurality of legal discourses, except in the debate initiated by the work of Robert Cover and continued by Gunther Teubner and David Trubek.[13] I will call this the 'third wave' of legal pluralism, whereby legal scholarship developed a rich analytical approach for the study of different modes of law and the struggle amongst them within a dynamic normative landscape embodying imminent tensions. In this context, the work of contemporary legal scholars such as Ruth Buchanan, Martti Koskenniemi, Rajagopal Balakrishnan and Issa Shivji, among others, sufficiently attends to the conundrums of the multiplicity of meanings in international law. This latest wave of scholarship does not assume that pluralism in law is merely exhibited in a multiplicity of 'semi-autonomous' systems separated by territory, culture or history. Rather, an attempt is made to theorize law as a process in which legal actors, legal subjects and legal norms are interdependent and effected by power and politics at large. They took the legal pluralist premise that law cannot be defined according to a fixed set of criteria one step further, and began to ask what 'other' criteria are to be used for the identification of different forms of law and legal regimes, distinct from those espoused by canonized theories of jurisprudence. As legal pluralism began to be reframed by critical international law scholarship from within the Global South exemplified by TWAIL, the establishment of a theoretical nexus between a plural view of law and the various manifestations of socio-economic and political power became increasingly manifest.[14]

Theoretically speaking, understanding legal plurality is conditional upon the recognition of irreducibly different accounts and experiences of law at a global scale. In this sense, there is a need for the legal pluralism debate to move beyond empirical descriptions of different legal regimes as straightforward socio-legal facts. Precisely in such a spirit, the third wave of legal pluralism attends to the conceptual complexities inherent in the production and maintenance of legal regimes in a world-historical context. This genre of thinking about law and legality is capable of attending to the ways normative systems are construed as discursive practices rather than as mere products of institutions. In addition, the ideals of closure and order are coupled with an appetite for understanding disorder, chaos, change and exceptionalities. In this sense, as Brian Tamanaha redefines it, the central question of legal pluralism can no longer be the different forms that 'law' takes, but what law is in its multifarious manifestations (Tamanaha, 2000).[15] Appreciation of incommensurably different conceptualizations of law also leads to a reflective analysis of the historical specificity of mainstream Western definitions of law, as seen in TWAIL scholarship (Zumbansen, 2010).[16] By moving beyond descriptive recognition of the multitude of legal or law-like normative systems, a critically oriented pluralism could allow for the discussion of plural sources, plural modes of reasoning, and complex forms of interaction between different legal regimes.

Finally, in terms of jurisprudential debates, law is incapable of grounding itself, and its conceptual foundations rest on other elements that are traditionally regarded as outside law. These elements also provide the contextual meaning of law in socio-political terms. Acceptance of the necessary relationship between internal and external elements of law is a foundational premise of legal pluralism.[17] Indeed, critiques of the autonomy of law begin with questioning the internal coherence of law.[18] In this sense, the third wave of legal pluralism is of direct use for the study of international law in a global context, and more specifically for attending to what emerged as transnational law in the age of late capitalism and neocolonialism.[19]

A. The Legacy of the New Haven School

During the roughly four decades in which the concept legal pluralism has been used in legal scholarship, it has become the subject of many a politically charged debate. Starting with Brian Tamanaha's article on the 'folly of legal pluralism' (1993), attention was drawn to the 'legal pluralist movement' associated with the *Commission on Folk Law and Legal Pluralism* and the *Journal of Legal Pluralism*. Tamanaha posited that equalizing normative orders that are fundamentally different from each other and calling them all 'law' was a questionable practice. The response from legal pluralist scholars was unequivocal: reserving the concept of law for only state-made law leads to an essentialist and ahistorical conception of law. Legal pluralism was guilty as charged for being the first one pointing to the elephant in the room (Teubner, 1991).[20]

In legal scholarship, thinking about law above and beyond the state, both domestically and globally, constitutes a methodological challenge. According to the critical understanding of law developed by legal pluralism, the two frames of local and global inform each other. This debate refers to what is now known as transnational law. The subject matter of this work is universal jurisdiction and accountability regimes pertaining to state criminality as exemplified by crimes against humanity. In this specific context, the most recent wave of legal pluralist scholarship engaged in transnational law provides a direct entry to the discussion on the relationship between globalization of law, and, local interpretations and interventions. The scope of analysis and conceptual aspirations delivered by the term transnational law are categorically different from what pertains to traditional depictions of international law. As marked by the canonized Yale lectures of Philip Jessup, transnational law undoes the frame of thinking that long characterized international law, and supplements it with a framework that allows for grasping the plurality of interactions among state and non-state actors as well as between states.[21] Yet, whether transcendence of national frontiers is the main criteria for deeming forms of law and practices of regulation 'transnational' and, if so, whether this is enough to require a significant change of focus in legal scholarship remains open to debate. Other such queries include whether the observable increase in the multitude of norm-producing institutions and actors constitutes a good enough reason for coming up with a different term for the legal universe that lies beyond the nation-state. Or, what is the main impetus behind the uprooting of 'dearly-held convictions of jurisdictional boundaries and competences'?[22] Would it not be better to refer to the phenomena under discussion as the 'law of globalization' rather than transnational law?

These questions are not new in the realm of legal scholarship and, what is more, they are not unique to the area of international law. As the debates examined in this section will reveal, discussions concerning the role of law across dispersed and fragmented spaces of norm production were held since the early days of legal pluralism and critical legal studies.[23] What is perhaps novel is the thorough consideration of the effects related to power and legitimacy of law at a global scale.[24] This shift in focus constitutes a significant challenge to the state-centred view of not only international law, but also constitutional and regulatory law. Furthermore, the recognition of private actors' and organized interests' growing relevance for law and legal regimes allows for a much more nuanced and dynamic understanding of the relationship between state and non-state actors, among states, and, between various legal actors and institutions in general. The growing complexity of de-centred or multi-centric socio-legal and political discourses addressing transnational activities requires an equally diverse and flexible frame of reference. The term 'transnational', conjoined with pluralism, is supposed to be that very frame.[25] However, a change of terms alone by no means produces all-encompassing solutions to theoretical or practical problems. Besides, there is an ongoing debate within the field of transnational law over the characterization of this field, that is whether it is fluid, semi-structured and cooperative, or simply a mirror image of power inequalities, antagonistic relations and anarchistic tendencies projected onto the area of law.[26] Transnational law, deemed neither domestic nor international but both and more, is equally important for constitutional and administrative law in a global context. For some, transnational law is where real change will emerge, dethroning the monstrosity of global capitalism and neo-liberal empires. For those who hold this viewpoint, transnational law, by way of providing a platform for new forms of governance, is expected to overcome the alleged separation of domestic and international realms and provide a global sense of transparency for conflicts and clashes of interest.[27]

At the juncture of international law and legal pluralism scholarship that led to the current debate on transnationalism, the New Haven School played a pivotal role. Its scholars, including Myres S. McDougal, Harold D. Lasswell and Michael Reisman, were among the most influential groups of legal thinkers in the field of international law since the Second World War.[28] In their spirited response to Cold War realism, they put their faith in legal processes, rules and norms, at the expense of the might of naked power in world politics. Theirs was a choice made in the name of recognizing the transformative normative power of what they saw as international legal practices. Their departure both from legal positivism and political realism[29] saved them from the pitfalls of a doctrinal quest for 'what law is'. Instead, they turned their gaze to issues concerning how non-state law is created, how it operates, how it affects domestic decisions, and how it influences the shaping of multiple legal regimes. The legacy of the New Haven School is perhaps best summarized in two basic questions: What is international law made of, and, who makes it? Deriving from these two questions, other concerns emerged, such as determining whether international law is primarily a system of edicts or rather a complex process with indeterminate ends. In their charting of the topography of international law, adherents of the New Haven School challenged the foundational assumptions about the nature of law and legal regimes that had dominated legal scholarship until then. The School's main impetus for engaging in this kind of critique was their belief in the possibility of 'bottom-up international law making' with respect to the codification of international rules and norms, as opposed to a top-down understanding of formal legal systems obsessed with state sovereignty.[30] They certainly did not regard the nation-state as the primary law-maker. They also refused to privilege treaty law as the pre-eminent form of international law. They denied that international law was simply an elite-orchestrated process of hegemonic power-building under the cloak of legality. Instead, they saw it as an uneven and yet lively battlefield of variant stakeholders and interests. Consequently, it became possible to regard international law as a legal universe made up of multiple and semi-overlapping law-making communities.

Almost fifty years after the School's protests against nationalist and power-centred conceptions of international law, an influential group of American law professors launched a new attack, but this time riding the tide of neo-conservatism in the United States. Jack Goldsmith and Eric Posner, in particular, emerged as two of the leading spokespeople for the neo-conservative study of international law, though their followers come from what may be called a 'rainbow coalition' of ideologies within a growing international audience.[31] In the ensuing debates critiquing the isolationist US stance against international law and the current responses to neo-conservative, formalist and doctrinal trends in legal scholarship, one could sense a strong resemblance to the stance taken by the New Haven School back in 1970s. There emerged a tradition of critique adjusting to the demands of the changing times. Along that trajectory, there are at least three other schools, namely TWAIL, Critical International Law and Radical Pluralism debates, which take issue with international law as it has been traditionally perceived and taught. They all take the inequalities and historical injustices endemic to the current state of world capitalism as their point of departure, rather than engaging mainly with an internal critique of how international law works. These latter bodies of scholarship have more kinship with the articulation of international law as globalization of law or transnational law, and are prone to overlook the nation-state much more readily. In this changed context, though the legacy of the New Heaven School is indeed an important one, to globalize its kind of critique requires a vision that looks above and beyond the way things appear from the Global North alone. And that has indeed been the desire of the new wave of discontented work on international law.

B. TWAIL Scholarship and the Radical Pluralism Debate

As already introduced at the opening of this work, Third World Approaches to International Law (TWAIL) is a critical approach to international law that has assumed a distinguished status in the overall questioning of the history and legacies of international law, an endeavour that started with the first and second waves of legal pluralism discussed above. However, TWAIL comes with a marked distinction. It is an approach to law that is unified by a particular set of concerns endemic to the application and imposition of law in the Global South. It draws its methodology primarily from the history of the encounter between international law and colonized peoples and post-colonial societies. In this regard, TWAIL shares a common heritage and an arsenal of analytical tools with post-colonial studies, feminist theory, critical race theory, critical legal studies and Marxism, as well as with legal pluralism. TWAIL scholarship capitalizes on the power dynamic between the largely Developed Core and the mostly Dependent Periphery in the world capitalist economy, following the terms used by world systems analysis.[32] Overall, it highlights the role of international law in legitimizing the subjugation and oppression of societies in the Global South. TWAIL scholars strive to avoid presenting the 'Third World' as a unified, coherent place and instead put emphasis on the shared experiences of underdevelopment, imposed dependency and marginalization. They also try to salvage at least some parts of the overall project of international law to aid struggles for justice in the Global South. Contemporary TWAIL scholarship has its origins in works of jurists such as Georges Abi-Saab, F. Garcia-Amador, R. P. Anand, Mohammed Bedjaoui and Taslim O. Elias. They were later joined by

Antony Anghie, Bhupinder Chimni, Karin Mickelson, Obiora Chinedu Okafor, Wa Makau Mutua, Balkrishnan Rajagopal and Issa Shivji.[33] Here, I will only discuss the TWAIL project's significance for the debate on transnational law, despite the vast array of contributions each of the aforementioned names otherwise made to legal scholarship.

Overall, the frame of thinking used by scholars associated with TWAIL represents a distinct form of historical analysis concerning the development of international law. TWAIL scholarship adheres to the description of international law as a set of practices that led to the continual subordination and marginalization of the experiences of Third World societies. In this regard, Makau Mutua describes Bandung, Indonesia as the symbolic birthplace of the TWAIL discourse, although the school is heavily indebted to the Non-Alignment Movement as well.[34] Overall, TWAIL emerged as a response to repressive and disciplinary strategies of de-colonization in the Global South. It was developed due to the urgent need to understand why liberation projects in the post-colonial world could hardly ever deliver what they promised. TWAIL scholarship also attends to historical experiences in non-European and post-colonial societies that have given rise to unique forms of political consciousness about the law. As such, TWAIL is dedicated to unpacking the uses of international law as a medium for the creation and perpetuation of racialized hierarchies, to historicizing the development and evolution of international law as a repressive universalist discourse, and to critically assessing its uses for the subordination of peoples and their realities across the Global South.[35] TWAIL claims to be counter-hegemonic, anti-hierarchical, and also coalition-prone.

Keeping with the spirit of legal pluralism though not necessarily identifying with it, TWAIL discourse thus assumes a moral equivalence of cultures and peoples. It is in this light that it considers the current regime of international law as illegitimate, since what exists today is seen as being based almost entirely on the intellectual, historical and cultural experiences of one particular region of the world – that is, Europe. Finally, TWAIL is positioned as a reconstructive project that aims at eradicating the conditions of underdevelopment in the Global South. Since international law has been instrumental in regulating encounters between Europe and the rest of the world through the rules of both sovereignty and self-determination, TWAIL scholars argue that international law has been used for the forced assimilation of non-European peoples into a legal regime within which they had no voice.[36] In order to build strong alliances to counter the position that post-colonial societies have been locked into, TWAIL scholarship has asserted itself through the formation of transnational movements committed to de-centring the European–North American domination of international law.

Despite this highly charged political stance, TWAIL scholars express the need to be self-critical, aware of the limitations of the school and the voices it may have yet excluded. Their emphasis remains on the international legal regime's complicity in the maintenance of colonial legacies during the post-colonial era. Consequently, international law is depicted as neither neutral nor impartial. Rather, it is marked by its indifference to human suffering and its own complicity with historical injustices. Mutua famously describes the relationship between the international legal regime and its players through the metaphor of savages–victims–saviours (Mutua, 2001).[37] Accordingly, the state is depicted as the operational instrument of savagery in international law. The victim, on the other hand, is described as the human being whose dignity and worth have been violated by the system as a whole. Of course, the victim is non-white, highlighting the racial divide endemic particularly to human rights discourse in international law. The saviour, then, refers to the Eurocentric nature of the dominant international law paradigm, constructing the West as normatively superior.

Another notable critique of the international legal system offered by TWAIL scholarship is its outcry that the pioneering roles played by non-Western activists, judges, legal scholars and human rights actors are not at all acknowledged in the universal human rights discourse. In this vein, Issa Shivji calls for a re-conceptualized rights regime capable of challenging the hegemonic logic of international law by unpacking its imperialist and statist biases, at the same time providing space for registering Third World people's abilities to resist hegemony.[38] Overall, TWAIL scholars take a decided stance against the promotion of a sense of naturalness of international law, and treat it as a political project of homogenization in its current form. They assert that the lack of attention to influences from the Global South within human rights law leads to a significant erasure of the legitimacy of the discourse. As is, problems are expected to be solved without reference to those involved and affected in the first place. The inconspicuous absence of race and racial hierarchies within the human rights discourse and the international legal system in general is read as a pathology of self-redemption masking the international hierarchy of race and colour re-entrenched in the neo-liberal system of capitalist relations. In this light, TWAIL scholars continue to push for opening up the discourse of international law, strive to create a balance between individual and group rights, to give more substance to social and economic rights, to relate rights to duties and responsibilities, and to address the relationship between the corpus of law and global economic systems (Okafor, 2005).[39] As such, although internally fragmented, TWAILers thus far developed and sustained a strong argument concerning the importance of an in-depth understanding of the power dynamics and historical realities at play in international law. TWAIL work attacks widely accepted norms of international law that both victimize and blame the peoples of the Global South. As it invites more actors onto the stage, it detests normative hierarchies in the construction of international law as a regime of hegemonic practices. For these reasons, although not formally included in the registers of legal pluralism scholarship, I believe there is a valid case to be made for TWAIL scholarship to be construed as part and parcel of what I call the third wave of legal pluralism/radical pluralism.

C. Radical Pluralism and Beyond

In the remainder of this discussion on legal pluralism, I will concentrate specifically on Martti Koskenniemi and Ruth Buchanan's work on international law and globalization. This choice is by no means to suggest that the work of other legal scholars is not important in marking the contours of radical pluralism. Peer Zumbansen and Gunther Teubner's works, in particular, are far too influential to omit from any such discussion (Teubner, 1991; 1997; 2004).[40] But for the purposes of this chapter, I choose this duo of legal scholars, as Buchanan engages in a debate with Koskenniemi from within legal pluralist discourse itself, while also utilizing many of the conceptual reference points of the latest phase of legal pluralism, including Teubner's work.

From the late 1980s onwards, Koskenniemi engaged in an embedded discussion on international law, the tenor of which was spelled out in his *From Apology to Utopia: The Structure of International Legal Argument* (first published in 1989). In this early work, Koskenniemi presented a critical view of international law as a discursive practice that attempts to remove politics from law. If so, international law would be nothing more than either an irrelevant moralist utopia or an apology to global power politics. In his later work, including *The Gentle Civilizer of Nations: The Rise and Fall of International Law 1870–1960* (2001), Koskenniemi diversified his agenda. He first developed an intellectual history of international law, and then offered a critique of that history. This led to a highly pessimistic account of the content and workings of international law. In this sense, Koskenniemi follows a similar trope to what one finds in Michael Mandel's, Tony Evans's or Steve Ratner's critiques of different branches of international law.[41] Overall, Koskenniemi seems to have finally given up on the formal, classical legal ideal of international law in search of a normatively endowed, Kantian ideal. This was perhaps to be expected, as he is an intellectual historian of international law rather than a jurist. In fact, his critique of international law eventually led him to attack the methodology of the profession.[42] This new turn in his work is most observable in the International Law Commission (ILC) Report titled *Fragmentation of International Law: Difficulties Arising from the Diversification and Expansion of International Law* (2007), the conclusion of which is penned by Martti Koskenniemi himself. The report organizes and synthesizes the various debates and discussions that relate to the breaking up of international law into several distinct regimes. It also presents practical suggestions for mitigating some of the problems associated with its increasing fragmentation.

At this point, I turn to Ruth Buchanan's critique of Koskenniemi's work and her reintroduction of legal pluralism, not as historical critique or background for policy suggestions but as a legal theoretical method of dealing with international law while critically addressing its contradictions. In her work, Buchanan provides both a critique of and a possible alternative to Koskenniemi's internal remedies for the failings of international law.[43] She argues that as long as globalization is reframed as an external problem for legal theory, the solutions envisaged will be determined by the limited parameters of already existing legal discourses. Global legal pluralism could invoke or illustrate the multiple, diverse and contested sources of law on a transnational plane and could allow us to think about law differently, rather than focusing on how to respond to globalization within existing frameworks of legality. Buchanan's work, like TWAIL scholarship, is squarely opposed to a positivist conception of law. She also refutes the reduction of legal plurality to descriptive claims and instead subscribes to it as an *ethos* and a form of critical theory. Her approach to legal pluralism takes as its starting point a critique of the practice of defining law as a privileged domain of aspiration, responsiveness and precision. She thus endorses an understanding of legal forms and institutions as both contingent and revisable, which in turn allows for opportunities for those whose interests are inadequately addressed by current institutions and legal regimes.

Specifically, Buchanan's critique of Koskenniemi is twofold. She states that while law and politics are interrelated, legal discourses cannot be equated with political outcomes. Moreover, she argues that while a critical investigation of politics of law is helpful in revealing law's failures and exclusions, this kind of analysis does not shed light on the production of law, or the capacities of legal subjects to contest, change or add legal meanings. Although she appreciates Koskenniemi's attempt to imagine law as inherently plural, her emphasis is more on the plurality of law-creating subjects. In comparison to Koskenniemi's worries about diplomats, jurists and international lawyers, Buchanan would like to think of a much wider range of law-creating subjects. She also refuses recourse to a unifying image of a constitutional moment, and instead chooses to live with a 'radically legal pluralist' topography of multiple and diverse subjects and regimes, and a transnational legality without a centre or normative hierarchy. The implication of her reframing of international law is that emergent transnational regulatory regimes need not be reduced to relations of superiority/inferiority based on the degrees of their legal or constitutional character. Instead, furthering the work of Cover, Teubner and Trubek[44] among others, Buchanan presents international law as an amalgamation of competing, interpenetrating, and mutually constitutive regimes at a transnational scale (Buchanan, 2008).[45] She hopes that by allowing such plurality into legal scholarship, public discussions about the emergence and evolution of transnational legal norms might include a much wider range of institutional and discursive mechanisms. In my view, Buchanan's unique contribution to the third wave of legal pluralism debate is her insistence that we give up our obsession with legal forms and start dealing with matters of substance, content and agency, and deal with these in terms of processes rather than formal rules. For her, the lens of legal pluralism leads us to understand the construction and contestation of normative frameworks by legal subjects. This is the reflexive approach to the relationship between law and politics in the international realm, whereby competing and conflicting normative claims are engaged with, negotiated, compromised or reconfigured.

II. Transnational Character of Accountability Regimes in International Law and Multicentricity of Legal Practices

In this section, I will narrow down the debate on the applicability of legal pluralism to international law and concentrate on the specific field of accountability regimes in international criminal law, the subject matter of this work. A well-functioning accountability regime in international law may be the ultimate dream of legal scholars and jurists alike. However, crystallization of a unitary legal system is an elusive goal.[46] Coherence and efficacy of the overall international legal order, with its fragmented and diversified structure and processes, could not be achieved by an imposed set of primary rules. The multitude of 'secondary rules' in international law – referring to Hart's list of recognition, change and adjudication – is a constant force to be reckoned with. Nor could we do away with the proliferation of 'third party forums', quasi-legal institutions or hybrid bodies in international law that are integral to both law-making and adjudication at the national and regional levels as well as in expertise subject areas. If we follow the lead of Jonathan Charney, who gave up on the dream of a unitary regime of international law as early as 1988, clearly pronouncing so during his Hague Lectures, cross-fertilization and variegation are to be seen as improvements to the overall quality of international law, rather than a gradual undoing that must be opposed at all cost.[47] Observable changes in the global network of legal systems, which are indicative of a decisive move away from an exclusive focus on state parties, undo the majestic assumption of the structural unity of international law. In this case, how could we pronounce a singular international accountability regime that is far-reaching, flexible, adaptable? Furthermore, is it desirable to have such a regime in the face of histories of discontent and injustice?

No doubt, these issues are of import not only for international criminal law, but have implications for all areas of international public law. However, they are particularly troubling for international criminal law due to the heavy weight of *jus cogens* norms and *ergo omnes* obligations dictating a regime of universal jurisdiction in areas such as crimes against humanity. In the institution of permanent courts such as the International Criminal Court (ICC), for instance, universal jurisdiction delivers the meaning of rules of legal codification to be diffused by the central legal authority of the Court itself. The Rome Statute provides specific guidelines for this centrifugal procedure. However, the way it was designed to be ratified and embedded in the constitutional realm of individual states does not consider the socio-political investment required for the domestic adoptions of international criminal law that fall under the ICC's mandate. In this regard, while an increasing number of legal practitioners, jurists and scholars note the hybridization, fragmentation and cross-fertilization of international law – and even opt for the term 'transnational law' in its place – legal discourse in the field of international criminal law remains obsessed with centralization and standardization, with the universal reach of a single institution and it jurisgenerative conduct.

A. Fragmentation in International Law and the Fragile Balance of Primary and Secondary Rules in Accountability Regimes

Institutions like the ICC in fact perform a double action. They engage in both *jurisgenerative* and *jurispathic* conduct, though which one of these practices is more important for the legacy and saliency of the institution, or indeed for the effectiveness of punishment of international crimes, is highly debatable. To put it differently, the ICC engages in both primary and secondary rule-making in contemporary accountability regimes, though they are often discussed as if almost entirely separate from one another. Such concerns about the increasing diversity of secondary rules and the desired unity of primary rules of international law reveal themselves fully in the context of debates on the sources of international law, responsibilities of legal institutions and normative conflicts. As suggested earlier in this chapter, the relative autonomy of a wide range of coexisting regimes is seen by some as a guarantee of its growing effectiveness in terms of its primary rules, rather than as jeopardizing the unity and coherence of the overall structure of the international legal order (Hart, [1961] 2012). If diversification and differences in interpretation are seen as an integral part of the general enterprise, secondary rules do not constitute a threat to primary ones. The apparent coherence of the doctrines espoused by international courts and tribunals is taken as further proof that it is possible to talk about a single, unitary accountability regime in international criminal law that can accommodate variations between judgments produced by international, domestic and regional legal regimes.[48]

Meanwhile, for there to be a legal accountability regime in any branch of international law, there has to be an identifiable remedial aspect of its judicial functions. There is a significant difference between substantive and remedial law. The former is generally understood to stand for statutory or written law that governs the rights and obligations of those who are subject to it. Therefore, it defines the legal relationship of individuals and the society, or the relationship between society and the state. Remedial law, on the other hand, is a version of procedural law. It comprises the rules by which a court hears and determines what happens in civil or criminal proceedings. Procedural law – including remedial law – provides the method and means by which substantive law is made and administered. While substantive law defines rights and duties, procedural law corresponds to the body of legal rules for enforcing those rights and duties. The principle of delivering and promoting justice requires both substantive and procedural law to be effective. In Hart's language of jurisprudence, law has to embody a strong link between primary and secondary rules. Organs of international law are not only fragmented, they operate at multiple levels of jurisdiction and face a variety of claimants, the state being one amongst many. These multiple *fora* entertain different procedural rules and substantive norms, and could yield different results attending to the same type of case. Their limited *locus standi* and restrictive jurisdiction directly affects their competency. However, if we go back to the debate on transnational law and radical pluralism, neither variations in procedures nor in competency constitute a death sentence for a nascent legal regime. Instead, it is possible to argue that in the area of international law, and specifically with regards to accountability regimes, work on primary and secondary rules is often undertaken almost simultaneously. This is precisely what organs like the ICC have embarked upon. In that sense, determination of the success of a regime of universal jurisdiction should not be undertaken solely in terms of whether domestic courts adopt the Rome Statute *verbatim*. Equally important is the spirit of the laws endorsed by the ICC and the harmonization they may induce in regional and state practices concerning adjudication of state criminality. We must keep our focus on the primary rules of international criminal law falling under the mandate of such legal bodies, and examine whether the Court initiated a process of transnational regime formation in this regard. Procedural/remedial aspects of international criminal law, otherwise known as the secondary rules, should not become the end game in this determination.

B. The Project of International Law and the Jurisprudential Promise of the ICC: Disciplining the Domestic Realm through International Criminal Law?

Public international law is traditionally viewed as oscillating between a Kantian cosmopolitan *ethos* and negotiated regimes of adjudication regarding conflict of laws and other jurisdictional matters at the international level.[49] Regimes of trade law, human rights law, environmental law, and of course international criminal law are all testimony to the latter tendency. The former, cosmopolitan impetus to manage and resolve 'global problems', on the other hand, often finds its best expression in the form of institution-building with a global reach and a purportedly global mandate. Standard political responses to institutional developments in the area of international legal regime formation took two forms: the constitutionalist defence disputing the accountability of transnational institutions, or invitations extended by the legal pluralism of earlier decades celebrating institution-building as a possible platform for dialogue. In my view, both are inadequate to deal with the task of redefining the project of international law in the age of late capitalism, neocolonialism and globalization. The knee-jerk reaction of reducing international public law to a phantom mechanism built to advance functional objectives of neo-liberal harmonization, and serving only the interests of the powerful, is a similarly misleading take on this issue. Surely, the managerial vocabulary of international regulatory and legal practices fit the definition of an overarching plan of neo-liberal global constitutionalism, as do the markedly negative implications of acts committed by select international institutions concerning the interests of the societies in the Global South. Still, not all new formations in public international law could be explained by these broad strokes and not all of them herald the impending doomsday.

The establishment of the permanent International Criminal Court is one such area that has a double-edged quality vis-à-vis the post–Second World War history of public international law. Strictly speaking, the ICC does not entertain legal pluralist renditions of criminality into its chosen areas of authority. Despite the worries about it being an integral part of the neo-liberal agenda of forcing post-colonial and post-imperial societies into submission for further capitalist expansion and deeper forms of accumulation, its nexus lies in the area of what may be called 'disciplining practices' emanating from a normative standpoint regarding egregious crimes committed by states and state-like legal actors such as war crimes, genocide, slavery, and crimes against humanity.[50] In addition, its existence owes much to widespread NGO movements both within Europe and the Global South, as these actors struggled for decades and made alliances with each other to counter the American hegemonic position in the area of international criminal law.[51] This aspect of the ICC's history gave the institution an unusual degree of legitimacy for an organ with such outreach – at least this was the case at the outset. Last but not least, the regime of international criminal law envisaged by the ICC cannot be grasped merely through the language of sovereign acts of states culminating in customary practices or treaty obligations. There is a clear transnational quality to the ICC's mandate. The institution is designed to resolve cases of state criminality within the parameters of a legally defined exercise of international public authority and based on the principle of universal jurisdiction. As such, the subject matter jurisdiction of the Court does not refer to disputes arising between states. Rather, it primarily concerns the criminal acts of states against their own societies.

In terms of its jurisdictional reach, the ICC operates on the principle of complementarity/subsidiarity. Thus, the first choice for adjudication of crimes falling under its jurisdiction is identified as domestic courts acting in accordance with domestic law, or specialized hybrid tribunals subject to supervision by domestic courts. The founding document of the ICC – the Rome Statute – clearly indicates that in cases when such remedies are deemed not available or not realizable, general international consent authorizes the adjudication of such crimes by the ICC itself. Whether resolved by resort to domestic or international courts, international crimes falling under the ICC's mandate are therefore squarely identified as matters of international law. The criminal law regime attending to them is to be distinguished from reciprocal and consensual agreements dictated by treaty law. Furthermore, the ICC is a court of prosecution, and not a civil court. In this context, international criminal law as codified by the ICC is not based on the regulation of a relationship between juridical equals. Following the standard criminal law format, it accrues a privileged position to the party representing public authority, and calls upon those who allegedly committed crimes against the society. In the specific case of crimes against humanity jurisprudence, the violated party is in principle defined as the whole of humanity. If so, the ICC, as one of the prime institutional embodiments of transnational law, acts as a semi-autonomous supranational adjudicative body.

The ICC is semi-autonomous because its decisions are insulated from higher court supervision or judicial review mechanisms, and its ties with the UN are symbolic rather than legislative even in the case referrals arriving by way of the UN Security Council. It is supranational because its authority derives from a treaty, the Rome Statute, as well as customary understanding of the crimes listed under its jurisdiction. Constituted at the transnational level, the ICC thus embraces the role of disciplining the governmental actions of states in the personhood of individuals representing states and state-like actors committing crimes against their societies, as defined by the normative architecture of international criminal law. In this context, what makes the ICC a noteworthy specimen of transnational law is not its reach *per se*. Nor is it the ICC's inevitable exposure to forces of legal fragmentation and hybridity of international law in the global realm. The ICC's capacity for legal norm and conduct building is what makes it worthy of attention.

Owing to its transnational mandate, tribunals established under the law of individual states are invested with authority to try crimes defined by the ICC on the basis of universal jurisdiction. As such, the ICC not only produces but also perpetuates a specific legal discourse, even when it does not try a given case itself. According to the dictate of universal jurisdiction, although the ICC is uniquely removed from the domestic legal system of any given state, its codes are to be integrated into the domestic enforcement structures of all states. As a result, the power of this institution to make and enforce legal claims of criminality stands apart from its predecessors such as the Nuremberg and Tokyo military trials, or even the International Court of Justice. For this reason, the regime of international criminal law most clearly embodied by the ICC's Rome Statute should be recognized as constituting an exceptionally powerful manifestation of transnational law. No other system of court-based international adjudication has as much sway in terms of substantiating forms of criminality and enforcing methods of adjudication within a global compass. Even if a given state has not signed and ratified the Rome Statute, the dictate of universal jurisdiction obliges its articles to be considered as positive international law, and to be taken into direct consideration in the domestic realm. In this context, it would be apt to identify ICC-based codification of international crimes as the full-fledged exercise of a disciplinary regime with transnational qualities.

These developments are symptomatic of changes in public international law readily identified by the third wave of legal pluralist scholarship. In order to understand the workings of international criminal law, the manner in which ICC operates needs to be examined closely. This includes topics such as the court's determination of the exhaustion of all local remedies, the establishment of hybrid tribunals based on the principle of universal jurisdiction, and the adaptation of the Rome Statute by domestic courts, with the implications of this process for national law. While all of these issues clearly invite further inquiry, the remainder of this chapter will only focus on the politico-legal reasoning upon which the ratification of the Rome Statute in the realm of domestic law has been envisaged, and how this process relates to the 'international law as transnational law' debate.

C. International Criminal Court and the Ideal of Complementarity in International Law

A key statement that defines the ICC's ideal role in public international law was uttered in 2003, just after the Court's founding, by none other than Luis Moreno-Ocampo, Chief Prosecutor of the Court. As he was sworn into office, he declared that 'the absence of trials before this Court, as a consequence of the regular functioning of national institutions, would be a major success.'[52] The legal reference here is to the Rome Statute's complementarity principle,[53] which permits the Court to exercise its jurisdiction over a serious international crime only if no State is willing and able to prosecute the crime. The determination of the likelihood that defendants will receive due process in national proceedings is part and parcel of this legal stipulation.[54] The fact that most national criminal justice systems may not provide such guarantees in states where atrocities have been committed, or where a civil war ensued, no doubt renders this picture somewhat idealistic, unless the assumption is that such trials will then take place in other states capable of sustaining such standards.

In some instances, the ICC's deferrals may in fact expose the alleged perpetrators of atrocities to national judicial systems which may not be interested in or capable of providing them with due process. This in turn may increase the likelihood of wrongful convictions, which in turn would erode the ICC's legacy, if not credibility. Furthermore, the ICC was never envisaged as an appellate body to review decisions of domestic courts or as a human rights monitoring organ. In this regard, making decisions about the legality of procedural matters in domestic courts in cases related to international crimes does not fall within its mandate. At best, the Court has the authority to determine the unwillingness or inability of a state party to prosecute a 'situation' on a case-by-case basis, inquiring whether national proceedings were fair given the totality of the circumstances in a particular setting. However, if a trial proceeds in a domestic court, the ICC has no authority to vacate a conviction resulting from a trial deemed not to have been conducted independently or impartially in accordance with the norms of due process that the Court itself upholds.[55] In other instances, the ICC's identification of specific crimes may never be fully approved by the domestic courts that claim jurisdiction over the criminal trial of alleged individuals. A case in point is that of Augusto Pinochet, and the 'Bermuda triangle' that formed between the Spanish Judge who claimed universal jurisdiction to try the retired dictator for crimes against humanity, the British House of Lords that erred, at least to an extent, on the side of diplomatic immunity, and the Chilean domestic courts that were at best hesitant to try the case.[56] Similar issues transpired vis-à-vis the ICC's direct or indirect involvement in Sierra Leone, Cambodia, Lebanon, Sudan and Iraq. Therefore, the issue of complementarity could be said to provide more questions than answers in public international law. However, if we shift our lens from international criminal law to transnational law, another picture emerges.

D. Mandate of the International Criminal Court: Jurisprudential versus Political Realities

In reality, the discrepancies observed in the application of universal jurisdiction of the ICC's codification of international crimes are indicative of the gap between the jurisprudential and political dimensions of accountability regimes in international law. The issues and concerns articulated above are informed by my conviction that in order to make a categorical observation about international legal institutions with a transnational mandate, we must first attend to the normative underpinnings of their legal operations as well as the symbolic and political value of their jurisdictional characteristics. Determining the significance of ICC-like institutions with respect to the grand project of launching a post-Westphalian regime of international law is a crucial step in this direction. Indeed, the ICC has often been presented as a *tour de force* heralding a new age, wherein state interests are trumped by universal, transnational and, of course, humanitarian ones. Similarly, from a jurisprudential point of view, the Rome Statute is considered to have made a marked change in the attribution of responsibility and the curtailment of impunity for crimes of grave nature and exceptionally wide scope.

Historically speaking, the trend of building a regime of international criminal law that started with the Nuremberg and Tokyo trials significantly lost steam during the Cold War years.[57] Following the cascade of developments including the endorsement of the International Military Tribunals of Nuremberg and Tokyo in 1946, the charting of the Genocide Convention in 1948, the Geneva Convention on armed conflict in 1949, and the attached Code of Offences against Peace and Security of Mankind, and subsequent UN covenants related to human rights law, not much more was done. Until the unfolding of the catastrophic events in the former Yugoslavia and Rwanda, the constitution of a system of substantive international law to attend to human rights atrocities committed during war *or* peace was not a priority for the UN's bureaucratic and legal circles. This was despite the fact that crimes against humanity were not at all absent from the international scene, and there were a wide range of disturbing developments in the former

Soviet Union and Eastern bloc, Latin America, the Middle East, Asia, and Africa.

In summary, the unique kind of intersection that the international tribunals of the 1990s came to embody – signifying a calculated overlap between international human rights law, humanitarian law and international criminal law – was perhaps intimated and yet by no means fully articulated during the immediate post-war trials and the trajectory that followed from there onwards. Even the International Law Commission's resumption of work in 1983, after a long hiatus of almost thirty-five years, was tainted by the debate among states concerning how to define 'aggression' committed by states.[58] It took another thirteen years to reach a state of semi-resolution in the form of a Draft Code. The culmination of these efforts finally came in the form of the constitution of a permanent International Criminal Court in 2002. Yet, for jurisdiction-related matters, whether this should be regarded as a watermark remains far from obvious. What could be argued with much greater comfort is that the ICC is part and parcel of a sea change in norm creation and norm inducement at the transnational level. Its internal logic may be at odds with the traditional operations of international law, and from that angle, applications of universal jurisdiction lacks jurisdictional certainty. If, however, universal jurisdiction is taken as a discursive tool honed to circumscribe domestic variations in the determination of criminality in categories delineated by the ICC, then the matter assumes novel dimensions, as will be discussed in the remaining chapters of this work.

Conclusion

This chapter provided a conceptual map of existing scholarship on the workings of international law and applied it to the dictum of universal jurisdiction. Though the review presented here is by no means comprehensive, it is symptomatic of most pronounced trends in the current reconfiguration of the debate on the nature and reach of international law. In this context, I analysed the merits and failings of the model of centrifugal diffusion regarding international regimes of accountability, particularly in light of the claims made by select schools of thought related to legal pluralism. Based on the foundational premises of the third wave of radical legal pluralistic scholarship, I commenced an examination of the normative boundaries of the applicability of international criminal law codified by a supranational body with a transnational reach such as the International Criminal Court (ICC) in domestic settings. This examination will be continued in the remainder of this work. With particular reference to crimes against humanity, and attending to the institutional, normative and political aspects of universal jurisdiction, the following chapters will analyse the context and efficacy of attempts at their adjudication in the Global South. The aim of this chapter was to foreground this particular debate in legal theory.

The history of politico-legal practices leading to the foundation of a permanent court is primarily Europe-bound, though its emergence involved a strong component of Global South and non-state participation. As is, the ICC's mandate defined by the Rome Statute has far-reaching global implications. A crucial part of its operations and the principle of universal jurisdiction embraced by the court depend on the unassailable equation of morality and law, especially so in the case of crimes against humanity. Meanwhile, the absence of a widespread ethics of responsibility to provide international criminal law with a final say in this area cannot be overlooked. Hence, we witness a clearly identifiable contradiction between the mandate of a transnational legal institution and the realities of the application and adaptation of international (criminal) law produced or endorsed by it. This is a delicate disjuncture, and one that cannot be handled solely by legal pluralism in its early or later versions.

The original concern behind the debate on the ICC presented in this chapter was to determine whether international tribunals and courts indeed embody a new kind of relationship between socio-political, substantive/normative and legal aspects of public international law and thus constitute an exemplary case for transnational law. A related query was whether international criminal law has achieved the status of a transnational legal regime and assumed a position above and beyond the interests and immediate involvement of the states and societies affected by it. If so, could it indeed sustain the kind of criticism that was raised by schools of thought such as TWAIL scholarship? The answers to both lines of inquiry proved to be highly conditional. Here, the issue is no longer the codification of law or even juridification processes themselves. In public international law, codification customarily refers to the articulation of binding legal rules, otherwise known as 'positive law'. The 'codification movement' in legal conduct emerged out of the post-Enlightenment context, and took root in European societies during the late eighteenth century in the form of civil and criminal codes. It reached its high point with the enactment of the French Napoleonic Code in 1804.[59] No doubt the relationship between domestic and international criminal codes, and in particular the embedding of international law within constitutional or domestic criminal law, is a complex one. However, the applicability of transnational law in domestic contexts is only a small part of the problem. Legal pluralism scholarship reveals that the substantive meaning of law in changed contexts and scales is a much more significant issue concerning the workings of transnational law.

International criminal law jurisprudence is considered an 'autonomous branch' of criminal law, as it only deals with international crimes. Similarly, the institutions adjudicating such crimes are designated courts and tribunals, set up to try natural and artificial legal persons who have incurred an international criminal responsibility. And yet, in the case of the ICC, the court's emergence was predicated upon state consent and the continuation of its operations also demands long-term state support. Herein lies the conundrum for legal scholars and international jurists alike. Although the ICC and similar transnational organs do not constitute a unified legal system, they strive for the establishment of universal rules of adjudication for crimes codified under their aegis. They push for the enforcement of standard practices via public international law. However, the way they go about implementing this project matches the definition of transnational law, due to the nature of fragmented, overlapping regimes held together through persuasion, disciplining strategies, harmonization practices and at times by force. Indeed, global disorder, a multiplicity of regimes, and polycentric systems much more readily describe the *status quo* for international law (Dunoff, Ratner and Wippman, 2015). The unique offer of radical legal pluralism and reflexive legal theory is that such disorder is not seen as symptomatic of chaos. On the contrary, it is regarded as a necessary expression of conflicting norms, and different articulations of the desire for socio-political change.[60] According to this depiction of diversification and conflict as essential features of transnational legal regimes, the tensions endemic to the mandate of institutions such as the ICC are *pro forma*. The issue is no more how to make domestic courts and legal systems adapt the ICC's definition of criminality, and adjust their codes of legal conduct according to what the Court dictates as proper adjudication. Even in the presence of a comprehensive criminal code substantiated by an enforcement architecture, limitations of their applicability will continue to exist. Diverse norms entertained by different domestic constituencies as to what constitutes state criminality, the power dynamics affecting the addressing of problem cases, and the determination of the venue and form of trials directly influence both the scope of 'domesticated' international criminal law and the set of mechanisms availed for adjudication.

The grand project of selective and targeted erosion of state sovereignty in the name of a higher common good for global society may well be an esteemed legal prescription; its socio-political validation, however, is an entirely different matter.[61] As the practices of public international law evolved, they did so in the context of conflicts of interest, wars, negotiations, and always under the shadow of global power struggles and historically embedded forms of domination. Therefore, a truthful appraisal of the attainability of the goal of institutionalizing accountability for crimes against humanity requires that legal scholarship expand beyond the realm of assessment of criminal liability and judicial certainty. In this regard, transnational law, as tackled by recent debates within legal pluralism debates, is one venue within which we may be able to link accountability regimes to other areas of law in a global context. This would not only reduce the burden of the ICC's exceptional and yet fragile status regarding the application of the principle of universal jurisdiction. It could also bring us closer to the substantiation of injurious acts specified by crimes against humanity jurisprudence in local contexts through domestic absorption of their normative address of state criminality.

In conclusion, as I have highlighted, the historical use of notions of universality and objectivity in international law have long served First World socio-economic and political interests. These interests have now taken on a transnational character and are being pursued through an elaborate network of meta-regulatory regimes beneficial to emergent transnational capitalist classes cutting across the North and the South.[62] Critical international law scholars appear somewhat ambivalent in their efforts to craft disciplinary proposals for revealing this dark underbelly of the global legal order, with the exception of TWAIL and post-Marxist legal pluralism. While a reflective type of global legal pluralism recognizes the legitimacy of law-making as executed by non-institutional actors, the field of legal theory remains perplexed about how we reconcile the pursuit of legal accountability for state criminality and egregious mass political crimes with histories of international law clearly reflecting a highly stratified and unjust world.[63]

2

Universal Jurisdiction and Genealogies of International Criminal Law

Introduction

Over the past hundred years, there have been at least three attempts at the creation of an institutionalized system of international criminal law. The notion of a universally enforceable criminal law dates back to the Treaty of Versailles in 1919.[1] This was also when the idea of an international criminal court first emerged.[2] The realization, implementation and application of such a court, however, were not tried until after the Second World War. To address the crimes committed under the National Socialist regime in Germany, an international military tribunal was erected in Nuremberg, based on the London Charter of the International Military Tribunal, which was followed by the Tokyo Tribunal.[3] After the Cold War years (1947–91), the United Nations decided to establish *ad hoc* courts against the backdrop of gross humanitarian and human rights law violations in the former Yugoslavia and Rwanda. Then in 1998 the Rome Statute of the International Criminal Court (ICC) was adopted, which came into effect on 1 July 2002. The ICC was followed by various internationalized and hybrid courts, set up *inter alia* to cope with the conflicts in Kosovo, Sierra Leone, East Timor and Cambodia. All of these post-ICC institutions sought the ideal of a standardized legal frame of reference for the adjudication of international crimes. Alas, this yearning did not alleviate the problem of the state-centric nature of international criminal law and the limitations that come with it.

In this chapter, the issue of causes of compliance (or lack thereof) with international law is addressed in the specific context of the debate concerning the emergence of a standardized frame of reference for universal jurisdiction. This is a continuation of the questioning developed in the first chapter concerning the nature of transnational law as it applies to the condition of states and societies in the Global South. During the last few decades, the long-standing divide between those who believed that international rules have an effect on shaping state behaviour and those who saw such rules as epiphenomenal or, worse, as imposed, has given way to an increasingly acrimonious debate. The proliferation and evolution of international legal agreements, organizations and quasi-judicial bodies in the aftermath of the Cold War years led to attention being paid to the role of public international law in determining interstate and transnational politics. Meanwhile, the phenomenon of legalization and adjudication of state criminality under the aegis of international criminal law raised several new questions. What factors affect the choice to resort to international criminal law? When is such a recourse a choice and when is it imposed? Upon whom is international criminal law 'imposed' and under which circumstances? Does the use of international criminal law make a difference in how governments behave when states are faced with their own criminal conduct? What issues emerge from critiques emanating from the post-colonial world and the Global South at large concerning the use and abuse of international criminal law? These are just a few of the rather troubling concerns emerging in the post-ICC landscape criminal adjudication.

Here, I would start with positing that compliance is to be distinguished from the related but distinct concepts of implementation and effectiveness.[4] Broadly speaking, the focus of the present discussion is not compliance with treaties, but rather with the broader category of rules that constitute 'customary international law'. In studies on international criminal law, comparatively little attention has been paid to theoretical questions pertaining to universal jurisdiction. However, this chapter focuses less on the legal validity of universal jurisdiction and more on the way it relates to the conception of the state as the basic unit of international law. This is of utmost importance in terms of developing a framework for identifying the limits of universal jurisdiction in international criminal law and for thinking about criminal jurisdiction measures beyond the dictates of an overarching, formulaic regime of accountability.

I. *Nemo Me Impuna Lacessit?* The Ethos of Universal Jurisdiction[5]

Universal jurisdiction is a specific legal doctrine dictating that domestic courts try and punish perpetrators of a select set of crimes so heinous that they amount to crimes against the whole of humanity, regardless of where they occurred, the nationality of the victim or the perpetrator, the triplet which otherwise constitutes the standard nexus requirements in international law. Under its purview fall piracy, slavery, crimes against humanity, war crimes, torture, and genocide.[6] In other words, universal jurisdiction constitutes a significant departure from the traditional maxim of international criminal law that requires a direct connection between the prosecuting state and a particular crime. Specifically, states could bestow upon domestic courts the power to assert universal jurisdiction over select crimes in tandem with the capabilities of international courts such as the ICC with the power to litigate such crimes. Meanwhile, the scope and content of universal jurisdiction vary significantly despite the fact that the contemporary framework of international criminal law provides ample grounds for its exercise by states parties.

The doctrine of universal jurisdiction asserts that for a select body of international crimes, the perpetrators in question should not escape trial by invoking doctrines of sovereign immunity used as a standard defence preventing governments or their political subdivisions, departments and agencies from being brought to trial without their consent, otherwise known as the sacrosanct principle of state sovereignty. Proponents of widespread exercise of universal jurisdiction further argue that it is not always possible to prosecute crimes committed by states in the very locale where they were committed. For example, after a devastating civil conflict or inter-ethnic war, states often lack the necessary legal infrastructure and resources to carry out investigation and prosecution of state criminality. Alternatively, governments may intentionally fail or refuse to prosecute such crimes. Even worse, conduct subject to prosecution may have been sanctioned or supported by the state itself, or the perpetrators of such crimes may still be serving as government officials or could have allies within the ruling regime and the judiciary. Thus, there may be a lack of political will to pursue investigations, preventing the prosecution of alleged crimes. At least in theory, in the absence of accountability, other states may seek to initiate prosecutions on the basis of universal jurisdiction in order to prevent impunity and provide justice for victims of such crimes subject to universal jurisdiction.[7] States may also be put under pressure to pursue prosecutions due the presence of a perpetrator within their borders, for their territory not to be regarded as a safe haven for criminals.

Still, universal jurisdiction remains a controversial principle and practice in international law due to the state-centric nature of the very enterprise, as well as the power dynamics that shape the relations between states, regions and international courts in terms of the selection of cases that have been subject to investigations and prosecutions. There are three historical instances that need to be re-examined to provide a background to this unique practice in international criminal law. With the Treaty of Versailles in 1919, President Woodrow Wilson's new agenda for Europe led to the development of the League of Nations, and the emergence of the Permanent Court of International Justice.[8] However, this court was seen as a victor's court by many rather than having universal legitimacy. In 1945, the allied powers replaced the (by then defunct) League with the United Nations, which was followed by the establishment of Nuremberg and Tokyo military trials.[9] These too have been generally named as trials that led to victor's justice, despite the very valid reasons for which they tried war criminals, albeit one-sidedly. The UN Security Council itself proved heavily problem-laden in terms of misuse of its powers during the Cold War years. Following the collapse of the Soviet Union in November 1989, for instance, permanent members of the Security Council cooperated in the unprecedented UN-backed strike against Iraq's invasion of Kuwait in August 1990. This is commonly cited – both positively and negatively – as the beginning of a 'new world order'.[10] The Iraq decision was followed by the establishment of two *ad hoc* tribunals for the prosecution of crimes against humanity regarding the former Yugoslavia (1993) and Rwanda (1994). Considerations of the desirability and sustainability of institutionalized organs of international criminal law such as the International Criminal Court (ICC) developed against this background. The ICC has also been under heavy attack from states in the Global South, as well as some in the West such as the USA, who claim that it delivers justice based on selective criteria and picks its cases according to political reasons rather than purely justice-related ones.[11] This is the historical context that determined the limits of a full-fledged embrace of the doctrine of universal jurisdiction.

In addition, regional hubs of economic activity, political alignment, power and hegemony are becoming more pronounced, often rendering the state as a secondary actor compared to transnational corporations and private interests. In such a multifaceted environment, domestic courts, national regulatory agencies and legislatures are networking with their counterparts across the globe, espousing a transnational system of governance and regulation albeit not always for the benefit of the concerned public.[12] This has been the reality of neo-liberalism since the 1990s. Curiously, international criminal law lags behind and lacks answers to many of the most pressing challenges of the twenty-first century while being obsessed with state criminality defined in traditional terms. Dominant schools of thought in this field continue to hold the state so dear that all else fades into relative obscurity. Perhaps this is the real tragedy of the debate on universal jurisdiction, more so than the letter of the law itself or the uncertainties concerning its application. In the following pages, interpretations of the fragmentation manifest in contemporary international law are canvassed. The issues addressed here specifically deal with collisions between international law and state sovereignty, and incompatibilities of select international legal regimes in terms of their effects in the Global South. This debate has direct repercussions concerning the merits and applicability of crimes against humanity jurisprudence under the purview of the universal jurisdiction principle. Assuming harmony and normative unity to be the foundational characteristic of international criminal law is a prescriptive suggestion more than a historical reality. Furthermore, there are conflicts between international, regional and domestic regimes presenting problems of overlap in terms of jurisdictional limits, uncertainties regarding applications of the law, and divergences in its interpretation.

Specialized organs of international law often come into conflict with domestic institutions over what a particular section of international law means, and how to determine compliance. There may also be disagreements about the meaning of particular rules in international law, and who should have the authority to interpret them with certainty. These disagreements may lead to divergent decisions concerning legal obligations. In the following discussion, such conflicts are considered to be endemic to the long history of the post-imperial and post-colonial roots of international law. To this end, this chapter highlights the kinds of interaction between multiple regimes of accountability that provide political, legal and historical content to the fragmentation of international law. The chapter concludes with the suggestion that the plurality of regulatory institutions, normative values and adjudication *fora* in international law are in fact necessary components of the existing system of international criminal law given its genealogy.[13] Seeking unity and coherence in any branch of international law, including international criminal law, without addressing the violent histories it represents and through the application of traditional legal techniques of institutionalization to harmonize adjudication is a futile exercise at its best, and one that yields very antagonistic results at its worst.

II. Divided We Unite? Fragmentation and Legitimacy in International Law

As already discussed, the fragmentation of international law is a substantial enough issue to have merited an official recognition. Indeed, back in 2000, the International Law Commission decided to add to its programme of work the topic 'Risks ensuing from the fragmentation of international law'.[14] The proliferation of regional and hybrid criminal courts and tribunals should be treated as part of this larger debate on fragmentation. While some fragmentation theorists posit a non-hierarchical set of relations between general and specialized areas of international law, adherents of global constitutionalism in its positive rendition depict a gradual transformation from horizontal and consent-based forms of law towards a definite hierarchical structure built upon commonly shared fundamental principles.[15] In this latter context, the development of a series of smaller scale and sometimes *sui generis* regimes of legal accountability is perceived as a risk to the coherence and presumed homogeneity of international law.[16] According to the former take, however, institutional fragmentation could be seen as a key factor that strengthens the role of specialized regimes including regional courts, and, regional human rights and environmental regulation bodies, thus infusing public international law with fresh blood and vitality. Either way, in this increasingly variegated landscape of legal accountability and regulation, the question of normative conflicts amongst coexisting regimes and between established and emergent ones is no longer an abstract one. In fact, as the Chairman of the ILC Study Group on Fragmentation of International Law, Martti Koskenniemi was almost forced to emphasize the maxim of *lex specialis* in his report in order to address the relation between these seemingly self-contained regimes and general international law. Meanwhile, *lex specialis* suffers from a marked degree of conceptual vagueness. The fragmentation of international law made new types of conflicts visible, and heightened some of the old ones concerning historical injustices. As such, *lex specialis* may not be enough to address the current challenges faced by international law while a transnational approach may soothe some of these anxieties. Combined with the maxims of reflexive legal pluralism on the one hand, and TWAIL scholarship on the other, it may indeed be possible to chart a different trajectory for understanding the present and future of international law in its heavily fragmented *modus operandi* and contested *modus vivendi*.[17]

In the area of international criminal law (ICL), much of the worry over fragmentation originated from the collision between the ICJ and the ICTY (International Criminal Court for the former Yugoslavia) over the 'overall control' test in the Tadić case, whereby the ICTY departed from settled ICJ law on the attribution of liability and the qualification of the nature of an armed conflict, employing instead a standard of 'effective control'.[18] Since the establishment of the ICTY, the fragmentation/pluralism debate has proliferated to yet new heights. With a well-developed body of *ad hoc* tribunal case law, an emerging body of case law at the ICC, judgments produced by hybrid courts such as the Cambodia Tribunal, as well as a number of domestic prosecutions under the dictate of universal jurisdiction, fragmentation and pluralism in ICL have become serious matters for legal realists, legal positivists and monists alike. While there are still those who express concern over heterogeneity in ICL, contemporary legal scholarship by and large acknowledges the field's pluralistic nature.[19] In contradistinction, the ICC (and other institutions) continues to dwell on its cosmopolitan ethos and technical specialization for charting out all possible routes for attaining justice for international crimes falling under its purview.[20] Alas, concerns and misgivings about the asymmetry in the applications of related jurisprudence, as well as historical conflicts lying at the roots of the Court's formation, cannot be wished away.[21]

As argued by the latest generation of TWAIL scholars, notwithstanding ICL's historically troubling past and violent track record, international criminal justice is still embraced, at least in some parts of the Global South, as a potentially emancipatory project. And yet, the main impediment to the fulfilment of such a desire remains ICC's continuing operational selectivity and geopolitical bias. ICL may indeed be capable of overcoming deficiencies in national legal systems.[22] However, ICL in and of itself cannot provide a panacea for the partiality, lack of accountability, and/or ineffectiveness of domestic measures concerning mass political crimes.[23] Furthermore, if ICL and the values it promotes are provided primarily by international entities with European ancestry, what sort of legitimacy could these organs claim by virtue of the letter of the law they purport to adhere to? For the protagonists of ICL claiming it to be a universalist enterprise, the solution lies in what is called 'robust internationalism'.[24] Accordingly, the courts and tribunals tasked with applying ICL jurisprudence are seen as sufficient to successfully fulfil their mission by virtue of the delegational role they have. Seen from that angle, the way ICL currently works becomes the embodiment of global constitutionalization *par excellence*. Constitutionalism in this specific context assumes unity even where there are no grounds for the presumption of universality in international law.

In historical terms the emergence of multiple regimes of accountability in international law followed the rise of nation-states at the dusk of the European Empires. As nations were imagined into being, so were legal accountability regimes.[25] Debates over pluralism and fragmentation in ICL urge us to consider alternative accounts of how international law works. Regional legal bodies, quasi-legal regimes, subnational rights struggles, hybrid criminal tribunals, restorative justice projects, societal reconciliation mechanisms, global social and political movements for substantive legal reforms are not to be considered as complementary to international law.[26] They are essential parts of it. Divided we cannot simply unite under the charms of a universalist ICL, as there is a lot to be accounted for at the very point of origin that led to these divisions in the first place.

III. Legitimacy of International Law: Lingering Questions

The regime of international law is illegitimate. *Makau Mutua*[27]

In this section, perceptions of the legitimacy of international law in the Global South will be examined. This is an essential discussion for understanding the limits of universal jurisdiction in terms of its global applications. In this specific context, we turn to TWAIL scholarship yet again. It was more than two decades ago that James Thuo Gathii published a critical overview of the Special Symposium Issue of the *Harvard International Law Journal* titled 'Alternative and Critical: The Contribution of Research and Scholarship on Developing Countries to International Legal Theory'.[28] There, he rightfully stated that what began as a lecture series during the 1990s at the Harvard School of Law has grown into an enterprise worthy of international law scholars' attention. The aforementioned special issue on 'international law and the developing world' was planned as a flagship publication to alert the world of legal scholarship to a renewal in interest, research and publication in the area of 'Third World' contributions to the field. Gathii noted with pride that the articles included in the volume explored important and novel ways of understanding the most urgent themes in international law affecting 'developing countries' over the last several decades, and the challenges these societies face in the new millennium. The articles listed were penned by a consortium of scholars with varied experiences, perspectives and national backgrounds, though with a common focus on the interaction between international law and the Global South.[29] They fit into roughly three distinct theoretical frameworks in terms of their contributions to legal theory. The first set of articles provided an explanation of international law as culturally constitutive and historically contingent. Obiora Okafor's work in the collection, for instance, underlined the frailty of the nation-state model in Africa, as a legacy of the impositions of Eurocentric notions of legitimacy on culturally heterogeneous landscapes, which in turn led sub-state groups to view it as illegitimate.[30] Similarly, Balakrishnan Rajagopal's piece engaged in an alternative reading of international legal history, showing how Third World resistance was an important factor, although often overlooked or underestimated in the expansion, consolidation and renewal of international institutions.[31] These pieces signalled the coming trend of critical historical analysis of international law as seen, perceived and experienced in the Global South. For the purposes of the present work, what emerged as the TWAIL's overall approach to international law constitutes the backbone of the methodologies used to decipher perceptions and formulations of international criminal law from within the Global South.

The other two theoretical frameworks celebrated in the special issue are also of great significance. The second one called for international law to play a mediating role in addressing noticeable legal gaps in the global restructuring of capitalism, while the third one was built on the premise that notions of international law, development policy or local practices do not have predetermined outcomes. Overall, TWAIL scholarship achieved its initial goal, securing growing number of followers as a school of thought as well as in terms of the reception of its interventions to mainstream law curricula. It has driven home the point that international law's claims to universality must be replaced with an acceptance of legal and normative pluralism, and that international law bears the imprint of the hegemonic architecture of North–South relations starting with European imperialism, colonialism, and now neo-colonialisms. Furthermore, new generations of African, Middle Eastern, Latin American and Asian international law scholars have produced increasingly subtle readings of how international law functions across the North–South divide and internal debates flourished.

Within the first generation of international law scholars from the Global South, thinkers like Elias Olawale Taslim and Sinha Prakash had argued that Africa in particular, and the Global South in general, had directly participated in creating the civilizational pluralism from which international law was created.[32] Scholars like U. O. Omozurike, S. B. O. Gutto and Mohammed Bedjaoui, however, insisted that despite its potential for harbouring plurality, international law continues to reflect the structural and economic inequalities produced by former regimes of colonial rule.[33] By the time the third generation of scholars joined this conversation, there were marked tensions building within TWAIL itself. The work of Antony Anghie and Siba Grovogui, for instance, traces the origins of international law and identifies distinctions made by leading jurists such as Vitoria between Europeans and non-Europeans. Their analysis clearly signals continued wariness concerning the legacy of contemporary international law doctrines and institutions. Overall, TWAIL scholarship provides an insistent counterweight to the overwhelming dominance of American and European legal scholarship, offering alternatives to traditional paradigms of understanding and producing knowledge about legitimacy in international law. Speaking from a variety of views on the nature and implications of the hegemonic Euro-American framing of international law represented by liberal internationalism, institutionalism, constitutionalism, and of course by neo-conservative realism in international law scholarship, TWAIL scholars have also been asking markedly difficult questions about the origins of the existing state system (Okafor, 2000, 2005,

2008; Mutua and Anghie, 2000).[34] The critical issue here is not so much producing accounts of countervailing or 'more authentic' notions of legitimacy, but opening up a space for scholarly and political projects that are capable of formulating change while acknowledging genealogies of injustice.

In the following narrative, working from within the TWAIL perspective, some of the key arguments commonly used in defence of the neutrality of international law will be refuted, though to a somewhat unusual end: to foreground *jus cogens* norms in a more palatable context for the societies in the Global South. These norms form the foundation of the universal jurisdiction doctrine and, as such, they are essential for deciphering the trends in the adjudication of crimes against humanity at a global scale. In the case of *jus cogens* norms, even the most inclusive brands of legal positivism or legal pluralism do not succeed in estranging themselves adequately from the traditional, apoliticized conception of international law (Rajagopal, 2003).[35] If canonized debates about the legitimacy of international law were to shed their state-centric approach along with their Eurocentricity, and if the field could be re-contextualized in terms of the history of global capitalism and the legacy of North–South relations, a much richer discourse would emerge. Prior to the emergence of TWAIL as a formidable school of thought, the conventional view tended to characterize 'Third World legal discourses on international law' as *ad hoc* and reactive rather than as a distinctive mode of analysis.[36] Now that we have reached a juncture where, for a growing number of scholars, thinkers and legal activists, TWAIL offers both theories of and methodologies for analysing international law and its institutions, the questions of both legitimacy and universality in international law are to be duly reframed.

IV. The Question of the State in International Law as Seen from the Global South: A Chance to Start Anew?

Post–Cold War rejuvenation of enthusiasm about international law has been attributed in part to the way critical legal scholarship, in particular the TWAIL work, has reshaped the discipline and provided it with new sensibilities and perspectives, hence increasing its appeal to larger audiences.[37] Still, the increasingly adversarial and divisive debate about how to embrace the study of international law remains as a Herculean task.[38] The state must be problematized rather than being treated as a political given or a historical *fait accompli*. Instead, the historical importance of the state in the emergence of international law must be revisited from the perspective of the Global South. The classical mode of thinking on international law in terms of the perception of its building blocs and key conceptual tools for understanding how law works need to be re-examined. To this end, a brief discussion of the treatment of the state in international law scholarship will be undertaken in order to underline the possibility of a different take on this particular issue for the future studies of international law.

There is a series of fundamental conflicts over both the meaning and workings of international law as it relates to the history of the nation-state since the Treaty of Westphalia (1648). Well into the mid-1800s, the classic form of the state was a multi-ethnic empire.[39] The populations of such states belonged to many ethno-religious groups and spoke different languages. These empires were often dominated by a particular ethno-religious group, and the language of this group was declared to be the language of public administration, though the identity and composition of such ruling groups changed over time. Internal state structures also exhibited a considerable degree of variation despite the overarching imperial format.[40] Finally, some of the smaller European states were not ethnically or religiously diverse, and yet possessed considerable territorial sovereignty due to their 'successful' imperial and colonial expansion strategies. In examining these smaller states prior to the advent of the nation-state, one must keep in mind either their religio-political significance, as in the case of Spain, or their overseas connections, as in the case the Netherlands, when judging the political power they possessed and the bargaining power they could levy in their dealings with other states.[41] It was against the background of this general imperial mould that, from the late eighteenth century onwards, and for reasons far too complex to be adequately covered here, the ideal of the nation-state took root. No doubt, the origins of the nation-state are highly contested.[42]

Canonical figures in the field such as Benedict Anderson have even suggested that nationalism was actually a product of what happened in the overseas colonies rather than in Europe proper. It was 'over there' that the spark was set off, giving the idea to peoples ruled by imperial powers that 'another world was possible'.[43] For many other scholars, however, it is from within Europe that we should read the histories of both the nation-state and nationalism, initiated by the transformations of the absolutist state on the Continent.[44] Across Europe, some regions grew into nation-statehood through unification via trade relations and political integration, while others were brought into the fold by military force and invasions – for which the French are singularly blamed. Meanwhile, despite their differences, scholars of nationalism do agree on one issue: the so-called nation-state emerged at the end of a particularly brutal trajectory of homogenization and organized violence during the eighteenth and nineteenth centuries. Secondly, it was the political entity of the nation-state that sought to define a firm national identity in order to justify its existence, internally and externally, and not *vice versa*. This is not to suggest that nationalism was purely myth and invention, or that it did not have historical roots. This observation does indicate, however, that there was as much politics involved in the emergence of modern nations as there was culture. Furthermore, it is also generally agreed that with the growth of not only the concept but also the reality of the nation-state came along the idea of societies-cum-nations to be controlled by a centralized system of government with a *complete* say over the livelihood of its subjects-turned-citizens. And here lie the beginnings of international law as known today.[45]

But what kind of international law? Until the beginning of the twentieth century, relations between nation-states were almost exclusively dictated by treaties, which are in essence agreements obliging the concerned states to behave in a certain way towards each other or another state, based on the threat of use of force.[46] At the other end of the spectrum were customary practices, mainly applicable in the field of warfare, such as *jus in bello* and *jus ad bellum*. As the twentieth century progressed, a number of extremely destructive armed conflicts and unprecedented forms of organized violence, particularly the First and

Second World Wars and the Holocaust, starkly exposed the underbelly of this semi-voluntary system of international law, as far as relations between states were concerned. After the First World War, a new model of international law as it pertained to interstate relations was provided by the League of Nations, which however lasted only until the outbreak of the Second World War. In the aftermath of the two World Wars, in an attempt to create a more entrenched and encompassing system of rules and laws to prevent similar future conflicts, a new vehicle for the application of international law was found in the form of the United Nations (UN), which in turn came to encompass several international law-making bodies. So far, this narrative follows a standardized and also, at least in the eyes of critical international law scholars, apoliticized history of public international law.[47] A sceptical reading of this account points out that international law is essentially Eurocentric. While some strands of legal scholarship in this area dictate that the idea of international law was extant before the nation-state system became the dominant form of statehood, others make every conceivable effort to separate the worlds of Grotius, Vattel and Kant from that of the International Court of Justice and similar legal bodies with an international mandate. For the purposes of the present study, the question that binds these categorically different takes on the origins and meaning of international law together is whether or not system-oriented developments in international law have managed, at least in select areas, to take power away from states and governments, and to cede it to international bodies.[48] Alternatively, is state sovereignty still to be regarded as the only working principle of international law?[49] For any of these questions to find satisfactory answers, the sources of international law need to be re-examined.

Legal scholarship posits that there are three recognized sources of international law: international treaties, customary law and general principles of law.[50] Specifically, international treaty law is comprised of obligations that states expressly and voluntarily accept among themselves through treaties. Customary international law, on the other hand, is assumed to have derived from the consistent practice of states accompanied by *opinio juris*, referring to the subjective element of international law including judgments of international tribunals and courts, as well as legal scholarship, all of which are traditionally regarded as a source for international law.[51] Accordingly, the common account concerning the emergence of the current regime of international law suggests that attempts to codify customary international law assumed a decisive momentum after the Second World War with the formation of the International Law Commission (ILC).[52] The ILC was established by the General Assembly of the United Nations in 1947, with the specific purpose of codifying and promoting international law, although this project itself had begun with the activities of the League of Nations from 1924 onwards.[53]

In general, codification in international law is achieved either through the production of a binding interpretation of an underlying customary practice by agreement, or through a treaty. What was unique about the ILC was that in the case of acts of codification undertaken by this body, states not party to such treaties were nonetheless expected to accept the work of the ILC as an expression of customary law.[54] Meanwhile, only a very small section of international law presumes the binding force of peremptory norms (*jus cogens*) and thus allows for no permissible derogations. Furthermore, unlike treaty law that traditionally requires consent and is open to alteration of obligations by states, *jus cogens* norms could not be questioned by any state.[55] An added complication is that the actual list of peremptory norms is not exclusively catalogued. In legal terms, they are not defined by any singular authoritative body. Rather, they arise out of case law, customary law, and, in cases such as crimes against humanity, as a direct result of changing social and political attitudes within the institutional bodies authorized to produce new laws, such as the International Criminal Court (ICC). Generally included in this list are prohibitions on waging aggressive war, war crimes, piracy, genocide, slavery, racial discrimination and torture, and of course crimes against humanity. Despite the seemingly clear principle of condemnation related to these state practices, there are disagreements over whether a particular case violates a peremptory norm, otherwise known as the threshold question, and how and by whom such an occurrence is to be determined. As in other areas of international law, states generally insist on reserving the right to interpret these norms. Where there are disputes about the exact meaning and application of international criminal law, ultimately their resolution is deemed to be the responsibility of national courts, unless otherwise specified by international courts such as the ICJ or ICC. In other words, decisions concerning the determination of violations of international criminal law categorically rest with the superior domestic courts, unless extenuating circumstance dictate otherwise.[56]

Meanwhile, domestic practices of providing a rendition for *jus cogens* norms often lead to a compromise between three different forms of legal interpretation.[57] The textual approach dictates a restrictive interpretation based on the 'ordinary meaning' of the norm or ruling in question;[58] the subjective approach considers the idea or fundamental assumptions and beliefs behind the letter of the law, as well as the context within which it came into existence; and, finally, interpretation could be conducted in the light of the purpose of a given norm or ruling. These variations in interpretation imply differences in the understanding and application of international criminal law within the domestic sphere.[59] In other words, as much as legal scholarship would like to capitalize singular readings of *jus cogens*, the highly political nature of these norms cannot be dismissed, shaping an entire debate on the legitimacy of international criminal law.

V. *Jus Gentium* and the Outer Limits of International Law

Historically, although the world of all things legal distinctly assumes its autonomy, this self-perception and self-presentation may well be seen as nothing more than a comforting illusion for those who subscribe to it.[60] In particular, lack of systemic inclusion of the issue of the exercise of power by states into the study of legal processes and structures has been taken as a clear demonstration that legal scholarship avoids discussions on how power is organized, operationalized, and, of course, maintained.[61] This disjunct is particularly relevant for determining the limitations of universalized applications of international law, which is the focus of this work.

A judicious assessment of both the limits of and possibilities inherent in the conduct of international law means two main issues must be addressed in this context.[62] First and foremost, debates on both the sources and the meaning of customary international law start with the assumption of the 'legal personhood of the state'. It then becomes extremely difficult to identify the distinction made between *opinio juris* and consensual state practices. Secondly, what states might be legally obligated to do under the rubric of international law, and what they actually do and for which specific reasons (apart from legal ones), is essential to unpack the historically contingent notion of *jus gentium*.[63] Concomitantly, the first critical issue concerning the cross-disciplinary study of international law is to determine whether *opinio juris* stands for more than a widespread consensus symbolizing a shared, though contextually bound, understanding among states. Only on the condition that *opinio juris* stands for something larger and deeper than occasional moments of forced or voluntary consensus on specific issues would *jus gentium* become relevant. The next question is related to the codification of *jus gentium* related law. Customary processes are often deemed inadequate to create widespread consensus regarding what *jus gentium* requires of states. Consequently, the differences between articulations of customary international law, its codification practices, and exercises of power in international politics constitute a real divide between legal and political realities of international law.[64] That is an essential part of what is being attacked and systemically unpacked in terms of the stabilized understanding of international law by TWAIL scholarship and critical debates emanating from the Global South.

Power comes in many forms and disguises. Both consent and coercion are essential means through which power is exercised. Effective control and dispensation of force, as well as claims of legitimate authority, are equally needed for the use of power. As such, the question remains as to why legal scholarship on international law privileges or isolates legal rules as the ultimate tool for constraining, persuading and guiding state behaviour at the expense of phenomena that are overtly political in their nature.[65] Could developments in international law solely be explained by the histories of jurisprudence in international law alone? Could international law generate its own source of legitimacy? How could we understand the foundational principles of international law, such as reciprocity, justificability, legal personality and legitimate expectations, and their effects in constraining and influencing state behaviour, without paying attention to the mechanisms that define and sustain these very states? Why is it that the idea of obligation constitutes the distinguishing mark of international law scholarship, as opposed to the idea of conflict, especially when obligations and rules sanctified by international law are often used to qualify the abuse of power within the international system by bigger and richer states against others?[66]

We could of course posit that the obligations determined by international law are designed, first and foremost, to constrain violence and excessive use or abuse of power, in addition to framing rights that are at least in principle applicable to all members of the 'international community'.[67] Yet, what about subsections of international law, such as humanitarian law, that can generate a correlative right to apply power against select states despite the right to territorial integrity or immunity from interference, as exemplified by the invasions of Afghanistan, Iraq or most recently Syria, by coalitions of states?[68] Even if the foundational principles of international law are indeed there to condition states in their attempts to modify customary international legal rules within the bounds of judicial merit and legitimate expectation, explicit respect is paid to the legal personhood of the state at the expense of other international entities. Furthermore, even if international law is open to change emanating from within the system – as long as it is consistent with its founding premises – this basically amounts to a protection of the status quo of unequal relations and historical injustices.

Among the principles of international law cited above, reciprocity emerges as paramount in international legal relations. It is assumed to ensure that the activities and claims of powerful states could be moderated by the knowledge that other states or conglomerations of states have the right to engage in similar activities or to make similar claims.[69] However, critical readings on international law openly depreciate the principle of reciprocity as a mere front, and not an effective device in regulating interstate relations – or indeed any other form of inter- or transnational politics.[70] This is despite the fact that the legal principle of legitimate expectation encompasses powerful norms such as *pacta sunt servanda*.[71] In contrast, from the classical legal scholarship point of view, the principle of legitimate expectation combined with the principle of reciprocity could build into the system of international law the desired degree of stability, both for the operation of its rules and for the workings of its institutions. Here, the assumption is that there is a stable set of constraints operating on powerful states in international law, and thus fears that it will only serve the interests of the mighty are regarded as unjustified.

And yet, legal scholarship on international law cannot avoid debates on the power/law nexus entirely. The contributions of critical legal studies scholarship, debates on transnational law, and TWAIL scholarship readily attest to this uncomfortable fact.[72] Starting back in the 1940s, the 'realist' international relations scholarship already expressed a strong dislike for the 'idealist' international law of the inter-war, and later on post-war, period. Scholars as high profile as Hans Morgenthau branded international law scholarship – referring explicitly not only to legal positivism but also to liberal idealism – as naïve, dangerous and morally dubious.[73] Suffice it to state that legal positivism and its state-centric logic explaining how international law works is a common target not just for the realists, but also for liberal internationalists, transnationalists, cosmopolitanists, Marxists and neo-Marxists, constructivists, institutionalists, and of course critical theorists of a post-modernist persuasion. And yet, whether it is the same state we are talking about in each case is a question mostly avoided outside the domain of TWAIL scholarship.[74]

VI. *Jus Cogens* or Not – Dilemmas?

The standard account of customary international law is that it arises from the widespread and consistent practice of states acting out of a sense of legal obligation, though this is in turn owed at least in part to hegemonic practices and global hierarchies.[75] A fundamental problem with much theorizing about international law is that it fails to identify the decision-maker(s) under study. Instead, the discussion proceeds as if international law exists in the abstract, without any particular political entity to interpret and apply it (Shelton, 2006). In contradistinction, applications of a fundamental norm like *jus cogens* cannot be understood without paying attention to the relevant legal actors.[76] Immunities in international law expose multifaceted tensions between the conflicting goals of international stability of the state-system and legal accountability of the states. The laws arranging immunities do not provide conceptual and doctrinal coherence in terms of the relationship between state immunity and jurisdictional universalism. Foreign sovereign immunity and official status-based immunity are protective of the existing state system in that they block the exercise of adjudicative jurisdiction by other states' courts. However, these immunities do not pre-empt the prescriptive jurisdiction of foreign states' laws to regulate conduct – even conduct inside other states – if a basis of prescriptive jurisdiction exists in international law such as the kind dictated by *jus cogens* norms. The question is to understand what determines a particular violation's status as subject to peremptory norms and prescriptive jurisdiction in international law. Considering the notion of a hierarchical international legal order whereby (certain) norms are elevated to a superior level, the concept of *jus cogens* denotes a substantive superiority in international criminal law. Yet it remains highly questionable whether the suggested norm hierarchy is anything more than aspirational. Due to the rather narrow interpretation of the scope of *jus cogens* norms in both domestic and international judicial practice, in reality they remain within the horizontal scope of international law, unless used by powerful legal actors.[77]

This dynamic endemic to the relationship between state sovereignty and universal jurisdiction has two important implications for international law. The connection between immunities and applications of *jus cogens* is a very important one as the latter introduces practices that are against the mandate of the former in international criminal law. A few caveats are necessary here. First, the relevant law pre-empting immunities normally accorded to the state is the law in existence when a court determines whether to entertain a suit, and not the law in existence at the time of the domestic conduct leading to the international adjudication of the issue. This in turn causes complaints concerning legal certainty of issues subject to adjudication under the aegis of international criminal law. Secondly, peremptory norms doctrine lacks rule-of-law coherence, since it is often embroiled with problems of its possible retroactive applications. This has been particularly troubling in the interpretation of ICC judgments discussed previously, and it is an issue receiving further elaboration in Chapter 5 on hybrid courts and tribunals. Compared with the relatively settled laws of foreign sovereign and status-based immunities, conduct-based accountability determinations and removal of immunities are in a state of flux. Since customary international law arises from state practices and *opinio juris*, arguments used to avoid collisions between state sovereignty and *jus cogens* do not lend themselves to a distinct doctrine of international law. Suggesting *jus cogens* norms address substantive prohibitions under international law may not even hold when the acts at issue are to be brought to trial according to conduct-based jurisprudence and in *ad hoc* settings. Ascertaining accountability criteria whereby the law about state criminality is as unsettled is risk-laden. The only exception to this seems to be when international legal bodies are engaged in determining culpability and accountability concerning the acts of the states and high-ranking officials representing the state in the Global South. Only then, it appears, do *jus cogens* norms become alive. In actual practice, the presumption that peremptory norms are binding on all states translates into something else. As such, the nature of peremptory norms cannot be adequately explained by positivist, institutionalist or voluntarist explanations. Perhaps the only other option available is an explanation based on natural law or its derivatives.[78] This issue is to be further investigated in the context of collective responsibility and societal wrongdoing as they relate to virtue ethics on the one hand, and natural law theories on the other.

Meanwhile, in the next two chapters of this work, I will first attend to the applicability of the principle of legal certainty to the category of crimes against humanity and highlight some of the missing connections between *jus cogens* norms, *erga omnes* obligations and actual international law adjudication of egregious criminal conduct. My misgivings concerning the application of universal jurisdiction in the context of crimes against humanity jurisprudence find further expression in the discussion on the limits of ICC jurisprudence and askance of potential avenues for alternative practices in the form of hybrid courts and tribunals. However, before advancing the debate on universal jurisdiction in that particular direction, first we must be clear about the doctrinal limits of universal jurisdiction in terms of its applications in the Global South.

Conclusion

The thrust of this chapter has been the critical examination of the matter of the state in contemporary international law, and to determine pertinent issues concerning statehood and sovereignty in the Global South in the context of the global application of *jus cogens* norms. This type of examination is essential for understanding the limits of universal jurisdiction, which is a key part of adjudication of crimes against humanity.

Conceptualizations of the state – as emblematic of power relations in general – shape the context of processes and practices of international criminal law in the Global South. Treating the state either as a relic or as a nuisance is not a helpful approach in this regard. Similarly, there is no foundation upon which one can appeal for a common understanding of international law other than the one that engages with power, hegemony and histories of discontent. In this sense, the most distinctive feature of the current study of international criminal law is the decisive conflation of its subject and its object, the state. The possibility of finding an external international normative order as an autonomous producer of legal sources and processes is a grand illusion. The evasive rhetoric regarding the state in particular, and power relations in general, provides the ultimate guarantee for the intellectual and professional autonomy of international law. In this context, the suggestion made in this chapter is twofold. First and foremost, the debate about the state should at least remain a point of discomfort for international law scholarship. Secondly, the grammar of legal theory attending to international law should include the state as a problem-laden point of reference, and contextualize it both geographically and historically. Perhaps then we could start a genuine conversation about why the state no longer seems to matter as much as international law once assumed it to. International law's secretive over-dependency on the state is at odds with the realities of the Global South only at the surface, as the state re-emerged as a bastion of hope against the invasive forces of global constitutionalism, and hence many of the maxims of contemporary international law.

Coming back full circle, a major consequence of the new global restructuring of states, societies and economies has been the double process of further and deeper integration to the global market on the one hand, and social exclusion, dispossession and emergence of novel forms of widespread insecurity and precarity, on the other. These processes have led to an exponential growth of marginalized and deinstitutionalized subaltern classes, especially in the Global South, rendering them all the more vulnerable to becoming subjects of state criminality.[79] Critically navigating through prevailing perspectives on international criminal law pertaining to violent acts and crimes committed by states against their own people – otherwise known as crimes against humanity – the remaining chapters of this work will thus strive to propose an alternative outlook. In the spirit of a 'quiet encroachment of the ordinary', I will address crimes against humanity first in doctrinal terms, then as seen through the mechanisms of international law as it is applied in the Global South, then normatively, and finally from within the states and societies wherein they are committed.[80]

International law, and in particular international criminal law, reproduces many of the oligarchic tendencies in global governance, while also creating ambiguities and a multilateral ethos of indifference. Within the parameters of a dialectics of stability and change, international legal practices and processes not only inhibit global transformations and reproduce some of the most oppressive conditions of the existing order, they also lead to new openings. As the following discussion on crimes against humanity will illuminate, international criminal law is not immune to these coexisting forces, and it too harbours promises as much as casting long dark shadows.

3

Crimes Against Humanity Jurisprudence in International Law and the Conundrum of Jurisdictional Certainty

Introduction

This chapter pursues the question of what distinguishes crimes against humanity from other international crimes, as well as why and how they fall under the purview of universal jurisdiction. To this end, the normative architecture of crimes against humanity jurisprudence is examined in order to determine whether jurisdictional certainty alone would suffice for establishing the basis for their adjudication. Crimes against humanity is the key category of criminal conduct codified by international law that I chose to use as the basis of my analysis concerning *limits* of universal jurisdiction. This is despite the fact that these crimes constitute a frontal assault on human dignity and humanity at large. The conundrum we are faced with concerns the impossibility of removing the vestiges of a historically skewed regime of accountability in international law regardless of the severity of such crimes. In other words, the problem rests with the way international (criminal) law is perceived and operationalized and not with the applicability of universal jurisdiction to crimes against humanity. In this context, let me start this somewhat unsettling discussion with the citation of a recent incidence befitting the definition of these crimes, and use this vignette as a starting point to analyse the limits of legislating an applicable punishment scheme.

In August 2016, the Syrian Network for Human Rights (SNHR) published a report in which it documents in detail the crimes against humanity and war crimes that led to the complete depopulation of Darayya city.[1] The SNHR is an independent, non-governmental human rights organization founded in June 2011, and is a certified source for the United Nations concerning statistics about human rights violations in Syria. The report notes that truces and reconciliations regarding circumstances in Darayya were implemented while negating basic international humanitarian and human rights law.[2] Negotiations were carried out under oppression and dictated by siege, indiscriminate bombing, starvation, and the prohibition of civilian residents and aid from getting into or out of the city. According to the report, the crime of *en masse* forced displacement was carried out in a blatant manner in Homs, Darayya and Banyas.[3] This particular report is one example amongst many documenting mass political violence committed by states against their own citizens since 1945. In this sense, it does more than simply shedding light on the drastic changes in the demography of Syria since 2011 as a result of the killing, indiscriminate and deliberate bombing, and destruction of livelihood of civilian communities. It also provides an inlet into a more nuanced understanding of the limits of the applications of crimes against humanity jurisprudence *in situ*. In Syria, more than eight million people have been displaced and become refugees, while an estimated seven million people have become IDPs.[4] Such demographic changes undoubtedly pose threats to the well-being of the peoples of the entire region. Equally importantly, they raise the additional challenge of establishing an accountability regime in the aftermath of the still-ongoing war. In the specific case of Darayya city, for instance, the report records the killing of no less than 817 civilians, including 67 children and 98 women, during the limited time period covered. These numbers and associated circumstances of the killing of civilian population constitute a serious concern for the determination of the extent of crimes against humanity committed during the Syrian War, even if they are to be categorized as wartime casualties. According to the same report, government forces-owned helicopters dropped no less than 7,846 bombs on the city, including barrel bombs loaded with a flammable substance that is evidently identified as napalm. It also documents that the siege imposed on the city and its fallouts, such as shortages in food and medicine, resulted in further civilian deaths. Finally, it notes that there are 4,311 forcibly-disappeared persons from Darayya who were arrested by government forces, while the authorities denied their existence.[5]

The commonly accepted understanding of the modern concept and related jurisprudence of crimes against humanity is that it is a product of the horror of the crimes committed during the two World Wars. It was codified and later on revitalized due to the growing consensus amongst both European and post-colonial states that certain crimes committed by states against their own citizens should be legitimate subjects of international criminal law and adjudication.[6] However, unlike war crimes and genocide, crimes against humanity jurisprudence developed through piecemeal additions to customary international law.[7] Today, the statutes of most international and internationalized tribunals, including but not limited to the International Criminal Court's Rome Statute, contain definitions of these crimes. However, there are significant differences in terms of the jurisprudence employed by different international, regional and hybrid legal bodies.[8] To say the least, the evolution of the definition of crimes against humanity as an international instrument has not been linear.[9] As far as the practices of international courts are concerned, later definitions are often more expansive, while at the regional level domesticated definitions tend to be narrower compared with their international counterparts. Furthermore, the contents of both *jus cogens* norms and *erga omnes* obligations dictating that state parties punish crimes against humanity remain subject to greater controversy than has been the case in the prescribing of punishment for genocide and war crimes.[10]

Perhaps one might argue that these are merely jurisprudential matters to be settled in the courts that have subject matter jurisdiction. Throughout this work, I argue otherwise, and posit that many of these seemingly jurisprudential disputes actually relate to the criteria used for the determination of what constitutes crimes against humanity and determination of the criminal threshold. As such, there is actually an intrinsic politico-normative challenge concerning the issue of their universal applicability. In jurisprudential terms, the primary challenge in defining crimes against humanity is to identify the precise elements that distinguish these offences from crimes exclusively subject to national laws. The definition itself not only determines the scope of international jurisdiction, it also gives rise to a number of important consequences concerning trial structure, conditional and selective removal of immunities and the commuting of sentences. Unlike the majority of domestic crimes, these offences are generally considered outside the purview of statute of limitations. Equally importantly, the immunities that often shield state representatives and high-ranking public and military officers from criminal responsibility are categorically removed in the context of crimes against humanity, at least when trials are held before international tribunals or domestic courts employing universal jurisdiction. Although applications of universal jurisdiction remain controversial vis-à-vis the capacities of domestic courts, proponents of the norm invariably include crimes against humanity within its scope. Its practice would deliver the following result: while the crime of murder could only be tried in a court with a jurisdictional link to the act, a murder committed as a crime against humanity could be tried in any criminal court in any state.

The prohibition of crimes against humanity falls strictly under the purview of *jus cogens* norms in international law. At least in theory, states have an obligation under international law either to prosecute perpetrators of crimes against humanity or to extradite them to states intending to pursue prosecutions, hence the *erga omnes* obligation pertaining to this particular set of crimes. In light of the serious legal consequences of designating an offence a crime against humanity, in addition to the severe moral condemnation the label entails, the importance of understanding the exact juridical nature of these offences needs no further explanation. However, this chapter is not an exercise in that vein. Although it does provide a brief historical sketch of the evolution of the norms and jurisprudence prohibiting crimes against humanity, as well as an assessment of its constitutive crimes, the core of the argument developed in the following narrrative pertains to another and, I would purport, an equally important issue: the politico-normative framework within which these offences find meaning and are deemed worthy of trial under the aegis of universal jurisdiction. The ultimate aim of this exercise is to determine whether the focus of their adjudication could be shifted away from institutions such as the ICC to hybrid or national courts, thus examining the possibility of 'domesticating' this particular category of state criminality.

In essence, crimes against humanity are mass crimes committed against the fundamental human rights of a civilian population. If so, their common inclusion under humanitarian, rather than human rights, law is misleading and has grave consequences. They are distinguished from egregious state crimes such as genocide in that they need not target a specific group, but may aim at the civilian population in general. Thus, they create conditions of generalized trauma and loss. Similarly, crimes against humanity are regarded different from war crimes insofar as the criminal conduct is directed not towards an enemy's population but against the perpetrators' own; hence the difficulty of their adjudication. In the following discussion, an appeal is made to understand the politico-normative precepts of crimes against humanity jurisprudence in an attempt to render them meaningful and useful within the domestic realm, where these crimes are perpetrated, rather than being seen as an imposition by an international court or a consortium of states (the latter format commonly known as 'victor's justice').

I. The Normative Architecture of Crimes Against Humanity Jurisprudence

In international law, crimes against humanity found their first explicit formulation as a category of crime in Article 6(c) of the Nürnberg/Nuremberg Charter which emerged from the Tribunal.[11] The offences categorized as crimes against humanity were also included in Article 5(c) of the Tokyo Charter and Article II(1) of Control Council Law No. 10.[12] While the Nuremberg and Tokyo Charters required that crimes against humanity evidence a connection to aggressive war or war crimes, this supplementary requirement was later on left out of Control Council Law No. 10, The Statutes of the Yugoslavia and Rwanda Tribunals. The ICC then reaffirmed the customary law character of crimes against humanity, and the prohibition of crimes against humanity was recognized as having the status of *jus cogens* and its adjudication belonging to the domain of *erga omnes* obligations.

It is worthy of note that the legal phrase 'crimes against humanity' was first employed earlier, in a 1915 Declaration by the governments of Great Britain, France and Russia which condemned the Ottoman Empire for the reported massacres of Armenians as 'crimes against humanity and civilization for which all the members of the Turkish [*sic* Ottoman] Government will be held responsible together with its agents implicated in the massacres' (Robertson, 2013).[13] Despite this early use of the term, the first full prosecutions of crimes against humanity did not take place until after the Second World War in 1945, in the form of the International Military Tribunal (IMT) at Nuremberg, Germany. The charter establishing the Nuremberg IMT defined crimes against humanity as murder, extermination, enslavement, deportation and other inhuman acts committed against any civilian population, before or during the war, or prosecutions on political, racial or religious grounds in the execution of or in connection with any crime within the jurisdiction of the Tribunal, whether or not in violation of the domestic law of the country where they were perpetrated. Subsequent to the Nuremberg Charter, the Tokyo Charter of 1946 established the International Military Tribunal for the Far East, incorporating the same definition of crimes against humanity. Following the Nuremberg and Tokyo trials of 1945–6, no other international tribunal with jurisdiction over crimes against humanity was established until the *ad hoc* Yugoslav and Rwanda Tribunals.

Meanwhile, in 1947, the International Law Commission was charged by the United Nations General Assembly with the formulation of the principles of international law recognized and reinforced in the Nuremberg Charter, and drafted a 'code of offenses against the peace and security of mankind', which included crimes against humanity.[14] In 1996, this Draft Code from 1947 was brought to the attention of jurists who then reinstated crimes against humanity as inhumane acts including murder, extermination, torture, enslavement, persecution on political, racial, religious or ethnic grounds, institutionalized discrimination, arbitrary deportation or forcible transfer of population, arbitrary imprisonment, rape, enforced prostitution, and other inhuman acts committed in a systematic manner or on a large scale, and, instigated or directed by a Government or by any organization or group within the boundaries of a state.[15] This latter definition differs from the one used in Nuremberg in the sense that, as stated above, the former only targeted criminal acts that were committed 'before or during the war', thus establishing a prescriptive nexus between crimes against humanity and armed conflict.

Prior to this expanded 1996 definition, in 1993 the International Criminal Tribunal for the Former Yugoslavia (ICTY), established by the UN Security Council in order to investigate and prosecute genocide, war crimes and crimes against humanity which had taken place in the former Yugoslavia, had already opened up the 1947 draft definition. Although the ICTY's connecting of crimes against humanity to both international and non-international armed conflict led to the expansion of the list of criminal acts used in Nuremberg to include imprisonment, torture and rape, as per Article 5 of the ICTY Statute, this was done with reference to a specific case. In 1994, the UN Security Council established the International Criminal Tribunal for Rwanda (ICTR) pursuant to the genocide that had taken place between April and July 1994. This second *ad hoc* international criminal tribunal yet again changed the scope of the definition of crimes against humanity. In the ICTR Statute, the linkage between crimes against humanity and an armed conflict of any kind was dropped. Rather, a new requirement was added, stipulating that the committal of such inhumane acts must be part of a 'systematic or widespread attack against any civilian population on national, political, ethnic, racial or religious grounds', as per Article 3 of the ICTR Statute.[16] This change was introduced due to the concern that, given the internal nature of the conflict in Rwanda, crimes against humanity would likely not have been applicable if the nexus of armed conflict had been maintained.

Post-1996, the most up-to-date definition of crimes against humanity came with the establishment of a permanent international court, the ICC, in 2002. In its founding treaty, the Rome Statute, crimes against humanity are stated somewhat differently than in any of the preceding legal definitions. For the purpose of this Statute, crimes against humanity denote any of the following acts when committed as part of a widespread or systematic attack directed against a civilian population: murder; extermination; enslavement; deportation or forcible transfer of population; imprisonment or other severe deprivation of physical liberty in violation of fundamental rules of international law; torture; rape, sexual slavery, enforced prostitution, forced pregnancy, enforced sterilization, or any other form of sexual violence of comparable gravity; persecution against any identifiable group or collectivity on political, racial, national, ethnic, cultural, religious, gender as defined in paragraph 3, or other grounds that are universally recognized as impermissible under international law, in connection with any act referred to in this paragraph or any crime within the jurisdiction of the Court; enforced disappearance of persons; the crime of apartheid; and other inhumane acts of a similar character intentionally causing great suffering, or serious injury to body or to mental or physical health.[17] Essentially, the Rome Statute employs the same definition of crimes against humanity that the ICTR does. However, it removes the requirement that the attack must have been carried out 'on national, political, ethnic, racial or religious grounds'. In addition, the Rome Statute definition offers the most expansive list of specific criminal acts to be covered by international criminal law.

Against the extensive nature of this jurisprudence, however, international law scholars have repeatedly pointed out the need for a more specialized convention for the determination of crimes against humanity (Bassiouni, 2008). This is in part due to the fact that its current framing could be problematic in light of the limited application of principles of legality to such crimes. For instance, the maxim *nullum crimen sine lege*, a fundamental principle of criminal law writ large, dictates that an individual can only be convicted for specific acts which, at the time of their commission, were known to be of criminal nature. The aforementioned *ad hoc* tribunals could not limit their jurisdiction with that maxim. However, there is at least a partial solution offered to this conundrum by international criminal law jurisprudence. Fundamentally, crimes against humanity are inhumane acts committed as part of a widespread or systematic attack against civilians by their own state or by an organized political authority with jurisdiction over that territory. Their connection to a broader or systematic attack is what justifies the exercise of criminal jurisdiction and thus removes the burden of such crimes not being already codified within the confines of domestic jurisprudence. Similarly, the *erga omnes* category of obligations dictates the necessity for any legal party to pursue punishment, even in the likely event of the impossibility of domestic adjudication of crimes against humanity. In normative terms, the *erga omnes* obligation is weaker than the *nullum crimen sine lege* dictum, though together with the systematic attack component, it forms a defence for the applicability of crimes against humanity jurisprudence for both past and present cases.

It is also true that some scholars make a distinction between substantive and procedural law in the context of *nullum crimen sine lege*.[18] According to this view, a change in substantive law leading to liability must occur before a criminal act is committed for it to be suitable for adjudication, but a change in procedural aspects of the law leading to liability may occur after the act is committed. For example, extending the statute of limitations to allow the prosecution of crimes that occurred in the past would constitute a change in procedural law and thus make it possible to qualify the *nullum crimen sine lege* restriction in the specific context of crimes against humanity.[19] This would directly apply to acts punished by international criminal tribunals whose status were legally ambiguous in the immediate context of the conflict or atrocity situations. Finally, though the exact wording of the definitions of crimes against humanity differ in the cornerstone documents that provide it a juridical standing, each definition is made up of similar underlying criminal elements (e.g. murder, extermination, rape, and so forth) as well as common contextual elements under which the criminal act must have been committed. Therefore, the foundational meaning attributed to this category of crimes is not available for a wide reading of the law.

As far as the structure of these crimes is concerned, the material element of crimes against humanity determination requires the commission of a specific individual act in the course of a widespread or systematic attack against a civilian population.[20] The attack on the civilian population also represents the contextual element of the crime. The mental element requires intent and knowledge regarding the material elements of the crime, including the contextual element. These crimes affect not only the individual victim(s), but as already mentioned, they constitute a systematic or widespread denial of the fundamental human rights of a civilian population as a whole. This particular characteristic of organized violence calls into question the responsibilities of humanity as a whole against the atrocities committed. In principle, the norm also protects individual human rights, including the right to life, health, freedom and dignity.[21]

Secondly, the primary object of these crimes is harming the civilian population, though this explicit focus does not apply to the category of war crimes targeting both military personnel and civilian populations as victims. Furthermore, crimes against humanity are directed against a civilian population at large and not merely against select individuals. A civilian population is any plurality of persons that are connected with each other by common characteristics, including but not limited to ethnicity, religion, race, nationality and political belief, and any one of these characteristics could render them the target of an attack. The most contentious part of this generic definition is the criterion that the presence of a limited number of combatants among an attacked civilian population does not negate its civilian character. Accordingly, at times of ethnic civil war, the state cannot justify its actions in attacking civilian populations through the reasoning that they have a military/guerilla arm. Neither is it necessary for the entire population of a state or territory to be affected by the attack. The civilian character of the attacked population and persons as a threshold requirement applies both in civil war or occupation and during peacetime. Therefore, for the purpose of determining the criminal element, a distinction between civilians and non-civilians is not possible solely by applying the terms of customary international humanitarian law.

In the context of crimes against humanity, application of the notion of harming the civilian population for criminal adjudication aims to protect the fundamental rights of every human being against any form of systematic violence. The determining factor for adjudication is the victims' need for protection, and the presumption of their defencelessness vis-à-vis the state, the military or other types of politically organized force. By derivation, anyone who is *not* part of this organized political power using force is considered a civilian and hence a potential victim. Furthermore, it is not the formal status – such as membership in the military forces – but a person's actual role at the time of the commission of these crimes that determines their culpability under the purview of crimes against humanity. In other words, members of military forces or other armed groups who have laid down their arms or have otherwise been rendered *hors de combat* are not to be subjected to culpability criteria. By the same token, paramilitary forces who engage in acts qualified as state criminality would be subject to adjudication even though they are not formally regarded as members of the military or the police.

Another very important feature concerning the normative architecture of these crimes concerns the definition of an 'attack'. This element describes a specific course of conduct involving the commission of acts of violence. In its latest iteration, such a course of conduct must include the 'multiple commission' of acts listed in Article 7(1) of the ICC Statute. However, this does not mean that the perpetrator needs to act repeatedly by him- or herself (Luban, 2004). Rather, what is in question is the widespread or systematic character of these acts of violence. Specifically, the criterion 'widespread' describes a quantitative element related to the crimes committed. The widespread nature of the attack can arise either from the number of victims targeted or from the extension of its effects over a broad geographic area. The criterion of a systematic attack, on the other hand, is a qualitative qualifier. It refers to the organized nature of the committed acts of violence, and thus serves to exclude isolated acts from the notion of crimes against humanity. Earlier case law of the *ad hoc* tribunals required that an individual act that is adjudicated based on the definition of crimes against humanity must follow a predetermined plan or policy. However, the Appeals Chamber of the Yugoslavia Tribunal distanced itself from such a requirement and set a precedent for its limited application.[22] Accordingly, although attacks on a civilian population typically follow a predetermined plan, this does not make the existence of a plan or policy an essential element of the crime. This argument relies on the principle that, under customary international law, crimes against humanity do not call for the proven presence of a policy element. However, Article 7(2)(a) of the ICC Statute extended the definition again and stipulated that crimes against humanity jurisprudence dictates that the attack on a civilian population must have been carried out 'pursuant to or in furtherance of a State or organizational policy to commit such attack'.[23]

Finally, there is the issue of perpetrators and victims. Perpetrators need not be members of the State or an organization involved in the crime. This category could include all persons who act to implement or support the policies of the State or the organization in question. In its most current rendition, the list of such acts include killing (Art. 7(1)(a) of the ICC Statute); extermination (Art. 7(1)(b)); enslavement (Art. 7(1)(c)); deportation or forcible transfer of population (Art. 7(1)(d)); imprisonment (Art. 7(1)(e)); torture (Art. 7(1)(f)); sexual violence (Art. 7(1)(g)); persecution (Art. 7(1)(h)); enforced disappearance (Art. 7(1)(i)); apartheid (Art. 7(1)(j)), and 'other inhumane acts' (Art. 7(1)(k)). In all cases, it must be proven beyond doubt that the perpetrator acted with intent and was fully cognizant that their actions constituted a part of the attack on the civilian population.[24] Furthermore, there are criteria to be fulfilled for the possibility of prosecution of crimes against humanity in keeping with prior post–Second World War jurisprudence, which led to an even narrower interpretation of the term 'civilian'. In some earlier cases, courts have interpreted the term by incorporating *hors de combat*. However, both the ICTY and the ICC have moved towards a restrictive interpretation of the term, potentially excluding members of the armed forces. This move may be regarded as regressive, leading to a protection gap which crimes against humanity jurisprudence was initially intended to close. In hindsight, the exclusion of members of the armed forces from the definition of 'civilian' may well have been a concession extended to increase the number of signatory states to the Rome Statute.[25]

Overall, crimes against humanity pertain to both past and present atrocities, and two new concepts have been introduced into the landscape of international law as a result: the first one describes the violence, oppression or persecution undertaken or allowed by the state itself (international crime component), and the second one encompasses the variety of responses to these acts of violence, oppression or persecution (transitional justice component). With the establishment of the ICC, a new hope arose that common citizens, whose lives were marked by the violence of genocide, crimes of war, and crimes against humanity, have finally found a platform to ask for justice and seek the punishment of persons responsible for these atrocities. However, the truth is much more complicated, and justice for crimes against humanity is far more evasive than what a flat reading of the Rome Statute might suggest. In this regard, a re-examination of the Tokyo Trial in comparison with the ICC reveals interesting characteristics concerning the evolution of international criminal law. The background of the Tokyo Trial was somewhat different from that of the Nuremberg Trial, as it had a unique jurisprudential context due to the declarations made specifically on Japan by the principal Allied Powers. Among the crimes provided for in Article 5 of the Tokyo Charter, crimes against peace, for which there was to be individual responsibility, were the most disputed jurisprudence during the proceedings. Furthermore, war crimes and crimes against humanity were not clearly distinguished in either the Indictment or the Judgment of the Trial.[26]

Furthermore, later discussions on international criminal law also led to the necessity of clearly defining peremptory norms, which were not addressed during the Tokyo Trials. As a safeguard, the 1969 Vienna Convention on the Law of Treaties introduced the concept of *jus cogens* into international law.[27] Meanwhile, the related category of *erga omnes* obligations remains one of the most problem-laden areas in international law. Contrary to what the term may imply in its first reading, the rule that every state has the right to define its international legal position vis-à-vis these obligations remains in force. In this regard, the judgment of the English House of Lords in the Pinochet case is of special interest,[28] as the problem of criminal responsibility of individuals for grave violations of international law was trumped by political concerns amounting to the personal immunity of heads of state.[29]

In comparison, the emergence of legal rules governing criminal liability for genocide represents a different response in international criminal law. Punishing those responsible for committing such abominations required an unequivocal consecration of the criminality of mass killings in the hands of the state in international humanitarian law. Regulations concerning the methods and means of war, limiting or prohibiting the use of certain types of weapons and ammunition, and protection of victims of armed conflict, all together constituting a body of jurisprudence known as war crimes, is another example. Unlike these two other prototypical international crimes – war crimes and genocide – the proscription against crimes against humanity remains to be enshrined in such clear terms. While the former two are primarily used for international law purposes outside the domain of domestic jurisdiction, and historically in international courts, crimes against humanity relates to internal affairs of the state and, as such, requires additional steps to be taken at the national level to enable its adjudication. As discussed above, the jurisprudence pertaining to crimes against humanity has developed largely through the various international courts and tribunals established since the end of the Second World War. This process has yielded enduring normative difficulties as well as doctrinal ambiguities. Still, the law against crimes against humanity promises to fulfil a function that no other body of jurisprudence has been capable of in the context of human rights law or humanitarian law.

II. Competing Politico-Normative Visions

Despite the avowed desire to reach a certain level of legal certainty, there are foundational normative questions that crimes against humanity jurisprudence is not fully poised to answer, such as what makes an inhumane act a crime against humanity, or, the distinct purpose of establishing such a category of crimes. This is the case despite the fact that, in the drafting of the Rome Statute, the differentiation of these crimes from war crimes and genocide was fortified with substantive legal reasoning.[30] However, both during the Rome Conference and in its aftermath normative discussions were always circumscribed by the conflicting political goals of individual states (May, 2005).[31] As a result, delegations were often willing to compromise their vision of crimes against humanity if the alternative was to write off the prospect of a permanent international criminal court. As such, the Rome Conference produced jurisprudence on the issue without an underlying or overtly expressed normative consensus. Instead, several normative visions of crimes against humanity competed, and continue to do so, for recognition in the law, jurisprudence and scholarship related to this specific category of crimes. In order for the ICC or other national and international judicial bodies to be able to exercise adequate jurisdiction over crimes against humanity, an accurate and consistent assessment of situations in which these crimes have been committed must be achieved. This is not an exclusively jurisdictional matter, either. For the aforementioned judicial bodies to attribute individual criminal responsibility for these crimes without violating the principles of legality or legal certainty, they must have clear guidance regarding the core principles with reference to indictment, defence and sentencing. This again is not simply a jurisdictional matter but requires (political) recognition of the Rome Statute as a binding document. Finally, in order for states to justify resorting to universal jurisdiction in addressing crimes against humanity, the scope of these crimes must be clearly defined. This is perhaps the only aspect of crimes against humanity jurisprudence with an exclusive legislative focus. Even there, politico-normative concerns determine the threshold for resorting to the exercise of universal jurisdiction, that is trying nationals of another country above and beyond the requirements of nationality–territoriality nexus in international criminal law.

Despite this notably normative nature of the determination, adoption and application of definitions pertaining to crimes against humanity, declaring them as worthy of international law jurisdiction simply on the basis that they threaten the peace and security of the world was the central argument posed by the Nuremberg Charter and

Judgments (Robertson, 2013).[32] In other words, it was the context of the Second World War and its aftermath that justified the initial adjudication of such crimes. Atrocities committed within a state with no connection to war were regarded as a matter concerning that state alone. Indeed, some participants in the Rome Conference continued to endorse this perspective as late as 1998. With the Rome Statute's coming into effect, however, a broader view of the peace and security rationale was adopted, which encompasses internal armed conflict and civil war as well.[33] Ultimately, the elimination of the requirement of the context of armed conflict from the definition trumped the peace and security rationale for these crimes. However, what is to replace the war nexus is yet to be determined. Crimes committed against civilian populations in peacetime by a sovereign state pose unique challenges for international law. The trials about the horrendous crimes of the Khmer Rouge provide an apt example. In justifying the continued detention of one of the defendants charged with crimes against humanity, the Extraordinary Chambers in the Courts of Cambodia ('ECCC') echoed the old peace and security rationale.[34] The Rome Statute's rationale, on the other hand, rests more on the gravity of the crimes. In this latter context, one of the most frequently invoked justifications for crimes against humanity is that they 'shock the conscience of humanity'.[35]

The ICC-endorsed view of crimes against humanity is duly appreciated in the international human rights law framework, as a result of which crimes against humanity are depicted as particularly severe violations of fundamental human rights. Accordingly, the purpose of the overarching category of crimes against humanity is to capture this seriousness related to a targeted 'population' and a 'widespread or systematic attack'. Meanwhile, proponents of the gravity rationale amongst the human rights scholars employ a generously wide reading of the jurisprudence and reject the notion that crimes against humanity should require a government or organizational policy or a discriminatory intent to be present. Unfortunately, the difficulty with this particular normative vision is that it calls for the application of a scale for judging the gravity of the crimes in question. Such a task is not a legitimate component of international law, much less of the jurisprudence pertaining to crimes against humanity.[36]

In addition to the peace and security argument and the justification for adjudication based on the gravity of the offences, there is a third normative perspective that envisions the ethos of crimes against humanity as punishment for the misuse of state power to attack rather than to protect.[37] If so, it is the misuse and abuse of state power that renders these crimes non-justiciable in the domestic sphere, and the likelihood they will go unpunished mandates the availability of universal jurisdiction. Proponents of this view promote the inclusion of a state policy element in the definition of crimes against humanity. If so, only inhumane acts dictated by official policy measures to commit such violence would merit designation as crimes against humanity. This last vision reflects an overreliance on a rigid understanding of state sovereignty, especially concerning crimes perpetrated by regional alliances and non-state actors intervening in a civil war situation or during a military occupation, not to mention state-like actors in international law such as transnational corporations especially active in extractive industries across the Global South.

Despite their differences, all three instances of normative justification provided for the crimes against humanity jurisprudence share a blind spot: while it is true that domestic legal systems are generally unwilling or unable to prosecute their own state or state-like actors, it is far from clear that an international court could easily step in to remedy the lacunae for the adjudication of such crimes. In this regard, even though the critique of state sovereignty is the strongest normative standpoint for the justification for crimes against humanity jurisprudence, even it falls short of identifying the political and institutional route required to try these cases in non-domestic courts other than its reliance on universal jurisdiction. This weakness is only partially remedied by a select emphasis on the group-based harm element of the crimes against humanity jurisprudence, which could in some instances counter-balance the lack of official policy measures dictating mass violence (Luban, 2004).[38] This aspect of the jurisprudence requires that the targeted group share particular characteristics beyond the geographic proximity of its members, such as nationality, race, religion or ethnicity.[39] Such a definition brings the normative basis of crimes against humanity jurisprudence close to the prohibition against genocide, although without the requirement of intent to destroy the group in whole or in part. Still, exclusive emphasis on this element lacks adequate attention being paid to the large-scale and systemic attack component, and thus weakening the coverage of the overall definition of these crimes concerning their effects on the whole of society.

In this list of normative justifications, we must also include the ILC and its experimentation with different rationales in the immediate post-war years. Accordingly, its 1954 Draft Code adopted a combination of state action and discrimination, while the 1991 Draft Code relied on seriousness, introducing the criteria of 'systematic' or 'mass scale'. Finally, the 1996 Draft Code combined the seriousness and state action requirements. Overall, all of the post-Nuremberg statutes pertaining to crimes against humanity have carried forward inconsistencies in their justifications. The ICTY resurrected the nexus with armed conflict; the ICTR required both seriousness and discrimination; the ICC injected a requirement of state – or at least group – action; the Special Court for Sierra Leone (SCSL) relied almost exclusively on seriousness; and the ECCC re-injected the element of discrimination. The resultant lack of normative uniformity in the jurisprudence has led to important doctrinal questions which remain unresolved. Aside from jurisprudential debates, the current state of affairs clearly indicates the importance of the politico-normative context of the adoption and usage of crimes against humanity jurisprudence. Consequently, no single vision of crimes against humanity emerged despite the jurisprudential authority of the Rome Statute. Instead, from the Nuremberg judgment onwards, various approaches continue to compete for the provision of a solid basis for the adjudication of these crimes.

III. Adjudication, Responsibility and the Law: Limits of Universal Jurisdiction

Since 1945, there have been myriad kinds of prosecutions for crimes against humanity. In addition, charges for particular instances of crimes against humanity are often brought in conjunction with charges for war crimes.[40] The changing nexus requirements according to which these prosecutions took place has already been discussed. In this section, this debate will be extended to address another issue, that of collective responsibility. As already stated, under Article 7(2)(a) of the ICC Statute, crimes against humanity require that a widespread or systematic attack on a civilian population be committed 'pursuant to or in furtherance of a State or organizational policy to commit such attack'. Here, both the term 'state policy' and the interpretation of the term 'organization' remain controversial. Normative and jurisprudential debates on the exact meanings of these terms lead to varying conclusions. Now, if these terms were understood as reflecting the ordinary meaning of the concepts and include any association of persons with an established structure of political authority, perhaps the dubiousness of their coverage would erode. What is it, then, that makes such a simple interpretation, thereby associating responsibility with the state or state-like organizations and people acting on their behalf, so cumbersome a task?

The missing link between the adjudication of crimes against humanity and a principled acknowledgement of their relationship with the acts of the state or state-like political authority harks back to the 1961 Eichmann trial in Jerusalem.[41] The Eichmann trial is part of a series of Holocaust-related trials widely known and studied among Holocaust scholars. Specifically, Holocaust scholars have come to employ the tripartite concept of information, knowledge and awareness for the determination of criminal accountability for crimes against humanity based on the study of these of trials. Their work maintains that an awareness gap exists between information flow, its processing and interpretation into general knowledge, and crystallization of the recognition of the consequences of criminal actions.[42] These trials directly contributed to building a consciousness about individual responsibility for state crimes. In this regard, in addition to the Nuremberg Trial, the trials of Jewish functionaries during the Holocaust (otherwise known as the Kapo trials), the Malkiel Gruenwald trial (otherwise known as the Kastner trial) and the Eichmann trial are cornerstones of legally inclined Holocaust research.[43] Insofar as the Holocaust was so aberrant and unprecedented an event, these trials also set a formidable precedent for tracing the complex paths that acts constituting crimes against humanity follow before they amount to mass destruction.

These trials are thus generally accepted as offering significant clues concerning the politico-normative underpinnings of crimes against humanity adjudication. The Nuremberg trials (1945–7) in particular, which took place during the period immediately prior to the establishment of the state of Israel, were marked by the intensive diplomatic and military struggle against the British for Jewish independence in Mandate Palestine and the sanctification of Jewish national freedom. The 'Kapo trials' and the Kastner trial (1948–59) also occurred during the transition from a pre-state community (*Yishuv*) to sovereign statehood, and took place under the circumstances of Israel's War of Independence, mass immigration, and the building of the new state's legal, economic and security infrastructure. At this time, Israeli jurors also crafted the Law no. 64, 'Nazi and Nazi Collaborators Punishment Law' (1950), designed to bring Nazis and their proxies to justice through the quasi-legal practice of universal jurisdiction.[44] The Eichmann trial (1960–7) came after these two initial sets of trials; it received public attention at a time of economic and political growth of the Israeli state and was used to make that state's voice audible in international law. Holocaust scholars are not at all reticent in stating that each of these trials proceeded according to the national spirit and political environment of the times. Each trial was also associated with a specific agenda: the Nuremberg trials reflected the Allies' victory over Nazi Germany, while the Kapo trials were an expression of the post-war mass immigration that put its stamp on Israeli society. Finally, the political dimension of awareness of the Holocaust as an international crime stood at the core of the Kastner trial. The Eichmann trial, on the other hand, focused on the operative meaning of state sovereignty, the privatization of the Holocaust, and the place of crimes against humanity in the wider context of the Second World War. In the post-Nuremberg era, we rarely associate political agendas with courts, tribunals and trials working towards the adjudication of crimes against humanity, but in the 1960s Holocaust scholars readily did so.

The remainder of this section will focus on the interpretation of crimes against humanity during and in the aftermath of the Eichmann trial, and compare the context within which this debate took place with the current obsession on the universality of the Rome Statute. According to Hannah Arendt, men are not capable of forgiving what they cannot punish, nor are they capable of adequately punishing what is unforgivable. Indeed, the most distinguishing feature of crimes against humanity, in the form that they were articulated during the Eichmann trials, is their imprescriptibility.[45] The Arendtian claim concerning the impossibility of punishment in certain cases such as crimes against humanity is a clear indicator of the limits of positive law. This is what Arendt alludes to in her discussion on the 'radical evil', the inadequacy of existing sentences and punishment schemes in addressing the damage caused, both because of the unprecedented nature of the crimes committed and due to their extreme cruelty constituting an obstacle to the very idea of adequate punishment. According to Arendt, during the Eichmann trial, the monstrous scale of the Nazi crimes made any punishment provided for them not just inadequate but also absurd.[46] Specifically, in 'Personal Responsibility under Dictatorship', Arendt stated that the horror of the Nazi crimes themselves, in their naked monstrosity, transcended all moral categories and exploded existing standards of jurisdiction.[47] Hence she reached the conclusion that such crimes were neither adequately punishable nor suitable for forgiveness. In the same text, she further claimed that, contrary to the statements made by the Israeli courts, reasons such as the need for society to be protected against these kinds of crimes, the rehabilitation of criminals, the dissuasive force of the example, or measures of retributive justice would not bring a complete closure. Thus, our ordinary sense of justice does not suffice in the case of crimes against humanity.

In her later work, in particular in *The Human Condition*, it is true that Arendt admitted a possible combination of forgiveness and punishment concerning crimes against humanity.[48] Still, she clearly stated that punishment is a mere alternative to forced forgiveness by the dictates of history.[49] Punishment and forgiveness have one crucial aim in common: an attempt to put an end to something that without interference would lack closure. Forgiveness is not alien to politico-normative judgment. And yet, forgiveness could not be routinized, and it remains an exceptional act. Meanwhile, we make the opposite claim for crimes against humanity jurisprudence: it is meant to be the supreme example of the regularization of forgiveness in international law, presumably finding a suitable universal codification. To think more deeply about this antinomy, it is necessary to consider the context in which both the 'globalization of forgiveness' and universal jurisdiction pertaining to crimes against humanity emerged.[50] Especially in the Global South, but also in the heart of what were once the colonial empires, scenarios of repentance, confession and forgiveness have multiplied since the end of the Second World War. The Catholic Church's request for forgiveness for the Second World War crimes, that of the Prime Minister of Japan towards the Korean and Chinese societies, that of the Belgian government for not having acted on the genocide in Rwanda, the Chilean armed forces' confession of their crimes, and the Canadian prime minister's apology to the Native Peoples of Canada are just a few examples widely advertised in this avalanche of a desire for forgiveness for crimes that cannot be punished or forgotten. This proliferation of scenes of regret and requests for forgiveness coincides with the renewed urgency of memorials, and of institutional repentance. It appears to be a symptom of a larger yearning for redemption. As such, forgiveness and its solicitation are directly conditioned by the weight of guilt felt on the shoulders of the public. What is worrisome about this trend is not so much that we choose to remember and to give account for past wrongs, but the *simulacrum* of healing that comes with repentance. This calculative aspect of public apology is indeed troubling, considering the egregious nature of the crimes committed that constitute the subject matter of such historical apologies. Consequently, the general character of requests for forgiveness could be paramount to collective guilt rather than collective responsibility.

Perhaps this is one of the strongest reasons to re-embrace the jurisprudence of crimes against humanity in international law. This particular branch of criminal jurisprudence emerges as a chance for freeing societies from the repentance-redemption equation or its opposite, the total denial of heinous and most egregious crimes. A publicly appointed body could not forgive on behalf of either the direct victims of egregious crimes or the public at large who suffered in relation to or as a result of such crimes. The State, its institutions and courts cannot force wronged peoples to forgive simply because an official apology has been extended to them. Through the adjudication of crimes against humanity, on the other hand, the culpable person(s) is called upon in relation to unforgivable acts, and yet without being redeemed. That is a much stronger form of seeking accountability and as a society, claiming responsibility for mass violence, rooted in politics, history and normative grounds, than what forced forgiveness alone could provide.[51]

Conclusion

Despite the universal jurisdiction clause attached to them, much like forgiveness, crimes against humanity have politico-normative foundations that determine the form of their adjudication. I would further argue that crimes against humanity jurisprudence should not be normalized in international law. By the very nature of the crimes it attends, this body of jurisprudence must remain exceptional and extraordinary, putting impossibility to the test, as if it interrupts the ordinary course of human sociality. Only then it would assume the power to intercept the flow of events that sanctify egregious crimes. This chapter started with the question of what distinguishes crimes against humanity from other international crimes. The answer to this question cannot be determined solely on the basis of the doctrinal qualities of crimes against humanity jurisprudence; we need to closely attend to their normative architecture. Their distinct status in this regard has a deep connection with Hannah Arendt's narration of the 'banality of evil/radical evil' duality with reference to the Eichmann trials. More than half a century ago, as Arendt witnessed the proceedings of the trial of Adolf Eichmann as one of the major figures in the organization and conduct of the Holocaust, she coined these two separate and yet related terms. The former term has since become something of a legal conundrum though it constitutes the beginning point for the study of authoritarian regimes cloaked in legality. Arendt certainly did not mean evil had become ordinary, or that Eichmann and his Nazi cohorts had committed ordinary crimes. Rather, she was convinced that the crimes committed were so exceptional, they demanded a new approach to legal judgment itself.[52] Concomitantly, she offered several challenges to traditional conceptions of legal judgment. The first one was related to *legal intention*. The key question here is whether the courts had to prove that Eichmann intended to commit genocide in order for him to be convicted of the crime. Eichmann may well have lacked the required legal intention, insofar as he failed to even think about his acts as constitutive of a crime. Though Eichmann acted in full conscious capacity and without being affected by insanity, he lacked a mode of rationality that would yield intentionality. This observation led Arendt to claim that although national socialism was capable of making individuals implement policies that led to egregious crimes, it also equipped them with a cathartic state of assuming no responsibility for their actions and attributing no intentionality to their involvement in the making and sustenance of a criminal regime. In order to claim intentionality, one has to convey the capacity or knowledge needed to think reflectively about the consequences of one's wilful actions. The banality Arendt named thus corresponds to the inability to think and understand the weight of one's own actions as a legal/political being.

Furthermore, Arendt was not trying to establish an exceptional case for Israel or the Jewish people. Rather, she was striving to articulate the backbone of a theory of crimes against humanity, one that would acknowledge the destruction of not just Jews, but also Catholics, Gypsies, gay people, communists, the disabled and the ill under the Nazi regime.[53] In her thinking, the destruction and displacement of these populations on a categorical basis was an attack not only on those specific groups, but on humanity itself. As a result, Arendt objected to a specific nation-state such as Israel conducting the trial of Eichmann exclusively in the name of its own population. She was cursed and almost crucified for her interpretation of the crimes of the Nazis. And yet her interventions also made it possible to talk about crimes against humanity above and beyond the Jewish case and the Holocaust. As the history of crimes against humanity jurisprudence proves, after the particular historical juncture of the Eichmann trial it indeed became necessary to devise new codes of international law that identify and propose punishment for crimes against humanity in a generic sense.

Finally, there is a critical aspect of Arendt's observations of the Eichmann trial that fell aside in the debate on later developments of international jurisprudence in this area. It concerns the 'banality' of such crimes, indicating that they were committed in the midst of daily life and routines, without notable opposition to their conduct, and without being named as a crime at the time they were committed. In a sense, Arendt's calling a crime against humanity banal allows us to conceptualize the socially accepted, routinized nature of these crimes which are committed mostly through policy enactments and under institutional guidelines and, as such, without moral revulsion, political indignation or public resistance. Hence, her interpretation of crimes against humanity calls for a new mode of political and legal reflection. This opposition between the radical nature of the crimes committed and the ordinariness that their committal assumes invites us to rethink the almost mechanical reiteration of crimes against humanity jurisprudence in the post–Rome Statute era of international law.

Arendt was also long blamed for trivializing the Holocaust and the Nazi crimes, as she was seen as attributing them to the Nazis' and their collaborators' simple failure to think before they act. For her, however, the degradation of thinking worked hand in hand with the systematic destruction of populations. What drew the ire against Arendt's interpretation of the Eichmann trials was related to the fact that she showed the audacity of confronting the Israeli courts in terms of their legal reasoning and conduct, though not their final verdict. She thought the trial needed to focus more on the acts that Eichmann committed, acts that left an imprint on the whole of humanity, not only the millions of European Jews who perished as a result. This is partly due to the fact that, similar to the legal philosopher Yosal Rogat before her, Arendt did not think that anti-semitism in Germany could be tried in a courthouse.[54] She thus objected to the ways Israel used the Eichmann trial to establish and legitimate its own legal authority and national aspirations as a Jewish state. She was severely displeased by the fact that Eichmann was made to stand for all of anti-semitism and for every Nazi. In her view, this was far too simplistic an interpretation of who Eichmann was and what he stood for. Finally, for Arendt, the Eichmann trial necessitated a deep critique of the idea of collective guilt, as well as a broader reflection on the historically specific challenges to assuming collective and moral responsibility under dictatorships and authoritarian rule. Eichmann was guilty because he failed to take distance from the requirements that Nazi law and policy imposed upon him in a legal order that was impeccably legitimate on paper.

There remains, then, a question that still lacks a definitive answer. It pertains to the politico-normative foundations of the adjudication of egregious crimes such as crimes against humanity. The first time we heard of acts that could be defined as crimes against humanity was around one hundred years ago, in 1915, when France, Great Britain and Russia used this concept in a diplomatic note. They were considering issuing a warning concerning the massacre of the Armenians at the hands of the Ottoman elite and military. The first legally sanctioned instance of the adjudication of this category of crimes appeared four decades later, at the Nuremberg trials, set up to judge major Nazi criminals. At Nuremberg, it became a practical necessity to create a special category of crimes that did not fit into the conduct commonly classified as war crimes. This need to create a new framework was partly due to the fact that Germany's persecution of its own citizens could not be classified as a war crime. It is true that a country's expulsion, deportation and mass murder of its own citizens was not unheard of in the history of war or state-making alike. However, the degree to which these acts were orchestrated and publicly condoned by the German state constituted a unique case. The trouble is, what was once considered unique became a normalized category on its own, expected to deliver a sense of closure for societal morass and lack of collective responsibility. Thus, the current normative framework characterizing crimes against humanity as a frontal attack on plurality and human diversity in effect became a *pro forma* acknowledgement of the conducts that constitute crimes against humanity as part of the maintenance of the current system of sovereign statehood. Addressing this issue requires a closer look at the way that international law has played out in court and litigation-based accountability measures, with a particular emphasis on the Global South. Not only did crimes against humanity become normalized, they were regularly attributed to only states and societies in the post-colonial geographies.

4

Mea Culpa, Sua Culpa, Tua Maxima Culpa: Collective Responsibility, Societal Wrongdoing and Legal Judgment[1]

Introduction

> *ad auctores reddit sceleris coacti culpa* – the guilt of imposed crimes lies on those who impose them *Seneca*[2]

If only we could abide by the ethical guidelines offered by the Romans, problematic aspects of collective responsibility in law and legal morality could perhaps be avoided. However, a harmonious relationship between social life and political peace is not so easy to attain or sustain in an era marked by deep crises and normalization of mass violence. Issues concerning justice and personal desert at times of turmoil and uproar such as genocidal violence, ethnic cleansing, or crimes against humanity cannot be reduced to proven links between punishable individual actions, international criminal law and regimes of accountability. This chapter thus invites the reader to consider the limitations of seeking societal peace and political transformation mainly through achieving criminal accountability concerning the 'individual perpetrators' of mass atrocities. Almost all of the examples covered in the previous pages pertain to post–Second World War applications of universal jurisdiction concerning egregious crimes. But they also belong to a particularly difficult field of inquiry: transitional justice. The field of transitional justice is increasingly characterized by the dominance of legalism to the detriment of advocacy, politics, scholarship and practice.[3] My fear is that correctives to such leanings are by and large missing in legal scholarship. Furthermore, the tendency towards aggrandizement of litigation-related measures is furthered by hybrid courts and other localized applications of international criminal law. In this chapter, I will thus venture a politico-philosophical inquiry underlining the importance of legal humility and contextualizing the criminology of transitional justice. As law's place at the heart of transition from societal and political conflicts becomes increasingly insecure, the time is right for a more honest appraisal of the limitations of legalism vis-à-vis accountability for mass atrocities.

Let me begin this discussion with an innocent looking but potent question: how much responsibility falls on our shoulders concerning the harms that flow from the social, economic and political institutions in which we are embedded, even if we do not personally inflict harm while occupying positions of authority? Furthermore, do our relations as individuals to spheres of collective existence lead to complicity and/or collective responsibility in the event that they lead to harm for select populations in society?[4] In the following discussion, I will argue that the relationship between collective responsibility, societal wrongdoing, individual guilt and criminal accountability is a very critical albeit difficult one, often entirely avoided in international criminal law. And yet, it provides a precious point of entry to the nature of our relations with society and the state, of which we are a part and for which we are the harbingers of legitimacy. Here, I posit that international criminal law scholarship needs a richer theory of accountability, in which our understanding of individual responsibility in relation to societal acts of violence not only allows for but demands an analysis of collective action and thus contextualizes litigation in this select area. Specifically, in instances such as crimes against humanity, what should be sought after is not more complicated punishment schemes but rather a substantive and all-encompassing way of addressing harm both by commission and by omission.[5] In this context, intentional and purposeful collective action, collective moral responsibility and collective guilt, individual responsibility for (and in) societal wrongs, collective legal obligations to victims of societal and political crimes, and individual moral responsibility with regard to wrongful social and political acts constitute key entries for a meaningful politico-legal debate on collective responsibility and legal judgment. I will pursue these questions in a context originally set by Hannah Arendt's work on legal judgment as summarized at the end of the preceding chapter.

In *Eichmann in Jerusalem*, her account of the trial of Adolf Eichmann, Arendt used the phrase 'the banality of evil' to describe how a man who was neither a monster nor a demon could nevertheless be an agent of the most extreme and evil acts of violence and destruction.[6] This subsequently prompted her to readdress fundamental questions and concerns about the nature of (collective) violence and our making of moral choices. *Responsibility and Judgment*, a sequel to her work on Eichmann in this regard, gathers unpublished writings from the last decade of Arendt's life.[7] In these later works, she strived to further explicate the meaning of the Eichmann trial in Jerusalem. At the heart of this series of essays lies a profound ethical concern regarding the use of traditional moral truths as politico-legal standards to judge criminality as it relates to mass violence. In this regard, Arendt's analysis of judgment tests to its limits our ability to distinguish good from evil and right from wrong. The radical evil she had addressed in her earlier work on totalitarianism evolves into a much more pernicious account of evil in this later context, whose execution is limitless when the perpetrator feels no remorse and can erase the memory of his or her acts as soon as they are committed. For such acts, individual criminal responsibility, even if it comes tied to mass crimes such as crimes against humanity, does not suffice for us to understand the true nature of the harm and wrong implicated by these acts.

Arendt's conclusion has serious repercussions for contemporary conceptions of accountability in international criminal law, and the debate presented here is a token of dedication to think further in that vein. We are currently witnessing a bewildering variety of developments in regimes of control in domestic jurisprudence of criminal justice. These range from demands for preventive detention of asylum seekers and suspected migrants to the development of dispersed regimes for the continual, silent and largely invisible work of surveillance, leading to the perpetual assessment, management, communication and control of risk-laden groups deemed prone to commit crimes. Nonetheless, little attention is paid to the inner workings of mass political violence and systemic societal crimes. In keeping with this circumscribed understanding of criminality, accountability regimes in international criminal law have also been severely individualized with regard to state criminality. In the post–Rome Statute era of international criminal law, the trial of individual perpetrator of mass crimes as the juridical subject of the rule of law is no doubt a great leap forward towards the erosion of the unjustified defence of state sovereignty and related immunities. However, the forms of legal knowledge and modes of jurisprudential expertise that are implicated in these new techniques and rationalities of criminalization of state conduct also carry the danger of blinding us towards larger socio-political realities of mass crimes.

In criminal justice, individual autonomy is used as a benchmark and an ideal that refers to the capacity to be one's own person, and to live one's life according to reasons and motives that are taken as one's own and not as the product of manipulative, coercive or distorting external forces. Individual autonomy is also the central value in the Enlightenment tradition of moral philosophy. Examination of the concept of autonomy is similarly central for debates over legal freedoms and rights, as well as moral and political theory pertaining to justice.[8] Autonomy has traditionally connoted independence, and hence prioritized individual agency in moral thinking and political decision-making. Finally, in the realm of moral theory, seeing autonomy as a foundational value stands in contrast with alternative frameworks, such as ethics of care and ethics of virtue.

In the specific context of individual autonomy and its relation to the banality of evil connoting societal crimes, the existing arsenal of concepts hence does not suffice to deal with the problem in hand: namely, how to understand the weight of individual choices in producing unforgivable forms of societal and mass harm. In the following debate, we therefore turn to another concept, albeit one that Arendt did not contend with at all. In order to make sense of the conundrum of commonplace and rule-bound choices made by individuals leading to collective forms of violence and societal wrongdoing, I will examine the idea of *collective responsibility* but couple it with the notion of societal wrong to remove the adage of collective guilt attached to it.[9] In legal philosophy, starting with Joel Feinberg's work, the debate on collective responsibility has been kept alive like a slowly burning flame, looming at the background of questions concerning accountability but rarely entering the registers of litigation-oriented takes on applications of international law, particularly in the context of transitional justice measures and post-conflict societies where applications of crimes against humanity jurisprudence are most relevant.[10]

Collective responsibility has received ire from many corners, a reaction most predictable as it goes against the basic principle that no one can be responsible, in the properly ethical or criminal sense, for the conduct of another, and that criminal responsibility squarely belongs to the individual. However, concerning mass political violence and state criminality, the implications of exclusive reliance on the principle of individual criminal liability are more damaging than is evident at first.[11] In international criminal law, reverting to the barbarous notion of collective or group responsibility for litigation purposes is considered an absolute derogation of rights, and rightfully so. What I am pursuing here is rather different: it is the notion of accountability for atrocities as societal responsibility in a distinctively socio-political sense, and as an element that foregrounds the legitimacy of criminal trials targeting egregious acts such as crimes against humanity (Kutz, 2007).[12] In other words, my purpose is not to attribute diminishing importance to causation in criminal law, whether domestic or international in its application. In ideal circumstances where harm is not involved, the outcome of an act does not and should not affect our assessment of the act. In cases of acts *blameworthy* due to their resulting in harm or near harm, however, should our moral assessment be neutral? Furthermore, concerning acts that are committed or condoned under the aegis of state criminality, should we not look elsewhere than the individual *mens rea* component? Do such criminal acts not require societal endorsement and support? Should larger outcomes never matter in our assessment of a person's individual criminal conduct?

Back in 1968, when D. E. Cooper proposed the thesis that collectives can be held responsible in a sense not reducible to the individual responsibility of members of the collective, he also stated clearly that it is not *moral* responsibility which is involved in such a reassessment of accountability.[13] I strongly concur with Cooper, and invite us to revisit the collective responsibility debate[14] at the current historical junction of criminal acts pertaining to state criminality, civil war, military occupation and neocolonialism, almost all of which are now within the reach of the current regime of accountability in international criminal law and, to a lesser degree, universal jurisdiction. We have much to gain by at least temporarily suspending our overdependence on legal institutions for finding cures to our societal ills via litigation of state criminality and political violence solely based on individual accountability.

I. Beyond Eichmann: On the Necessity of Judgment

While writing *Eichmann in Jerusalem*, Arendt truly struggled to defend the possibility of judgment against the manifold problems we encounter in our attempts to offer legally valid and morally meaningful verdicts concerning those who have committed crimes in morally bankrupt and legally defunct communities.[15] No doubt some of Arendt's conclusions concerning Eichmann are equivocal. Her theory of judgment in the *Eichmann* manuscript itself could even suggest that Arendt may have remained trapped within a set of Kantian assumptions in her philosophy of history, and thus ended up defining the question of freedom to act in a binary way. In contradistinction, proposing that judgment has an antinomical character and emphasizing the importance of elements of reason and sense as well as circumstance and context may allow for a better understanding of the collective nature of responsibility for societal crimes.[16] In Theodor Adorno's terms, judgment becomes the very test for the limits of agency and autonomy suffered by the potentially free but essentially 'unfree subjects' of modernity.[17]

Contemporary readers of *Eichmann in Jerusalem* sometimes cast it as a juridical text, due to the fact that it is presumably more concerned with justice than with politics or ethics. Such readings of Arendt's work on Eichmann in particular, and crimes against humanity in general, focus attention on what Arendt calls the primary challenge of the case – namely, the trial of Eichmann's unprecedented crimes against humanity in a domestic court.[18] However, putting so much emphasis on the nature of crimes against humanity jurisprudence leads to our failing to attend to Arendt's principled resistance to a merely juridical response. This is clearly evidenced in her criticism of both procedural and substantive aspects of the Jerusalem Court's ruling. Taking my cue from Arendt's resistance to the Israeli Court's approach, here I argue that *Eichmann in Jerusalem* does not authorize a solely juridical approach to the unprecedented and egregious crimes under discussion. Instead, it could lead us to think about the importance of an 'agonistic understanding of law',[19] emphasizing law's dependence on the political acceptance or contestation of legal strictures, maxims and constraints. Especially with the advent of mass crimes such as crimes against humanity, Arendt asks us to attend to law's dependence on the human capacity to resist 'illegal' compulsions, and urges us to redefine the meaning and merit of legal institutions in light of the responsibility of all concerned for their maintenance, sustenance, and functioning.[20]

Foregrounding this debate, in her *Lectures on Kant's Political Philosophy*, Arendt detranscendentalizes Kant by linking Kant's judgment of taste to empirical sociability and lived experience.[21] However, she does not confuse Kant's idea of enlarged thinking with an actual dialogue with others. Instead, she introduces the notion of interdependence between judgment and speech (or communication). In this sense, Arendt interprets Kant's *Critique of Judgment* not as a theory of aesthetic judgment, but as an answer to the more general question of 'how do I judge?' She also draws a distinction between common sense and community sense, a notion further explored in the work of Jennifer Nedelsky and others writing in the area of human rights. Working with the notion of community sense, Arendt uncovers a foundation not only for humans as political beings but also for the idea of humanity at large, a finding that is often overlooked in the literature on her theory of judgment (Berkowitz, Katz and Keenan,

2010).[22] Here, I would like to capitalize on this sense of the political groundedness of action and judgment vis-à-vis the notion of collective responsibility.

Of Arendt's completed works, the 'Postscriptum' to *Thinking*, the first volume of *The Life of the Mind*, and her Lectures on *Kant's Political Philosophy* are widely considered to be her definitive remarks on judgment. These texts are privileged for two reasons. First, they were written after *Eichmann in Jerusalem*. Arendt's recognition of the role that Eichmann's inability to think played in his war crimes motivated her to analyse more fully not only the 'human activity' of thinking, but those of willing and judging as well. In addition, in both *The Life of the Mind* and the *Kant Lectures*, Arendt treats judgment as a distinct human activity with a unique potential. In these later works, though Arendt does indeed reformulate her notion of judgment, she does not depoliticize it. On the contrary, the effects of what Arendt refers to as 'dark times' are considered as long-term and pervasive. Moreover, the weight of making judgments remains as politically germane as it was in the immediate aftermath of the Second World War.

The basic project of Arendt's *Lectures on Kant's Political Philosophy* is to ground the idea of human dignity within the context of the publicly displayed 'words and deeds' that constitute the realm of human affairs and, of course, politics. Her attempt to redefine human dignity also involves a strong philosophical response to Plato's impugning of dignity from the *polis*. The Kant Lectures bring this distinct take on the political nature of genuine human conduct to its completion: the enactment of public deeds presupposes a company of engaged spectators who draw meaning by judging what is enacted in the public sphere. In other words, Arendt appropriates and reconceptualizes Kant's work in such a way that judgment, while a distinct faculty, nonetheless retains an utmost political character. If we were to put Arendt's conclusion in the context of crimes against humanity, it would not be possible to kill, plunder, violate, rape and decimate entire populations using state power or official condonement unless there was widespread societal involvement and/or complicity for such egregious acts.

II. Towards an Engaged Theory of Judgment and Collective Responsibility

The notion of collective responsibility indeed proves legally and morally unsustainable if it is taken to be an unqualified application of the Kantian model of individual moral responsibility to society at large.[23] However, it emerges as a more coherent phenomenon if we formulate it in terms of moral choices leading to wilful acts producing results that are above and beyond the singular capacity of autonomous individual agents.[24] Accountability for actions of groups and institutions that cause harm and injustice for the larger society demands us to remove our singular focus on intentionality of harm and attend to wider processes concerning its production, and possible curtailment.[25]

The biggest controversy concerning collective responsibility involves the method of its attribution. Without ascertaining collective responsibility 'beyond reasonable doubt', there is no possibility for judgment. Legally speaking, collective responsibility is defined in literal terms and refers to the duty to respond to the suffering of victims of collective crimes. Therefore, it invokes a reverse reading that is heavily situation-bound. Reasonable fear on the part of victimized groups and communities creates a kind of responsibility that concerns the society at large. This bracketed account of collective responsibility may offer a justification for making judgments that are compatible with the principles of separateness and autonomy of persons. However, it still leaves a number of critical questions unattended in terms of the overall project of justice in post-conflict settings. For the purpose of examining the nature of legal judgment concerning egregious crimes, here I would argue that collective responsibility is best understood in terms of *societal duties* to respond to the victims of collective crimes rather than attribution of collective guilt and culpability.[26] If applied to individual accountability-based adjudication of state criminality, for instance, this would translate into the need to determine whether a person in a position of high office and responsibility used all available means to subvert and constrain damages that were implicated by egregious acts committed using public resources, in addition to the determination of whether the individual in question partook in these acts.

The responsibilities moral agents have in relation to social and political processes with unjust consequences constitute another case in point for further debate on the inadequacies of existing criminal liability schemes concerning mass crimes. How ought moral agents, whether individual or institutional, conceptualize their responsibilities in relation to global injustice, for instance, if they do so at all? In this case, a model of collective responsibility deriving from global social connections and interdependencies may serve as the foundation for defining obligations of justice that arise from structural social processes. As detailed in the work of Iris Marion Young, a social connection model of responsibility dictates that all agents who contribute by their actions to the structural processes that produce injustice have responsibilities to remedy these injustices.[27] This is quite different from the standard model of criminal responsibility that puts emphasis on liability. This alternative model does not isolate perpetrators. Instead, it examines background conditions of action as well as its consequences. It is forward-looking and relies upon shared responsibility. Furthermore, it can be discharged only through collective action and, as such, would not fit into a strict criminal justice model per se but would necessitate the inclusion of alternative modes of justice. As such, Marion Young's social connection model and Arendt's notion of community sense have more in common than at first meets the eye, and this is a hopeful overlap for any future discussion on collective responsibility in international criminal law under circumstances dictated by mass atrocities and state criminality.

A. The Threshold Question

In terms of commission of mass crimes such as those defined by crimes against humanity, which is the subject matter of this work, could we define the legal threshold to determine whether members of a collective share the intention to harm a select group, which is the distinctive feature of collective (as opposed to individual) responsibility? There are at least three criteria of adequacy for an account of shared criminal intention, namely disjunction, concurrence and obligation.[28] Accordingly, people share an intention when and only when they are jointly committed as a body to perform an act in the future. In other words, there is the element of premeditation as well as active participation in the commission of a violent act. The problem is, in the case of societal and political crimes, many instances of wrongdoing appear to be of a distinctly spontaneous kind, without clear signs of premeditation. It is true that when one group commits genocide against another, the genocide is collective in the sense that the wrongfulness of genocide is morally distinct from the aggregation of individual murders that make up the genocidal killings in their entirety. Even then, however, it may not be possible to prove, or indeed to find a clear framework for determining, shared intentions for committing genocidal acts. The problem, which I would rephrase as that of *collective wrongdoing*, is how to assign blame to individual contributors for distinctly collective acts of violence, when none of those individual contributors is singularly guilty of the Wrongdoing (with a capital W) in question.

In such instances, intention is not merely a private mental act. Rather, intention is a communal and a public act. Meanwhile, it is only observable circumstances and consequences that determine the justiciability of intention in criminal law. Here, Christopher Kutz's *Complicity Principle* provides a good starting point for tackling the problem of intentionality in societal and political mass crimes (Kutz, 2007).[29] Kutz's work examines the relationship between collective responsibility and individual guilt. He presents a rigorous philosophical account of the nature of our relations to social groups in which we participate, and links this debate to contemporary moral theory. For him, there are two prevailing theories of moral philosophy, Kantianism and consequentialism, both of which have difficulties dealing with the issue of complicity in a legal context. For Kutz, similar to Arendt, a richer and more grounded theory of accountability demands that our understanding of collective action not only allow but call for redefining individual responsibility in collective settings via complicity.

No doubt Kutz's principle ought to be expanded to link it with the legal phenomenon of attribution of collective responsibility. In this context, the view I purport is that individuals are blameworthy for collective harms insofar as they knowingly participate in those harms, and that said individuals remain blameworthy regardless of whether they succeed in making a causal contribution to those harms.[30] In this sense, my argument for collective responsibility is based on contra-factual reasoning. For instance, if a collective takes no active responsibility for the conservation of life and livelihood of all of its members but especially ignores those with vulnerabilities, then it is right to presume that there emerges collective responsibility for the harm that ensues from lack of provision for any necessary protections.[31] This is one way to avoid the problem of intentionality that clouded Arendt's path, in terms of identifying wrongdoing that is not seen or known as wrongdoing by either the person who commits it or by those who condone it.

At this point, the writings of David Miller on national responsibility, read alongside Karl Jasper's work on societal responsibility, are of great relevance. In his work on national responsibility and global justice, Miller conceptualizes and justifies a particular model of national responsibility – a model that may be helpful in devising a wholesome approach to collective responsibility in terms of mass crimes.[32] His conceptualization proceeds in two steps. He starts by developing two models of collective responsibility, the like-minded group model and the cooperative practice model. He then proceeds to discuss national responsibility as a species of collective responsibility, and argues that nations have features such that both models of collective responsibility may apply to them. I would argue that Miller's like-minded model does not provide a plausible conceptualization of collective responsibility in the politico-legal realm at all, as it tends to rely upon a bucolic, romanticized notion of a nation as an ethically cohesive unit.[33] The collective practice model, on the other hand, could provide a strong argument for formulating state criminality-related collective responsibility. The standard example used in this context is the conceptualization of crimes pertaining to societal and political violence under the Third Reich.[34]

Miller attempts to attribute to nations the kind of responsibility that is generally vested in states as legal actors. Unfortunately, models of statist legal responsibility disregard society's inner dynamics. In addition, they sanction the differences between intrastate and interstate forms of law as irremovable. Miller aims to build up the moral and historical prestige of the nation-state to make it a viable agent embracing a claim of universal morality. Miller's nations thus become political organizations capable of instantiating great moral truths. This results in an account that is compassionately cosmopolitan, and yet with very little interest in or engagement with local forms of delivery of justice that relate to mass violence either within state perimeters or globally.[35] Overall, however, Miller's work raises a number of interesting questions concerning both weak and strong variants of collective responsibility and state-centric law.[36] For instance, he defends a theory of connections to address remedial responsibilities amongst states. His interventions on the subject of cosmopolitanism in particular endorse a position where states that are causally and morally responsible for deprivation and suffering in other states may be held remedially responsible for their actions. This is despite the fact that there is no international mechanism to ensure that remedially responsible states would assume accountability for the suffering of affected states and societies. As such, Miller's claims of universal morality as applied to international or transnational law are severely idealistic. In contradiction, I would argue that we must initiate deflation of both the nation and the state as foundational moral agents in international criminal law. Just as the diminution of responsibility for mass crimes from the collective to the individual is faulty, the aggrandizement of individual moral agency and accountability to the grandiose entity of the state or the construct of the nation as the ultimate truth bearer is equally hyperbolical.

B. The Outcomes Perspective

At this point, as an alternative to cosmopolitan and liberal accounts such as Miller's work, I will examine collective responsibility from an 'outcomes perspective'. My starting point is that moral responsibility for criminal acts implies a reasonable possibility that an agent should have acted otherwise. Furthermore, allocation of moral responsibility to individuals concerning complex collective actions that result in mass harm is an issue that goes well beyond 'the problem of many hands' as exemplified by the classic Frankfurt counter-examples.[37] Philosophers usually discuss responsibility in terms of responsibility for past actions or as a question about the nature of moral agency. Yet the word responsibility also ushers in deep concerns about human agency defined above and beyond legal terms. This particular take on responsibility relates it to civic virtues that can be demonstrated both by individuals and organizations or institutions. Such a virtue-based account of responsibility occupies a distinctive place in the context of discussions of the moral and political needs of societies, especially those that have survived mass political violence and trauma.

This is an opportune moment to bring in Karl Jaspers's work. When Hitler came to power in 1933, Jaspers was taken by some degree of surprise, as he had thought that this movement would destroy itself from within, leading to the reorganization and liberation of other political forces active at the time.[38] His expectations did not materialize, and because his wife was Jewish, Jaspers qualified as an enemy of the German state. Consequently, from 1933 onwards, he was excluded from the higher councils of the university. In 1935 the first part of his work on logic, entitled *Vernunft und Existenz* (*Reason and Existence*, 1955), appeared. This was followed by a book on Nietzsche in 1936, an essay on Descartes in 1937, and in 1938 his *Existenzphilosophie*.[39] Meanwhile, a series of decrees were promulgated against him, including his removal from professorship and a total ban on any further publication. These measures effectively barred him from living and working in Germany. Permission was finally granted to him in 1942 to go to Switzerland, but a condition was imposed by the Nazis that required his wife to remain behind in Germany. Jaspers chose to stay with his wife and remained in Germany. Both of them had decided, in case of an arrest, to commit suicide. In 1945 he was told that his deportation was scheduled to take place on 14 April. On 30 March, Heidelberg was occupied by the American forces and Jaspers and his wife thus avoided deportation by merely fourteen days.

Ironically, marked only by the events of the pre-war years as yet, Jaspers's detailed philosophical examination of the contemporary state and nature of humankind, titled *Man in the Modern Age*, touches upon precisely the issue of our responsibility for our own and others' future.[40]

Elucidating his theories on a variety of topics pertaining to contemporary and future human existence, the volume meditates upon the tension between mass-order and individual human life, our present conception of human life, and the potential for a better future. Jaspers wrote this work before the advent of the Second World War, but at a time when Nazi ideology and institutional practices were beginning to run rampant in Germany.

Jaspers's contribution to the literature on collective responsibility took an even more pointed form with the publication of *Die Schuldfrage* [The Guilt Question], which addressed the question of collective responsibility of the German people for the criminal actions of their government.[41] In that short treatise, Jaspers listed four types of guilt. The first category, criminal guilt, derives from violating unequivocal laws and could be determined based on objective proof. Its jurisdiction rests with the courts. The second category, political guilt, involves the deeds of statesmen and implicates the citizens as having to bear the consequences of the deeds of the state under whose order they live. Jurisdiction of this type of guilt rests with the power and will of the victor if the state was defeated militarily, or, again, with the courts if this was a civil war situation. The charge would be failure to exercise political prudence to mitigate arbitrary use of power. Thirdly, there is the category of the moral guilt, which pertains to the actions of those who cannot act otherwise in an individual capacity. They are nonetheless deemed morally responsible for their deeds, including the execution of political and military orders. Its jurisdiction, however, purely rests with one's conscience, and is retained within the community. This particular text was written prior to the Nuremberg and Eichmann Trials. In this regard, Jaspers's last category, that of metaphysical guilt, is the most troubling one, and it became a point of contention in his lengthy exchanges with Arendt during the post-war years. Accordingly, Jaspers assumes that there exists a solidarity among men as humans that makes each co-responsible for crimes committed in his presence or with his knowledge.

No doubt, the underlying assumptions of Jasper's work on guilt could lead to a sanctimonious political moralism that has often been used to justify acts of vengeance and collective punishment. It may also support a conception of war as a crusade that requires unconditional surrender by the enemy.[42] Still, there is room for further deliberation. Jaspers acknowledges that jurisdiction over metaphysical guilt for mass political violence lies with no court. As such, this easily abused concept reminds us of the myriad ways in which our lives are entangled with, and may profit from, the suffering of others, and for which we must assume at least some degree of accountability.

III. Collective Responsibility and Legal Judgment in International Law: The Jaspers Alternative?

Ascertaining litigation for crimes reaching the dimensions of what Jaspers had in mind remains an ongoing quest, starting with the precedents set by post–Second World War trials. As already discussed at length in previous chapters, the trial of major Nazi war criminals in Nuremberg (1949) is considered a landmark event in the development of international criminal law, and continues to be highly influential in our understanding of international criminal law in post-conflict settings.[43] The plethora of essays and manuscripts written on the Trial, discussing key legal, political and philosophical questions raised both at the time and in historical perspective, are indicative of the crowned position it occupies in legal history. Ranging from the contribution of Nuremberg, to the substantive developments in international criminal law, to the philosophical evaluation of legalism in post-conflict systems of justice, the persistent significance of Nuremberg is worthy of attention (Ratner, Abrams and Bischoff, 2009).[44]

However, the reason why I include a discussion of the Nuremberg Trials in this particular debate on collective responsibility for mass crimes is somewhat different from what is covered in the canonized literature on international criminal law. The Nuremberg Judgment is often regarded as the benchmark in international law for the definition and adjudication of individual accountability for human rights abuses at a mass scale. It constitutes a tipping point in the context of legal doctrines concerning the nature of legal responsibility. Still, as I will argue in the following paragraphs, this achievement did not alleviate Jaspers's concern that, for such crimes, judgment cannot emanate from the courtroom alone. During the Trial, the concept of *Nullum Crimen Sine Lege* was put to the test of war crimes and, despite a degree of inexactitude, both crimes against humanity and genocide have been retroactively codified as a result.[45] These developments in adjudication of international crimes were then followed by the codification of slavery, forced labour, torture, forced disappearances, racial discrimination and apartheid as indictable crimes. In this sense, the Trial also redefined the notion of culpability in international law. It introduced significant changes to our understanding of individual criminal responsibility, and, despite statutes of limitations and the reasonable time period clauses concerning the duration of the proceedings, it opened the path for reinstituting the threshold of legal requirements for individual accountability for mass crimes.

The Nuremberg Trial forced us to address the problem of whether and on what basis a successor government must prosecute the human rights abuses of a prior regime. Contending that the rule of law and natural justice principles require that the very worst crimes be prosecuted no matter what the rank and status of the accused person(s), Nuremberg judges proposed that principles of international law, both in its customary and conventional forms, impose a duty to investigate and prosecute in such extreme cases.[46] This take on legality and judgment has been accepted as a foundational premise for contemporary international criminal courts.[47] However, in terms of the defences available for the accused in international criminal law pertaining to war crimes and crimes against humanity, the generic standardization of prosecutions in national courts as well as in international tribunals is causing an increasing number of problems, with significant socio-political repercussions. The most notable substantive defences at the international level include superior orders, command responsibility, *tu quoque* as a subcategory of *argumentum ad hominem*,[48] military necessity, proportionality, and reprisals. Jurisdictional defences applicable in national tribunals, on the other hand, include personal jurisdiction, subject-matter jurisdiction, and double jeopardy. Then there are defences concerning the issue of the location of the tribunal or the trial, the status of the presiding judge or judges, and the legitimacy of the court producing the judgment.[49]

In this context, if we look at the victor's justice argument posed about Nuremberg and Tokto trials from the point of view of the victims, although forgiveness is often taken to bear a close connection to societal reconciliation, there is a good deal of scepticism about its role in situations where there is no consensus on the moral complexion of the past and no clear admission of guilt on the part of the perpetrator. In other words, the conviction-oriented framework of these post–Second World War Military Tribunals are indeed troubling for closure on societal and political crimes (Isaacs, 2011).[50] Forgiveness without perpetrator acknowledgement aggravates the risk of recidivism, yields a substandard and morally compromised form of political accommodation, and leads to the silencing and patronizing of the victims, therefore potentially causing further social and political alienation, and new forms of victimization. Guilt becomes inscribed in the collective memory of nations as a dividing line, and neither forgiveness nor true understanding emanates from the litigation of these crimes alone. Hence the need to underline the importance of legal humility concerning mass violence as the impetus for the penning of this chapter.

IV. Moral Responsibility as an Epicurian Cure for the Conundrums of International Criminal Law?

Inspired by Arendt's insistence on the unique nature of judgment, I will now turn to another philosopher for whom morality carried a politically relevant meaning. Indeed, from Epicurus onwards, the notion of moral responsibility based on a moral agent's causal ownership of his or her actions, as opposed to the agent's ability to act or choose otherwise, has troubled legal thinking. This is indeed the crux on which the aforementioned Frankfurt examples were built. On the issue of free will and moral responsibility, Harry Frankfurt's argument that moral responsibility does not require the freedom to do otherwise echoes the Epicurean call for deciphering individual agency in collective acts. It also relates to the puzzle surrounding Arendt's view on the banality of evil and the possibility/impossibility of the punishment of the unforgiveable. Epicurus considered it a necessary condition for praising or blaming an agent for an action, that it has been the agent and not anything else that brought the action about.[51] Thus, the central question of moral responsibility was whether the agent was a cause of the action, or whether the agent was forced to act by some other force. Accordingly, actions are to be attributed to agents if it is in their actions that agents, *qua* moral beings, manifest themselves. Here, the question of moral engagement becomes the most important component of (criminal) acts, which significantly differs from the 'outcomes perspective' discussed above.[52] In his narration of how humans become moral beings, Epicurus envisaged a complex theory of moral responsibility and moral development, which could indeed find application in the area of collective responsibility for societal wrongdoing and mass crimes. Epicurean ethics does not suggest a moral system that allows for the effective allocation of praise and blame (Braham and van Hees, 2012).[53] Instead, it looks at the choices people make regardless of the system they are surrounded by.

Furthermore, some instances of wrongdoing are of a distinctly collective kind: when, for example, genocide is a collective act in the sense that the wrongness of genocide is morally distinct from the aggregation of individual murders that make up the genocide. The problem, which I will refer to as the problem of accountability for collective wrongs, is that in traditional criminal law, how to assign blame for collective wrongdoing to individual contributors, when at least some of those individual contributors are not directly guilty of the wrongdoing in question, is a question habitually left unclear. I have already offered Christopher Kutz's *Complicity Principle* as a starting point for solving this particular problem, although the principle ought to be expanded to include a broader and more appropriate range of cases than Kutz initially intended. The view I ultimately defend is that individuals are blameworthy for collective harms insofar as they knowingly participate or collaborate in the committal of those harms, and that said individuals remain blameworthy regardless of whether they succeed in making a causal contribution to those harms (Lawson, 2013). This is a distinctly Epicurean take on societal crimes and opposes the traditional outcome-oriented litigation methods. Suffice to say, I am not making this suggestion for it to be incorporated into the relevant bodies of international criminal law. Rather, the issue here is how to address mass crimes in a contextualized manner and with reference to forms of justice other than restitution.

Regarding this issue of (criminal) intent, another prominent political philosopher of the post–Second World War era, Michael Bratman, made critical contributions to our understanding of the notion of intention and how it relates to criminal action in particular. In Bratman's view, when we settle on a plan for action we are committing ourselves to future conduct. The commitment involved in intending, and its implications for our understanding of shared intention and cooperative activity, lead to a richer discussion on moral responsibility (Bratman, 1999). In the context of philosophy of action and moral philosophy, issues about intention and practical reason, free will and moral responsibility, and shared agency are brought to the fore with relative ease in comparison to the difficulties we face with in this regard in the context of philosophy of law. Bratman's work *Intention, Plans, and Practical Reason* (1987) permanently altered the landscape of both the philosophy of action and theory of practical rationality by drawing our attention to the complex, constitutive roles that intention plays in human agency.[54] In particular, his essays on shared agency are of utmost significance for the debate on collective responsibility.[55] If we accept Bratman's description, the notion of collective responsibility would refer to both the responsibility of moral agents for causing harm in the world and the blameworthiness we ascribe to them for having caused such harm. Hence, it would assume both a *moral* and a *causal* component. Criminal law does associate causal responsibility and blameworthiness with groups in rare cases such as genocide and crimes against humanity, but for litigation purposes the line in the sand is always drawn at individual culpability. Specifically, criminal jurisprudence locates the source of moral responsibility in collective actions only if collectives were directly involved in these acts of harm.[56] Here, I beg to differ from this commonplace reference to the notion of collective responsibility as derivative of an assumed group morality. I am also standing against the assumption that collective responsibility violates principles of individual responsibility and fairness concerning criminal attribution. On the contrary, collective responsibility as related to societal wrongdoing – as well as group intentions, collective action and group blameworthiness – is a coherent construct, and can be ascribed to moral agents fairly in cases of mass political crimes. This attribution, however, does not have to be punitive in nature.

My reservations about associating collective responsibility with group morality could be explicated further in the context of the structure of the argument that was augmented by traditions of religious thought, such as those found in the Old Testament (*Tanakh*) referring to the accounts of the Flood, the Tower of Babel, or Sodom and Gomorrah, as well as the New Testament blaming Jews as an entire race for the killing of Jesus Christ. In these narratives, entire communities were deemed punishable for their supposed deeds, and to set an example for the rest of humanity. In Biblical narratives pertaining to the death of Jesus, for instance, the blame was cast not only on the Jews of the time but upon all future generations to come. The core of these religious arguments reveals a desire for communal punishment for collective harms. Secular forms of this logic are equally widespread and troubling. Post-9/11 trends of anti-Islamism and resultant public policy measures are an all too familiar case in point. Collective responsibility translated into a rationale for collective punishment is also regularly used as a disciplinary measure in military units, prisons and psychiatric facilities used for political crimes, such as those operated in Russia or in the post-Guantanamo Bay United States.[57] Without fail, these measures breed distrust and desire for vengeance among the members of the punished group and their communities at large. These punishment schemes are also commonly practised in situations of war, based on the presupposition of collective guilt. Collective guilt, or guilt by association, is a dangerous claim that assumes groups of humans should be subject to punishment above and beyond the guilt of individual members. Luckily, contemporary criminal law operates on the principle that guilt shall only be attributed to a legal person and not to a group or community. Keeping these intricacies and problem-laden historical examples of attribution of collective guilt in mind, one must not equate collective responsibility either with collective punishment or the collective assignment of presumed moral failure to groups, communities or societies. And yet, this precaution should not restrain us from seeking a substantive definition of collective responsibility for mass crimes either.

While the majority of debates on collective responsibility continue to deliberate on the very possibility of it, a select group of scholars have ushered in two further concerns. The first is whether groups can meet stringent conditions of moral responsibility that individuals do. Intentionality, as I touched upon briefly, becomes key in this context. The second concern is the advantages and disadvantages of holding particular kinds of groups, such as communities or particular ethno-religious groups, or even states, morally responsible for harm caused by their direct or indirect actions.[58] One key example to consider in this area is that of lustration. Often, after a regime-changing war, a state engages in lustration in order to secure the condemnation and punishment of dangerous, corrupt or culpable members of the previous political system. Changes in the political structure of post-Apartheid South Africa, post–Second World War de-Nazification of Germany, or the recent de-Ba'athification in Iraq are commonly referred cases of lustration. This practice poses an important dilemma from the perspective of how to define and put into practice collective responsibility, because even well-planned, legally sound and nuanced lustration involves condemning entire groups of people.[59] It also raises additional questions about collective agency and the rectification of historical injustices. While group treatment might be justified on grounds of convenience and political peace in times of transitional justice, there are also valid arguments consistent with due process requirements waged against wholesale group punishment.[60]

Concomitantly, I would posit a theory of combined criminal and political accountability based on an understanding of collective action and collective responsibility that not only allows for but demands individual responsibility (Kutz, 2007). Instead of generalizing the sum total of individuals as a collective, the causation I propose implicates a movement from the collective back to the individual. No doubt, there is not a single, simple and all-encompassing solution to the problem of the relationship between individual and collective responsibility for wrongdoing and harm. The one component that most obscures the fundamental requirement for ascribing responsibility is that of moral agency. Closer attention to matters of individual and collective agency may provide a defensible criterion for establishing when an individual is or is not responsible for the untoward consequences of a collective act (Held, 1970).[61] For instance, not only individuals but organizations, institutions and corporations can act and exercise power, and thus could be deemed as accountable for harm. This is possible because they possess decision-making structures that are formal. As such, they could be deemed as 'legal persons'. The actions of such legal actors are not reducible to the actions of their individual members. Since these legal actors/agents could have acted differently or could have been re-organized to change the course of their harmful acts, they could be deemed as morally responsible for the untoward effects of the power they exercise upon the larger population. Thus, at least in principle, they are blameworthy and could be subject to legal judgments. The ability to exercise power purposely and knowingly as opposed to recklessly or negligently, reveals a particular disposition to abusing power when it is concentrated and institutionalized. Finally, I would argue that such legal actors' disposition for wrongdoing is not reducible to the dispositions or degrees of blame applicable to their individual members who participated in the internal decision-making processes, or even those who led these organizations and institutions, which is the dictum used for litigation against crimes against humanity, for instance. Instead, there is a need for a larger discussion on the interdependent relationship between the individual and the collective in upholding a system of abuse, harm and danger. Here, the Epicurean cure for the conundrums of the debate on moral responsibility comes to our rescue as the foreground allowing us to think about intentionality and causal involvement in collective acts, and as a call to assume responsibility for our own decisions to act or not to act.

V. Collective Responsibility and the Distribution of Blameworthiness

Whether collective responsibility makes sense as a non-distributive phenomenon, that is to say whether it transcends the contributions of particular group members, is a pivotal debate for legal theory. In this context, two claims are crucial. The first is that groups, unlike individuals, cannot be accountable for intentions, and hence cannot act or cause harm *qua* groups. The second is that groups, as distinct from their individual members, cannot be understood as morally blameworthy according to the criteria required by moral responsibility argument. Accordingly, we cannot isolate genuinely collective actions, as distinct from the identical actions of many persons; and groups, unlike the individuals who belong to them, cannot formulate intentions of the kind thought to be necessary for criminal actions. Here, the main worry is about the fairness of ascribing collective responsibility to individuals who do not themselves directly cause harm, or who do not bring about harm purposefully (Narveson, 2002).[62]

If group intention is a necessary condition of attributing collective responsibility, the question then becomes how it can be ascertained.[63] At this point, I would argue that collective behaviours are separated from *collective actions*, the latter caused by the beliefs, desires and wants of the collective itself. As such, moral blameworthiness is grounded in the intentions of moral agents who cause harm, which is applicable to both individual and collective responsibility. If so, how can groups, as distinct from their individual members, be said to have intentions and demonstrate the ability to act on them? Could entire communities be deemed as appropriate bearers of moral blameworthiness, guilt or shame? Critics of the collective responsibility argument concentrate on showing either that actions are associated exclusively with individuals, not groups or communities, or that groups cannot make choices or hold beliefs in the sense required by the formulation of intention as defined by criminal law (Lewis, 1948; Cooper, 1968; Downie, 1969). Meanwhile, these same critics pay much less attention to the nature of collective actions. Collectivities cannot have moral faults. And yet, does that mean by default that they cannot properly be ascribed moral responsibility for harmful actions that are only possible if and when individuals act collectively?

At the other end of the spectrum, defenders of the collective responsibility argument feel compelled to justify both the moral possibility of collective responsibility and the coherence of collective responsibility as a moral, and hence possibly legal, construct. To start with, precepts of methodological individualism are brought under attack (Cooper, 1968; McGary, 1986).[64] Accordingly, the collective blame that we ascribe in mass crimes cannot be realized in terms of individual blameworthiness. Furthermore, as exemplified by Larry May's work, there is a class of predicates that can only be true of collectives. May uses the relational theory of Jean-Paul Sartre to argue that groups can legitimately be ascribed actions in cases where individuals act together in a manner that would not be possible if they acted alone (May and Hoffman, 1992).[65] On the issue of group intentions, however, the legal problem of ascertaining intentionality is not easy to tackle, and it remains a threshold issue for criminal law-related determinations. If intentions play a fundamental role in an agent's practical deliberation and volition, the prospect of a shared intention introduces the spectre of shared mental states. This is *not* included in the standards of proof for criminal law litigation and for very valid reasons, as it would lead to collective punishment.

If the possibility of collective responsibility supposedly requires a collective mind, we might as well give up on the notion of collective responsibility altogether. Groups can legitimately be said to have shared beliefs and convictions, yet this is quite distinct from the proposition of a collective mindset. These convictions are otherwise known as institutional culture, ideology, political movements, and so on. Hence, looking for a collective mindset to ascertain collective responsibility for societal harm and wrongdoings is not the business of criminal justice litigation (Gilbert, 1996; 2000; 2009 and Bratman, 1999).[66] And yet, it is a very important component of how to rebuild a sense of trust and societal peace in the aftermath of mass crimes. In the area of political philosophy, in Raimo Tuomela and Kaarlo Miller's work these factors are named as 'we intentions', and they provide the springboard for joint commitments and actions for rebuilding societies.[67] According to Tuomela, actions by collectives build upon the actions of the operative members of the collective in such a way that the properties of collectives, such as their intentions, beliefs and desires, are both embodied and determined by the perspectives of individual members or representatives of the collective in question. This is an unusual intervention, with very important implications for the production of legal judgments concerning collective or societal wrongs. Larry May similarly offers one of the most interesting arguments of this sort in his defence of collective moral agency. Although he rejects accounts of group intentions that are tied to Kantian notions of moral agency, he reformulates group intentions with reference to a theory of interdependence and sociality.

Historically, for those who work on collective responsibility as a necessary notion for applied philosophy, ethics and legal theory, the focus has been on states, corporations and other entities that have an institutional backbone and well-ordered decision-making processes in place. Organizational and institutional mechanisms through which courses of concerted action have been decided upon and justified as rule-bound are deemed particularly important. Similarly, enforced standards of conduct for individuals that are stringent and disciplinarian constitute a crucial aspect of such forms of action. In turn, purposeful, planned and institutionally controlled actions could render groups and communities collectively responsible for harm caused by their joint acts, though most likely not in a criminal sense. In the case of social and political movements, as discussed in detail by Joel Feinberg in his body of work on collective responsibility, there is the added element of ideological directives and the resultant group solidarity leading individuals to pursue projects together as a collective agent (Feinberg, 1970).[68] All of these are aspects of a very germane debate on collective responsibility that has been thus far overlooked by theories of international criminal law pertaining to mass crimes, war crimes and crimes against humanity. This is a deep chasm that must be addressed without further ado, and this chapter has endeavoured to provide a critical review of some of the key connections already built in this regard.

Conclusion: The Dilemma of the Sum Total versus Its Constitutive Parts

Since collective responsibility refers to the addressing of widespread harm and wrongdoing associated with the actions of collectivities, groups, societies and institutional bodies, the key components of its adjudication are directly related to constitutive aspects of social, cultural and political life. While there is a broad, often tacit, agreement regarding the basic model of moral and criminal responsibility when it is applied to individuals, there is considerable doubt about how this notion might be applied to collectivities and their members at large. First and foremost, even the thought of adjudicating collective responsibility leads to disagreements about the very conception of collective responsibility (Jaspers, 2009).[69] One version maintains that only individual human agents can be held morally and criminally responsible for harmful acts, while another conception insists that groups, collectivities and institutions can be held morally and criminally responsible as collectivities, independent of their members' individual actions. The former conception has, as its departure point, the conviction that collectivities and institutions are capable of actions that cannot be reduced to the actions and interests of their individual members.[70] This conviction alone does not render adjudication of collective responsibility a straightforward process. It does, however, indicate that the courtroom alone is not the solution for mass crimes. Furthermore, adjudicating egregious acts such as crimes against humanity does require societal action and wilful participation, particularly if these litigation-oriented strategies of transitional justice are to be pursued at the local and domestic level.

In this context, Joel Feinberg's now largely forgotten taxonomy of collective responsibility arrangements constitutes a critical contribution to the exploration of issues regarding the culpability of collectives and their members. In his classic treatise written back in 1970, *Doing and Deserving*, Feinberg presents four distinct responsibility arrangements: (a) 'Whole groups can be held liable even though not all of their members are at fault'; (b) 'A group can be held collectively responsible through the fault, contributory or noncontributory, of each member'; (c) 'Group liability [could be attributed] through the contributory faults of each and every member'; and (d) 'Through the collective ... fault of the group itself [the collective] bears liability independently of its members' (Feinberg, 1970).[71] If we are to consider Feinberg's constructs in order to reach a conclusion pertaining to the justiciability of collective acts leading to harm, the complications involved need to be adequately addressed.[72]

In Feinberg's first case, if a whole group is liable for the faulty and harmful actions of one or several members of the group, there must be the accompanying assumption that this sort of collectivity possesses a significant degree of solidarity. No doubt, this presumption stands against the ideal of individual responsibility and autonomy. Punishment of all for the wrongdoing of a few is not defensible on moral or legal grounds. For both goods and harms to be defined as collective and shared, would promotion of a mutual sense of collective destiny suffice? Looked at through the lens of justiciability, the answer is negative. Courts often invoke one of the justiciability doctrines – standing, ripeness and mootness – to bring potentially important public litigation to a definite conclusion. According to orthodox understandings of justiciability, these doctrines disempower courts from deciding certain kinds of cases. Of the three, mootness is the most relevant for our purposes, as it has the strongest moral moorings in terms of law's compass in society. Collectives are not punishable where individual autonomy is held as a supreme value in the constitutional order. Furthermore, constitutional schemes often create a presumption in favour of preserving a degree of legislative control over jurisdiction. In the case of collective responsibility, courts would need to transform mootness from a constitutional doctrine into a prudential doctrine that would enable them to decide otherwise 'moot cases' whenever a decision would help give true and concrete meaning to important public values. That is, however, an idealistic future projection rather than the present-day reality of litigation for societal and political crimes.

Furthermore, in a standard criminal law setting, arrangements in which the whole group is punished for the faults or wrongdoing of a few constitute *vicarious liability*, since a person punished on account of another's wrongdoing is said to have been punished vicariously. Vicarious liability squarely conflicts with individual moral responsibility and, of course, the principle of individual accountability for criminal acts.[73] For litigation purposes, vicarious attribution of group or collective liability is an arrangement unsuitable for most forms of harm or wrongdoing.[74] However, the issue is not so clear when we are dealing with the actions of state institutions, for instance. In this changed setting,

Feinberg's second arrangement of collective responsibility comes into the picture, which is based on the examination of implications for a group of individuals sharing a common agenda, or who could possibly have engaged in a similar harmful act. As such, the ascription of criminal or moral responsibility requires that an act causing harm has actually occurred rather than simply been intended.[75]

In summary, as I have discussed thus far, legal-philosophical debates in the field of collective responsibility prove that an exaggerated conception of fault and responsibility could easily lead to the ascription of blameworthiness to groups and communities without having a solid ground for justiciability. This is clearly observable in Feinberg's categorizations, which constitute one of the finest examples of the legal-philosophical analysis of collective responsibility. If so, formal organizations, such as business corporations, nation-states, armies or public bureaucracies appear to be the only legal actors to which we could accrue justiciable forms of collective responsibility. That locks us back into the problem of responsibility being allocated only to formal units and their representatives thereof, and leaves us astray when it comes to societal accountability for mass political crimes.

Whether a true and systemic rectification of injury and harm aiming for corrective justice is at all possible concerning mass political crimes thus remains as a troubling question. By whom justice must be performed is where almost all attention seems to have focused on up until now. If the injuries in question are divided into components of harm and wrong, each component's rectification would have to be considered separately. Although pecuniary compensation for such harms is practically plausible, money cannot act as a mediator between severely damaged lives and abusers of political power. Not all harms could be compensated, nor can it be said that when compensation is paid, the *status quo ante* should be restored. There is no normative or conceptual reason for regarding compensation as the main remedy for societal harms. On the issue of the wrong, on the other hand, standard methods of rectification may or may not work, depending on the specific context of the injustice in question. For instance, to correct wrongdoing by rectifying harm may not be at all possible in the event of mass civilian deaths and disappearances. Deploying only punitive damages may not be of much benefit for hundreds of thousands or millions of displaced populations, either. The third, most common option embraced by international criminal law, individual incarceration and punishment, remains by and large symbolic. There may well be a need for an admission of causal and moral responsibility, public and institutional repudiation of the criminal act, substantive reforms at the state level, and, in some cases, disgorgement and reparations to be performed as a sign of a good faith effort to share the burden of the victims' suffering by the society at large. Although these cannot be forced onto members of the society, the state and its institutions are obligated to take a lead in this regard. However, how much of a restoration these measures would yield is truly dependent on how the society at large deals with the issue of collective responsibility for mass crimes in a non-criminal sense, as well.

In this vein, this chapter has offered a refutation of the litigation-heavy focus of international criminal law as it has been applied to mass societal and political crimes. Instead, it embraced the view that if so used, criminal law essentially becomes a stunted system of corrective and restitutional rather than restorative justice. The concept of corrective justice is neither capable of offering solutions to society-wide problems nor is it poised to deliver restorative justice for historical wrongdoings. In contradistinction, what is required in instances such as crimes against humanity is an essentially future-oriented vision. The aim is the protection of legal subjects and valuable social interests from such harms in future. Here, I have also tried to address the question of whether a statute of limitations on a historical injustice is morally justified. In essence, rectificatory justice calls for the ascription of a right to ask for rectification once an injustice has been perpetrated, without reference to a set time frame. To claim a statute of limitations on historical injustices amounts to inserting a temporal limit on the legitimacy of a right to rectification – a set amount of time following injustice after which claims of rectification could no longer be considered valid. However, since ascribing a right to rectification for an injustice is a requirement of fundamental justice, and since the temporal limit called for by a statute of limitations is a constraint on that requirement, it is morally justified only if one has substantive reasons for accepting this constraint, such as the establishment and maintenance of societal peace.

As a footnote to this entire debate, in legal philosophy there is a peculiar argument that has been widely applied to substantiate the validity of claims for obtaining historic justice. It is known as the 'non-identity argument'.[76] Accordingly, the harm to descendants of historically wronged peoples is not only derived from the historic wrongs themselves, but from the failure to provide rectification to the previous generation for the harm they suffered. In a chain of injustices, each failure to provide rectification becomes the source of the next wrongful act and harm. Non-identity philosophers argue that such chains form a bridge between the historic wrong and the harm suffered by living individuals today. In other words, past wrongs, for which only original wrongdoers are responsible, in turn harm descendants of original victims. A supplementary solution may be offered in the form of focusing on group harm and group membership. This approach ties individual harm to group harm rather than limiting justice claims to individual restitution or compensation. For instance, did slavery not harm the descendants of slaves? This is the classical example proving the shortcomings of the individual responsibility argument applied to reject the validity of claims for historic justice based on harms to descendants of victims of historic wrongs. According to the individual responsibility argument, if descendants are never harmed directly and personally by historic wrongs, they have no right to ask for rectification. Beyond doubt, although this conclusion may be legally sound, it is morally unintuitive and must be debunked.

To conclude, due to the extensive nature of harm involved in historic injustices, one must try in earnest to overcome the hurdle posed by the individual responsibility argument wielded against justice claims regarding mass crimes. Many of the crimes adjudicated under the aegis of crimes against humanity do constitute or lead to historical injustices. These forms of injustice and the harms they generate are best understood as group or collective harms. If so, the response to group harms has to have a collective component as well, because the remedies offered are again only meaningful in a social and political context. Claims for justice under such circumstances have to be grounded in harms currently suffered by living individuals as a function of the harms their group or community were subject to as part of historic wrongs. One common form of such harm, constitutive harm, significantly differs from the aggregative accounts of harm generally used by standard criminal litigation processes. Constitutive harm could not be addressed in that limited context at all. It is the type of harm people suffer as members of historically wronged groups and communities. Therefore, historic injustice cases require a different account of responsibility, one that cannot be harnessed solely based on individual responsibility argumentation within the context of criminal justice jurisprudence. With all the reservations carefully examined in this chapter, we must make room for considerations pertaining to collective responsibility as a moral obligation, providing a social and political context within which legal judgment should be firmly situated, though itself not catapulted to the status of a criminal charge.

This chapter might at first seem to be an aberration in terms of both its methodology and its subject matter vis-à-vis the core subject matter of this work: universal jurisdiction and adjudication of crimes against humanity. However, the frame within which these two issues are debated throughout includes the parameters of 'limitations' and the 'Global South', which changes the tenor of the arguments made and encourages a layered and historically informed understanding of how international law works in settings wherein it assumes a very problem-laden identity. In this regard, I believe it is apt to look for societal and political sources that establish or increase the legitimacy of criminal litigation against mass crimes and societal violence from within as well as through the use of international law jurisprudence concerning egregious acts such as crimes against humanity. This latter, I believe, could significantly benefit from an integrated discussion of collective responsibility in a non-criminal sense, as a foundational tenet of establishing the normative grounds for the desirability of trials and courts that attend to state criminality locally and regionally. Though not to be an end in themselves, localized bodies of international criminal law could well serve as a powerful beginning to hearing an untold story of restitutive justice in the aftermath of the traumas related to crimes against humanity suffered by entire populations.

5

Through the Looking Glass: Hybrid Courts and International Criminal Law in the Global South

Introduction

This chapter offers a critical analysis of a particular set of organs in international criminal law, which have emerged since the 1990s. This is a continuation of the debate over the limits of universal jurisdiction in the Global South and will bring it to its logical culmination. There is significant merit in examining the promise or potential benefits of hybrid courts and tribunals concerning the future of international criminal law in the Global South as an alternative to the ICC-led centrifugal model, which has severe limitations in terms of the application of the universal jurisdiction norm concerning crimes against humanity jurisprudence. This chapter thus attempts to identify the distinct features of hybrid courts while acknowledging the variation amongst the ones created thus far. The literature in the field has moved away from analysing or attempting to examine the promise of hybrid courts. Current commentaries on existing hybrid tribunals or courts are more inclined to examine specific issues or areas in their jurisprudence or statutes. The approach presented here still focuses on the general promise of the mechanisms offered by hybrid courts as an important tool to be used for criminal adjudication albeit within the larger context of transitional justice in the Global South. To this end, I re-examine TWAIL scholarship's take on the effects of the Global North–South dichotomy on a globalized regime of accountability, I explore hybrid courts as viable mechanisms of delivering criminal justice *in situ* concerning cases of state criminality; and readdress the ICC-endorsed principles of universal jurisdiction and complementarity in terms of their global applications.

Hybrid courts and tribunals are commonly referred to as the third generation of international criminal bodies.[1] The term hybrid court was initially used to address three jurisdictions, all of which were created between 1999 and 2001. These were the Crimes Panels of the District Court of Dili, the 'Regulation 64' Panels in the Courts of Kosovo and the Court for Sierra Leone.[2] This list now includes the Extraordinary Chambers in the Courts of Cambodia,[3] and the Extraordinary African Union Chamber in the Court of Senegal among others.[4] The earlier hybrid courts have closed their operations and thus it is possible to ascertain at least some of the outcomes of these trials. Both older and more recent formations of hybrid courts are composed of independent judges, working on the basis of predetermined rules of procedure, and rendering binding decisions. They are subject to the same principles governing the work of other international judiciaries, including but not limited to due process, impartiality and independence. Within the wider class of international courts, however, hybrid courts belong to a specific order. They are specialized criminal organs with a limited mandate, and prescribed to fulfil their function with reference to a predetermined time period. Meanwhile, although their goal is to sanction serious violations of international criminal law, and in particular international humanitarian law and human rights law, they are part of transitional justice regimes rather than permanent features of the legal system in any of the given constituencies. Similarly, although they impose criminal penalties, their primary obligations are to the society within which they are situated, rather than addressing a presumed international community.

Akin to the ICTY and the ICTR, but unlike the ICC, they are *ad hoc* institutions, created as the result of singular political and historical circumstances. Similar to other international criminal institutions, in order to carry out their mission, hybrid courts need to rely on international jurisprudence and judicial assistance from states and international organizations. And yet, their peculiar legal status gives utmost priority to the bridging act of creating hybrid jurisprudence which resonates with the national legal system. In some cases, they are part of the judiciary of a given country, while in others they have been grafted onto the local judicial system through the intermediary action of international bodies. One constant feature they exhibit is that their jurisdictional portfolio is mixed, incorporating international and national features.[5] This chapter thus argues that on the critical issues of criminal accountability and responsibility, hybrid courts exhibit a unique promise for states and societies in the Global South.

The literature on international criminal law has already welcomed hybrid courts as a new type of international crimes courts, asserting that they have the benefits, while avoiding the drawbacks, of both purely international and purely domestic trials. A closer examination of examples of hybrid courts, however, in Kosovo, East Timor, Sierra Leone, Cambodia and Bosnia and Herzegovina, reveals something else as well. Attributing a promise to hybrid courts as a fixed category has raised false expectations, as each court has fundamental differences and distinct features. Here, I will argue that this variation is endemic to any genuine transitional justice project, and should be welcomed rather than shunned. Hybrid domestic-international trials offer an important new angle to jurisprudential properties of international law and to transitional justice in general. The processes by which societies provide accountability and reconciliation for mass atrocity in their own terms is often overlooked. Since these courts have developed in an *ad hoc* way, as a result of on-the-ground innovation rather than grand institutional design, they carry the seed of a genuine political involvement from within and have the potential to override the mechanized narratives of transitional justice.

I. Mapping Out Responsibility for Mass Atrocities

Theories of transgovernmental and transnational networks, when applied to cross-border regulation regimes in areas such as international finance, antitrust regulation, environmental protection or securities law, have steady purchase amongst international law scholars. One area to which this type of theorization has not yet been fully applied is international criminal law.[6] Until recently, international criminal law had not been conceptualized within the framework of the transnational networks that have caught our attention in other legal fields (Turner, 2007: 1020–5). With few exceptions, the predominant conception has been that international criminal law is to be enforced primarily through a universalized idiom and with a top-down jurisprudential approach. However, as critical debates in the area of human rights scholarship amply demonstrate, this prescription is far from helpful. Human rights lawyers, activists and advocates as well as investigators, prosecutors and judges dealing with specific categories of state criminality have long been acting in collaboration or consultation with their peers across borders and with their counterparts at regional or international courts and regulatory bodies.[7] In the following discussion, some of these developments are evaluated with reference to hybrid courts dealing with cases of mass atrocities. In the context of state criminality, providing a conceptual framework within which transnational networks are not seen as an anomaly is essential in this regard. International human rights law, which in essence embodies a constant mediation between claims about the core values of justice and dignity, on the one hand, and hard-fought contingent politico-historical battles, on the other, is in particular need of a substantive exchange between the North and South. As amply illustrated by TWAIL scholarship, political geography has much to contribute to the critical study of international law, above and beyond connecting rights discourse with contemporary justice agendas.[8] As TWAIL scholars declare, for instance, human rights struggles reveal a global map of consistent practices of violence, which necessitated current human rights struggles in the first place.[9] The ways that responsibility for systemic and structural violence has been claimed, denied, ascribed, enacted or avoided have cartographical anchorage. The North takes the credit for creating legal discourse and jurisprudence, while the South carries the burden of the heaviest violations and at the same time is singled out as the worst violator. We need a more evocative lens for understanding the place of human rights law and state criminality within a global framework of emancipatory politics.[10]

As Vijay Prashad puts it so succinctly, 'The Third World was not a place. It was a project.'[11] TWAIL scholarship both specifies and expands upon the sense in which Third World or Global South was never a place *per se*. In the same spirit, in the following discussion the Global South, as well as the North–South divide, are treated as part of a grand political project of some elusive universal legal order, which is constantly reinvented. Here, the emphasis will be put on alternative lineages of international criminal law in the Global South, and outside the realm of state-based narrations of post-colonial politics, as explicated in the methodology section of the Introduction to this work. It is essential to foreground aspects of the North–South divide that hinge upon the premise of intertwined regimes of accumulation, regulation, culpability and responsibility. Only then can we truly challenge the top-down approach – the siren call of international human rights law and international criminal law in the Global South – and offer something more palatable in its place, based on a transnational politics of rights struggles, accountability for mass crimes, and substantive human emancipation.

A. More Than Each unto His Own – Hybrid Courts in the Global South

This chapter singularly focuses on the distinctive characteristics of regional, sub-regional and hybrid courts operating mainly in the Global South. Their workings suggest that in terms of universal jurisdiction and globalized applications of international law, the Global South is *not* an unwilling participant at best and an afterthought of an addendum at worst. Tailgating TWAIL scholarship, I strongly argue otherwise, and the examples chosen here amply illuminate the reasons for insisting upon an alternative vantage point.

To begin with, there is a growing number of regional courts, tribunals and quasi-judicial review bodies that exercise compulsory jurisdiction over states parties which are located in the Global South. Secondly, established hybrid and international tribunals, despite their failings, trials and tribulations, have been steadily expanding their authority over a wide range of legal actors, including but not limited to states. Many of these courts owe their strength to their limited-subject-matter mandate and conscribed geographic and chronological reach. The majority of these courts and tribunals attend to regional affairs and internal conflicts that entail mass human rights violations. As such, they symbolize the stabilization of a fragmented and yet reasonably operational accountability regime in the Global South. It is true there are grounds for fear of a growing trend towards the judicialization of politics at a global scale in this regard. We certainly cannot take it on faith that creating new regional courts or hybrid tribunals will necessarily provide solutions to deep-seated societal and political problems. Rather, the role of law in various struggles for social and political justice in the Global South, some of which are waged against post-colonial states themselves by their own citizens, is the focus here. The case of hybrid courts signals the emergence of alternative forms of utilization of international law, and call for new legal theories capable of capturing the potential of, as well as the tensions endemic to, counter-hegemonic forms of globalization of law.

Although the legitimacy of domestic courts is no doubt more established than that of their international or hybrid counterparts, the risks of depending solely on domestic adjudication at historical junctions of transition from civil war, ethnic cleansing, genocide, occupation, etc. are far greater than resorting to divergent interpretations of international criminal law in these settings. Furthermore, third-generation judicial bodies are often regional in scope and thus cover both states and subterranean or non-state actors within their jurisdiction. This is yet another advantage they have over both domestic and international courts. They have the ability to contextualize a given conflict, a most urgent need in cases of mass political violence in Africa, the Middle East, the Balkans, or South East Asia. Equally importantly, while international courts have shallow – that is optional – jurisdictional powers, hybrid courts tend to have a deeper jurisdictional basis that leads to compulsory jurisdiction, since they act over a limited number of issues in conjunction with a set number of parties and they are often an integral part of ongoing peace negotiations.

Based on the increasing number of rulings produced by regional tribunals and hybrid courts in the Global South, an emerging litigation pattern is becoming evident that may be significantly different from those corresponding with international or European courts.[12] Their rulings span a broad range of subjects, including customs, taxes, and tariffs and non-tariff barriers to trade, as well as criminal proceedings. In these alternative settings of international jurisdiction, national as well as international judges, administrative officials and private parties participate in litigation. The symbiotic relationship between international and national law exemplified by these courts and tribunals has a broader significance. Even when (national) law proves moot, a distinctive group of sub-state actors including human rights movements, NGOs, political movements, and judges, can serve as conduits to bypass the indifference or even the resistance of governmental institutions to delivering justice where (though rarely when) it is due.

II. The Clarion Call of Universal Jurisdiction in the Global South

One of the more recent and noteworthy episodes in international criminal law pertaining to a rising demand for hybrid courts is the Darfur crisis. In July 2008, the chief prosecutor of the International Criminal Court (ICC) in the Hague sought the indictment of the Sudanese president, Omar al-Bashir, on charges of genocide and war crimes.[13] Subsequently, foreign diplomats, regional leaders and many Sudanese activists, including members of the political opposition in the country, expressed divided opinions in their evaluation of this indictment. It is true that some supported the idea of prosecuting President Bashir and his leading cadres for the human catastrophe they are alleged to have inflicted on Sudan's western province of Darfur in an international court.[14] However, a significant number of NGOs, political groups and legal scholars in the Global South were not comfortable with the indictment of a serving president by an international court situated in Europe due to two factors: its neocolonialist optics, and the indictment's possible negative effects on the Sudanese society. For instance, human rights circles repeatedly stated that a vindictive Bashir could resort to a number of violent strategies in response to the ICC's indictment, which would make the situation in Sudan worse than before.[15] They argued that President Bashir's repertoire of retaliation could include ending the already fragile peace process in Darfur, expelling UN troops from the region, and retarding the implementation of a peace agreement between his government and the former rebels in south Sudan.[16] Differences in interpretation grew further when in April 2010 President al-Bashir won Sudan's first multi-party elections in twenty-four years, despite the fact that observers criticized the election as falling short of international standards. Indeed, many opposition parties withdrew from the race, alleging widespread vote rigging and intimidation. Still, al-Bashir re-emerged victoriously and despite or, some would suggest, thanks to the indictment presented as a Western imperialist plot.

In the light of the developments and concerns exemplified by the case of Sudan, it is timely to ask whether a sound mechanism of international criminal law could be envisaged to hold individuals responsible for the type of atrocities perpetrated in Darfur, and elsewhere in the Global South, without jeopardizing the safety of local populations or creating an aura of neocolonial moral and legal superiority. This inquiry is linked with the larger question that runs through this entire work: how meaningful and beneficial is it for crimes against humanity to be subject to universal jurisdiction if the local constituency, including the victims' groups, rejects or disagrees with the charges, methods of trial, or both? What are the implications of trials held in an international court, removed from the original locale where these crimes were committed, rather than being handled as an internal or regional affair of the societies in question? In Sudan, for instance, in response to significant worries about escalation of violence in the aftermath of the ICC indictment against President al-Bashir, Sadıq al-Mahdi, the country's most prominent opposition politician, urged for a 'third way' solution.[17] Like many in human rights circles in the Global South, he believed that the ICC indictment of President Bashir would lead to further chaos in Sudan.[18] He did not agree that hauling the Sudanese president to the Hague would achieve much in terms of accountability for the mass crimes committed in Darfur. Instead, he suggested setting up an independent hybrid court for Darfur, which would have both

Sudanese and international judges, and would sit in Sudan as opposed to in Europe, the land of ex-colonial powers. The idea of mixing national and international jurisprudence and legal procedures, and of holding politically charged trials for international crimes on home turf, has already been welcomed in Sierra Leone and Cambodia.[19] It is true that these two examples have thus far yielded only mixed success. Still, the overall prospect of hybrid courts possesses unmatched legal and political attractiveness. In the case of Sudan, a hybrid or 'internationalized' court could dispense justice close to the scene of the crime, and at the heart of the society directly affected by the atrocities committed. Additionally, if such a special court were deemed to be a genuine, impartial attempt to obtain justice, the ICC could defer its indictment of President Bashir under Article 16 of the Rome Statute.[20] Finally, a hybrid court with a strong domestic element would have the strength to counter the furious denunciations of the ICC charges and indictments as a Western imperialist intervention in Sudan.

Based on the understanding of their potential gains for transitional justice as a societal project with a strong historical dimension, rather than a package of mechanized and juridified solutions, the remainder of this chapter will examine select examples of hybrid courts as relevant cases for an emerging model for the dissemination of international criminal law jurisdiction. The fragmented nature of the globalized legal regime of accountability – despite the post-ICC solidification of the doctrine of universal jurisdiction for international crimes – is not something to be shunned but a development to be embraced. The benefits of a limited or circumscribed application of universal jurisdiction, as endorsed by the hybrid courts that have emerged during the last decade, must be fully explored. Legal literature has already welcomed hybrid courts as a new type of international crimes courts, asserting that they could avoid the drawbacks of purely international and purely domestic trials.[21] Upon closer examination of the recent examples of hybrid courts in Kosovo, East Timor, Sierra Leone, Cambodia, and Bosnia and Herzegovina, it becomes clear, however, that the current set of hybrid courts differs from one another in critical respects. The next step requires the evaluation of hybrid courts as part of a continuum of fragmented practices, which include truth and reconciliation commissions, local adaptations of the Rome Statute, and an expansive application of human rights mechanisms to improve general standards of societal responsibility for mass crimes and historical injustices, which were the subject matter of the last two chapters.

To start with, there is no doubt that hybrid mechanisms blending international and domestic elements have the capacity to deliver improved justice measures – especially when they are undertaken via judicial reforms, thus initiating the process of a serious commitment to legal accountability for war crimes and crimes against humanity in post-atrocity states. In this regard, at the institutional level, the claim of universal jurisdiction put forward by the ICC has severe limitations. To begin with, many crimes currently ailing post-conflict societies cannot be tried by the ICC, since conflicts occurred before the Rome Statute went into effect; or ongoing conflicts in non-signatory nations lie beyond the jurisdiction of the Court unless brought forward politically. Secondly, even when the ICC has jurisdiction over a set of crimes, its mandate is primarily limited to trial of a handful of senior figures. In other words, societal responsibility is not within the reach or the mandate of the Court with reference to the overall process of transitional justice. In the light of these concerns, a closer look into the promise of a fragmented embrace of universal jurisdiction in the form of hybrid courts must be synchronized with a tally of local endeavours for transitional justice and societal accountability for mass atrocities.

Going back to the case of Sudan, on 13 October 2016 the African Union Commission (AUC) launched a campaign to 'restore the dignity of women and to ensure accountability in South Sudan'.[22] This campaign was intended to lobby for accountability and an end to the atrocities that have disproportionately affected women in South Sudan. It was organized in solidarity with the women of South Sudan, and spearheaded by the AU Special Envoy on Women, Peace, and Security in Addis Ababa.[23] The outcomes of the campaign were to be presented to high-ranking South Sudanese officials. These were indeed hopeful times. And yet, while accountability has been touted as a key element for peace and reconciliation in South Sudan, it remains to be seen whether the envisaged hybrid court for South Sudan would be able to try sitting leaders and senior government officials who had involvements with the atrocities in the country, including mass rapes.[24] Human rights reports on the South Sudanese conflict consistently point out that the country's leaders bear responsibility for the war crimes and crimes against humanity perpetrated in the country, and have in fact benefited from these offences.[25] Thus any real effort to ensure accountability in South Sudan needs to engage the role of the South Sudanese leaders. Efforts continued at the legal affairs department of the AUC to mobilize funds and finalize the memorandum of understanding (MoU) for the establishment of the hybrid court. This was in line with the Agreement on the Resolution of the Conflict in the Republic of South Sudan, signed by former vice-president Riek Machar and President Salva Kiir.[26] According to the peace agreement and the MoU, the mandate and the jurisdiction of the proposed hybrid court should have been finalized within six months of the formation of the government of national unity, which took place in April 2016. The hybrid court was to be operational within twelve months of that date, April 2017. However, the ongoing violence, and the replacement of Machar with Taban Deng Gai as vice president of the government of national unity, stalled this process, and attention is instead focused on ending the most recent crisis. As it is, the situation in Darfur, Blue Nile and South Kordofan states remains dire, with widespread violations of international humanitarian and human rights law. Furthermore, evidence points to the use of chemical weapons by government forces in Darfur. The rights to freedom of expression, association and peaceful assembly are repeatedly and arbitrarily restricted and critics and suspected opponents of the government have been regularly subjected to arbitrary arrest, detention and other violations.

If so, will the AU Assembly of heads of state and government – its highest decision-making body – draw up jurisprudence for a hybrid court that enables it to try leaders and senior government officials? For instance, Chapter 5 of the peace agreement stipulates that the hybrid court 'shall not be impeded or constrained by any statutes of limitations or the granting of pardons, immunities or amnesties. No one shall be exempt from criminal responsibility on account of their official capacity as a government official, an elected official or claiming the defense of superior orders.'[27] In addition, the AU remains in favour of immunity for sitting heads of state and senior government officials. What is even more alarming is the fact that this development came after the ICC's issuance of an arrest warrant for President Omar al-Bashir of Sudan in 2009. The AU's new immunity stance led to the inclusion of an immunity clause in Article 46A of the 2014 Protocol on Amendments to the Protocol on the Statute of the African Court of Justice and Human Rights, as well.[28]

In effect, prior to the Sudan issue, the AU has fought desperately, in the case of Kenya and Sudan, for the lifting of ICC charges against leaders in office. The AU also recently called for an inquiry into a collective withdrawal from the ICC based on the differences over immunity concerns in Africa.[29] Burundi, South Africa and The Gambia have already announced their withdrawal from the ICC.[30] The dilemma is that, according to the peace deal, the same leaders who would have to be tried by the hybrid court are meant to occupy leadership positions in the transitional government of national unity. In other words, the South Sudanese deal kept South Sudanese leaders in the positions they occupied before the war started. The dynamics among the member states of the Intergovernmental Authority on Development (IGAD), who were mediating in the South Sudan conflict, indicated that the question of leadership accountability is a highly contested issue. Hence, there is not enough regional support for the issue to deter South Sudanese leaders from orchestrating further violent atrocities. The hybrid court for South Sudan could thus end up prosecuting lesser officials and soldiers of both Kiir and Machar factions. Due to these concerns, some observers have recommended that an alternative international body should provide the necessary checks and balances.[31] Yet others have recommended that the South Sudanese leaders should be bound through the peace agreement to ratify the Rome Statute, thereby enabling the ICC to intervene if they attempt to undermine the efforts of the hybrid court – though no doubt this is one of the most unrealistic solutions proposed. Although the peace agreement is vague about the role of the transitional government in the workings of the hybrid court, Chapter 5(1.1) of the agreement states that the transitional government 'shall initiate jurisprudence for the establishment of the transitional justice institutions', and Chapter 5(1.5) expects the hybrid court to cooperate with the AU and the international community in its operationalization.[32] This gives the transitional government some leverage to influence the establishment and mandate of the hybrid court from the outset. In the end, however, the liability of South Sudanese leaders for the heinous atrocities and human rights violations in the country rests on the balance of societal pressure and political negotiations, and not just on the form or legislative intent of the proposed hybrid court *per se*. Neither could these dynamics be undone by the sheer presence of ICC indictments. In the case of mass political violence, (criminal) law and politics go hand in hand to introduce change, rather than the former leading the latter in providing solutions and rectificatory and restitutive justice. Hence the clarion call of universal jurisdiction in the Global South in its present from and applications.

A. The ICC and Domestic Applications of the Rome Statute

Overall, this chapter purports that the establishment of the ICC by no means lessened the need for regional, lesser or hybrid courts. Instead, a strong case is made for the increased appreciation of the fragmented nature of international criminal law as an accountability regime. Even in treaty terms, pursuant to Article 11 of the Rome Statute, the ICC has jurisdiction only with respect to crimes committed after the Treaty came into force in 2002. Consequently, there is a judicial vacuum concerning crimes identified by the Rome Statute as subject to universal jurisdiction in the period prior to ICC's establishment, as well as regarding countries that are not signatories.[33] With reference to these limitations, hybrid forms of endorsing international legal accountability have become the focal point of a growing number of discussions on the ICC.[34] Those who support hybrid courts' functioning in tandem with the Rome Statute argue that national/municipal courts and the ICC constitute 'two layers of judicial institutions' that can cooperate in bringing perpetrators of international crimes to justice.[35] This heightened expectation from multi-level judicial performance is partly due to the fact that the question of the limited potential of the ICC to affect the international criminal justice system, and more specifically to sustain an international legal regime of accountability as the leading institution, remains questionable. In reality, the ICC is a carefully constrained legal institution in its structure and reach, despite the fact that it relies on universal jurisdiction for at least some of the crimes falling under its purview.[36] Not only is the jurisdiction of the court limited, as exemplified by discussions of the above-cited Article 11. The Rome Statute also requires that either the state where the crimes have occurred, or the state of which the accused is a national, must be a party to the Statute for the Court to intervene, unless dictated by the UN Security Council. This has been a problem clouding the prospects of, for instance, those who wish to bring the case of Israeli war crimes in Gaza to the Court's attention.[37] The limitations that come with a territoriality or nationality-based nexus to the crime in question could be overcome only to a certain extent through the exercise of universal jurisdiction by states that are a party to the Rome Statute. For universal jurisdiction to take effect, these state-parties must be willing to try the case in their own courts in accordance with international criminal law. With reference to the case of Israel, for instance, so far only Belgian courts have expressed a willingness to consider a trial at a future date. Added to these constraints are the complexities of the complementarity principle, as well as limitations regarding subject-matter jurisdiction and the parliamentary overview of critical judicial matters, as exemplified by the final decision concerning the Pinochet extradition case in the United Kingdom.

Given all these limitations and complications, what does universal jurisdiction [re]defined by the Rome Statute of the ICC add to the already existing regime of accountability in international criminal law?[38] The core idea of universal jurisdiction is the following: some crimes are so heinous that they lead to a duty, in every society and in every system of substantive law, to prosecute the perpetrators when the opportunity arises. The category of crimes against humanity captures this notion at its best: it refers to criminal acts that constitute an offence to every human being, giving rise to a corresponding obligation to take action against the perpetrator(s) regardless of the specific circumstances of the crime or limitations ordinarily caused by jurisdictional restrictions.[39]

Although the concept of crimes against humanity had specific roots as one of the key justifications for the Nuremberg trials of Second World War criminals from 1945 to 1949, it began to be put to common use again shortly after the collapse of dictatorships in Latin America during the 1980s.[40]

Meanwhile, something is amiss in these debates, namely, the context within which these crimes were committed. Here attention should be turned to transitional justice measures and their relationship to accountability regimes in international criminal law. The overall aim of transitional justice projects is to end impunity deriving from official or personal immunities accorded to representatives of the state and high-ranking officers, and to guarantee personal accountability for gross human rights abuses and societal crimes. In this vein, for instance, the impetus behind the reactivation of the legal category of crimes against humanity against Latin American dictatorships was the hope that universal jurisdiction in relation to these crimes would help to bring torturers and murderers to justice when national jurisdictions were failing to try them. Another pertinent reason for the call for universal jurisdiction is that many deposed oppressors have sought amnesty outside their own country of origin and claimed asylum on neutral grounds. By removing the territoriality nexus of the crime, it was hoped that universal jurisdiction litigation would allow for the capture of fugitive statesmen, army officers and former dictators. In summary, universal jurisdiction for international crimes would, at least in principle, obligate governments to prosecute the perpetrators of these crimes wherever they were found. While the government of the country where the atrocities occurred might be severely compromised to prosecute these persons, the idea is that another government without a history of complicity could punish the concerned criminals based on the principle of universal jurisdiction.

As early as 1999, the very date that marks the formulation of the ICC jurisprudence on crimes against humanity, Amnesty International reported that twenty-four national jurisdictions had adopted universal jurisdiction for serious international crimes such as genocide, among them Spain and Belgium.[41] Since then, there have been very few prosecutions. Perhaps as to be expected, the most notable case was in Britain and Spain against the Chilean ex-dictator Augusto Pinochet, prior to the establishment of the International Criminal Court (ICC) in 2002. The success of this particular rendition of universal jurisdiction, however, remains far from obvious.[42] The Pinochet case is of interest for understanding both the internal and institutional limitations of universal jurisdiction as endorsed by the ICC. As far as the ICC is concerned, the claim in its statute that the Court's jurisdiction is 'complementary' to that of the states that endorse it reveals its underlying purpose: to drive societies to prosecute criminals in the places where the crimes were committed, or in countries which are signatories to the Rome Statue, but not at the Hague itself. The Court is constituted as a transnational tribunal to try only a select set of international crimes and only when all else fails. If it is to provide outreach services or to act as a centrifugal force, this is to take place at the level of jurisprudential framing provided by the Rome Statute. A legitimate question that needs an answer in the context of the Pinochet case, for instance, is the following: if Chile, currently a democratic state peopled by many of the victims of Pinochet's regime, did not want to prosecute the ex-dictator in 1998, on what basis could a magistrate in Spain interfere in Chile's internal affairs or past crimes committed by its state officers? The answer came in the form of crimes committed against Spanish citizens. However, when a Spanish court claims to exercise universal jurisdiction over Pinochet's crimes, how could Britain refuse to honour Spain's request for extradition, despite the fact that Britain herself is a signatory to the Rome Statute and a dedicated state-party to the ICC?

The internal and historical facts of the Pinochet case allow us to examine a different and mostly overlooked dimension of the universal jurisdiction debate. Chile granted amnesty to Pinochet as a way to break his grip on local politics and to return to democratic governance.[43] Still, this should not have shielded the retired General from justice for his gross human rights violations, and specifically the crimes against humanity associated with his regime. The only reasonable explanation for this local lapse of justice is that Chilean prosecutors and investigating magistrates, while enjoying institutional independence, were bound to operate within the strictures of Chilean law and politics. These legal authorities had to answer to appellate courts and the executive, and they had to honour statutory obligations, one of which gave immunity to General Pinochet in perpetuity. A legal authority outside Chile may not claim to have a direct interest in the affairs of the nation where the crime occurred. And yet, under the principle of universal jurisdiction, they would have the freedom to indict and to prosecute if there is evidence that crimes of most egregious nature were committed. This paradox repeats itself in African and other cases as well, namely, egregious crimes were committed directly indicating state criminality, there is a formally independent judiciary, and yet no prosecution for the perpetrators from within for political reasons.

A more recent example that illustrates the pros and cons of universal jurisdiction exercised by foreign courts taking on cases pertaining to international crimes, rather than the issue being referred to the ICC or handled by a domestic court *in situ*, is the investigation Belgium launched against Israel's military offensives in Gaza and Lebanon during the last few decades.[44] Human rights groups hailed the Belgian Supreme Court's decision as another stepping stone for establishing a regime of international criminal justice. The high-profile Sharon case followed from the 1993 Belgian universal jurisdiction law.[45] It permits lawsuits to be filed in Belgian courts for war crimes, crimes against humanity, torture and genocide regardless of the time and place of their commission or any national or geographical link to Belgium by the plaintiffs or the accused.[46] The specific case against Sharon was brought by a group of Lebanese citizens, who asked for him to be charged with war crimes in connection to his indirect role in the 1982 massacre of at least 800 Palestinians by Phalangist troops in the Sabra and Shatila refugee camps outside Beirut while the camps were under Israeli control. Sharon was found 'indirectly responsible' for the massacre by an Israeli judicial commission in 1983, and was barred for a time from holding high office in Israel. In 2002, a Belgian appeals court ruled that Sharon could not be tried in Belgium because he was not physically present in the country; the Belgian Supreme Court reversed that ruling in 2003. This latter decision acknowledged diplomatic immunity only for serving heads of state or ministers. Based on this nuanced reading of immunity, Belgian prosecutors could then start proceedings against other Israeli officials allegedly involved in the massacre, including former Israeli army chief of staff Rafael Eitan and former Defense Ministry Director General Amos Yaron, who was the Israeli army commander in Beirut at the time. Consequently, in addition to the possibility of arrest on Belgian soil, Israeli officials became worried about possible extradition demands from other European states. Israel has extradition treaties with most European countries, and all members of the European Union have conventions requiring that an extradition request by a member state is be considered by others.

The plot thickened in January 2017, as a Belgian court ordered the arrest of former Israeli Minister of Foreign Affairs, Tzipi Livni, when she disembarked the plane on her scheduled trip to Belgium. Livni was accused of committing war crimes and crimes against humanity during her time as Minister of Foreign Affairs from 2006 to 2009. She oversaw the Israeli military operation 'Cast Lead' in the Gaza Strip, from which the crimes allegedly stemmed. In effect, Livni was one of several Israeli officials named in the lawsuit filed by a group of victims in 2010 in response to the military activities in Gaza. Livni, a member of the Israeli parliament, was set to meet with Jewish leaders in Brussels, but cancelled the trip before the report of the arrest order came out. Back in 2010, Livni had been set to speak at the Jewish National Fund Vision 2010 conference in London, but again cancelled her travel plans after a British court issued an arrest warrant for her. In 2011, however, the UK announced that Livni would enjoy diplomatic immunity. The practice of giving immunity to foreign officials who are accused of serious crimes under international law, in order for the host country to avoid having to arrest them, readily receives criticism. Proponents of the warrants argue that countries giving immunity to these officials are not living up to their responsibility under international law, and are thus complicit in creating impunity for international crimes.[47] Regardless of the repeated failures of the UK courts to prosecute despite the mandate of universal jurisdiction, worthy of note is the fact that Belgium and the UK are two of the growing number of countries to enshrine elements of universal jurisdiction in their laws. With Spain and Canada recently coming on board, the endorsement of the Rome Statute in terms of domestic law's engagement with international criminal law according to the principle of universal jurisdiction is emerging as a trend albeit in limited circles.[48] Other notable examples opting for institutionalizing universal jurisdiction as defined by the Rome Statute include Australia, Germany, New Zealand, and South Africa, all of which have amended their laws to provide for the opening of investigations without any of the traditional *nexus* requirements.[49]

Situated at the other end of this spectrum, where rejection of 'international jurisprudential intervention' constitutes the distinguishing feature of the domestic take on international law, are the United States and Israel. Still, even these states have legal mechanisms that allow foreign criminal acts to be prosecuted in their courts. For instance, the Alien Torts Act allows foreigners to sue in United States Federal Court if the subject acts were committed against them in violation of international law or an American treaty. This act was used by a group of Bosnians against Serb leader Radovan Karadzic for crimes committed during the Yugoslav civil war. Similarly, in Israel, the Knesset passed an amendment to the Penal Code in 1995 that is almost identical to Belgium's 1993 law.[50] Israel also approved jurisprudence making it responsible for the protection of every Jew around the world, whether or not such protection is requested. According to this law, anyone committing a crime against a Jew anywhere in the world breaks Israeli law and is liable to punishment by the Jewish state. In this sense, Israel herself has long been engaged in forcefully applying universal jurisdiction, though only in select areas and many argue with a distinct bias of Jewish nationalism.[51]

Based on the two examples of the Pinochet case and the Belgian law for universal jurisdiction, the key question concerning the limits of universal jurisdiction as it is applied in domestic courts is whether the problems that are appearing in its current applications are likely to weaken its legitimacy. Hybrid courts established closer to the scene of the crimes to be adjudicated and in direct contact with the societies involved could be more effective in delivering justice (Dickinson,

2003).[52] Where the scope of a state's application of universal jurisdiction is wide, as seen in Belgium for instance, additional problems may emerge. As a case in point, in 2000 Belgium sought to extradite the Congolese Minister of Foreign Affairs for speeches that allegedly incited the public to race-hatred in the Congo.[53] Given Belgium's troubled history of colonial engagements in the Congo, these proceedings opened the country to a charge of neocolonialism. In response, the International Court of Justice (ICJ) stepped in and declared that an incumbent minister of foreign affairs was immune from Belgian criminal proceedings. The principal problem in this case was less with the process of filing and administering complaints than with its political character. In contemporary international criminal law, many of the states that ratified and embedded the Rome Statute into their constitution and/or criminal law are ex-colonial powers. Complicating matters further, the majority of the cases that fall under universal jurisdiction take place in the Global South, and therefore in ex-colonies. This brings forth the critical issue of trust, and opens domestic courts such as the Belgian courts to charges of neocolonial domination of the Global South through the means of international criminal law, and via the premise of universal jurisdiction.

There is another concern, too, when domestic courts take on international criminal cases above and beyond traditional nexus requirements. They tend to act as a magnet for complaints, regardless of their merit, leading to arguments that both the claims and the resultant complaints against the claims are rooted in regional or global political vendettas. On the other hand, international power politics could narrow applications of universal jurisdiction and silence complaints, as in the case of claims made against Israel. This latter situation leads to the argument that when domestic courts exercise universal jurisdiction concerning cases that affect other societies, meritorious complaints could be stifled due to extraneous issues not germane to the case itself. Domestic criminal jurisdiction, when it embraces universal jurisdiction, aspires to be free of politics but rarely achieves it. International criminal jurisdiction, despite all of its shortcomings, has been compensating for the failures of domestic courts. If this is so, the solution is not simply a matter of someone else's domestic courts doing the difficult work. If high-ranking

Israeli soldiers and leaders could not be tried in Israel, their trial in Belgium cannot be the ultimate solution to the suspicion and accusation of war crimes.

By virtue of being complementary to the domestic system, the workings of international criminal justice organs such as the ICC could create a dialogue, however limited, that in turn would increase the possibility of establishing a legal regime of accountability for state criminality. In the Pinochet case, the British authorities managed to avoid his extradition based on the defendant's alleged illness. However, the British courts also recognized that his crimes were heinous enough to support extradition to Spain where he would have had to stand trial. That development alone could be considered a key element that has finally driven Chilean courts to start their own case against Pinochet, despite the many internal obstacles leading them to avoid this for decades. This has been pinpointed by legal scholars such as Stephen Ratner as the 'democratizing effect' of international law, despite the fact that international law itself does not qualify as a democratic edifice in its origins (Ratner, Abrams and Bischoff, 2009).[54] The second point to be made is that unless and until we accept international accountability regimes such as international human rights law or international criminal law as fragmented and composed of variant elements, rather than centre-heavy and fixed structures, we will continue to have far too many (and often unrealistic) expectations from organs such as the ICC. This in turn creates effects to the detriment of the very regime we purport to uphold, as these courts and their proceedings often reflect power dynamics in global politics that render their reach uneven, and often problem-laden. This is in addition to the fact that, unlike the ICJ for instance, ICC is defined as a court of last and not first resort.

In the remainder of this section, the critical role of the complementarity principle as a defining feature of the post-ICC regime of accountability for international crimes will be examined. Select cases of hybrid courts will also be brought into the picture, to determine the degree of their contribution to international criminal law in terms of the expansion of universal jurisdiction, especially in the context of transitional justice. The goal of this exercise is to determine the relationship between international, domestic and hybrid courts, and to firmly establish the idea of a fragmented international criminal law as an accountability regime with future promise.

B. The ICC and the Importance of the Complementarity Principle for the International Legal Accountability

The basic stated objective of the establishment of a permanent international criminal court was to replace a culture of impunity for the commission of very serious crimes with an international legal regime of accountability.[55] To this end, the provisions of the Rome Statute expressly address a specific set of crimes – that is genocide, war crimes, crimes against humanity, and the crime of aggression – as indictable crimes. Prior bodies such as the *ad hoc* Tribunals for Former Yugoslavia and Rwanda were necessarily limited in their scope, due to their context-specific and time-sensitive jurisprudence. To a certain degree, the idea of a permanent court was also a response to the UN Security Council's monopoly on international tribunals, which many states in the Global South deemed as being far too selective in 'distributing' international justice.[56] Still, there is continued suspicion about the deterrent effect of international tribunals or courts, whether permanent or *ad hoc* in their constitution. There is also the much larger question of what universal jurisdiction means for different societies, and whether some are treated 'more equal' than others concerning its reach, especially under the purview of Europe-based international courts such as the ICC.[57]

The common response to the establishment of the ICC emanating from scholars and practitioners of international law is that the effectiveness of such organs must be judged within a long-term perspective.[58] Accordingly, the impact of these relatively new institutions should not be compared to that of long-standing institutions such as the ICJ. Specifically, the ICC is seen as part of a framework of measures brought into effect in order to establish and sustain a new international regime of accountability, including increased domestic prosecution of state criminality, wider use of international jurisprudence, and greater international and transnational cooperation and coordination in the addressing of heinous crimes. The cornerstone of this anticipated legal regime is the principle of complementarity, as reflected in Articles 18 and 19 (containing procedures) and Articles 17 and 20 (containing the substantive criteria) of the Rome Statute.[59] This principle was agreed upon as a result of long negotiations. It was put in place to ensure that State Parties will always have primacy if they choose to investigate and prosecute crimes within their domestic courts or in accordance with the jurisdiction of the Court. It is only where States are unwilling or unable to act within the meaning of the Statute, or where they are simply inactive, that the ICC would take on a case. Moreover, if a State has started proceedings, the ICC would only be able to take over the case if it is shown that domestic authorities acted with an intention to shield the person(s) concerned, or in a manner that was inconsistent with the intent to bring the person(s) concerned to justice. Without such findings, lack of observance of standards of due process or differences in sentencing practices do not constitute a valid reason for the ICC to step in. At the same time, there are complementarity provisions to guide national authorities for incorporating the Rome Statute definitions of genocide, crimes against humanity and war crimes into their domestic law. As such, the primacy of State Parties for investigation and trial purposes does not go against the principle of universal jurisdiction and the demand for the faithful adoption of the Rome Statute in part or as a whole. On the contrary, the complementarity principle reflects the belief that universal jurisdiction is best achieved through a multi-level and complex model of jurisprudential expansion that links international and domestic spheres. This is a centrifugal model. The ICC acts as the epicentre, and produces the blueprint to be appropriated wherever a certain set of international crimes are concerned. Both State and non-State Parties are expected to adopt the principles and format of codification developed by the Court, in order to make a legitimate claim that their legal regime is on par with the dictates of international criminal law.

In this context, the 'proper implementation' of the Rome Statute within the national law of States Parties is of key importance for the establishment and sustenance of a globalized legal regime of accountability. This is in addition to the required cooperation between the ICC and affected States Parties in the investigation and preparation of cases, as outlined by the elaborate machinery set out in Part IX of the Statute.[60] Indeed, there are specific stipulations put in place to ensure the desired coordination for investigative and adjudicative purposes. First, States Parties are under an unequivocal obligation to cooperate fully with the Court (Article 86) and to modify national laws as necessary to allow the forms of cooperation required by the Statute (Article 88).[61] States Parties are also obliged to arrest and surrender suspects to the Court (Article 89), and to provide other forms of cooperation as requested, such as the questioning of witnesses, the conduct of searches and seizure of evidence, the protection of witnesses, and the tracing, freezing and seizure of assets related to the crimes under investigation (Article 93). The grounds allowed for refusing cooperation are extremely limited. States Parties cannot refuse to extradite their own nationals, and immunities available under national law cannot be used to refuse the handing over of one's own nationals to the Court. Notwithstanding these mechanisms, national security concerns could provide a limited basis for refusal to cooperate with the Court, provided all the consultation measures set out in Article 72 of the Statute are undertaken.

In this larger context of complementarity, ICC and the Rome Statute function as guideposts for the exercise of universal jurisdiction. The domestic jurisprudence of a State Party to the ICC provides the critical mass of laws and principles specifically designed to govern and protect its people within its borders. However, the majority of recent cases brought to the attention of the ICC proved that while these domestic laws can prosecute individuals for crimes such as murder, rape, armed robbery and larceny, they do not equip the national judicial system with the competence to try perpetrators of serious violations of International Human Rights Law or International Humanitarian Law.[62] Hence the need to enact laws that can address egregious crimes committed both in conflict and during peacetime. The standard route for this is the domestication of the Rome Statute by the State Parties.[63] The assumption behind this prescription is that the domestication process would provide the legal framework for the implementation of ICC jurisprudence, inching towards the establishment of a wider network of universal jurisdiction in the case of select international crimes, and a sustainable global regime of accountability.

On a final note, the Rome Statute makes provision for victims' participation at all stages of the proceedings. At least in principle, the ICC assures the victims' access to and participation in the adjudication process. In international law, this is regarded as a unique development in the operations of international tribunals. The ICC also attends to issues of reparations for victims beyond the traditional punishment and deterrence objectives of domestic courts. Specifically, Article 79 of the Rome Statute provides for the establishment of a trust fund for victims and their families.[64] The court can determine the extent of the damages, and can order perpetrators to compensate victims as such. Furthermore, adhering to international standards, the ICC does not use the death penalty as punishment. Article 77 of the ICC's Statute provides that the court can only institute penalties such as life imprisonment, imprisonment for a designated number of years, and fines.[65] Domesticating the Rome Statute could therefore constitute a significant step towards expunging capital punishment from domestic trials.

These points may appear as tangential to the issue of universal jurisdiction. However, they could also be seen as part and parcel of the transfusion of a legal culture of accountability and globalized endorsement of a new approach to international crimes, especially those committed by state authorities and people in position of power. In summary, the ICC's complementarity principle is essential to the establishment of a new legal regime of accountability especially for state criminality. This principle operates at three levels. First, it dictates the set of crimes that fall under the purview of universal jurisdiction. If local, domestic legal authorities and courts do not act on these crimes, and if these crimes are brought to the attention of the Court, it then becomes a court of last resort and could proceed to try those accountable for the identified crimes. Alternatively, if there is not a case brought directly to ICC's attention, or, if there are local attempts to achieve accountability that are hindered by domestic circumstances, the ICC could provide a reservoir of legal expertise, as well as guidelines for juridification concerning such trials and transitional justice projects-in-the-making. The functioning of hybrid courts falls under this last category. In the remainder of this chapter, examples of hybrid courts and their workings will be presented in order to illustrate their potential, but also to underline the fact that they are not the ultimate solution to the problems emanating from this centrifugal model of universal jurisdiction. Indeed, their operations are much more complex than have thus far been foreseen by proponents of universal jurisdiction in international criminal law.

III. Hybrid Courts: Fractured or Overlapping Legal Regimes of Accountability?

To reiterate, due to disappointments and difficulties with both local trials and international tribunals, in international criminal law, hybrid courts and tribunals are increasingly seen as a compromise that could benefit from the strengths of international jurisprudence while minimizing the weaknesses and 'side effects' of central institutions such as the ICC, particularly concerning the charge of neocolonialism.[66] A hybrid court is indeed a distinct instrument. It is a court in which international judges and local judges sit side-by-side, drawing their decisions from a blend of local and international jurisprudence. From the point of view of an international/transnational regime of accountability, hybrid courts are expected to benefit from the outreach of universal jurisdiction and the codification of international criminal law achieved by various conventions and the Rome Statute, while honouring domestic legal traditions. During the post-ICC era, the first hybrid court was established in Kosovo in 2000. As discussed, this was followed by hybrid courts in East Timor, Sierra Leone and Bosnia. Cambodia is completing the final stages of a hybrid court addressing crimes committed by the Khmer Rouge.[67] Lebanon is yet another country to have expressed desire to create a hybrid tribunal.[68] There have also been internal and external political demands for the Sudan's former President al-Bashir to be tried by a hybrid court rather than by the ICC. Then there is the successful resolution of the trial of the former dictator of Chad, Hissène Habré, in the Senegalese hybrid court. Concerning this last example, Amendments to the Protocol on the Statute of the African

Court of Justice and Human Rights, known as the Malabo Protocol,[69] truly reconceptualized the idea of transitional justice mechanisms and purported that they should encompass regional and transnational efforts to respond to mass political violence. In this sense, the Protocol actively sought to correct perceived biases in international criminal justice. As such, it offered the Continent, and Global South at large, a substantive alternative vision of local and regional criminal justice and accountability for state criminality.[70] In keeping with these developments, in the final section of this chapter, the workings and institutional characteristics of some hybrid courts established since the establishment of the ICC and the coming into effect of the Rome Statute will be further scrutinized.

My starting premise on hybrid courts has been that domestic criminal justice systems have options for flexible responses not currently available to the ICC, and that these options extend beyond criminal proceedings to encompass civil ones. The right to sue governments and out-of-court settlements supervised by judges that allow for the participation of those harmed promises a wider range of potentially satisfying compensatory activities for government-induced harms. These and other strategies of litigation are indicative of restorative justice measures, and they do not limit accountability for societal harm to the court room alone. That is also where hybrid courts have so far been underutilized, due to their dependency on the list of crimes and trial procedures defined by the Rome Statute. Restorative justice, in contrast to retributive justice as embodied in international criminal law, does not focus solely on the punishment of the offender. Rather, it seeks to address the needs of both the victim and the offender, with the goal of restoring the broader well-being of the individuals and communities involved as well as the society at large.[71] Contemporary prosecutions at international criminal courts and tribunals have demonstrated that, where individuals are convicted of core international crimes, the resources available for reparations are grossly insufficient to meet even the basic restitution needs of the victims. Most of the wealth that might have been accrued as a result of crimes such as crimes against humanity or war crimes is likely to be in the hands of individuals via corporations or other artificial legal persons who have gained prominence via these mass human rights violations. None of the international criminal courts and tribunals (together known as the ICCTs) has adjudicative jurisdiction over artificial legal persons of any sort. This means that any progress on large-scale restitution and restorative justice must come through domestic or hybrid courts and tribunals. This applies to both core international crimes and the broader category of human rights treaty crimes, which remain outside the authority of ICCTs.[72]

Meanwhile, translating restorative justice measures into international criminal law dealing with mass atrocities is not simple. This is despite the fact that while restorative justice is traditionally used in response to lower-impact crimes such as property damage or fraud, it has also been successfully used in response to higher-order offences where traditional retributive forms of punishment, such as imprisonment, could not resolve the issue of long-standing damages. As a case in point, the potential utility of restorative justice measures in the context of hybrid court trials for past mass atrocities became a lively public debate during the Juba Peace Talks in Uganda.[73] The July 2007 agreement between the Ugandan Government and the LRA on Accountability and Reconciliation stated that traditional justice mechanisms practised in the communities affected by the conflict shall be promoted, with necessary modifications, and that restorative justice measures would be treated as a central part of the framework for accountability and reconciliation.[74] Although the Final Peace Agreement was not signed, traditional restorative justice mechanisms of northern Uganda have been used extensively with lower-level LRA members who have returned to their communities.[75]

There are no doubt some inherent problems with traditional forms of justice, and overreliance on them could lead to an evasion of the retributive justice embodied in indictments by the ICCTs. Still, some of the practical questions faced during the Uganda peace talks reveal the limitations posed by criminal trials alone. For instance, how should abducted children who committed atrocities be treated, when they are both victims and perpetrators? Can traditional justice work both for formerly abducted children who became LRA fighters under duress, and for LRA commanders and those who enlisted voluntarily as adults? Suffice to say that traditional forms of restorative justice that are locally rooted and adapted for the purpose of reconciliation, truth-telling and advancing peace for a just social and political future order do not have to take place in opposition to or in isolation from ICCT involvement.[76] The question remains as to whether simply prosecuting and convicting Kony and a few of his senior commanders would indeed satisfy the needs of justice in the Ugandan context.[77] A multi-layered, locally nuanced set of approaches to justice and peace is more likely to deliver the needed results, a possibility that could be made into reality through the workings of a hybrid court.

Overall, the verdict emerging from the Global South is that the ICC in particular pursued a narrow criminal justice mandate under the Rome Statute to investigate and prosecute those primarily responsible for committing mass atrocities.[78] As stated, according to the ICC's defining principle of complementarity, the Court will take on an atrocities case only if domestic courts are 'unable or unwilling' to do so. The Court may also agree to hand over the prosecution of a case in midstream, if its judges are convinced that the proposed special domestic (or hybrid) court would be as strict and fair in its application of justice – including its sanctions – as the ICC itself. This is an option that could be put into practice for cases pertaining to countries such as Sudan and Uganda. It may indeed become a necessary route to take, as in recent years the ICC has faced a growing degree of suspicion since its first trial was suspended and the defendant, the Congolese warlord Thomas Lubanga, was subsequently ordered to be released.[79] In the meantime, a decade of war began in the Democratic Republic of Congo (DRC) with Laurent-Désiré Kabila's 1996–7 campaign to overthrow the repressive rule of Mobutu Sese Seko in the country then known as Zaire.

Here is how this peculiar story unfolded: in resource-rich Ituri province in the country's north-east, Thomas Lubanga led the Union des Patriotes Congolais (UPC) and its militia, the Forces Patriotiques pour la Libération du Congo. In 2004, the DRC herself invited the ICC to investigate and prosecute war crimes that had occurred in the DRC since 1 July 1 2002.[80] Meanwhile, DRC authorities arrested Lubanga in March 2005 and charged him with genocide and crimes against humanity, based on provisions of the DRC's military criminal code. These charges concerned the UPC's alleged participation in the killing of civilians in the villages they attacked. In March 2005, DRC authorities issued a second warrant charging Lubanga with illegal detention and murder. After these two warrants, the ICC issued a complementary arrest warrant accusing Thomas Lubanga Dyilo of war crimes for conscripting children as soldiers in 2006. However, the Court had to cancel the beginning of his trial in June 2008 because of what is stated as 'complex procedural issues'. The two other Congolese warlords, Mathieu Ngudjolo Chui and Germain Katanga, are awaiting trial in The Hague, while a fourth, Bosco Ntaganda, has been indicted but is still at large.[81] None of these long-drawn-out proceedings has helped matters concerning how to address the ICC in particular, and ICCTs in general, as they become involved with mass crimes in the post-colonial world. Instead, there is now a growing desire to see locally rooted and regionally legitimate institutions come on board instead.[82]

Conclusion: Hybrid Courts as New Actors of International Criminal Law in the Global South?

Major cases that have taken place before hybrid tribunals merit close examination in terms of their legal and political properties, as well as their procedural details and jurisdictional outcomes. In the Extraordinary Chambers of the Courts of Cambodia (ECCC), for instance, there are two particularly critical cases: Case 001 (Kaing Guek Eav a.k.a. 'Duch'), and Case 002 (with defendants Nuon Chea, Khieu Samphan, Ieng Sary and Ieng Thirith). The individuals mentioned were each charged with war crimes, genocide, crimes against humanity and crimes under Cambodian Law.[83] Meanwhile, Case 003 and Case 004 have been opposed by the Cambodian government, as a result of which several members of the court's international staff resigned from the tribunal, a circumstance which is reflective of the tense political context. At the Special Court for Sierra Leone (SCSL), the trials for the Civil Defence Forces (CDF) leads including Sam Hinga Norman, Moinina Fofana and Allieu Kondewa, the Revolutionary United Front (RUF) including the surviving leaders Issay Sesay, Morris Kallon and Augustine Gbao, and the Armed Forces Revolutionary Council (AFRC) including Alex Tamba Brima, Brima Bazzy Kamara and Santigie Borbor Kanu, along with the indictment, arrest and prosecution of Charles Taylor, are of particular concern for the future of international criminal law from the perspective of the Global South.[84] There are also the cases of Julio Fernandez and Joao Fernandez, The Los Palos Case, and the indictment of General Wiranto before the Special Panel for Serious Crimes, Dili. At the Bosnia War Crimes Chamber, the Foča Rape Camp Trials as well as the Kravica Case, focusing on violence related to the Srebrenica massacres in 1995, are of significant concern. Similarly, in Kosovo, the trial of Milos Jokic as well as the trials concerning the Racak massacre and the 2001 bombing of the Nis Express (Florim Ejupi) are to be attended closely, in terms of both their results and their reception in the larger context of bringing closure to the war and atrocities that marred former Yugoslav Republics in South-Eastern Europe.

All of these hybrid courts in the Global South operate based on the same principles that guide international criminal law and human rights law nexus in larger regional and international courts. First and foremost, whether they appear as witnesses, victim participants or civil parties in mass crimes proceedings, victims contribute vital evidence and insight bearing on the guilt or innocence of the accused. Their testimonies are accepted as a categorically valid contribution to the truth-telling function of the process, and under some circumstances are used as a means for coming to terms with societal trauma. However, as has been widely discussed, victim testimonies can also lead to re-traumatization.[85] Furthermore, from a jurisdictional point of view, they could compromise the fairness or efficiency of the judicial process if emotional distress is regarded as a factor that undermines the testimony's relevance, credibility or focus. Inherent tensions are inevitable due to the nature of courtroom experience for victims, who are subjected to pointed questioning and cross-examination on the details of very traumatic events as part of standard procedures that are essential for a fair criminal trial. What is unique about the hybrid courts is the way they deal with such tensions, and the flexibility and innovativeness they exhibit compared to the much more rigid structures embraced by the larger courts. A key example in this regard is the UN-backed hybrid court established to address crimes of the Pol Pot era. The ECCC has tried to facilitate victim testimonies both through formal procedures and through informal trial management strategies, including two important innovations in international criminal justice. Specifically, the ECCC spearheaded the special 'victim impact hearings' and 'statements of suffering', both of which allow civil parties to describe harms they endured under Khmer Rouge rule before a judgment is reached. These types of interventions help ease the tension between survivors' interests and the rights of the accused, which is for the benefit of the society at large.[86]

When it comes to mass atrocities and egregious crimes, the techno-legal transitional justice paradigm and the lustre of transitional justice institutions funded by the global North but operating across the Global South are beginning to fade. Therapeutic legalism did not deliver.[87] This in effect creates a real window of opportunity for the societies in the Global South. Similar to standard international judicial bodies, such as the International Criminal Court or the European Court of Human Rights, the hybrid and 'internationalized' criminal organs are composed of independent judges, working on the basis of predetermined rules of procedure, and rendering binding decisions. They are subject to the same principles governing the work of all international judiciaries, including due process, impartiality and independence.[88] Within this wider class of international judicial bodies, however, hybrid courts belong to a specific order. Similar to the ICC, ICTY and ICTR, their goal has been to sanction serious violations of international humanitarian law and human rights law, to secure individual accountability, and to act as a deterrence mechanism against future violations emanating from state criminality. To serve these functions, they impose criminal penalties, but they also increasingly engage with restorative justice mechanisms. This is perhaps the most critical feature setting hybrid courts and tribunals apart from other international judicial bodies. Moreover, like the ICTY and ICTR, but unlike the ICC, they are by their nature *ad hoc* institutions. They have been created to address particular situations, for a limited period of time, and they respond to singular political and historical circumstances. Finally, in order to carry out their mission the hybrid courts rely on cooperation from international legal organs such as the ICC, judicial assistance by individual states, as well as the endorsement of international organizations such as the UN. As a specific form of internationalized criminal institutions, they constitute a group of their own, and yet they operate within the larger field of other international judicial and political institutions and entities. In some cases, they are part of the judiciary of a given country, while in others, they may have been grafted onto the local judicial system by outside actors and posses a semi-independent status. In all the cases covered in this chapter, however, their make-up is markedly mixed, incorporating international and national features, and their mandate is circumscribed and issue-specific. They all are composed of international and local staff (judges, prosecutors, support staff), and apply a compound of international and national substantial and procedural law.

The remaining question is whether hybrid courts and tribunals constitute the future of international criminal law in terms of the dissemination of jurisprudence produced and endorsed by central institutions such as the ICC. What is their significance in terms of establishing an international regime of accountability regarding the crimes that now fall under the purview of the Rome Statute? Perhaps this question itself needs to be reformulated, and we must come to terms with the transnational and fragmented nature of international criminal law as a necessary aspect of its working. Throughout this chapter, I posited that international criminal law on war crimes, crimes against humanity, and genocide – perhaps better clustered together as societal crimes – constitutes a fragmented accountability regime. The common mistake regarding this regime is to limit the roster of actors that constitute it to state parties and international institutions such as the ICC. The ICC is an independent, permanent court that tries persons accused of the most serious crimes of international concern under its aegis. The ICC was established based on a treaty, which was originally joined by 108 countries.[89] However, the ICC is a court of last resort and should remain so. In addition, the ICC can only try those accused of the gravest crimes. One of the great innovations of the Statute of the International Criminal Court and its Rules of Procedure and Evidence is the series of rights granted to victims. For the first time in the history of international criminal justice, barring the Eichmann trials that took place in a domestic court, victims have the possibility to present their views and observations. Furthermore, participation may occur at various stages of proceedings, and it may take different forms. Although it is up to the judges to give directions as to the timing and manner of participation, the victim-based provisions within the Rome Statute provide post-conflict societies with the opportunity to have victims' voices heard and to obtain, where appropriate, different forms of reparation. But this would be infinitely more effective if practised in situ and as part of a larger scheme of restorative justice. It is this balance between retributive and restorative justice that enables the crimes against humanity jurisprudence formalized by the Rome Statute to carry out a mandate of not only bringing criminals to justice, but also helping the victims to obtain a sense of closure. In reality, hybrid courts are much better equipped than the ICC to ensure such results.

In setting up the ICC, its founders stated two main aims: to end impunity for the worst mass crimes, and to deter would-be perpetrators.[90] Three State Parties to the Rome Statute – Uganda, the Democratic Republic of the Congo (DRC) and the Central African Republic – have referred situations occurring on their territories to the Court. In addition, the Security Council has referred the situation in Darfur, Sudan – a non-State Party. The Court's Prosecutor has opened and conducted investigations in all of the above-mentioned cases.[91] Given that the Court's first four cases were all in Africa, the accusation of neocolonial bias raised its head. This is despite the fact that, in Congo, Uganda and the Central African Republic, it was the governments themselves that requested the court to investigate. On this second issue, there are now charges that accuse the Court of being used by corrupt leaders and dictators in the Global South, who use the Court as a stage to wage battles against the opposition in their countries. In this heated political context, hybrid courts seem to offer a much-needed new platform for accountability in international criminal law.

Another case that caused immense controversy but also revealed further advantages regarding the workings of hybrid courts is that of Charles Taylor. In May 2010, the trial of Charles Taylor at the Special Court for Sierra Leone (SCSL) took a dramatic twist as prosecutors requested the judges to issue a subpoena to supermodel Naomi Campbell, requiring her appearance before the Chambers.[92] The SCSL Prosecutors made an application that they be allowed to reopen their case, which was closed in February 2009, or to bring evidence in rebuttal against Taylor by calling three additional witnesses, Campbell, Carole White and Mia Farrow. Campbell was required to testify as a witness about a diamond gift she allegedly received from Taylor in South Africa in 1997. Campbell's evidence supported the prosecution's allegations that the accused used rough diamonds for personal enrichment and arms purchases for Sierra Leone, particularly during the AFRC/RUF period. As the actual recipient of the gift of diamonds from the accused, Campbell was in a position to provide material evidence. This case also indicated that the cooperation of states whose citizens are subpoenaed is essential to the functioning of hybrid judicial bodies.

Still, concerns remain about the efficacy of hybrid courts in carrying forward the mandate of the Rome Statute. Yet, what is the alternative? Perhaps the problem lies with our expectations from international criminal law, and our principled distancing of it from transitional justice, the rigidity of institutional forms that the existing framework for international criminal law imposes, rather than the hybrid courts themselves. On a similar note, scholarship on sentencing remains surprisingly universalist. Leading scholars and jurists advance sentencing principles that are intended to apply to international crimes, no matter where they are prosecuted.[93] Here, I also wish to challenge this viewpoint and the resultant flat reading of ICC jurisprudence in that regard, both empirically and normatively. Expectations of sentencing consistency in international criminal law are premised on the misguided and factually unsupported notion that there is a unified international criminal justice system represented by the jurisprudence of globalized courts such as the ICC. In contradistinction, I would argue that sentencing disparities across hybrid courts are both legally justifiable and normatively desirable since they respond to crucial differences in domestic criminal prosecutions pertaining to international crimes, including differences in the kinds of atrocities that occurred, the rank and status of the perpetrators who can be prosecuted, and the hybrid courts' own mandates. These differences create the need for differentiated sentencing schemes in different tribunals and courts. Without doubt, here I am not endorsing the use of death penalty. However, it is high time that we accept domestic sentencing norms as a particularly crucial factor that influences hybrid courts' specific sentencing practices and as an essential part of their political legitimacy. As I discussed in the opening chapter of this work, traditional accounts of international law entertain a distinction between monist and dualist legal systems.[94] According to the monist approach, courts must apply international law directly. According to the dualist accounts, unfettered application is not an option, so courts apply international law through the filters of domestic jurisprudence, or not at all. This distinction tells us very little about the functional role of hybrid courts in international criminal law. There is a lot to be learnt from the on-the-ground realities of hybrid courts in this regard.

In this final chapter, both a functional and a normative account of hybrid courts and tribunals were presented, with particular focus on the distinctions among the horizontal, vertical and transnational legal obligations and merits of such organs. International law regulates horizontal relationships between states, vertical relationships between states and private parties, and transnational relationships among private parties whose interactions cross state lines. In conjunction, the role of domestic courts in interpreting and applying international law varies greatly, depending on whether the international rule at issue is horizontal, vertical or transnational. As the cases examined here demonstrate, the willingness or the ability of state-based courts to apply international law is not solely a legal matter. It depends heavily on the political nature of the subject matter of the trials. In effect, domestic courts rarely interpret horizontal rules. Rather, they generally refer to treaties that regulate the horizontal relationship between states as *ultra vires* in nature. As a result, implementation of horizontal obligations as dictated by international law typically involves executive and not judicial action. However, the role of domestic courts in interpreting and applying vertical rules, such as human rights treaties, tends to be different. Particular political relationships may affect the willingness of domestic or hybrid courts to engage with international law, and to effect legal change based on their own initiative.

This chapter drew on materials from several jurisdictions, all of them situated in the Global South, to present a holistic account of the role played by hybrid courts in interpreting and applying horizontal, transnational and vertical international legal rules. As these cases demonstrate, the application of universal jurisdiction over core international crimes has been uneven. Non-governmental organization (NGO) activism has been regarded as a significant factor in this regard, but much less attention has been paid to the political engagement of the public in terms of their willingness to bring certain matters to the courtroom or even to seek address for state criminality. After the Pinochet debacle in the UK, the amputation of the universal jurisdiction laws in Belgium in 2003 and Spain in 2009 and 2014 made it clear that expecting one's unfinished business to be settled in another country's courts was not all that realistic. Subsequently, an alternative view is emerging in international criminal law. Universal jurisdiction is not necessarily on the decline. The number of universal jurisdiction-related statutes and trials has increased significantly in recent years, although the trajectory of applying universal jurisdiction is shifting towards hybrid and at-home courts. Perhaps it is time to revise received wisdom concerning the operation of international criminal law in this regard. Rather than seeing the matter as bipolar operation concerning the role states play in the applications of universal jurisdiction for international crimes (i.e. national versus international accountability and enforcement regimes), the emphasis could be put on the mandate of universal jurisdiction itself rather than the specific organs to carry it. States are not the 'global enforcers' of the Rome Statute *verbatim*. Although signatory states have a role in preventing and punishing core international crimes committed anywhere in the world, which is the 'no safe haven' conception, states should not be seen as the guardian of the victims of crimes perpetrated by other states, either.[95] More to the point, the anti-impunity rationale of international criminal law should not be reduced to a legalistic position and a zealously Northern rhetoric about practising universal jurisdiction. The radical pluralism approach to international law has already established a critical jurisprudential tradition that asks how actors use and apply law, in order to understand how law obtains meaning, is practised, and changes over time.[96] Combined with TWAIL scholarship, these kinds of critical engagements with international criminal law force us to ask a different set of questions about the possibility of life after Rome Statute, so to speak. Debates on universal jurisdiction concerning gross and systemic humanitarian law and human rights violations have long suffered from a single focus on jurisprudential certainties imposed by international organs or a neutered state-centric worldview.[97] It is time to look closely at the realities of universal jurisdiction on the ground, and to give up the obsession with what goes on in the chambers of international courts or indeed national courts in the North, and to come up with strategies and answers about human suffering in the Global South from within while also engaging with the globalized context of international crimes.

In Lieu of Conclusion: Deliverance of Justice in International Criminal Law and the Role of Political Judgment as Purposive Action

> … time shall in fine out breake
> When Ocean wave shall open every Realme
> The wandering World at will shall open lye,
> And Thyphis shall some newe founded Land Survay
> Some travellers shall the Countries farre escrye,
> Beyond small Thule, known farthest to this day.
>
> Seneca, *Medea*
> (from the John Studley translation of 1581)

Taken from Seneca's tragedy *Medea*, these lines have become symbolic of the prediction that a 'new found land' will indeed appear, located far beyond the edges of the known world. This utopian impulse, and the commitment to and desire for imagining a different, better or even perfect society is nothing new. In fact, there is always a dramatic increase in expressions of such yearnings when times get harder. This 'Wandering World' of Seneca's could take many forms, as it offers the potential actualization of novel ways of doing things, seeing things and understanding anew. From Platonic dialogues to architectural treatises and plans, from literary and theatrical works to historical documents and legal texts, expressions of a desire for *what we are told we cannot have* found their way into our existing order of things in myriad ways.

Law, its *ethos* and *pathos* constitute a triplet that looks rather unlikely at first sight as a harbinger for such utopian longings to transcend delimitations of existing regimes. Law imposes structure and discipline while striving for the creation of an ideal order. Clearly heralded by Plato's late dialogues many centuries ago – namely *Timaeus*, *Critias*, and the *Laws* – the yearning for a transformative ideal in the form of law has been a foundational belief. While Timaeus, Critias and Socrates are talking about the ideal society, Socrates wishes to see this ideal in action and find out if it works. Critias tells him that Athens once was this ideal society. He heard that from Solon, who heard it from an old man, who heard it from an Egyptian that Athens was that ideal at the time they defeated Atlantis. Having no writing, the Athenians apparently forgot their own history and are learning it all afresh. Timaeus then suggests that the world is a receptacle into which images of the eternal forms are stamped. Thus, physical things are copies of the eternal forms, and although these copies are continually decaying, their essence remains. Then comes the unique place for Law, delivering foundational truths.

These late dialogues suggest that Athenians who defeated Atlantis have degenerated to the extent that their laws and thoughts moved away from the original divine form. The Platonic hope is that the essence of things could be restored and preserved by creating pure laws and institutions to fight off any diversion from the spirit of the divine presence.[1] These ancient texts, as distinct from anything law-related as they may appear, speak in a language that one often hears about *jus cogens* norms and *erga omnes* obligations, and international criminal law in general. Something even more removed from international law, the *Ten Books of Architecture* by Vitruvius, similarly displays the belief in perfect geometric shapes forming the basis for universal order. The Renaissance embellished this idea of 'perfect reflection' further to include the human form: Leonardo da Vinci and Cesare Cesariano illustrated it in what is now known as Vitruvian Man, based on Vitruvius' discussion of the proportions of the human body inscribed in a circle and a square. From time immemorial, the ideal city, the ideal state, the ideal shape, the ideal order always hinged upon a strong sense of the existence of a self-contained system expressed in pure laws.

In this work, I attacked the common conceptions pertaining to the ideal of the state in international law and what they leave behind, the residue, so to speak. Deliverance of justice is a central, and yet highly contested, element in theories and debates on international law. As the justice claims of societies increasingly clash with the largely statist basis of existing legal practices and institutions operating at the transnational level, it has become critical that we question the role of international organizations, including the Courts, in creating and sustaining the illusion of a perfect global legal order.[2] As this multifaceted debate on the jurisprudential merits of international criminal law in the area of crimes against humanity proves, international organizations including courts such as the ICC will have to reconstitute some of their authoritative practices and render them open to the motives of both new and previously marginalized legal actors.[3] Furthermore, international organizations have to be open to potential norm change based on claims gone unaddressed in the past, as well as claims related to current and newly emerging forms of injustice.[4] This need is further underlined by the limited capacity of the existing legal regime of accountability for realizing such projects. Alternative models of adjudication should be welcome as a true feature of the fragmented regime of international criminal law, indicating poli-centricity and countering the prototypical approach of centrifugal norm production and dissemination. I have also argued that the institutional masking of the hegemony of key actors in the international legal domain creates a blind spot. International organizations have in the past, and might again at present, become the bulwark of hegemonic privilege.[5] The tempering of conflicting interests by doctrinal idealism does not guarantee that an international organization can or does provide a sufficient, widely recognized and inclusive mechanism for dealing with the justice-related claims of different actors. Ongoing conflicts in global politics are carried onto the institutional and organizational realms, and judicial organs such as international courts constitute no exception to this phenomenon. Thus, it is high time for welcoming a degree of utopian thinking in international criminal law.

As posited throughout this work, normative theories of international law promise to address these critical questions regarding the deliverance of justice.[6] However, a distinction is to be made between the deliverance of justice as a motive and as an authoritative legal practice. Rather than raising the spectre of lack of just practices in given areas of international law, organs such as the ICC are built upon the premise of deliverance of justice according to established legal norms and practices. On the surface, international legal obligations of a state are overwhelmingly based on consent. Their formal commitment to consent supposedly preserves the power of states, and yet with a bias towards the *status quo*. Historically, the regime of international law has not been equitable to all states that are a party to it.[7] International law, given its background, has developed a variety of ways to live with this specific problem of unequal beginnings and yet equal consent. The expectation from international criminal law has been for it to overcome this hurdle via normative prerogatives such as those exemplified by universal jurisdiction for crimes against humanity.[8] Meanwhile, international organizations such as the ICC have a life of their own. There is always the risk that the institution would develop its own interests and declare themselves as essential for the ideal of justice.[9] What is at stake here is life after the ICC for international criminal law.

As Kantian scholarship on international law has long insisted, seeking a legalized and institutionally guarded regime of accountability to constrain states has direct benefits in terms of avoiding random warfare in an age where such wars tend to bring more damage than profit.[10] As such, justice delivered via international criminal law is considered a virtue. This peculiar understanding of political order relies on standardized expectations, procedures and entitlements.[11] It has also been argued for decades that the essence of any meaningful and reasonable idea of peace dictates international law to be primarily about the rules and procedures that allow states to coexist.[12] This take on international law is quite similar in its logic to the way constitutions are defined as frames within which societies and polities can accommodate change and conflict without breaking existing political systems apart. In other words, international law is deemed purposive. And yet, is it not so much a maker as it is a protector of the *status quo*? Even the *jus cogens* norms and *erga omnes* obligations do not constitute major exceptions in this sense. Consequently, in international criminal law justice is defined mainly in formal procedural terms. There is very little room left for political judgment or norm creation to enter the debate, even concerning critical instances that challenge the founding pillars of the entire state system such as crimes against humanity.[13]

In this work, I have inquired about whether it is possible to strike a balance between normative and deliberative purposefulness and authoritative jurisdictional practices in international criminal law, in such a way that its legislative prowess is not just 'effective' but also legitimate. My examination of the limits of the application of universal jurisdiction in the context of crimes against humanity and particularly in the Global South was a testimony to the intrinsically challenging nature of this proposition. The anxiety about closing the gap between what legal theorists such as Hart named as primary and secondary rules is endemic to the dominant statist model of international law, and it bars us from seeing it for what it is – a transnational and fragmented enterprise. Acknowledgement of the plurality of political and legal actors, as well as forms of legal and restorative action, is essential for achieving a large enough scope of applicability for the model of deliverance of criminal justice beyond the confines of international courts. Needless to say, addressing this plurality alone cannot override the normative centrality of the state in international criminal law. However, as I indicated throughout the debate on hybrid courts, formalistic international criminal law is stagnating rather than liberating in its universalistic claims. Particularly disconcerting is its dubious status regarding the treatment of injurious acts such as crimes against humanity, which have implications for the past, present and future of societies. This results from an almost exclusive reliance on institutions like the ICC with their centrifugal mandate and procedural rigidities.

In this vein, we must pay closer attention to 'informal lawmaking' and variant forms of adjudication that involves new actors, new processes and new approaches concerning the most heinous forms of state criminality. The validation requirements of traditional international criminal law as it is spread through the adaptation of the Rome Statute have to be rethought. Crimes against humanity jurisprudence adapted to local realities by hybrid courts and regional organizations vividly prove this point. It is erroneous to use the example of Belgian or Spanish courts as the test case for universal jurisdiction, as there are

European states with their own burdensome history of colonial crimes and involvements. To recommend these precedents to be followed by states in the Global South only points to the continuing blindness of international law scholarship regarding the history and politics of how the post–Second World War state system was built, and at what costs it is maintained.

Throughout this work, I insisted on the necessary involvement of political judgment in the alignment of international and domestic law in cases concerning state criminality. This blending is essential for widespread endorsement and application of the current legal codification of crimes against humanity. In my view, it is a base requirement for international criminal law in this area to become purposive rather than merely formalistic. The development of a justice-based dialogue above and beyond the confines of the sovereign state is only possible via politically astute deliberation, legal arguments keen on persuasion rather than dictation, and the endorsement of multilateral legal premises rather than adherence to a monist or dualist legal frame of understanding being applied to international criminal law. Statist and intergovernmentalist models of international law require that demands for justice be either channelled through domestic policy processes, or appropriated within a top-down process of international jurisdiction. In the specific case of crimes against humanity, there are widely observed and profound structural tensions between the human rights and humanitarian norms introduced into the framework of international law since the Second World War. According to the existing model, international criminal law jurisprudence is attempting to adjudicate the crimes committed by the very actors that it protects, that is the state, by asking them to come to international courts or local courts of other states empowered by universal jurisdiction in the event these states fail to try their own leaders. In this sense, I believe the word 'transnational' continues to escape universal jurisdiction debates.[14] Yet when it comes to issues such as crimes against humanity, how could such an argument be maintained: that human rights and human dignity must be met within the parameters determined by the limits of either the 'national' understanding and domestic jurisdiction of such crimes, or via litigation sought in the chambers of a distant international court or a European domestic court armed with universal jurisdiction? This is precisely the conundrum that triggered the methodological investigations and conceptual worries presented in this work.

As signalled throughout this work, a post-statist and transnational conception of international law and international organizations helps the matters a great deal.[15] Ideally, in this new setting, the justice motives of a variety of actors beyond the state would become favourable to international law scholarship. However, the static and authoritative perception of law often acts as an impediment for such a hybrid understanding of justice. It is as if legal debates about the deliverance of justice are utterly uninterested in dealing with moral dilemmas, ethical concerns, normative reflections and political deliberations. By introducing the notions of political judgment and collective responsibility/wrongdoing concerning state criminality as necessary components of the debate on the deliverance of justice in the context of crimes against humanity, this work exemplifies a concerted effort to bypass the dichotomy between the domestic and international spheres in international law.[16]

Just as values and norms are affected by a plurality of actors and political forces both within and beyond states, so are the actual workings of international criminal law. It is not structurally sealed from the purposive claims of political agents and legal actors. The crucial matter concerning the category of supra-legal norms such as those pertaining to crimes against humanity is not so much the presence of value plurality that they have to address, but whether there are limits and thresholds beyond which they lose their validity. As the Sudan case clearly demonstrates, when imposed from outside despite the reservations of voices of dissent and victims' groups inside, their adjudication becomes an impediment to the deliverance of justice rather than aiding it. International criminal law cannot turn its back on voices of dissent, particularly those emanating from communities who currently suffer the most from state brutality and politically organized forms of criminality. In this regard, *ad hoc* and hybrid tribunals' jurisprudential contributions, their extra-legal impact and legacies, and the intrinsic relationship between transitional justice projects and international criminal law have to be brought into the canonized debates. Furthermore, in many cases of extended civil war, the concept of state legacy is itself contested and the appropriateness of international courts' efforts to consolidate it must be questioned. A normative (rather than procedural) critique of the history of international criminal law pertaining to the adjudication of crimes against humanity jurisprudence provides a perfect opportunity to reflect upon the need for the inclusion of more voices in justice claims and with an ear on the ground for historic grievances.[17]

I would like to conclude this treatise on a hopeful note, in keeping with the utopian impulse mentioned in the opening of this conclusion. In a series of speeches and occasional essays delivered in 1999 and 2000, Pierre Bourdieu, one of France's leading sociologists of culture, called for a new European social movement to unite existing and future unions, new social movements and intellectuals to struggle against globalization.[18] In his outcry, Bourdieu denounced numerous evils of globalization, especially its guiding philosophy of neo-liberalism, and he sketched specific roles that writers, scholars, artists and research workers – otherwise known as Bourdieu's 'intellectuals' – could play in this new composite movement. While this call to arms is not without contradictions, it offered encouragement to intellectuals to join with the working classes, farmers, the unemployed, immigrants, activists, students and militants to struggle against the depredations of the new world order. For Bourdieu, as for many other critics of globalization, what is particularly vexing is the recent retreat of national governments from funding welfare, medical care, housing, public transportation, education, and, of course, culture. The neo-liberal focus of the past few decades on privatization, deregulation and self-help, characteristic of the economies in the Global North but also becoming widespread policy initiatives in the Global South, argued Bourdieu, were unabashedly supported by international organizations such as the World Bank, International Monetary Fund and World Trade Organization (WTO). The quest for maximum short-term profits and reduced expenditures is seeping into the everyday life of citizens in an exponentially increasing number of states and creating a perpetual condition of insecurity. Ironically, noted Bourdieu, the transnational spread of this neo-liberal social insecurity provides a solid and tangible foundation for a new form of politics.[19]

The work of Pierre Bourdieu offers a potentially productive way to practise research in academia. Does it also offer us clues concerning how to practise international legal scholarship and advocacy perhaps with less jurisdictional certitude but more moral conviction and normative involvement with global injustices? Bourdieu invites academia to refuse the presumed opposition between general theory and everyday life. This relational approach also provides a protective shield against two of the biggest handicaps affecting international criminal law: essentialization and ahistoricism. In order to undo its state centrism and to discuss possible transformations of international criminal law, we must show the courage to reveal the power relations hidden beneath the perfect spectre of universal jurisdiction. This work attempted to do so within the specific context of the applications of universal jurisdiction to crimes against humanity, both within and beyond the confines of the ICC. Its findings encourage us to renew the debate on the growing network of international law institutions and the underpinnings of a transnational legal regime of accountability from the lens of regional, national and sub-national authorities and spaces including political movements and civic initiatives. The complex nature of crimes against humanity renders such a change of optics absolutely necessary. Amidst the rising tide of seeking justice for political and mass crimes, using the rubric of international criminal law for questioning individual responsibility for societal crimes has been a very important first step.[20] The next crucial step is the involvement of hybrid courts and other local mechanisms that do not exclusively rely on a centrifugal dictation of norms in matters concerning states and societies in the Global South. Furthermore, the normative frame of reference used to adjudicate crimes against humanity must be expanded to welcome debates on the notion of societal responsibility for mass crimes. This would introduce the elements of choice, volition and legitimation in the Global South for future uses of international criminal law jurisprudence. Only then, the prediction of Seneca cited here would truly resonate with international law scholarship: '… time shall in fine out breake / When Ocean wave shall open every Realme …'

Notes

Introduction

1. See Martti Koskenniemi, '"The Lady Doth Protest Too Much": Kosovo, and the Turn to Ethics in International Law' (2002) 65 *Modern Law Review* 159.
2. See Harold Hongju Koh, 'Transnational Legal Process' (1996) 75 *Neb. L. Rev.* 181, and Abram Chayes and Antonia Handler Chayes, *The New Sovereignty* (Harvard University Press, 1998).
3. See Jean Cohen, 'Whose sovereignty? Empire versus international law' (2004) 18 *Ethics & International Affairs* 1.
4. On the issue of the hegemonic purchase of international law, see Detlev F. Vagts, 'Hegemonic international law' (2001) 95 *Am. J. Int'l L.* 843; Martti Koskenniemi, 'International law and hegemony: a reconfiguration' (2004) 17 *Cambridge Review of International Affairs* 197, and, Nico Krisch, 'International law in times of hegemony: unequal power and the shaping of the international legal order' (2005) 16 *European Journal of International Law* 369.
5. Concerns regarding the role of international law are particularly evident in contemporary Europe. In Germany, for instance, the federal constitutional court has positioned itself as a bulwark between the national legal system and the two European legal orders the court is a part of – the European Union and the European Court of Human Rights. In the United Kingdom, long before Brexit, the government sought to derogate from the relevant provisions of the European Convention on Human Rights in specific cases related to terrorism. See Karen Alter, *Establishing the Supremacy of European Law: The Making of an International Rule of Law in Europe* (Oxford University Press, 2001); Lisa Conant, *Justice Contained: Law and Politics in the European Union* (Cornell University Press, 2002); and Rachel A. Cichowski, *The European Court and Civil Society: Litigation, Mobilization and Governance* (Cambridge University Press, 2007).
6. See the debate presented in the Special Issue of *American Journal of International Law*, in particular Gerald Neuman, 'The Uses of International Law in Constitutional Interpretation' (2004) 98 *Am. J. Int'l L.* 82 and Roger Alford, 'Misusing international sources to interpret the constitution' (2004) 98 *Am. J. Int'l L.* 57.

7. See Jonathan Turley, 'Dualistic Values in the Age of International Legisprudence' (1993) 44 *Hastings Law Journal* 185.
8. See Gerald L. Neuman, 'Human Rights and Constitutional Rights: Harmony and Dissonance' (2003) 55 *Stanford Law Review* 1863.
9. Seyla Benhabib, 'On the Alleged Conflict Between Democracy and International Law' (2005) 19 *Ethics and International Affairs* 85; Allen Buchanan, *Justice, Legitimacy, and Self-Determination: Moral Foundations for International Law* (Oxford University Press on Demand, 2007); Gregory Shaffer, 'International Law and Global Public Goods in a Legal Pluralist World' (2012) 23 *European Journal of International Law* 669; Nico Krisch, 'The Decay of Consent: International Law in an Age of Global Public Goods' (2014) 108 *Am. J. Int'l L.* 1; and Charles De Visscher, *Theory and Reality in Public International Law* (Princeton University Press, 2015).
10. See Gregg Barak (ed.), *Crimes by the Capitalist State: An Introduction to State Criminality* (SUNY Press, 1991); Nina Jørgensen, *The Responsibility of States for International Crimes* (Oxford University Press, 2000); Dawn L. Rothe, *State Criminality: The Crime of All Crimes* (Lexington Books, 2009); David Luban, 'State Criminality and the Ambition of International Criminal Law' in T. Isaacs and R. Vernon (eds), *Accountability for Collective Wrongdoing* (Cambridge University Press, 2011), pp. 61–91.
11. Martti Koskenniemi and Pkivi Lein, 'Fragmentation of International Law: Postmodern Anxieties' (2002) 5 *Leiden Journal of International Law* 556.
12. Hersch Lauterpacht, 'The Grotian Tradition in International Law' (1946) 23 *British Yearbook of International Law* 1.
13. International norms are bound by contractual regimes. Meanwhile, legal codes such as those exemplified by crimes against humanity jurisprudence indicate absolute terms as a result of which they are expected to be endorsed in *statu nascendi*.
14. See Frank Michelman, 'Reasonable Umbrage: Race and Constitutional Antidiscrimination Law in the United States and South Africa' (2004) 117 *Harvard Law Review* 1378.
15. See Thomas Nagel, 'The Problem of Global Justice' (2005) 33 *Philosophy and Public Affairs* 113.
16. See David Dyzenhaus, 'The Genealogy of Legal Positivism' (2004) 24 *Oxford Journal of Legal Studies* 39.
17. Balakrishnan Rajagopal, 'International Law and Its Discontents: Rethinking the Global South' (2012) 106th American Society of International Law Proceedings, p. 176, March 2012. Available at *http://ssrn.com/abstract=2304309* (accessed 25 May 2020).

18. See Obiora Chinedu Okafor, 'Critical Third World Approaches to International law (TWAIL): Theory, Methodology, or Both?' (2008) 10 *International Community Law Review* 371.
19. Asef Bayat, 'From Dangerous Classes' to Quiet Rebels' Politics of the Urban Subaltern in the Global South' (2000) 15 *International Sociology* 533.
20. Anne Orford et al., *The Oxford Handbook of the Theory of International Law* (Oxford University Press, 2016).
21. There are myriad examples of universalist international law scholarship, as it dominates the theoretical debates in this field. See, for instance, the overviews provided by Dennis Patterson, 'Cosmopolitanism and Global Legal Regimes' (2015) 67 *Rutgers U. L. Rev.* 7; and Cedric Ryngaert, *Jurisdiction in International Law*, 2nd edn (Oxford University Press, 2015).
22. Third Worldism joins together anti-colonial nationalisms and the utopianism of post-independence projects. The idea of the Third World dates back to the late 1940s. In the aftermath of the Second World War, the term was increasingly used to generate unity and support among an emergent group of nation-states whose governments were reluctant to take sides in the Cold War. These leaders and governments thus displaced the 'East–West' conflict with the 'North–South' conflict. The rise of Third Worldism as an ideology, on the other hand, coincides with the 1950s and early 1960s. The latter was closely connected with national liberation projects in Asia and Africa, the former mandates and new nation-states of the Middle East, as well as those in Latin America. Third Worldism in this period is linked to Pan-Asianism, Pan-Arabism, Pan-Africanism and Pan-Americanism. The demise of the first generation of Third Worldist regimes in the 1960s and 1970s was followed by the emergence of a second generation with an explicitly socialist vision. By the 1980s, however, Third Worldism began a dramatic decline. On the history of the term 'Third World', see Mark Berger, 'After the Third World? History, destiny and the fate of Third Worldism' (2004) 25 *Third World Quarterly* 9.
23. For an interdisciplinary historical account of the flirtatious relationship between Marxism, the Left in general, and legal theory, see Roberto Mangabeira Unger, *The Critical Legal Studies Movement: Another Time, a Greater Task* (Verso Books, 2015); Wesley Gould and Michael Barkun, *International Law and the Social Sciences* (Princeton University Press, 2015); Barbara Stark (ed.), *International Law and its Discontents: Confronting Crises* (Cambridge University Press, 2015).
24. Legal pluralism has become common currency in contemporary debates on law, globalization and post-coloniality since the 1980s. Its most recent proponents claim that a new form of global legal pluralism represents both the most accurate description of law in a global context and the best normative

option. At the descriptive level, transnational legal pluralism is considered more reliable than state-based accounts. At the normative level, legal pluralism is similarly trusted to open up spaces for previously unheard voices. On the issue of the limitations of legal pluralism, however, see Mariano Croce and Marco Goldoni, 'A Sense of Self-Suspicion: Global Legal Pluralism and the Claim to Legal Authority' (2015) 8 *Ethics & Global Politics* 1; Jiří Přibáň, 'Asking the Sovereignty Question in Global Legal Pluralism: From "Weak" Jurisprudence to "Strong" Socio-Legal Theories of Constitutional Power Operations' (2015) 28 *Ratio Juris* 31; Mireille Delmas-Marty, *Ordering Pluralism: A Conceptual Framework for Understanding the Transnational Legal World* (Bloomsbury Publishing, 2009).

25. See Math Noortmann, August Reinisch and Cedric Ryngaert (eds), *Non-State Actors in International Law* (Bloomsbury Publishing, 2015).
26. On the methodology of writing through the prism of the Global South, see the seminal work of Boike Rehbein, *Critical Theory After the Rise of the Global South: Kaleidoscopic Dialectic*, vol. 5 (Routledge, 2015). Also see R. Connell, *Southern Theory: The global dynamics of knowledge in social science* (Polity Press, 2007); G. Therborn, 'Entangled Modernities' (2003) 6 *European Journal of Social Theory* 293; S. Randeria, 'Entangled Histories of Uneven Modernities: Civil Society, Caste Solidarities and Legal Pluralism in Post-Colonial India' in Yehuda Elkana et al. (eds), *Unraveling Ties: From Social Cohesion to New Practices of Connectedness* (Campus Verlag, 2002), pp. 284–311; S. N. Eisenstadt, 'Multiple Modernities' (2002) 129 *Daedalus* 1.
27. See Antony Anghie, *Imperialism, Sovereignty and the Making of International Law*, Cambridge Studies in International and Comparative Law, vol. 37 (Cambridge University Press, 2007); Mark Goodale and Sally Engle Merry (eds), *The Practice of Human Rights: Tracking Law Between the Global and the Local* (Cambridge University Press, 2007); Bhupinder S. Chimni, 'Third World approaches to international law: a manifesto' (2006) 8 *Int'l Comm. L. Rev.* 3; Boaventura de Sousa Santos and César A. Rodríguez-Garavito (eds), *Law and Globalization from Below: Towards a Cosmopolitan Legality* (Cambridge University Press, 2005); Obiora Chinedu Okafor, 'Newness, imperialism, and international legal reform in our time: a TWAIL perspective' (2005) 43 *Osgoode Hall L. J.* 171; Balakrishnan Rajagopal, *International Law from Below: Development, Social Movements and Third World Resistance* (Cambridge University Press, 2003); and Boaventura de Sousa Santos, *Toward a New Legal Common Sense: Law, Globalization, and Emancipation* (Cambridge University Press, 2002).
28. For international criminal law regimes, the importance of the notion of crimes against humanity (CAH) is twofold. These are defined as offensive acts *against*

human dignity committed as *part of widespread or systemic attack* against *civilian populations*. They can be a series of events or a one-time event, planned and committed by state or non-state organized groups, supported by a distinct policy or ideology. Secondly, they signify a sense of justice that hinges upon dictates of the public conscience. See Eveylon Mack and Corrie Westbrook, 'Does Customary International Law Obligate States to Extradite or Prosecute Individuals Accused of Committing Crimes against Humanity' (2015) 24 *Minn. J. Int'l L.* 73; Leila N. Sadat, 'Codifying the "Laws of Humanity" and the "Dictates of the Public Conscience": Towards a New Global Treaty on Crimes Against Humanity' in Morten Bergsmo and Song Tianying (eds), *On the Proposed Crimes Against Humanity Convention* (Torkel Opsahl Academic EPublisher, 2014), pp. 17–46; M. Cherif Bassiouni, 'Crimes Against Humanity: The Case for a Specialized Convention' (2010) 9 *Wash. U. Global Stud. L. Rev.* 575.

Chapter 1

1. In *The Concept of Law* (Oxford University Press, Clarendon Law Series [1961] 2012), Herbert L. A. Hart provides a canonical analysis of the relation between law, coercion and morality, and addresses the question of whether and when law should be conceptualized as a coercive order or as a moral command. In Hart's view, there is no logically necessary connection between law and morality. He also takes a stance against imposing a misleading appearance of uniformity on different kinds of laws social functions that law may perform. Instead, he posits the existence of variety in the content, origin and range of applications of law. Accordingly, laws that impose duties or obligations on individuals are described as 'primary rules' of obligation. In order for a system of primary rules to function effectively, Hart argues that 'secondary rules' will be necessary to provide an authoritative statement of the primary rules. Secondary rules of a legal system include rules of recognition, rules of change, and rules of adjudication. Meanwhile, secondary rules themselves, i.e. the formal qualities of law, do not guarantee delivery of justice in and of themselves. If the primary rules are not sufficiently intelligible, there may be uncertainty about the obligations that have been imposed on individuals. Neither are primary rules sufficient, in and of themselves, to establish a system of laws that can be formally recognized or adjudicated. Primary rules must be combined with secondary rules in order to establish a functioning legal system. A second distinction Hart introduces is between 'external' and 'internal' points of view with respect to how the rules of a legal system may be described or evaluated. The external point of view is that of an observer who does not necessarily have to accept the rules of a given legal system.

The internal point of view, on the other hand, is that of individuals who are governed by the rules of a given legal system and who accept these rules as standards of conduct. According to Hart, there are two minimum requirements that must be satisfied in order for a legal system to exist: private citizens must obey the primary rules of obligation, and public officials must accept the secondary rules of recognition, change and adjudication as standards of official conduct. See Herbert L. A. Hart, 'Positivism and the Separation of Law and Morals' (1958) 71 *Harvard Law Review* 593. Hart's interpretation of the relation between law and morality significantly differs from that of Ronald Dworkin, who in *Law's Empire* (Harvard University Press, 1986) suggests that every legal action has a moral dimension. Dworkin rejects the concept of law as acceptance of conventional patterns of recognition, and describes law as an interpretive process combining jurisprudence and adjudication. In this general context, international law is seen as problem-laden by Hart, since it may not possess all of the elements of a fully developed legal system. International law lacks secondary rules since international legal bodies may not have the power to enforce sanctions or even the necessary jurisdiction. In contradistinction, according to Dworkin, a complete legal theory must consider not only the relation between law and coercion (i.e. the force of law), but also the relation between law and rightfulness or justifiability. See Andrzej Grabowski, 'The Missing Link in the Hart–Dworkin Debate' (2016) 36 *Oxford Journal of Legal Studies* 476.

2. For a hopeful account of the making of international law in the era of transnational politics and global economy, see Janet Koven Levit, 'A bottom-up approach to international lawmaking: the tale of three trade finance instruments' (2005) 30 *Yale J. Int'l L.* 125. Also see Ralf Michaels, 'The re-statement of non-state law: the state, choice of Law, and the challenge from global legal pluralism' (2005) 51 *Wayne L. Rev.* 1209; Balakrishnan Rajagopal, 'The role of law in counter-hegemonic globalization and global legal pluralism: lessons from the Narmada Valley struggle in India' (2005) 18 *Leiden Journal of International Law* 345; Paul Schiff Berman, 'Global legal pluralism' (2006) 80 *Cal. L. Rev.* 1155; Ralf Michaels, 'The true lex mercatoria: law beyond the state' (2007) 14 *Indiana Journal of Global Legal Studies* 447; Peer Zumbansen, 'The law of society: governance through contract' (2007) 14 *Indiana Journal of Global Legal Studies* 191.
3. Robert Cover theorizes 'jurisgenesis' or the creation of legal meaning as a process that is not reliant on the state or any given central authority. Instead, the normative world or *nomos* within which *jurisgenesis* occurs is defined as the amalgamation of multiple social, historical, cultural and political factors, leading to various 'interpretive commitments'. In Cover's work, the

pronouncements of judges and legislatures constitute only a particular *nomos* that cannot encompass all that is possible in terms of creation of legal meaning. In this sense, state law in its traditional definition is not considered the superior source of *jurisgenesis*. Cover's work on Talmudic traditions and other renditions of law provides examples of several religious communities inhabiting a distinct *nomos* in the context of their religious commitments. These traditions identify their own paradigms for lawful behaviour and reduce state-made law to one of the elements in their normative environment. While each *nomos* is constituted in part by state or central law, each has a different interpretation of it. Amongst this plurality of laws, Cover argues that the function of the state is *jurispathic*, or disciplinary and violence-prone, rather than engaged in norm creation. See Robert M. Cover, 'Nomos and Narrative' (1983) 97 *Harv. L. Rev.* 4.

4. The epistemological foundations of legal monism were most succinctly theorized by the Vienna School of Jurisprudence: the *Grundnorm*, the hierarchy of norms, and the unity of the law. Subsequently, the theory of legal monism was developed and defended against both dualism and pluralism in terms of its explanatory power in describing the trigonal relationship between national law, regional law and public international law. On the philosophical foundations of monism, see Luke MacInnis, 'Two Concepts of Monism: Axiomatic and Asymptotic' (2015) 77 *The Review of Politics* 603. For critiques of monism, see Roderick Macdonald, 'Metaphors of multiplicity: civil society, regimes and legal pluralism' (1998) 15 *Ariz. J. Int'l & Comp. L.* 69; Mirjam Künkler and Yüksel Sezgin, 'The unification of law and the postcolonial state: The limits of state Monism in India and Indonesia' (2016) 60 *American Behavioral Scientist* 987; Violeta Moreno-Lax and Paul Gragl, 'Introduction: Beyond Monism, Dualism, Pluralism. The Quest for a (Fully-Fledged) Theoretical Framework: Co-Implication, Embeddedness, and Interdependency between Public International Law and EU Law' (2016) 35 *Yearbook of European Law* 455.
5. See Peer Zumbansen, 'Transnational legal pluralism' (2010) 1 *Transnational Legal Theory* 141; and Emmanuel Melissaris, *Ubiquitous Law: Legal theory and the space for legal pluralism* (Routledge, 2016). Legal positivism's failure to adequately capture the complexity of contemporary legal orders makes legal pluralism all the more preferable as a descriptive theory of law. However, legal pluralism does not offer a normatively desirable view of law, unless it is supplemented by a theory of critical legal justice. On the limits of legal pluralism, see Sionaidh Douglas Scott, *Law after Modernity* (Bloomsbury Publishing, 2013).
6. See Margaret Davies, 'The Ethos of Legal Pluralism' (2005) 27 *Sydney Law Review* 317. Also see Jonathan Crowe, 'The limits of legal pluralism' (2015)

24 *Griffith Law Review* 314; and Margaret Davies, *Law Unlimited* (Routledge, 2017). This debate continues amongst legal theory scholars and remains loyal to the format that was originally defined by the Hart–Raz–Dworkin exchanges.

7. Scholars such as John Griffiths make the point of distinguishing between 'weak' and 'strong' pluralism. Weak legal pluralism indicates that differences are recognized and managed by a dominant legal system. An example for this in the area of international law would be the ironing out of inconsistencies between laws of the state and laws dictated by international bodies and covenants, a practice commonly known as harmonization. This definition, however, leaves out the importance of judiciary interpretation during and after the adaptation process. Perhaps better examples would be arbitration tribunals and alternative dispute resolution mechanisms operating within the parameters of existing national legal systems and in full regard of constitutional principles and premises. It should also be noted that the recognition of such normative/substantive differences, to the extent that they are contained and sealed within the realm of dominant law, does not constitute a threat to the doctrine of centralism. In contrast, 'strong' legal pluralism is defined as the irreducibility of differences of legal doctrines and/or applications and procedures under the rubric of a singular institutional authority such as a state or an international court. If so, two or more legal regimes coexist in tandem while a dynamic and often conflictual relationship exists between different bodies of law attending to same or similar realms. This is not simply a matter of jurisdictional reach as these conflicts may pertain to the substantive elements of the law. See John Griffiths, 'What is Legal Pluralism?' (1986) 24 *Journal of Legal Pluralism and Unofficial Law* 1. On varieties of legal pluralism without direct reference to international law, see *inter alia*, M. B. Hooker, *Legal Pluralism: An introduction to colonial and neo-colonial laws* (Clarendon Press, 1975); Sally Engle Merry, 'Legal pluralism' (1988) 22 *Law & Society Review* 869; Paul Ricoeur, 'The Plurality of Sources of Law' (1994) 7 *Ratio Juris* 272; Martha-Marie Kleinhans and Roderick MacDonald, 'What is a Critical Legal Pluralism?' (1997) 12 *Canadian Journal of Law and Society* 25; Brian Tamanaha, 'A Non-Essentialist Version of Legal Pluralism' (2000) 27 *Journal of Law & Society* 296; and Christoph Eberhard, 'Towards an Intercultural Legal Theory' (2001) 10 *Social & Legal Studies* 171.
8. See Peer Zumbansen, 'Transnational Law' in *The Encyclopedia of Comparative Law* (Edward Elgar, 2006), 738–54.
9. See Stephen Gill and A. C. Cutler, *New Constitutionalism and World Order* (Cambridge University Press, 2014).

10. The term 'two optics' as a methodological approach was originally coined by Robert Keohane. See Robert Keohane, 'International Relations and International Law: Two Optics' (1997) 38 *Harvard International Law Journal* 487.
11. See Jeffrey Dunoff, Steven Ratner and David Wippman, *International Law: Norms, Actors, Process* (Kluwer Law, 2015).
12. See Paul F. Diehl, Charlotte Ku and Daniel Zamora, 'The Dynamics of International Law: The Interaction of Normative and Operating Systems' (2003) 57 *Int'l Org.* 43. I am indebted to Craig Scott, Peer Zumbansen and Ruth Buchanan's work on Transnational Law and introducing me to this debate.
13. See Gunther Teubner, 'The Two Faces of Janus: Rethinking Legal Pluralism' (1991) 13 *Cardozo Law Review* 1443; Gunther Teubner, 'The Anonymous Matrix: Human Rights Violation by "Private" Transnational Actors' (2006) 69 *Modern Law Review* 327; Gunther Teubner, *Constitutional Fragments: Societal constitutionalism and globalization* (Oxford University Press, 2012). Also see David Trubek, Yves Dezalay, Ruth Buchanan and John R. Davis, 'Global Restructuring and the Law: Studies of the Internationalization of Legal Fields and the Creation of Transnational Arenas' (1993) 44 *Case W. Res. L. Rev.* 407; David Trubek, Jim Mosher and Jeffrey S. Rothstein, 'Transnationalism in the Regulation of Labor Relations' (2000) 25 *Law & Social Inquiry* 1187; and Andrew Lang, *World Trade Law after Neoliberalism: Reimagining the global economic order* (Oxford University Press, 2011).
14. This particular school of critique has already progressed through two historical phases: TWAIL I and TWAIL II. While TWAIL I had a heavy focus on colonization and the hegemonic use of international law by powerful nations, TWAIL II was more engaged with international institutions and the impact of globalization as well as possibilities of resistance. Current TWAIL scholarship responds to new challenges with the global rise of populism and oppressive conservative politics as well as the need to refocus on the inconsistent and untenable use of international law in order to rethink our understanding of international law in terms of global injustices. See Madhav Khosla, 'The TWAIL Discourse: The emergence of a new phase' (2007) 9 *International Community Law Review* 291, and Karin Mickelson, 'Taking stock of TWAIL histories' (2008) 10 *International Community Law Review* 355.
15. Also see Brian Z. Tamanaha, 'The folly of the "social scientific" concept of legal pluralism' (1993) 20 *Journal of Law and Society* 192.
16. There are strong connections between long-standing legal sociological insights into pluralistic legal orders and present concerns regarding the fragmentation of law outside the nation-state. Within the nation-state, legal pluralism was initiated by contestation of concepts of legal formalism, of the alleged unity of the legal order and institutionalized norms, despite the coexistence of different

levels and sites of norm creation. Contemporary calls for a just, democratic and equitable global legal order, including debates on the 'fragmentation of international law' or 'global administrative law', take place in the same spirit. On this issue, see Ruth Buchanan, 'Writing resistance into international law' (2008) 10 (4) *International Community Law Review* 445.

17. See Gunther Teubner, 'Substantive and reflexive elements in modern law' (1983) *Law and Society Review* 239.
18. See Gunther Teubner, *Law as an Autopoietic System* (Blackwell Publishers, 1993), Hugh Baxter, 'Autopoiesis and the Relative Autonomy of Law' (1997) 19 *Cardozo L. Rev.* 1987, and Jennifer Nedelsky, *Law's Relations: A relational theory of self, autonomy, and law* (Oxford University Press USA, 2011).
19. I define neocolonialism as colonialism stripped of its formal qualities, nonetheless producing the same set of effects, such as structural dependence, depletion of resources including human capital, and the subsuming of societies under the rubric of detrimental international class alliances.
20. Also see Franz von Benda-Beckmann, 'Who's afraid of legal pluralism?' (2002) 34 *Journal of Legal Pluralism and Unofficial Law* 37.
21. Philip Jessup, *Transnational Law* (Yale University Press, 1956). As Peer Zumbansen argues, the development of the concept of transnational law could be traced back to Philip Jessup's Storrs Lectures at the Yale Law School in 1955. Jessup famously challenged the doctrinal and conceptual boundaries of both public and private international law and suggested another concept better suited to capture the myriad normative and transactional relations across national borders. Transnational law has since become a promising perspective to assess particularly the regulatory challenges arising in late capitalism. See Peer Zumbansen, 'Law after the welfare state: Formalism, functionalism, and the ironic turn of reflexive law' (2008) 56 *American Journal of Comparative Law* 769.
22. Jessup (1956), pp. 72–7, cited in Zumbansen (2008).
23. See Andreas Fischer-Lescano and Gunther Teubner, 'Regime-Collisions: The Vain Search for Legal Unity in the Fragmentation of Global Law' (2004) 25 *Mich. J. Int'l L.* 999.
24. See Peer Zumbansen, 'Defining the space of transnational law: legal theory, global governance, and legal pluralism' (2012) 21 *Transnat'l L. & Contemp. Probs.* 305.
25. See Paul Schiff Berman, 'From international law to law and globalization' (2004) 43 *Colum. J. Transnat'l L.* 485 and 'A pluralist approach to international law' (2007) 32 *Yale J. Int'l L.* 301.
26. The former debate is best represented by Anne-Marie Slaughter's work. The latter viewpoint, on the other hand, is vividly discussed by Mary Kaldor,

Antony Anghie, James Tully and Robert Wai. See Anne-Marie Slaughter, 'International Law in a World of Liberal States' (1995) 6 *European Journal of International Law* 1, and her 'Judicial Globalization' (2000) 40 *Virginia Journal of International Law* 1103; James Tully, *Strange Multiplicity: Constitutionalism in an age of diversity* (Cambridge University Press, 1995); Robert Wai, 'In the Name of the International: The Supreme Court of Canada and the Internationalist Transformation of Canadian Private International Law' (2001) 39 *Canadian Yearbook of International Law* 117; Mary Kaldor, 'Civil society and accountability' (2003) 4 *Journal of Human Development* 5 and her *Global Civil Society: An Answer to War* (John Wiley & Sons, 2003); Antony Anghie et al., *The Third World and International Order: Law, Politics, and Globalization* (Martinus Nijhoff, 2003); Antony Anghie, *Imperialism, Sovereignty and the Making of International Law* (Cambridge University Press, 2007).

27. See Gunther Teubner, 'Global Bukowina: legal pluralism in the world society' in Gunther Teubner (ed.), *Global Law without a State* (Dartmouth Publishing, 1997) and Boaventura de Sousa Santos and César A. Rodríguez-Garavito (eds), *Law and Globalization from Below: Towards a Cosmopolitan Legality* (Cambridge University Press, 2005).
28. See Myres S. McDougal, Harold D. Lasswell and W. Michael Reisman, 'Theories about international law: prologue to a configurative jurisprudence' (1967) 8 *Va. J. Int'l L.* 188; Myres S. McDougal, Harold D. Lasswell and W. Michael Reisman, 'The World Constitutive Process of Authoritative Decision' (1967) 19 *Journal of Legal Education* 403; Myres S. McDougal and W. Michael Reisman, 'The Prescribing Function in World Constitutive Process: How International Law is Made' (1980) 6 *Yale Studies of World Public Order* 249.
29. See Lassa Francis Lawrence Oppenheim and Hersch Lauterpacht, *International Law: A Treatise* (Longmans Green, 1952) for classical legal positivist scholarship, and Hans Morgenthau, *Politics among Nations* (Alfred Kopf, 1948) for a classical realist viewpoint in the immediate aftermath of the Second World War.
30. See Janet Koven Levit, 'Bottom-Up International Lawmaking: Reflections on the New Haven School of International Law' (2007) 32 *Yale J. Int'l L.* 393.
31. See Jack L. Goldsmith and Eric A. Posner, *The Limits of International Law* (Oxford University Press, 2005).
32. See Immanuel Wallerstein, *The modern world-system I: Capitalist agriculture and the origins of the European world-economy in the sixteenth century, with a new prologue* (University of California Press, 2011).
33. See *inter alia*, Anghie, Antony, et al., *The Third World and International Order* (2003); Obiora Chinedu Okafor, 'Newness, imperialism, and international

legal reform in our time: a TWAIL perspective' (2005) 43 *Osgoode Hall LJ* 171; Obiora Chinedu Okafor, 'Critical Third World Approaches to International Law (TWAIL): Theory, Methodology, or Both?' (2008) 10 *Int'l Comm. L. Rev.* 371; Antony Anghie, 'TWAIL: Past and Future' (2008) 10 *Int'l Comm. L. Rev.* 479; Opeoluwa Adetoro Badaru, 'Examining the Utility of Third World Approaches to International Law for International Human Rights Law' (2008) 10 *Int'l Comm. L. Rev.* 379; Ibironke Odumosu, 'Challenges for the (Present/) Future of Third World Approaches to International Law' (2008) 10 *Int'l Comm. L. Rev.* 467; B. S. Chimni, 'The world of TWAIL: Introduction to the special issue' (2011); James Thuo Gathii, 'TWAIL: A brief history of its origins, its decentralized network, and a tentative bibliography' (2011) 3 *Trade L. & Dev.* 26; Luis Eslava and Sundhya Pahuja, 'Between resistance and reform: TWAIL and the universality of international law' (2011) 3 *Trade L. & Dev.* 103.

34. Makau W. Mutua 'What is TWAIL?' (2000) 94 *Proceedings of the Annual Meeting (American Society of International Law)* 31 and Makau W. Mutua, 'Savages, Victims, and Saviors: The Metaphor of Human Rights' (2001) 42 *Harvard International Law Journal* 201.
35. Anthony Carty, *Philosophy of International Law* (Edinburgh University Press, 2007).
36. Seth Gordon, 'Indigenous Rights in Modern International Law from a Critical Third World Perspective' (2007) 31 *Am. Ind. L. R.* 401.
37. Also see Balakrishnan Rajagopal, 'From Resistance to Renewal: The Third World, Social Movements, and the Expansion of International Institutions' (2000) 41 *Harv. Int'l L. J.* 529; Balakrishnan Rajagopal, *International Law from Below: Development, Social Movements and Third World Resistance* (Cambridge University Press, 2003); Balakrishnan Rajagopal, 'Counter-hegemonic international law: rethinking human rights and development as a Third World strategy' (2006) 27 *Third World Quarterly* 767.
38. See Issa Shivji, 'Constructing a New Rights Regime: Promises, Problems and Prospects' (1999) 8 *Soc. & Legal Studies* 243. Also see Samir Amin, *Capitalism in the Age of Globalization: The Management of Contemporary Society* (ZED Books, 2014).
39. See Obiora Chinedu Okafor, 'Is There a Legitimacy Deficit in International Legal Scholarship and Practice?' (1997) 13 *International Insights* 91.
40. See Gunther Teubner, 'The King's Many Bodies: The Self-Deconstruction of Law's Hierarchy' (1997) 31 *Law & Soc. R.* 76. Teubner envisages that a better understanding of global law needs different conceptions of the 'boundaries', 'sources', 'independence' and 'unity' of law in legal scholarship. Also see his 'Societal Constitutionalism: Alternatives to State-Centered Constitutional

Theory?' in Joerges, Sand and Teubner (eds), *Transnational Governance and Constitutionalism* (Hart, 2004).

41. See Steve Ratner, 'Corporations and Human Rights: A Theory of Legal Responsibility' (2001) 111 *Yale L. J.* 443; Michael Mandel, *How America Gets Away with Murder: Illegal Wars, Collateral Damage and Crimes Against Humanity* (Pluto Press, 2004); Tony Evans, 'International Human Rights Law as Power/Knowledge' (2005) 27 *Human Rights Quarterly* 1046.
42. Martti Koskenniemi, 'The Fate of Public International Law: Between Technique And Politics' (2007) 70 *Mod. L. R.* 1.
43. See Ruth Buchanan, 'Reconceptualizing Law and Politics in the Transnational: Constitutional and Legal Pluralist Approaches' (2008) 4 *Comparative Research in Law and Political Economy*; and Ruth Buchanan, 'Legitimating Global Trade Governance: Constitutional and Legal Pluralist Approaches' (2006) 57 *Northern Ireland Legal Quarterly* 1.
44. See David Trubek and Louise G. Trubek, 'Hard and Soft Law in the Construction of Social Europe: The Role of the Open Method of Co-ordination' (2005) 11 *European Law Journal* 343.
45. See Ruth Buchanan and Louise G. Trubek, 'Resistances and possibilities: A critical and practical look at public interest lawyering' (1992) 19 *New York University Review of Law and Social Change* 687; Ruth Buchanan and S. Pahuja, 'Legal Imperialism: Empire's Invisible Hand' in *Empire's New Clothes* (Routledge, 2004), pp. 73–95.
46. See Karel Wellens, 'Fragmentation of International Law and Establishing an Accountability Regime for International Organizations: The Role of the Judiciary in Closing the Gap' (2003) 25 *Mich. J. .Int'l L.* 1160; and his 'Diversity in secondary rules and the unity of international law: some reflections on current trends' (1994) 25 *Netherlands Yearbook of International Law* 3.
47. See Dinah Shelton, 'International law and "relative normativity"' (2006) 2 *International Law* 159; and René Provost (ed.), *State Responsibility in International Law* (Routledge, 2017).
48. The 'fragmentation' of international law has been a topic of discussion for the last three decades. Specifically, the increase in the number of international organizations, multilateral conventions and bilateral investment treaties, as well as the growth of international courts and tribunals, has led to concerns about the coherence and unity of international law. At issue was the destabilization of a totalizing international legal order and the emergence of competing and overlapping regimes. On this issue, see Jonathan Charney, 'The impact on the international legal system of the growth of international courts and tribunals' (1998) 31 *NYU J. Int'l L. & Pol.* 697; Pemmaraju Sreenivasa Rao, 'Multiple International Judicial Forums: A Reflection of the Growing

Strength of International Law or Its Fragmentation' (2003) 25 *Mich. J. Int'l L.* 929; William Burke-White, 'International Legal Pluralism' (2003) 25 *Mich. J. Int'l L.* 963; and Geert-Jan Knoops, *An Introduction to the Law of International Criminal Tribunals: A Comparative Study* (Martinus Nijhoff Publishers, 2014).

49. See Charles De Visscher, *Theory and Reality in Public International Law* (Princeton University Press, 2015); and Jean d'Aspremont, *Epistemic Forces in International Law* (Edward Elgar Publishing, 2015).
50. See Nicole Deitelhoff, 'The Discursive Process of Legalization: Charting Islands of Persuasion in the ICC Case' (2009) 63 *International Organization* 33.
51. On the history of the ICC in terms of activist politics, see Meghan Zacher, Hollie Nyseth Brehm and Joachim J. Savelsberg, 'NGOs, IOs, and the ICC: Diagnosing and Framing Darfur' (2014) 29 *Sociological Forum* 1; Todd Jonathan Ebling, 'History, Violence, and Legitimacy in Uganda: An Anthropological Analysis of Post-Colonial Politics and ICC Intervention' (2015) 7 *Journal of Collegiate Anthropology* 20; and also William Schabas, *The International Criminal Court: A Commentary on the Rome Statute* (Oxford University Press, 2017).
52. Statement by Luis Moreno-Ocampo, June 16, 2003, Ceremony for the Solemn Undertaking of the Chief Prosecutor, quoted in ICC Office of the Prosecutor, Informal Expert Paper (2003), cited in Kevin Jon Heller, 'The Shadow Side of Complementarity: The Effect of Article 17 of the Rome Statute on National Due Process' (2006) 17 *Criminal Law Forum* 255.
53. Article 1 of the Rome Statute provides that the ICC's jurisdiction 'shall be complementary to national criminal jurisdictions'. Article 17(1), in turn, specifies the four situations in which the Court must defer to a national proceeding, including exceptions: (a) the case must be investigated or prosecuted by a State which has jurisdiction over it, unless the State is unwilling or unable genuinely to carry out the investigation or prosecution; (b) the case has been investigated by a State which has jurisdiction over it and the State has decided not to prosecute the person concerned, unless the decision resulted from the unwillingness or inability of the State genuinely to prosecute; (c) the person concerned has already been tried for conduct which is the subject of the complaint, and a trial by the Court is not permitted under Article 20, paragraph 3; (d) the case is not of sufficient gravity to justify further action by the Court. (Citation from Statute of the International Criminal Court, UN Doc. A/CONF.183/9 (1998), art. 1 and art. 17.)
54. In principle, the ICC guarantees defendants all the procedural protections required by the International Covenant on Civil and Political Rights (ICCPR). It cannot, however, impose these principles upon national courts

whereby alleged perpetrators are to be tried. See Mark S. Ellis, 'The international criminal court and its implication for domestic law and national capacity building' (2002) 15 *Fla. J. Int'l L.* 215; Jann Kleffner, 'The impact of complementarity on national implementation of substantive international criminal law' (2003) 1 *Journal of International Criminal Justice* 86; Dwight Newman, 'The Rome Statute, Some Reservations Concerning Amnesties, and a Distributive Problem' (2004) 20 *Am. U. Int'l L. Rev.* 293; Carsten Stahn, 'Complementarity, amnesties and alternative forms of justice: some interpretative guidelines for the International Criminal Court' (2005) 3 *Journal of International Criminal Justice* 695; Simeon Sungi, 'Is it pragmatism or an injustice to victims? The use of plea bargaining in the International Criminal Court' (2015) 7 *Journal of Theoretical & Philosophical Criminology* 21; and Yitiha Simbeye, *Immunity and International Criminal Law* (Routledge, 2017).

55. See Marta Bo, 'The Situation in Libya and the ICC's Understanding of Complementarity in the Context of UNSC-Referred Cases' (2014) 25 *Criminal Law Forum* No. 3–4; Minhas Majeed Khan and Abbas Majeed Khan Marwat, 'International Criminal Court (ICC): An Analysis of Its Successes and Failures and Challenges Faced by the ICC Tribunals for War Crimes' (2016) 11 *Dialogue* 243.
56. On the Pinochet trial, see Cath Collins, Katherine Hite and Alfredo Joignant (eds), *The Politics of Memory in Chile: From Pinochet to Bachelet* (Lynne Rienner Publishers, 2013); and Daniela Accatino and Cath Collins, 'Truth, Evidence, Truth: The Deployment of Testimony, Archives and Technical Data in Domestic Human Rights Trials' (2016) 8 *Journal of Human Rights Practice* 81.
57. On the trajectory of developments linking the Nuremberg and Tokyo trials to the emergence of the ICC, see, *inter alia*, Steven Fogelson, 'The Nuremberg Legacy: An Unfulfilled Promise' (1989) 63 *S. Cal. L. Rev.* 833; Robert Wolfe, 'Flaws in the Nuremberg Legacy: An Impediment to International War Crimes Tribunals' Prosecution of Crimes Against Humanity' (1998) 12 *Holocaust and Genocide Studies* 434; Steven Ratner, Jason S. Abrams and James L. Bischoff, *Accountability for Human Rights Atrocities in International Law: Beyond the Nuremberg Legacy*, 3rd edn (Oxford University Press, 2009); Hans-Peter Kaul, 'The Nuremberg Legacy and the International Criminal Court – Lecture in Honor of Whitney R. Harris, Former Nuremberg Prosecutor' (2013) 12 *Wash. U. Global Stud. L. Rev.* 637; Benjamin Ferencz, 'A Nuremberg Legacy: The Crime of Aggression' (2016) 15 *Wash. U. Global Stud. L. Rev.* 555.
58. For details of this process, see Antonio Cassese and Paola Gaeta, *Cassese's International Criminal Law* (Oxford University Press, 2013).
59. The *Corpus Juris Civilis* was the formal compilation of Roman law commissioned by the sixth-century Roman emperor Justinian. Alongside scripture

and Greek philosophy, it ranks as one of the major classical texts studied or cited by medieval and modern political theorists including Thomas Aquinas, Marsilius, Bodin, Grotius, Hobbes, Montesquieu, Rousseau, Kant, Hegel, Tocqueville and Weber. See Neil MacCormick, Robert S. Summers and Arthur L. Goodhart (eds), *Interpreting Precedents: A Comparative Study* (Routledge, 2016).

60. See Alexis Galán and Dennis Patterson, 'The limits of normative legal pluralism: Review of Paul Schiff Berman, *Global Legal Pluralism: A Jurisprudence of Law beyond Borders*' (2013) 11 *International Journal of Constitutional Law* 783.
61. For a counter-argument, see Pablo Holmes, 'The politics of law and the laws of politics: The political paradoxes of transnational constitutionalism' (2014) 21/2 *Indiana Journal of Global Legal Studies* 553. Holmes subscribes to the view that transnational constitutionalism could be achieved in a fragmented manner and through local politicization of core principles of justice. On this issue, also see Turkuler Isiksel, 'Global legal pluralism as fact and norm' (2013) 2 *Global Constitutionalism* 160.
62. As a former graduate student of Immanuel Wallerstein and Giovanni Arrighi and a research fellow of Fernand Braudel Center, I am indebted to the vision of historical capitalism they developed back in the 1980s. In particular, I am very much at home with the late Arrighi's take on global class formations, both in economical and in legal-political terms. See Giovanni Arrighi, *The Long Twentieth Century: Money, Power and the Origins of our Times* (Verso, 1994); Giovanni Arrighi, 'Lineages of empire' (2002) 10 *Historical Materialism* 3; Giovanni Arrighi, 'Hegemony unravelling-2' (2005) 33 *New Left Review* 83; and Giovanni Arrighi, 'Spatial fixes, switching crises, and accumulation by dispossession' (2006) *Global social change: Historical and comparative perspectives* 201.
63. See Nancy Fraser, *Scales of Justice: Reimagining Political Space in a Globalizing World* (Columbia University Press, 2009).

Chapter 2

1. See the classic work of Ian McTaggart Sinclair, *The Vienna Convention on the Law of Treaties*, 2nd edn (Manchester University Press, 1984). Also see Mark Eugen Villiger, *Customary international law and treaties: a study of their interactions and interrelations, with special consideration of the 1969 Vienna Convention on the Law of Treaties*, vol. 7 (Brill Publishers, 1985).
2. See Gerry Simpson, *Law, War and Crime: War crimes, trials and the reinvention of international law* (Polity, 2007).
3. For the actual text of the Charter, see *http://avalon.law.yale.edu/imt/imtconst.asp* (accessed 25 May 2020).

4. See Kal Raustiala and Anne-Marie Slaughter, 'International law, international relations and compliance' in W. Carlsnaes, T. Risse and B. Simmons (eds), *Handbook of International Relations* (Sage, 2002).
5. This Latin phrase, literally meaning 'no one assails me with impunity', was the motto of the Royal Stuart Dynasty of Scotland from the reign of James VI onwards (1578–80). See Noreen Burrows, 'Nemo Me Impune Lacessit: The Scottish Right of Access to the European Courts' (2002) 8 *Eur. Pub. L.* 45.
6. There are two main approaches to universal jurisdiction. The first one seeks to apply the procedures of domestic criminal justice to violations befitting international criminal law standards. This is done with reference to legal codes embodied in United Nations conventions, or via authorization by national prosecutors to bring offenders into their jurisdiction through extradition from third countries. The second approach is endorsed by the ICC and is in accordance with its founding treaty of Rome Statute. The closest analogous historical concept to the contemporary notion of universal jurisdiction is *hostes humani generis* (enemies of the human race). However, this particular term has only been applied to pirates, hijackers and outlaws whose crimes were typically committed outside the territory of any state. A state engaged in adjudicating crimes based on universal jurisdiction backs its claim on the grounds that the crime committed is considered an international crime. The best example of this to date was Belgium's 1993 law of universal jurisdiction, though it was amended to reduce its scope in 2003. The creation of the ICC did *not* reduce the need to create further legislation in this area, since the Court is not entitled to judge crimes committed before 2002. For further debate on the intricacies of the concept of universal jurisdiction, see Anne-Marie Slaughter and William Burke-White, 'An international constitutional moment' (2002) 43 *Harv. Int'l L. J.* 1; William Burke-White, 'A community of courts: toward a system of international criminal law enforcement' (2002) 24 *Mich. J. Int'l L.* 1; William Burke-White, 'International legal pluralism' (2003) 25 *Mich. J. Int'l L.* 963; William Burke-White, 'Regionalization of International Criminal Law Enforcement: A Preliminary Exploration' (2003) 38 *Tex. Int'l L. J.* 729; David Wallach, 'The Irrationality of Universal Civil Jurisdiction' (2014) 46 *Geo. J. Int'l L.* 803; Abhimanyu George Jain, 'Universal civil jurisdiction in international law' (2015) 55 *Indian Journal of International Law* 209; Aisling O'Sullivan, *Universal Jurisdiction in International Criminal Law: The Debate and the Battle for Hegemony* (Routledge, 2017); and Erik Voeten, 'Competition and Complementarity between Global and Regional Human Rights Institutions' (2017) 8 *Global Policy* 119.
7. Recent examples of universal jurisdiction cases include: the prosecution and conviction of Nikola Jorgic, a former leader of a paramilitary Serb group,

and Novislav Djajic, a Serbian soldier, by German courts for acts of genocide committed in Bosnia and Herzegovina (1997); the extradition request by a Spanish Court seeking to try former Chilean President Augusto Pinochet for crimes such as torture, murder, illegal detention and forced disappearance (1998); the prosecution and conviction of two Rwandan nuns, Sister Maria Kisito and Sister Gertrude, by a domestic court in Belgium for war crimes committed during the 1994 Rwandan genocide (2001); and the investigation and indictment of the former president of Chad, Hissène Habré, by a Belgian court for crimes against humanity, torture, war crimes and other human rights violations committed during his presidency in Chad (2005).

8. See Yves Beigbeder, *International Justice against Impunity: Progress and new challenges* (Martinus Nijhoff Publishers, 2005); and Bill Bowring, *The Degradation of the International Legal Order?: The rehabilitation of law and the possibility of politics* (Routledge, 2008).
9. See Robert Walkinshaw, 'The Nuremberg and Tokyo trials: another step toward international justice' (1949) 35 *American Bar Association Journal* 299.
10. See Mara Bustelo, *Whose New World Order: What role for the United Nations?* (Wm Gaunt & Sons, 1991); Maz Singer and Aaron B. Wildavsky, *The Real World Order: Zones of peace, zones of turmoil* (Chatham House Pub., 1996); Stephen Gill, *Power and Resistance in the New World Order: Fully Revised and Updated* (Springer, 2008); and Anne-Marie Slaughter, *A New World Order* (Princeton University Press, 2009).
11. On critiques of ICC, see Shadrack Gutto, 'Created and Limited by Politics: A view of the ICC from Africa' (2003) 12 *African Security Studies* 127; Emmanuel Saffa Abdulai, 'The Standoff between ICC and African Leaders Debate Revisited' in The Foundation for Law, Justice and Society (ed.), *Oxford Transitional Justice Research: Debating International Justice in Africa* (2010); Wendy Laverick, *Global Injustice and Crime Control* (Routledge, 2016).
12. See Mark Rupert, *Ideologies of Globalization: Contending visions of a new world order* (Routledge, 2012). According to Rupert, the impoverishment of mainstream International Relations (IR) scholarship, especially in the bastions of academic power and respectability in the Global North, led to a conceptual blindness to mutually constitutive relations of governance/resistance at work in the production of global politics. Critical scholars of world politics have developed conceptual vocabularies with which to reconstruct aspects of these governance/resistance relations albeit with limited influence. For Stephen Gill, for instance, Marxist theory in its Gramscian version provides critical leverage for understanding the structures and dynamics of late capitalism, its relationship to the modern state, and class-based power dynamics. See Stephen Gill

and David Law, 'Global hegemony and the structural power of capital' (1993) 26 *Cambridge Studies in International Relations* 93.

13. See Ibrahim Gassama's work, including Ibrahim Gassama, 'Dealing with the world as it is: Reimagining collective international responsibility' (2013) 12 *Wash. U. Global Stud. L. Rev.* 695; Ibrahim Gassama, 'The Incoherence and Functional Incompetence of International Law: Toward a New Paradigm of Human Relationship' (2013) 37 *Fordham Int'l L. J.* 53; and also Thane Rosenbaum, 'Essay: the romance of Nuremberg and the tease of moral justice' (2005) 27 *Cardozo L. Rev.* 1731.
14. See Andreas Fischer-Lescano and Gunther Teubner, 'Regime-Collisions: The Vain Search for Legal Unity in the Fragmentation of Global Law' (2003) 25 *Mich. J. Int'l L.* 999. Also see Gerhard Hafner, 'Pros and Cons Ensuing from Fragmentation of International Law' (2003) 25 *Mich. J. Int'l L.* 849 in the same canonical issue.
15. See Collin Murray and Aoife O'Donoghue, 'A path already travelled in domestic orders? From fragmentation to constitutionalisation in the global legal order' (2017) *International Journal of Law in Context* 1. Murray and O'Donoghue argue that proliferation of international legal bodies enhances the trend towards constitutionalization.
16. For a counter-argument, see Christian Leathley, 'An institutional hierarchy to combat the fragmentation of international law: Has the ILC missed an opportunity?' (2007) 40 *NYU J. Int'l L. & Pol.* 259.
17. For a political economy-based understanding of fragmentation, see Eyal Benvenisti and George W. Downs, 'The empire's new clothes: political economy and the fragmentation of international law' (2007) 60 *Stanford Law Review* 595. Also see Eyal Benvenisti, 'Reclaiming democracy: the strategic uses of foreign and international law by national courts' (2008) 102 *American Journal of International Law* 241. Benvenisti's work is exemplary for her willingness to critique, as well as to usurp international law for causes of social justice, locally and globally.
18. In its related genocide judgment, the International Court of Justice addressed the question of whether the acts of genocide carried out at Srebrenica by Bosnian Serb armed forces must be attributed to the Federal Republic of Yugoslavia (FRY), as claimed by Bosnia. It applied the 'effective control' test set out in Nicaragua, thus reaching a negative conclusion. The Court also held that the broader 'overall control' test enunciated by the International Criminal Court for the former Yugoslavia (ICTY) in Tadić did not apply, on grounds of inefficient basis for claiming state responsibility. ICTY had to establish in Tadić whether the armed conflict in Bosnia was internal or international. However, as no rules of international humanitarian law were of assistance in

this case, the Tribunal had to rely on international rules on state responsibility. The ICTY thus advanced the 'overall control' test as a criterion valid for imputation of conduct of organized armed groups. For a detailed analysis of these two conflicting interpretations of the Tadić case, see Antonio Cassese, 'The Nicaragua and Tadić tests revisited in light of the ICJ judgment on genocide in Bosnia' (2007) 18 *European Journal of International Law* 649, and Davis Tyner, 'Internationalization of War Crimes Prosecutions: Correcting the International Criminal Tribunal for the Former Yugoslavia's Folly in Tadic' (2006) 18 *Fla. J. Int'l L.* 843.

19. See Martti Koskenniemi and Päivi Leino, 'Fragmentation of international law? Postmodern anxieties' (2002) 15 *Leiden Journal of International Law* 553. As Koskenniemi and Leino argue, successive International Court of Justice presidents have expressed concern about the proliferation of international tribunals and substantive fragmentation of international law. I fully agree with the authors that jurisdictional conflicts indeed reflect divergent political priorities, and that they cannot be done away with administrative coordination.
20. On this issue, see Robert Cryer, *Prosecuting International Crimes: Selectivity and the International Criminal Law Regime* (Cambridge University Press, 2005). Also see Robert Cryer, et al., *An Introduction to International Criminal Law and Procedure* (Cambridge University Press, 2014). In addition, the amicus brief prepared by him and three other legal scholars and submitted before the Extraordinary Chambers in the Courts of Cambodia is a key document on the issue of whether large-scale atrocities directed against members of a state or organization's own armed forces can constitute crimes against humanity: Darryl Robinson et al., 'Amicus Brief of Professors Robinson, De Guzman, Jalloh and Cryer on Crimes Against Humanity (Cases 003 and 004)' (2016). Cryer's work stands out in the canon of international criminal law texts, *inter alia*, Fabian Raimondo, *General Principles of Law in the Decisions of International Criminal Courts and Tribunals* (Brill, 2008); Ciara Damgaard, *Individual Criminal Responsibility for Core International Crimes: Selected Pertinent Issues* (Springer, 2008); Birgit Schlütte, *Theory and Practice of the ICJ and the International ad hoc Tribunals for Rwanda and Yugloslavia* (Martinus Nijhoff, 2010); and M. Cherif Bassiouni, *Crimes against Humanity: Historical Evolution and Contemporary Application* (Cambridge University Press, 2011).
21. See John Reynolds and Sujith Xavier, '"The Dark Corners of the World" TWAIL and International Criminal Justice' (2016) 14 *Journal of International Criminal Justice* 959.
22. See Sujith Xavier, 'False Universalism of Global Governance Theories: Global Constitutionalism, Global Administrative Law, International Criminal

Institutions & the Global South' (dissertation, Osgoode Hall Law School Toronto, Ontario, 2015).

23. The controversies arising from International Criminal Court interventions in Africa are a case in point. The deployment of the powers to refer and defer ICC cases central to Article 16 of the Rome Statute and the manner in which the UN Security Council has employed this power has led critics to conclude that geopolitics has severely undermined the judicial independence of the ICC. It is also argued that the drafting history of Article 16 of the Rome Statute reveals the political origins of international law and the manner in which historical inequalities were woven into the very fabric of it. If so, contemporary ontologies of international criminal law cannot escape the politics of its making. On the issue of rethinking and reworking of how complementarity and cooperation might work more effectively for the future of international criminal law, despite its history, see Kamari Maxine Clarke and Sarah-Jane Koulen, 'The Legal Politics of the Article 16 Decision: The International Criminal Court, the UN Security Council and Ontologies of a Contemporary Compromise' (2014) 7 *African Journal of Legal Studies* 297.
24. See Miriam Gur-Arye and Alon Harel, 'Taking Internationalism Seriously: Why International Criminal Law Matters' in Jens David Ohlin (ed.), *Oxford Handbook of International Criminal Law*, Hebrew University of Jerusalem Legal Research Paper No. 16-21 (2017).
25. See the classic text, Benedict Anderson, *Imagined Communities: Reflections on the origin and spread of nationalism* (Verso Books, 2006).
26. See Elies van Sliedregt and Sergey Vasiliev (eds), *Pluralism in International Criminal Law* (Oxford University Press, 2014).
27. Citation from Makau Mutua and Antony Anghie, 'What Is TWAIL?' (2000) 94 in *Proceedings of the Annual Meeting (American Society of International Law)* 31.
28. Thuo James Gathii, 'Alternative and Critical: The Contribution of Research and Scholarship on Developing Countries to International Legal Theory' (2000) 41 *Harv. Int'l L. J.* 263.
29. The keynote address of the symposium was delivered by the former Vice-President of the International Court of Justice, Christopher G. Weeramantry, who is widely respected for his historical perspective when addressing international law. Also see Christopher Gregory Weeramantry, *Universalising International Law*, vol. 48 (Martinus Nijhoff Publishers, 2014).
30. See Obiora Chinedu Okafor, 'After martyrdom: international law, sub-state groups, and the construction of legitimate statehood in Africa' (2000) 41 *Harv. Int'l L. J.* 503. Also see Obiora Chinedu Okafor, 'Newness, imperialism, and international legal reform in our time: a TWAIL perspective' (2005)

43 *Osgoode Hall L. J.* 171; Obiora Chinedu Okafor, 'Critical Third World approaches to international law (TWAIL): theory, methodology, or both?' (2008) 10 *International Community Law Review* 371. Okafor's later work rendered TWAIL scholarship a widely acceptable alternative to mainstream methodologies in international law. He directly engages with the question of whether TWAIL is a theory, a methodology, or both, and who has the right to define and determine the meaning of these terms other than the legal positivist school of thought. Accordingly, TWAIL offers both theories of, and methodologies for, analysing international law and institutions as a broad and historically conscious approach.

31. See Balakrishnan Rajagopal, 'From Resistance to Renewal: The Third World, Social Movements, and the Expansion of International Institutions' (2000) 41 *Harv. Int'l. L. J.* 529, as well as Balakrishnan Rajagopal, *International Law from Below: Development, social movements and third world resistance* (Cambridge University Press, 2003) and Balakrishnan Rajagopal, 'Counter-hegemonic international law: rethinking human rights and development as a Third World strategy' (2006) 27 *Third World Quarterly* 767.
32. See Mark Toufayan, 'When British Justice (in African Colonies) Points Two Ways: On Dualism, Hybridity, and the Genealogy of Juridical Negritude in Taslim Olawale Elias' in *African Legal Theory and Contemporary Problems* (Springer Netherlands, 2014), pp. 31–70.
33. See Anna Krueger, 'Conference Report: The Battle for International Law in the Decolonization Era' (2016) 49 *VRÜ Verfassung und Recht in Übersee* 80.
34. Also see D. Kennedy, 'The disciplines of international law and policy' (1999) 12/1 *Leiden Journal of International Law* 9–133; D. P. Fidler, 'Revolt Against or From Within the West? TWAIL, the Developing World, and the Future Direction of International Law' (2003) 2 *Chinese J. Int'l L.* 29; and J. Ngugi, 'Making new wine for old wineskins: can the reform of international law emancipate the Third World in the age of globalization' (2002) 8 *UC Davis J. Int'l L. & Pol'y* 73.
35. On the issue of how to salvage legal positivism, and how the effort fails, see Martti Koskenniemi, *The Gentle Civilizer of Nations: The rise and fall of international law 1870–1960*, vol. 14 (Cambridge University Press, 2001); Gerry Simpson, *Great Powers and Outlaw States: Unequal sovereigns in the international legal order*, vol. 32 (Cambridge University Press, 2004); Martti Koskenniemi, *From Apology to Utopia: The structure of international legal argument* (Cambridge University Press, 2006); Antony Anghie, *Imperialism, Sovereignty and the Making of International Law*, vol. 37 (Cambridge University Press, 2007). Back in 2004, B. S. Chimni argued that a growing network of international institutions constitutes a nascent global state in order to realize

the interests of an emerging transnational capitalist class, to the disadvantage of subaltern classes in the third and first worlds. Underpinning this emerging imperial global order, Chimni saw a web of sub-national authorities that represent, along with non-governmental organizations, its decentralized face and thus produce a false impression of an incomplete project. He contended that these developments seriously undermine substantive democracy at both inter-state and intra-state levels. Accordingly, it is not the form, but the content, that really matters. See Bhupinder S. Chimni, 'International institutions today: an imperial global state in the making' (2004) 15 *European Journal of International Law* 1.

36. Karin Mickelson, 'Rhetoric and Rage: Third World voices in International Legal discourse' (1998) 16/2 *Wisconsin International Law Journal* 353.
37. See Hugh Kindred et al., *International law, chiefly as interpreted and applied in Canada* (Emond Montgomery Publications, 2014); Gregory Shaffer, 'The New Empirical Turn in International Law Scholarship' (2014) 108 *Am. Soc'y Int'l L. Proc.* 369; Yannick Radi, 'In Defence of "Generalism" in International Legal Scholarship and Practice' (2014) 27 *Leiden Journal of International Law* 303; Sergey Vasiliev, 'On Trajectories and Destinations of International Criminal Law Scholarship' (2015) 28 *Leiden Journal of International Law* 701.
38. On the issue of IR scholarship on international law, see Karin Fierke and Knud Erik Jorgense, *Constructing International Relations: The next generation* (Routledge, 2015); and Ken Booth and Toni Erskine (eds), *International Relations Theory Today* (John Wiley & Sons, 2016).
39. On the resilience of the Westphalian state, see David Koller, 'The End of Geography: The Changing Nature of the International System and the Challenge to International Law: A Reply to Daniel Bethlehem' (2014) 25 *European Journal of International Law* 25; and Carl Landauer, 'The Ever-Ending Geography of International Law: The Changing Nature of the International System and the Challenge to International Law: A Reply to Daniel Bethlehem' (2014) 25 *European Journal of International Law* 31–4. For a counter-argument, see Andrea Bianchi (ed.), *Non-State Actors and International Law* (Routledge, 2017), and Claus Kreß, 'Major Post-Westphalian Shifts and Some Important Neo-Westphalian Hesitations in the State Practice on the International Law on the Use of Force' (2014) 1/1 *Journal of the Use of Force and International Law* 11–54.
40. See Antony Anghie, 'International Law and the Pre-History of Globalisation' (2015) 33 *Sing. L. Rev.* 3. Anghie posits that although imperialism has been crucial to the development of international law, the emphasis of the debate on international law gradually shifted elsewhere. As a result, 'colonial questions' have been reduced to political issues that didn't implicate the great theoretical

concerns of the time. See Antony Anghie, 'Imperialism and International Legal Theory' in A. Orford and F. Hoffmann (eds), *The Oxford Handbook of the Theory of International Law* (Oxford University Press, 2015).

41. The work of world-systems theorists on the history of the modern state system is of special import here. In particular, see Immanuel Wallerstein, *Modern World-System in the Longue Durée* (Routledge, 2015).
42. See the work of Anthony Smith, *Nations and Nationalism in a Global Era* (John Wiley & Sons, 2013); and Anthony Smith, *Nationalism and Modernism* (Routledge, 2013).
43. See Pheng Cheah and Jonathan Culler, *Grounds of Comparison: Around the work of Benedict Anderson* (Routledge, 2013).
44. See Eric Hobsbawm, *The Age of Extremes: A history of the world, 1914–1991* (Pantheon Books, 1995); Eric Hobsbawm, *Age of Capital: 1848–1875* (Hachette UK, 2010); and Eric Hobsbawm, *Nations and Nationalism since 1780: Programme, myth, reality* (Cambridge University Press, 2012). Also see John Breuilly, *Nationalism and the State* (Manchester University Press, 1993); Liah Greenfeld, *Nationalism: Five roads to modernity* (Harvard University Press, 1993); Michael Billig, *Banal Nationalism* (Sage, 1995); Dominique Schnapper, *La communauté des citoyens* (Gallimard, 2003); Ernest Gellner and John Breuilly, *Nations and Nationalism* (Cornell University Press, 2008).
45. See the seminal article of William Coplin, 'International law and assumptions about the state system' (1965) 17 *World Politics* 615. On the origins of international law in minority rights issues, see Jennifer Jackson Preece, 'Minority rights in Europe: from Westphalia to Helsinki' (1997) 23 *Review of International Studies* 75 and Jennifer Jackson Preece, *National Minorities and the European Nation-states System* (Oxford University Press, 1998).
46. See Martti Koskenniemi, 'What is international law for?' (2003) 89 *International law* 110 and Martti Koskenniemi, 'The fate of public international law: between technique and politics' (2007) 70 *Modern Law Review* 1.
47. See Antonio Cassese, *Self-Determination of Peoples: A legal reappraisal*, No. 12 (Cambridge University Press, 1995); Karen Knop, *Diversity and Self-Determination in International Law*, vol. 20 (Cambridge University Press, 2002); Hurst Hannum, *Autonomy, Sovereignty, and Self-Determination: The accommodation of conflicting rights* (University of Pennsylvania Press, 2011).
48. One of the most articulate accounts of this particular question is provided by O. A. Elias and C. L. Lim's work on consensualism in international law. Their work is complemented by Robert Keohane's take on reciprocity (2002). These two themes are further developed in Benedict Kingsbury's questioning of the meaning of public in international law. See Robert Keohane, 'Reciprocity in international relations' (1986) 40 *International organization*

1; Olufemi Adekunle Elias and Chin L. Lim, *The Paradox of Consensualism in International Law* (Kluwer Law International, 1998); Benedict Kingsbury, 'Sovereignty and inequality' (1998) 9 *European Journal of International Law* 599; Robert Keohane, *Power and Governance in a Partially Globalized World* (Routledge, 2002); Benedict Kingsbury, Nico Krisch and Richard B. Stewart, 'The emergence of global administrative law' (2005) 68 *Law and Contemporary Problems* 15; Joel Rosenthal, *Ethics and International Relations* (Routledge, 2017).

49. Stephen Krasner's markedly hostile take on sovereignty, as well as a growing field of scholarship in international relations questioning both the history and current validity of the notion of state sovereignty, merits attention here. See Stephen Krasner, 'The hole in the whole: Sovereignty, shared sovereignty, and international law' (2003) 25 *Mich. J. Int'l L.* 1075. On this issue, also see his earlier work, Stephen Krasner, 'Compromising Westphalia' (1995) 20 *International Security* 115, and Jack Goldsmith and Stephen D. Krasner, 'The limits of idealism' (2003) 132 *Daedalus* 47.
50. These are cited in Article 38 of the Statute of the International Court of Justice. For the full text, see the online version at *http://www.kentlaw.edu/faculty/bbrown/classes/HumanRightsSP10/CourseDocs/1ICJ%20Art_38.pdf* (accessed 25 May 2020).
51. On the publicists debate, see D. F. Vagts, 'Hegemonic International Law' (2001) 95 *Am. J. Int'l L.* 843 and S. Sivakumaran, 'The influence of teaching of publicists on the development of international law' (2017) 66 *Int. & Comp. Law Quarterly* 1.
52. See Umut Ozsu, *Formalizing Displacement: International law and population transfers* (Oxford University Press, 2015).
53. See Alina Kaczorowska-Ireland, *Public International Law* (Routledge, 2015).
54. On ILC's working principles, see Eyal Benvenisti and George W. Downs, 'The premises, assumptions, and implications of Van Gend en Loos: Viewed from the perspectives of democracy and legitimacy of international institutions' (2014) 25 *European Journal of International Law* 85; and Lusa Fernando Bordin, 'Reflections of Customary International Law: The Authority of Codification Conventions and ILC Draft Articles in International Law' (2014) 63 *Int. & Comp. Law Quarterly* 535.
55. Under the Vienna Convention on the Law of Treaties, which was adopted on 22 May 1969 and entered into force in January 1980, any treaty in violation of a peremptory norm is declared as null and void. The Convention is regarded as the primary source for the codification of pre-existing international customary law. The work on the Vienna Convention was conducted under the auspices of the International Law Commission. Although only 105 states

ratified the Convention, it is regarded as binding upon those who are not signatories as a founding pillar of customary international law. However, the scope of the Convention is limited. It only applies to treaties concluded between states (Article 1 of the Convention), and excludes treaties between states and international organizations as well as treaties among international organizations themselves. These other aspects of international law came to be governed under the subsequent 1986 Vienna Convention on the Law of Treaties Between States and International Organizations or Between International Organizations. See Ineta Ziemele, *Reservations to Human Rights Treaties and the Vienna Convention Regime: Conflict, Harmony or Reconciliation* (Springer, 2013).

56. In the case of the ICJ, states can, upon mutual consent, submit disputes for arbitration by the Court. The judgments given by the Court in these cases are binding, although the court possesses no means to enforce its rulings. The Court may also give an advisory opinion on any legal question at the request of whatever body may be authorized by or in accordance with the Charter of the United Nations to make such a request. There have been at least 150 primary cases receiving judgment since the ICJ evolved from the Permanent Court of International Justice in 1945. Decisions made through other means of international arbitration may be binding depending on the nature of the arbitration agreement, whereas decisions resulting from contentious cases argued before the ICJ are always binding on the involved states. See Taslim Elias, *The International Court of Justice and Some Contemporary Problems: Essays on International Law*, vol. 2 (Springer Science & Business Media, 2013); as well as Paula Almeida Wojcikiewicz and Jean-Marc Sorel (eds), *Latin America and the International Court of Justice: Contributions to International Law* (Routledge, 2016).

57. See Antonio Cassese et al., *Cassese's International Criminal Law* (Oxford University Press, 2013); Gerhard Werle and Florian Jessberger, *Principles of International Criminal Law* (Oxford University Press, 2014); Karel Wellens, *Negotiations in the Case Law of the International Court of Justice: A Functional Analysis* (Routledge, 2016).

58. On the issue of interpretation of international legal norms, see Anthony Clark Arend and Robert J. Beck, *International Law and the Use of Force: Beyond the UN Charter Paradigm* (Routledge, 2014).

59. The only area where interpretation is less open to differences of opinion is the UN Charter. Violations of the UN Charter by members of the United Nations are to be raised by the aggrieved state in the General Assembly for debate. The General Assembly cannot make binding resolutions, but under the resolution GA/RES/0377 it could authorize the use of force if there had been

what is considered as 'Breaches of the Peace' or 'Acts of Aggression', provided of course that the Security Council failed to act due to a negative vote of a permanent member in the first place. The United Nations General Assembly could also call for other collective measures such as economic sanctions if the situation is considered as constitutive of a milder threat to international peace. If these issues are raised at the level of the Security Council, this particular body is equipped to pass resolutions under Chapter VI of the UN Charter to recommend 'Pacific Resolution of Disputes'. Still, none of these resolutions are binding under international law, being *ad hoc* solutions to emergent problems. On the workings of the UN in the area of international law, see Thomas Weiss et al., *The United Nations and Changing World Politics* (Westview Press, 2016), and Simon Chesterman, Ian Johnstone and David M. Malone, *Law and Practice of the United Nations: Documents and Commentary* (Oxford University Press, 2016).

60. See David Kennedy, *A World of Struggle: How power, law, and expertise shape global political economy* (Princeton University Press, 2016).
61. See Simon Archer, Daniel Drache and Peer Zumbansen (eds), *The Daunting Enterprise of the Law: Essays in Honour of Harry Arthurs* (McGill-Queen's University Press, 2017).
62. See Anne-Marie Slaughter, Andrew S. Tulumello and Stepan Wood, 'International law and international relations theory: A new generation of interdisciplinary scholarship' (1998) 92 *Am. J. Int'l L.* 367–97; Kenneth Abbott, 'International relations theory, international law, and the regime governing atrocities in internal conflicts' (1999) 93 *The American Journal of International Law* 361; Anne-Marie Slaughter and Steven R. Ratner, 'Appraising the methods of international law: A prospectus for readers' (1999) 93 *Am. J. Int'l L.* 291.
63. The idealistic take on *opinio juris* suggests that international law has developed through a pluralistic process, its history revealing a pattern of proportionality. Accordingly, states as legal agencies are equipped, organized and empowered to participate actively in the interpretation and development of *opinio juris* on an equal basis. For a strong critique of this approach, see Andrew Guzman and Jerome Hsiang, 'Some Ways that Theories on Customary International Law Fail: A Reply to László Blutman' (2014) 25 *European Journal of International Law* 553.
64. On the development of *jus gentium*, see Arturo Escobar, 'Thinking-feeling with the Earth: Territorial Struggles and the Ontological Dimension of the Epistemologies of the South' (2016) 11 *AIBR. Revista de Antropología Iberoamericana* 11; and Edward Cavanagh, 'Prescription and Empire from Justinian to Grotius' (2017) 60 *The Historical Journal* 273.

65. See Charles De Visscher, *Theory and Reality in Public International Law* (Princeton University Press, 2015).
66. See Stephen Gill and A. Claire Cutler (eds), *New Constitutionalism and World Order* (Cambridge University Press, 2014). Gill and Cutler argue that the relationships between law, power and contestation in the global political economy are of paramount importance. Their analysis advances a radical critique of dominant understandings of the distinction between international and transnational law. Specifically, they argue that transnational law operates dialectically as the common sense of contemporary global capitalism to discipline the masses through hard, enforceable corporate trade and investor rights, whilst limiting corporate social responsibilities to soft, voluntary and unenforceable standards.
67. See Marie-Claire Cordonier Segger and Judge CG Weeramantry (eds), *Sustainable Development Principles in the Decisions of International Courts and Tribunals: 1992–2012* (Routledge, 2017).
68. See Michael Mandel, *How America Gets Away with Murder: Illegal wars, collateral damage and crimes against humanity* (Pluto Press, 2004).
69. See Michael Byers, *International Law and the Arctic* (Cambridge University Press, 2013). For an example of a strong counter-argument, see Wafula Okumu, 'Humanitarian international NGOs and African conflicts' (2003) 10 *International Peacekeeping* 120.
70. See Cedric Ryngaert, *Jurisdiction in International Law*, 2nd edn (Oxford University Press, 2015); Franz von Benda-Beckmann and Keebet von Benda-Beckmann, *Mobile People, Mobile Law: Expanding legal relations in a contracting world* (Routledge, 2017).
71. In its common use, *pacta sunt servanda* refers to private contracts and implies that contained pacts and clauses are to be considered with the weight of law between the engaged parties. In international law, *pacta sunt servanda* is regarded as a basic requirement for the efficacy of the whole system. See Hans Wehberg, 'Pacta sunt servanda' (1959) 53 *Am. J. of Int'l L.* 775; Jonathan Charney, 'Universal international law' (1983) 87 *Am. J. of Int'l L.* 529; Dinah Shelton, 'International law and "relative normativity"' (2006) 2 *International law* 159.
72. The theory of international law developed by the New Haven School (NHS) has been subject to criticism for over half a century. Members of the school are best known for their scepticism regarding the role of norms. Accordingly, norms are not to be viewed as operating autonomously, in as much as they cannot be understood separate from general legal principles. The NHS puts particular emphasis on how decision-makers make their choices in the context of conflicting drives and principles, such as the clash between *pacta*

sunt servanda and *clausula rebus sic stantibus*, the latter structuring the evolving regime of sovereign titles over natural resources. For the NHS, extra-legal factors at play, including the policy-relevant social and political interests of the actors in a position to make such choices are paramount. Particularly the Continental followers of Neo-Kantianism – which was developed by the Marburg School a hundred years ago and still provides the intellectual subtext for formal positivist legal scholarship today – exhibit an openly hostile attitude towards the NHS and its legacy. See Michael Reisman, 'Theory about law: Jurisprudence for a free society' (1999) 108 *Yale L. J.* 935–9; Janet Koven Levit, 'Bottom-up International Lawmaking: Reflections on the New Haven School of International Law' (2007) 32 *Yale J. Int'l L.* 393; Paul Schiff Berman, 'A Pluralist Approach to International Law' (2007) 32 *Yale J. Int'l L.* 301; Oona Hathaway, 'The Continuing Influence of the New Haven School' (2007) 32 *Yale J. Int'l L.* 553; Siegfried Weissner, 'Law as a Means to a Public Order of Human Dignity: The Jurisprudence of Michael Reisman' (2009) 34 *Yale J. Int'l L.* 525.

73. See Hans Morgenthau, *Politics Among Nations* (Alfred Kopf, 1948). Also see Gerry Simpson, 'The situation on the international legal theory front: the power of rules and the rule of power' (2000) 11 *European Journal of International Law* 439.
74. For an idealist take on the issue of the state in international law, see Malcolm Langford, *Global Justice, State Duties: The extraterritorial scope of economic, social, and cultural rights in international law* (Cambridge University Press, 2013). For a comparative analysis of the treatment of the state in international law scholarship, see David Bederman and Chimene Keitner, *International Law Frameworks*, 4th edn (West Academic, 2016). For a heavily critical take, see Gerry Simpson, 'The sentimental life of international law' (2015) 3 *London Review of International Law* 3.
75. See Leonard Hammer, *A Foucauldian Approach to International Law: Descriptive thoughts for normative issues* (Routledge 2007).
76. For an authoritative treatment of *jus cogens*, see Marteen den Heijer and Harmen van der Wilt (eds), *Netherlands Yearbook of International Law 2015: Jus Cogens: Quo Vadis?*, vol. 46 (Springer, 2016).
77. See William Conklin, 'The peremptory norms of the international community' (2012) 23 *European Journal of International Law* 837 and Robert Kolb, *Peremptory International Law –Jus Cogens: A General Inventory* (Bloomsbury Publishing, 2015).
78. See Dan Dubois, 'The authority of peremptory norms in international law: state consent or natural law?' (2009) 78 *Nordic Journal of International Law* 133.

79. See Boaventura de Sousa Santos and César A. Rodríguez-Garavito (eds), *Law and Globalization from Below: Towards a Cosmopolitan Legality* (Cambridge University Press, 2005) and Stephen Gill (ed.), *Globalization, Democratization and Multilateralism* (Springer, 2016).
80. For a similar use of the phrase of 'quiet encroachment of the ordinary' but in a different context, see Asef Bayat, 'From Dangerous Classes' to Quiet Rebels' Politics of the Urban Subaltern in the Global South' (2000) 15 *International Sociology* 533.

Chapter 3

1. See the Report, 'Crimes against Humanity and War Crimes are the reason behind the Forced Migration in Darayya: Siege, Chemical Weapons, Barrel Bombs, and International Silence' at *http://sn4hr.org/wpcontent/pdf/english/Crimes_against_humanity_forced_displacement_for_Daraya_en.pdf* (accessed 25 May 2020).
2. Regarding ICTY and ICTR case law, one of the main issues raised in the context of mass transfer of populations during armed conflict is the question of assessing whether people have chosen to leave conflict zones of their own free will. What counts as 'genuine choice' in each particular case cannot be established *a priori*. A careful consideration of the specific circumstances must be carried out before reaching a definitive conclusion. Secondly, international criminal law would benefit from further clarification of the meaning of the clause 'displacement of persons from the area in which they are lawfully present' as one of the constitutive elements of the crimes of deportation and forcible transfer. While the term 'lawfully' suggested by the ICTY is reasonable in the context of a conflict where different national groups and political parties confront each other in what effectively amounts to a civil war, this is not helpful in other circumstances. Internally displaced persons often lack residency permits or registration, and they move multiple times. Consequently, there might be 'penumbral' situations that are not straightforward for adjudication purposes. This is an area where greater cross-fertilization between international refugee law and international criminal law would lead to a better understanding of how to address mass human suffering. Even the difference established by the ICTY between deportation and forcible transfer does not change the basic point that forcibly transferring people within a country is as serious a threat to their livelihood as deporting them across a State border.
3. On the Lebanese case of the relationship between forced displacement and crimes against humanity, see *http://www.refworld.org/pdfid/4e09a5622.pdf* (accessed 25 May 2020).

4. See Nergis Canefe, 'Management of Irregular Migration: Syrians in Turkey as Paradigm Shifters for Forced Migration Studies' (2016) 54 *New Perspectives on Turkey* 9; and Nergis Canefe, 'Post-Colonial State and Violence: Rethinking the Middle East and North Africa outside the Blindfold of Area Studies' (2015) 45 *Refugee Watch* 7.
5. The description provided above shows the complexities of subsuming the atrocious crimes related to forced displacement under clear-cut legal categories for the purpose of international criminal prosecution. When committed with a discriminatory intent and as part of a widespread or systematic attack against civilians, this type of conduct falls under the purview of crimes against humanity. The case law in this area already established the criminal nature of certain types of forced displacement and the need to prosecute those responsible for forced displacement situations. The problem lies in finding the venue and the court, and, more generally, establishing political consent for the trial of these atrocities.
6. On politics of the establishment of the ICC and the drafting and ratification of the Rome Statute, see D. F. Orentlicher, 'Politics by Other Means: The Law of the International Criminal Court' (1999) 32 *Cornell Int'l L. J.* 489.
7. On the history of crimes against humanity in international law, see G. Robertson, *Crimes Against Humanity: The struggle for global justice* (The New Press, 2013); A. F. Lang Jr, *Punishment, Justice and International Relations: Ethics and order after the Cold War* (Routledge, 2009); M. Cherif Bassiouni (ed.), *International Criminal Law, vol. 2: Multilateral and Bilateral Enforcement Mechanisms* (Brill, 2008); L. May, *Crimes Against Humanity: A Normative Account* (Cambridge University Press, 2005); D. Luban, 'A theory of crimes against humanity' (2004) 29 *Yale J. Int'l L.* 85; D. Robinson, 'Defining "Crimes Against Humanity" at the Rome Conference' (1999) 93 *Am. J. Int'l L.* 43.
8. For a historical overview of the definition, see in chronological order:

   1945 London Charter of the International Military Tribunal (Nuremberg Charter), Article 6(c):

   > murder, extermination, enslavement, deportation, and other inhumane acts committed against civilian populations, before or during the war; or persecutions on political, racial or religious grounds in execution of or in connection with any crime within the jurisdiction of the Tribunal, whether or not in violation of the domestic law of the country where perpetrated. [*This definition was also used in the Charter of the International Military Tribunal for the Far East.*]

   The Statute of the International Criminal Tribunal for the former Yugoslavia (ICTY), Article 5:

> ... the following crimes when committed in armed conflict, whether international or internal in character, and directed against any civilian population: (a) murder; (b) extermination; (c) enslavement; (d) deportation; (e) imprisonment; (f) torture; (g) rape; (h) persecutions on political, racial and religious grounds; (i) other inhumane acts.

The Statute of the International Criminal Tribunal for Rwanda (ICTR), Article 3:

> ... the following crimes when committed as part of a widespread or systematic attack against any civilian population on national, political, ethnic, racial or religious grounds: (a) Murder; (b) Extermination; (c) Enslavement; (d) Deportation; (e) Imprisonment; (f) Torture; (g) Rape; (h) Persecutions on political, racial and religious grounds; (i) Other inhumane acts.

The Statute of the Special Court for Sierra Leone (SCSL), Article 2:

> ... the following crimes as part of a widespread or systematic attack against any civilian population: a. Murder; b. Extermination; c. Enslavement; d. Deportation; e. Imprisonment; f. Torture; g. Rape, sexual slavery, enforced prostitution, forced pregnancy and any other form of sexual violence; h. Persecution on political, racial, ethnic or religious grounds; i. Other inhumane acts.

The Law on the Establishment of the Extraordinary Chambers in the Courts of Cambodia (ECCC), Article 5

> ... any acts committed as part of a widespread or systematic attack directed against any civilian population, on national, political, ethnical, racial or religious grounds, such as: murder; extermination; enslavement; deportation; imprisonment; torture; rape; persecutions on political, racial, and religious grounds; other inhumane acts.

9. For instance, in 2002, the USA asked all countries who were part of the ratification scheme for the ICC to sign agreements exempting US citizens from prosecution by the Court, and threatened economic sanctions if they refused. Some countries yielded to this pressure even after ratifying the ICC Statute. What is important for the present and future context is the subsequent introduction of bilateral immunity agreements (BIAs) into the architecture of the Rome Statute. For further debate, see I. Nooruddin and Autumn Lockwood Payton, 'Dynamics of influence in international politics: The ICC, BIAs, and economic sanctions' (2010) 47 *Journal of Peace Research* 711.
10. On the disputed nature of the norm, see P. Wald, 'Genocide and crimes against humanity' (2007) 6 *Wash. U. Global Stud. L. Rev.* 621; R. K. Paterson,

'Resolving Material Culture Disputes: Human Rights, Property Rights and Crimes against Humanity' (2006) 14 *Willamette Journal of International Law and Dispute Resolution* 161.

11. See *The Charter and Judgment of the Nürnberg Tribunal – History and Analysis: Memorandum* submitted by the Secretary-General, Document A/CN.4/5, available at *http://www.cininas.lt/wpcontent/uploads/2015/06/1949_UN_ILC_N_statuto_koment.pdf* (accessed 25 May 2020).
12. For the full text, see *http://avalon.law.yale.edu/imt/imt10.asp* (accessed 25 May 2020). The list includes atrocities and offences, including but not limited to: murder, extermination, enslavement, deportation, imprisonment, torture, rape, or other inhumane acts committed against any civilian population, or persecutions on political, racial or religious grounds whether or not in violation of the domestic laws of the country where perpetrated.
13. Also see D. Matas, 'Prosecuting crimes against humanity: the lessons of World War I' (1989) 13 *Fordham Int'l L. J.* 86.
14. See the Commentaries document on the 1996 Draft Code of Crimes against Peace and Security of Mankind regarding the reference to International Law Commission, available at *http://legal.un.org/ilc/texts/instruments/english/commentaries/7_4_1996.pdf* (accessed 25 May 2020).
15. The International Law Commission's Draft Code of Crimes against the Peace and Security of Mankind (1996), Article 18 stated that:

    > [a]ny of the following acts, when committed in a systematic manner or on a large scale and instigated or directed by a Government or by any organization or group: (a) Murder; (b) Extermination; (c) Torture; (d) Enslavement; (e) Persecution on political, racial, religious or ethnic grounds; (f) Institutionalized discrimination on racial, ethnic or religious grounds involving the violation of fundamental human rights and freedoms and resulting in seriously disadvantaging a part of the population; (g) Arbitrary deportation or forcible transfer of population; (h) Arbitrary imprisonment; (i) Forced disappearance of persons; (j) Rape, enforced prostitution and other forms of sexual abuse; (k) Other inhumane acts which severely damage physical or mental integrity, health or human dignity, such as mutilation and severe bodily harm.

    http://legal.un.org/ilc/texts/instruments/english/draft_articles/7_4_1996.pdf (accessed 25 May 2020).
16. See the full body of the Statute at *http://legal.un.org/avl/pdf/ha/ictr_EF.pdf* (accessed 25 May 2020).
17. In treaty language, an 'attack directed against any civilian population' means a course of conduct involving the multiple commission of acts against any

civilian population, pursuant to or in furtherance of a State or organizational policy to commit such attack; 'Extermination' includes the intentional infliction of conditions of life, *inter alia* the deprivation of access to food and medicine, calculated to bring about the destruction of part of a population; 'Enslavement' means the exercise of any or all of the powers attaching to the right of ownership over a person and includes the exercise of such power in the course of trafficking in persons, in particular women and children; 'Deportation or forcible transfer of population' means forced displacement of the persons concerned by expulsion or other coercive acts from the area in which they are lawfully present, without grounds permitted under international law; 'Torture' means the intentional infliction of severe pain or suffering, whether physical or mental, upon a person in the custody or under the control of the accused; except that torture shall not include pain or suffering arising only from, inherent in or incidental to, lawful sanctions; 'Forced pregnancy' means the unlawful confinement of a woman forcibly made pregnant, with the intent of affecting the ethnic composition of any population or carrying out other grave violations of international law; 'Persecution' means the intentional and severe deprivation of fundamental rights contrary to international law by reason of the identity of the group or collectivity; 'The crime of apartheid' means inhumane acts … committed in the context of an institutionalized regime of systematic oppression and domination by one racial group over any other racial group or groups and committed with the intention of maintaining that regime; and, 'Enforced disappearance of persons' means the arrest, detention or abduction of persons by, or with the authorization, support or acquiescence of, a State or a political organization, followed by a refusal to acknowledge that deprivation of freedom or to give information on the fate or whereabouts of those persons, with the intention of removing them from the protection of the law for a prolonged period of time.

18. See M. Boot, *Genocide, Crimes Against Humanity, War Crimes: Nullum crimen sine lege and the subject matter jurisdiction of the International Criminal Court*, vol. 12 (Intersentia, 2002).
19. See G. Fletcher, *Basic Concepts of Criminal Law* (Oxford University Press, 1998).
20. See Article 7 of the ICC Statute as Doc. A/CONF.183/9 of 17 July 1998, available at *https://www.icc-cpi.int/nr/rdonlyres/ea9aeff7-5752-4f84-be94-0a655eb30e16/0/rome_statute_english.pdf* (accessed 25 May 2020).
21. According to the definition in Article 7(2)(a) of the ICC Statute, an 'attack on a civilian population' denotes 'a course of conduct involving the multiple commission of acts referred to in paragraph 1 against any civilian population,

pursuant to or in furtherance of a State or organizational policy to commit such attack.'

22. See the United Nations International Criminal Tribunal for the Former Yugoslavia jurisprudence in the section on judgment and sentencing at *http://www.icty.org/en/about/chambers* (accessed 25 May 2020).
23. Article 7(2)(a) clarifies that it needs to be a State or organizational policy. One Pre-Trial Chamber declared that the term 'State' was self-explanatory but added that the policy did not have to be conceived 'at the highest level of the State machinery' [*Situation in the Republic of Kenya*, ICC PT. Ch. II, Decision Pursuant to Article 15 of the Rome Statute on the Authorization of an Investigation into the Situation in the Republic of Kenya, ICC-01-09, 31 March 2010, para. 89, citing *Prosecutor v Blaškić*, ICTY T. Ch., Judgment, 3 March 2000, para. 205]. Therefore, also a policy adopted by regional or local organs of the State could satisfy this requirement (Ibid.). See *https://www.casematrixnetwork.org/cmn-knowledge-hub/icc-commentary-clicc/commentary-rome-statute/commentary-rome-statute-part-2-articles-5-10/* (accessed 25 May 2020).
24. On the issue of intent, see G. Werle, *Principles of International Criminal Law* (Oxford University Press, 2005) and G. Mettraux, *International Crimes and the* ad hoc *Tribunals* (Oxford University Press, 2005).
25. As Payam Akhavan argues, if conduct is consistent with the laws of war, it may be hard to prove that it nonetheless falls under a category of crimes against humanity during armed conflict. Initial jurisprudence pertaining to crimes against humanity extended the protection of the laws of war to a perpetrator's co-nationals. Although this new category requires a nexus with an international armed conflict, it has become an autonomous concept based on human rights law that criminalizes large-scale atrocities in *both war and peacetime*. Crimes against humanity committed during an armed conflict continue to be shaped by the laws of war. There is substantial convergence between the normative core of 'non-derogable' human rights and the minimum humane treatment standards in the Geneva Law. Still, there remains considerable divergence with respect to combat operations where the Hague Law applies as *lex specialis* concerning human rights norms. Akhavan states that the ICTY jurisprudence itself demonstrates tensions inherent in reconciling human rights law with armed conflict. A notable instance is the Gotovina case, in which the Trial Chamber held that the laws of war do not apply to 'deportation' qua crimes against humanity. In other words, there is no distinction to be made between forcible displacement of civilians in occupied territories as opposed to combat operations. Here, the temptation to dilute the laws of war through reclassification of the conduct as crimes against humanity should be

resisted, as it may lead to diminished protection for civilians during armed conflict. See P. Akhavan, 'Reconciling Crimes Against Humanity with the Laws of War Human Rights, Armed Conflict, and the Limits of Progressive Jurisprudence' (2008) 6 *Journal of International Criminal Justice* 21.

26. See M. Futamura, *War Crimes Tribunals and Transitional Justice: The Tokyo trial and the Nuremberg legacy* (Routledge, 2007), as well as Y. Tanaka, Tim McCormack and Gerry Simpson (eds), *Beyond Victor's Justice? The Tokyo War Crimes Trial Revisited* (Martinus Nifhoff, 2010), accessible at *https://www.researchgate.net/profile/Yoriko_Otomo/publication/282818305_The_Decision_Not_to_Prosecute_the_Emperor/links/561d6c5508aec7945a2532e9.pdf* (accessed 25 May 2020).
27. See M. E. Villiger, *Commentary on the 1969 Vienna Convention on the Law of Treaties* (Brill, 2009); and C. Bassiouni, 'International crimes: *jus cogens* and *obligatio erga omnes*' (1996) 59 *Law & Contemp. Probs.* 63.
28. This judgment was given on 25 November 1998. The appeal was allowed by a majority of three to two and the House restored the second warrant of 23 October 1998. As a result of this decision, Senator Pinochet was required to remain in the UK to await the decision of the Home Secretary whether to authorise the continuation of the proceedings for his extradition under section 7(1) of the Extradition Act 1989. See the actual text of the judgment at *https://publications.parliament.uk/pa/ld199899/ldjudgmt/jd990115/pino01.htm* (accessed 25 May 2020).
29. Since this case, the impact (if any) of Spanish and British Court rulings on the Pinochet case on the progress of human rights cases in Chilean courts has been widely debated. Chilean judges chafe at the notion that foreign courts exerted any influence on them, arguing that, based solely on Chilean law and the evidence already before them, they were empowered to strip Pinochet of his immunity. Human rights critics, on the other hand, allege that the courts had been thoroughly immobilized for decades by the authoritarian legacy to which they were enjoined. The botched trial at least shamed the Chilean Government into pressuring its own high courts to deliver a modicum of justice to the victims of Pinochet. See A. Bianchi, 'Immunity versus human rights: the Pinochet case' (1999) 10 *European Journal of International Law* 237.
30. See B. Wringe, 'Why punish war crimes? Victor's justice and expressive justifications of punishment' (2006) 25 *Law and Philosophy* 159.
31. As another case in point, the institutional design of the UN's new human rights organ, the Human Rights Council (HRC), was heavily contested, the options being an exclusive body with a high membership threshold, or an inclusive structure built upon cooperative mechanisms. The HRC features a moderate membership threshold. The same dynamic was in place during the

drafting of the Rome Statute. On this issue, see Larry May's work, including L. May, *Genocide: A Normative Account* (Cambridge University Press, 2010); L. May and Stacey Hoffman (eds), *Collective Responsibility: Five decades of debate in theoretical and applied ethics* (Rowman & Littlefield Publishers, 1992), as well as J. T. Kelly, 'The moral foundations of international criminal law' (2010) 9 *Journal of Human Rights* 502.

32. See M. Badar, 'From the Nuremberg Charter to the Rome Statute: defining the elements of crimes against humanity' (2004) 5 *San Diego Int'l L. J.* 73.
33. For Chapter VII of the UN Charter's full text, see *http://www.un.org/en/sections/un-charter/chapter-vii/* (accessed 25 May 2020). Chapter VII pertains to threats to peace, breaches of peace and acts of aggression.
34. Law on the Establishment of the Extraordinary Chambers in the Courts of Cambodia for the Prosecution of Crimes Committed During the Period of Democratic Kampuchea, NS/RKM/1004/006 (2004), Art. 5, and Nuon Chea (ECCC-002/14-08-2006), Provisional Detention Order, 19 September 2007, para. 5.
35. This language evokes the Martens' Clause's 'laws of humanity' and 'dictates of the public conscience' as stated in the Preamble to the Hague Conventions on the Laws and Customs of War on Land (1899). See T. Meron, 'The Martens Clause, principles of humanity, and dictates of public conscience' (2000) 94 *Am. J. Int'l L.* 78.
36. The contours of the prohibition of crimes against humanity with reference to proceedings before the ICTY and deliberations at the Diplomatic Conference of Plenipotentiaries on the Establishment of an International Criminal Court (ICC) prove that, because of the relatively contemporary status of these offences under international law, a particular reference to the genesis and re-interpretation of the war nexus requirement is essential. The task at hand was identifying the elements of these offences to distinguish them from 'ordinary' municipal crimes (e.g. murder, assault or false imprisonment) and to justify the exercise of international jurisdiction that would otherwise be the subject of domestic adjudication. For the drafters of the Nuremberg Judgment, the war nexus originally served precisely this purpose. The ICTY devised an ingenuous solution to the problem of delimiting international jurisdiction and distinguishing crimes against humanity from 'ordinary' crimes: the Trial Chamber did not require proof of a substantial link between the defendant's inhumane act and a state of war. Rather, the Chamber defined crimes against humanity in terms of the *mens rea* of the defendant and the existence of a widespread or systematic attack against a civilian population. It also added additional elements to the definition of crimes against humanity, further complicating the definition and the Prosecution's burden of proof. The Appeals

Chamber did overturn the Trial Chamber's decision in this regard in the Tadic case (INTERNATIONAL DECISION: Prosecutor V. Tadic (Judgement). Case No. IT-94-1-A. 38 ILM 1518 (1999). International Criminal Tribunal for the Former Yugoslavia, Appeals Chamber, 15 July 1999). During the drafting of the Statute for the permanent ICC, both the ICTY Statute and the work of the Tribunal were used for a consensus definition of crimes against humanity that will govern prosecutions before the new permanent international court. The drafters of the Rome Statute defined crimes against humanity with reference only to the existence of a widespread or systematic attack against a civilian population and the mental state of the individual defendant. In so doing, they recognized that once abuse of civilians surpasses a particular threshold, the prescriptions of international law are activated and individual perpetrators can be held internationally liable for their acts of murder, assault, rape or unlawful detention. See M. McAuliffe deGuzman, 'The road from Rome: the developing law of crimes against humanity' (2000) 22 *Human Rights Quarterly* 335.

37. Both Cherif Bassiouni and William Schabas state that the concept of crimes against humanity embraces only serious and egregious violations of human rights perpetrated by members of the state or state-like actors against their own citizens. See W. Schabas, 'State Policy as an Element of International Crimes' (2008) 98 *Journal of Criminal Law and Criminology* 959; M. Bassiouni, *The Legislative History of the International Criminal Court* (Transnational Publishers, 2005), particularly pp. 151–5; and R. Vernon, 'What is a Crime against Humanity?' (2002) 10 *Journal of Political Philosophy* 242.
38. For David Luban, for example, the rationale for crimes against humanity lies in the interest all humans share 'in ensuring people are not killed solely because of their group affiliation'.
39. Larry May also suggests that group-based harm can justify attaching the label crimes against humanity.
40. A lengthy list of crimes against humanity cases can be found in the International Criminal Database (ICD) at *http://www.internationalcrimesdatabase.org/Cases/ByName* (accessed 25 May 2020).
41. With regard to these trials, the primary text referred to throughout this section is H. Arendt, *Eichmann in Jerusalem* (Penguin, 1963).
42. H. Yablonka, 'The development of Holocaust consciousness in Israel: The Nuremberg, kapos, Kastner, and Eichmann trials' (2003) 8 *Israel Studies* 1.
43. See the judgment of the Nuremberg trials at *https://www.loc.gov/rr/frd/Military_Law/pdf/NT_Vol-I.pdf* (accessed 25 May 2020). For the case summaries of the remaining Holocaust trials, see M. J. Bazyler and Frank M. Tuerkheimer, *Forgotten Trials of the Holocaust* (NYU Press, 2015).

44. For the full text of the law, see the International Red Cross Archives at *https://ihl-databases.icrc.org/applic/ihl/ihl-nat.nsf/0/9D6164171FA43DE7C12575AE0034A437* (accessed 25 May 2020).
45. For the full text of the proceedings of the Eichmann trial, see *http://remember.org/eichmann/charges* (accessed 25 May 2020).
46. See H. Arendt, *The Origins of Totalitarianism* (Meridian Books, 1962). Similar to Arendt, philosopher Vladimir Jankélévitch advocated the idea that if no proportional punishment can be found, the crime remains unforgivable. According to him, forgiveness died in the death camps. See V. Jankélévitch, *L'imprescriptible. Pardonner? Dans l'honneur et la dignité* (Le Seuil, 2015).
47. H. Arendt, 'Personal responsibility under dictatorship' in *Responsibility and Judgment* (Schocken Books, 2003), pp. 17–48.
48. H. Arendt, *The Human Condition* (University of Chicago Press, 2013). On the issue of forgiveness, also see J. Derrida, *On Cosmopolitanism and Forgiveness* (Psychology Press, 2001).
49. This is despite the fact that confusion blurring the boundaries between forgiveness, apology, remorse, amnesty and prescription remains problem laden.
50. D. Levy and Natan Sznaider, 'Forgive and not forget: Reconciliation between forgiveness and resentment' in *Taking Wrongs Seriously: Apologies and reconciliation* (Stanford University Press, 2006), pp. 83–100, and R. Bernstein, 'Derrida: The aporia of forgiveness?' (2006) 13 *Constellations* 394.
51. For Arendt, forgiveness is a purely human experience, rather than having anything to do with divinity or sacred realms. Yet if forgiveness is a grand societal and historical gesture, the essence of which could not be captured by any existing, past or future law, we cannot sustain the presumption of symmetry between forgiveness and adequate punishment. This is also an important debate in the transitional justice literature pertaining to mass societal and political crimes. See P. Hazan, 'Measuring the impact of punishment and forgiveness: a framework for evaluating transitional justice' (2006) 88 *International Review of the Red Cross* 19.
52. In the works of the three post-Holocaust thinkers – Emmanuel Levinas, Hans Jonas and Hannah Arendt – radical evil, a term originally coined by the German philosopher Immanuel Kant, found a disturbing new meaning that casts a shadow over the gains of crimes against humanity jurisprudence. On the meaning and implications of both 'radical evil' and the 'banality of evil', see S. Neiman, *Evil in Modern Thought: An alternative history of philosophy* (Princeton University Press, 2015); and C. Card, *The Atrocity Paradigm: A theory of evil* (Oxford University Press, 2002).

53. See J. Kristeva, *Hannah Arendt*, vol. 1 (Columbia University Press, 2001); and R. Fine, 'Crimes against humanity: Hannah Arendt and the Nuremberg Debates' (2000) 3 *European Journal of Social Theory* 293.
54. See Y. Rogat, 'The Judge as Spectator' (1964) 31 *University of Chicago Law Review* 213.

Chapter 4

1. I am in debt to Les Jacobs for guiding me through the debate on Aristotelian ethics and re-reading Arendt. The latin term *mea culpa, sua culpa, tua maxima culpa* could be translated as 'through my fault, through your fault, we are where the fault lies most' and is an acknowledgement of having done wrong collectively.
2. For the full text of Seneca's work on Melancholy from which this quote comes, see *http://www.gutenberg.org/files/10800/10800-h/ampart1.html* (accessed 25 May 2020).
3. See Nergis Canefe (ed.), *Transitional Justice and Forced Migration: Critical Perspectives from the Global South* (Cambridge University Press, 2019).
4. Two of the prevailing theories of moral philosophy, Kantianism and consequentialism, both have difficulties resolving problems concerning complicity in collective violence. See Andrew Arato, 'The Bush Tribunals and the Specter of Dictatorship' (2002) 9 *Constellations* 457, and Christopher Kutz, *Complicity: Ethics and Law for a Collective Age* (Cambridge University Press, 2007).
5. See Larry May, *Crimes Against Humanity: A Normative Account* (Cambridge University Press, 2005). May focuses on the moral, legal and political questions that arise when individuals who commit collective crimes, such as crimes against humanity, are held accountable by international criminal tribunals. These tribunals challenge one of the most sacred prerogatives of states – their sovereignty. Breaches in sovereignty are justified only in limited circumstances, which constitutes the minimalist threshold of the justification for international prosecution. What I purport here is to carry this discussion forward in conjunction with moral theories of judgment in applied legal philosophy.
6. See Hannah Arendt, *Eichmann in Jerusalem* (Penguin, 1963). Also see Jacob Robinson, *And the Crooked Shall Be Made Straight: The Eichmann Trial, the Jewish Catastrophe, and Hannah Arendt's Narrative* (MacMillan, 1965); and Seyla Benhabib, 'Arendt's Eichmann in Jerusalem', in Dana Richard Villa (ed.), *The Cambridge Companion to Hannah Arendt* (Cambridge University Press, 2000), pp. 65–85.
7. See Hannah Arendt, *Responsibility and Judgment* (Schocken Books, 2003).
8. See Immanuel Kant, *Grounding for the Metaphysics of Morals*, in I. Kant, *Ethical Philosophy*, James W. Ellington, trans. (Hackett Publishing, [1785] 1983); and

his *Metaphysical Elements of Justice*, John Ladd (ed.) (Hackett, [1797] 1999); John Stuart Mill, *On Liberty*, David Spitz (ed.) (Norton, [1859] 1975). Also see Joseph Raz, *The Morality of Freedom* (Clarendon, 1986); Jennifer Nedelsky, 'Reconceiving Autonomy: Sources, Thoughts, and Possibilities' (1989) 1 *Yale Journal of Law and Feminism* 7; and Ben Coburn, *Autonomy and Liberalism* (Routledge, 2010).

9. In legal scholarship, the concept was taken up mainly in the context of blameworthiness for litigation purposes: actions could serve as legitimate bases for blame without objective wrongdoing *per se*. Here, intent is identified as the key. See Jan Narveson, 'Collective responsibility' (2002) 6 *The Journal of Ethics* 179.
10. See Joel Feinberg, 'Collective responsibility' (1968) 65 *Journal of Philosophy* 674. Also see Virginia Held, 'Can a random collection of individuals be morally responsible?' (1970) 67 *Journal of Philosophy* 471. Held's article was taken up and re-evaluated extensively in Stanley Bates, 'The Responsibility of Random Collections' (1971) 81 *Ethics* 343.
11. See Amy Harbin and Jennifer Lewelyn, 'Restorative Justice in Transitions: The Problem of "The Community" and Collective Responsibility', in Kerry Clamp (ed.), *Restorative Justice in Transitional Settings* (Routledge, 2016), pp. 133–51.
12. Starting with Hywel D. Lewis, 'Collective responsibility' (1948) 23 *Philosophy* 3, the spectrum of works consulted here includes Larry May, *Sharing Responsibility* (University of Chicago Press, 1992); Larry May & Stacey Hoffman (eds), *Collective Responsibility: Five decades of debate in theoretical and applied ethics* (Rowman & Littlefield Publishers, 1992); and Angelo Corlett, *Collective responsibility* (John Wiley & Sons, Ltd, 2001).
13. See the Cooper/Downie debate at David E. Cooper, 'Collective responsibility' (1968) 43 *Philosophy* 258, and Robert Silcock Downie, 'Collective responsibility' (1969) 44 *Philosophy* 66. Also see Howard McGary, 'Morality and collective liability' (1986) 20 *The Journal of Value Inquiry* 157.
14. See Mark Osiel, *Mass Atrocity, Ordinary Evil and Hannah Arendt: Criminal consciousness in Argentina's dirty war* (Yale University Press, 2001) and Mark Osiel, *Obeying orders: Atrocity, military discipline and the law of war* (Routledge, 2017); Robbie McVeigh, 'Hate and the State: Northern Ireland, Sectarian Violence and "Perpetrator-less Crime"', in A. Haynes et al. (eds), *Critical Perspectives on Hate Crime* (Palgrave Macmillan, 2017).
15. See Hannah Arendt, 'Eichmann in Jerusalem: An exchange of letters between Gershom Scholem and Hannah Arendt' (1964) 22 *Encounter* 51. Commentaries on Arendt's *Eichmann in Jerusalem* are generally one of two kinds. The first group confronts the historical relevance of Arendt's observations and

attempts to ascertain whether her presentation of Eichmann's trial complements or corresponds to the reality of the incommensurable suffering of the Jewish people during the Second World War. The second variety focuses on the meaning of her term 'banality of evil' by placing Arendt in a long tradition of moral and political philosophy concerned with the problem of judging evil and harm. See Peg Birmingham, 'Holes of Oblivion: The Banality of Radical Evil' (2003) 18 *Hypatia* 80. If one reads Arendt's treatise on Eichmann in light of Walter Benjamin's conceptions of history and storytelling, a third route emerges, and it becomes clear that *Eichmann in Jerusalem* was not intended to reflect reality objectively. On the contrary, Arendt aimed at avoiding the cold and detached neutrality of historicism, or as she calls it the 'tradition of *sine ira et studio*', the Latin term meaning without anger and fondness or without hate and zealousness. See Annabel Herzog, 'Reporting and Storytelling: Eichmann in Jerusalem as Political Testimony' (2002) 68 *Thesis Eleven* 83.

16. On the presence of 'ethical' narratives and images of the Holocaust in debates and demonstrations around the recent conflicts in Gaza and the need to form a new foundation for legal reflection, legal judgment and legal justice in the Arendtian tradition of rethinking law, see David Seymour, 'From Auschwitz to Jerusalem to Gaza: Ethics for the Want of Law' (2011) 6 *Journal of Global Ethics* 205.
17. During the 1960s, Theodor Adorno became the most prominent challenger of both Karl Popper's philosophy of science and Martin Heidegger's philosophy of existence. The scope of Adorno's influence stems from the interdisciplinary character of his research and the critical influence of Frankfurt School to which he belonged. For both Adorno and Arendt, a critical reading of Kant's *Third Critique* is the indispensable means by which it is possible to locate a path pointing beyond the chiasmic structure suggested by the modernist tradition of history. See Theodore Adorno, *Can One Live after Auschwitz?: A Philosophical Reader*, ed. R. Tiedemann, trans. R. Livingstone et al. (Stanford University Press, 2003). Also see Susan Buck-Morss, *The Origin of Negative Dialectics; Theodor W. Adorno, Walter Benjamin and the Frankfurt Institute* (Free Press, 1977).
18. In the course of her 1964 interview with Günter Gaus, Arendt stated her distaste for 'intellectual business' that arose from witnessing the widespread and 'relatively voluntary' Gleichshaltung (coordination) of German 'intellectuals' with the Nazis in 1933. This raises the following question: what does lack of conscientious engagement with one's own acts – as exemplified by Eichmann – tell us about the relation between reason, judgment and harm? Engaging with this very question, see Shoshana Felman, 'Theaters of Justice: Arendt in Jerusalem, the Eichmann Trial, and the Redefinition of Legal

Meaning in the Wake of Holocaust' (2001) 1 *Theoretical Inquiries in Law* 8; Paul Formosa, 'Thinking, Conscience and Acting in the Face of Mass Evil', in Andrew Schaap, Danielle Celermajer and Vrasidas Karalis (eds), *Power, Judgment and Political Evil: In Conversation with Arendt* (Ashgate, 2010); Roger Berkowitz, Jeffrey Katz and Thomas Keenan (eds), *Thinking in Dark Times: Hannah Arendt on Ethics and Politics* (Fordham University Press, 2010).

19. See Lida Maxwell, 'Towards an Agonistic Understanding of Law: Law and Politics in Hannah Arendt's Eichmann in Jerusalem' (2010) 11 *Contemporary Political Theory* 88. On the issue of morality and politics of law concerning Nazi crimes, see Diana Taylor, 'Hannah Arendt on Judgment: Thinking for Politics' (2002) 10 *International Journal of Philosophical Studies* 151; Craig Reeves, 'Exploding the Limits of Law: Judgment and Freedom in Arendt and Adorno' (2009) 15 *Res Publica* 137; Seyla Benhabib (ed.), *Politics in Dark Times: Encounters with Hannah Arendt* (Cambridge University Press, 2010).
20. The literature on this debate is immense. For a select set of critical readings that concentrates precisely on the subject, see Samir Gandesha, 'Writing and Judging: Adorno, Arendt and the Chiasmus of Natural History' (2004) 30 (4) *Philosophy and Social Criticism* 445; Serena Parekh, *Hannah Arendt and the Challenge of Modernity: A Phenomenology of Human Rights* (Routledge, 2018); Samir Gandesha and Avery Goldman, 'An Antinomy of Political Judgment: Kant, Arendt and the Role of Purposiveness in Reflective Judgment' (2010) 43 *Continental Philosophy Review* 331; Annelies Degryse, 'Sensus Communis as a Foundation for Men as Political Beings: Arendt's Reading of Kant's Critique of Judgment' (2011) 37 *Philosophy and Social Criticism* 345; Dana Villa, 'From the Critique of Identity to Plurality of Politics: Reconsidering Adorno and Arendt', in Lars Rensmann and Samir Gandesha (eds), *Arendt and Adorno: Political and Philosophical Investigations* (Stanford University Press, 2012).
21. See Hannah Arendt and Ronald Beiner, *Lectures on Kant's Political Philosophy* (University of Chicago Press, 1989).
22. See Ronald Beiner, 'Rereading Hannah Arendt's Kant Lectures' (1997) 23 *Philosophy and Social Criticism* 21; Paul Formosa, 'Thinking, Willing, Judging' (2009) 4 *Crossroads* 53; and Roger Berkowitz and Majid Yar, 'From Actor to Spectator: Hannah Arendt's Two Theories of Judgment' (2010) 26 *Philosophy and Social Criticism* 1.
23. For a strong philosophical critique of the application of the Kantian model with reference to legal obligations, see David Copp, 'What Collectives Are: Agency, Individualism and Legal Theory' (1984) 23 *Dialogue* 249; and Kendy M. Hess, 'Because They Can: The Basis for the Moral Obligations of Collectives' (2014) 38 *Midwest Studies in Philosophy* 203. Alienation of individuals from each other and from the society at large is taken up by

communitarian critiques of law in legal theory, as well. See, for instance, Chantal Mouffe, 'Democratic citizenship and the political community' in her *Dimensions of Radical Democracy: Pluralism, Citizenship, Community* (Verso, 1992), pp. 225–39.

24. On the legal significance of the concept, see Joel Feinberg's work, especially his *Doing and Deserving: Essays in the Theory of Responsibility* (Princeton University Press, 1970). Also see Linda Raznik, 'Collective Responsibility and Duties to Respond' (2001) 27 *Social Theory and Practice* 455; Iris Marion Young, 'Responsibility and Global Justice: A Social Connection Model' (2006) 23 *Social Philosophy and Policy* 102; Ronald Tinnevelt, 'Collective Responsibility, National Peoples and the International Order' (2009) 2 *Netherlands Journal of Legal Philosophy* 147; and Margaret Gilbert, 'Shared Intention and Personal Intentions' (2009) 144 *Philosophical Studies* 167.
25. Regarding 'communities of judgment', Jennifer Nedelsky makes a strong argument in support of the social foundations of judgment. Using Hannah Arendt's work on judgment as a starting point, she addresses the problems and possibilities that arise out of Arendt's view that judgment relies on a 'common sense' shared by members of a community. Nedelsky points out that 'common sense,' 'community' and 'other judging subjects' are concepts not fully developed in Arendt's theory. She then proposes the concept of 'enlarged mentality' as the basis for human rights. Nedelsky's insights on Arendt's theory of judgment prove most useful in the context of collective responsibility. See Jennifer Nedelsky, 'Communities of Judgment and Human Rights' (2000) 1 *Theoretical Inquiries in Law* 245.
26. Plausibly, only moral agents can bear action-demanding duties and thus only moral agents could be subjected to criminal attribution. This standard places serious constraints on the determination of which collectives can bear action-demanding duties or be rendered accountable for societal harm. It is erroneous to assume that individual agents can bear duties and full scale of legal obligations regarding actions that only a collective could perform. This leaves us at a loss when assigning duties in circumstances where only a collective could perform some morally desirable action and no collective exists. Collectivization of duties and introduction of notions such as 'public responsibility' may alleviate some of the problem. Specifically, we could define individual duties to take steps towards forming a collective sense of responsibility, which then incurs a duty over collective and cumulative action. See Marion Smiley, 'From Moral Agency to Collective Wrongs: Rethinking Collective Moral Responsibility' (2010) 1 *Journal of Law and Policy* 171.
27. See Iris Marion Young, *Responsibility for Justice* (Oxford University Press, 2011). On the application of restitutive justice at a global scale, see Jacob

Schiff, 'Confronting Political Responsibility: The Problem of Acknowledgement' (2008) 23 *Hypatia* 99; Henning Hahn, 'The Global Consequences of Participatory Responsibility' (2008) 5 *Journal of Global Ethics* 43; and Todd Calder, 'Shared Responsibility, Global Structural Injustice and Restitution' (2009) 36 *Social Theory and Practice* 263.

28. See Thomas Scanlon, *What We Owe to Each Other* (Belknap Press/Harvard University Press, 1998); Michael Bratman, *Faces of Intention: Selected Essays on Intention and Agency* (Cambridge University Press, 1999).
29. On the issue of collective complicity, also see Larry May, 'Complicity: Ethics and Law for a Collective Age' (2002) 111 *Philosophical Review* 483; Garrath Williams, 'No Participation without Implication: Understanding the Wrongs We Do Together' (2002) 8 *Res Publica* 201; Torbjorn Tannsjo, 'The Myth of Innocence: On Collective Responsibility and Collective Punishment' (2007) 36 *Philosophical Papers* 295; Tracy Isaacs, *Moral Responsibility in Collective Contexts* (Oxford University Press, 2011); and Brian Lawson, 'Individual Complicity in Collective Wrongdoing' (2013) 16 *Ethical Theory and Moral Practice* 227.
30. In support of my proposition, see Margaret Gilbert, *Sociality and Responsibility: New Essays in Plural Subject Theory* (Rowman & Littlefield Publishers, 2000). Gilbert develops her arguments around a plural subject theory of human sociality, first introduced in her *On Social Facts* and *Living Together*. See Margaret Gilbert, *Living Together: Rationality, sociality, and obligation* (Rowman & Littlefield Publishers, 1996), and her earlier work, *On Social Facts* (Princeton University Press, 1992). In *Sociality and Responsibility*, Gilbert presents an extended discussion of her proposal that joint commitments inherently involve obligations and rights, and proposes a new theory of obligations and rights that deviates from individualistic agency arguments. Presenting political obligation, collective remorse, collective guilt, shared intention, and important classes of rights and obligations from a plural subject theory perspective, Gilbert's work is highly relevant to legal scholars who engage the subject of collective responsibility. Also see Margaret Gilbert, 'Collective guilt and collective guilt feelings' (2002) 6 *Journal of Ethics* 115; and her *Joint Commitment: How we make the social world* (Oxford University Press, 2015).
31. On environmental justice and collective responsibility, see Mary Oksanen, 'Species Extinction and Collective Responsibility' (2007) in *The Proceedings of the Twenty-First World Congress of Philosophy* (Vol. 3 at 179–83). Concerning the issue of what we owe to the world at large, David Zoller argues that while it is well-recognized that many everyday consumer behaviours, such as the purchasing of sweatshop goods, come at a heavy cost to the global poor, it has proven difficult to argue that contributors are somehow morally complicit in

those outcomes. The problem concerning marginal contributions to distant harms stems from lack of explicit knowledge of the aforementioned consequences. Distant and inadvertent acts that lead to harm provide insufficient grounds for moral or legal blame. However, contributors who knowingly disregard distant harms, rather than being reckless or negligent about consequences they could have foreseen, directly perpetuate the moral invisibility and the lack of recognition from which the global poor generally suffer. For Zoller, this provides agents with reasons to refrain from knowing participation in unstructured collective harms. See David Zoller, 'Moral Responsibility for Distant Collective Harms' (2015) 18 *Ethical Theory and Moral Practice* 995. Also see Bjorn Petersson, 'Co-responsibility and Causal Involvement' (2013) 41 *Philosophia* 847.

32. See David Miller, 'National responsibility and global justice' (2008) 11 *Critical Review of International Social and Political Philosophy* 383.
33. For a critique of Miller's work, see Roland Pierik, 'Collective responsibility and national responsibility' (2008) 11 *Critical Review of International Social and Political Philosophy* 465; and K. Lippert-Rasmussen, 'Responsible nations: Miller on national responsibility' (2009) 2 *Ethics & Global Politics* 21.
34. For a detailed account of law during the Third Reich, see the historical pieces written and published during the Second World War: K. Loewenstein, 'Law in the Third Reich' (1936) 45 *Yale L. J.* 716; V. L. Gott, 'The National Socialist theory of international law' (1938) 32 *Am. J. Int'l L.* 704; as well as the more recent debates such as D. F. Vagts, 'International Law in the Third Reich' (1990) 84 *Am. J. Int'l L.* 661; Martin Lippman, 'They Shoot Lawyers Don't They: Law in the Third Reich and the Global Threat to the Independence of the Judiciary' (1992) 23 *Cal. W. Int'l L. J.* 257; and David Dyzenhaus, 'Legal theory in the collapse of Weimar: contemporary lessons?' (1997) 91 *American Political Science Review* 121.
35. See T. J. Levy, 'National and statist responsibility' (2008) 11 *Critical Review of International Social and Political Philosophy* 485; and Margaret Moore, 'Global justice, climate change and Miller's theory of responsibility' (2008) 11 *Critical Review of International Social and Political Philosophy* 501.
36. See David Miller, 'Collective responsibility and international inequality in the law of peoples', in *Rawls's Law of Peoples: A Realistic Utopia?* (2006), pp. 191–205.
37. Matthew Braham and Martin Van Hees, 'An Anatomy of Moral Responsibility' (2012) 121 *Mind* 601. As discussed in detail by Braham and Van Hees, Frankfurt cases (also known as Frankfurt counter-examples) were presented by philosopher Harry Frankfurt in 1969 as counter-examples to the 'principle of alternate possibilities', which holds that an agent is morally responsible

for an action only if that person could have done otherwise. Frankfurt infers that a person could still be morally responsible for what he has done even if he could not have done otherwise. Frankfurt's examples involve agents who are intuitively responsible for their behaviour even though they lack the freedom to act otherwise. Frankfurt thus suggests that we question the fallacy of the notion that coercion precludes an agent from moral responsibility. See Harry G. Frankfurt, 'Alternate possibilities and moral responsibility' (1969) 23 *Journal of Philosophy* 829. This debate on responsibility under coercion resurfaced in more recent work such as Jay R. Wallace, *Responsibility and the Moral Sentiments* (Harvard University Press, 1984); John Martin Fischer and Mark Ravizza, *Responsibility and Control: A Theory of Moral Responsibility* (Cambridge University Press, 2000); and Derk Pereboom, *Living without Free Will* (Cambridge University Press, 2006).

38. See the Karl Jaspers entry of Encyclopaedia Britannica by Hans Saner at *https://www.britannica.com/biography/Karl-Jaspers* (accessed 25 May 2020).
39. See Karl Jaspers, *Vernunft und Existenz* (Groningen: Wolters). Translated as *Reason and Existenz*, trans. W. Earle (Noonday Press, 1955); *Nietzsche: Einführung in das Verständnis seines Philosophierens* (Berlin: de Gruyter). Translated as *Nietzsche: An Introduction to his Philosophical Activity*, trans. C. F. Wallraff and F. J. Schmitz (University of Arizona Press, 1965); and *Existenzphilosophie* (Berlin: de Gruyter). Translated as *Philosophy of Existence*, trans. R. F. Grabau (University of Pennsylvania Press, 1971).
40. See Karl Jaspers, *Die Geistige Situation der Zeit* (Berlin: de Gruyter). Translated as *Man in the Modern Age*, trans. E. Paul and C. Paul (Routledge, 1933). The original volume in German came out in 1931.
41. See the English translation, Karl Jaspers, *The Question of German Guilt* (Fordham University Press, 2009). This work was translated by E. B. Ashton and it was published in a series edited by John Caputo. The original version came out in German back in 1946 and the first English edition was published in 1947. See Karl Jaspers, *Die Schuldfrage* (Heidelberg: Schneider) ([translated as *The Question of German Guilt*, trans. E. B. Ashton] The Dial Press, 1947).
42. See Hannah Arendt et al., *Hannah Arendt/Karl Jaspers Correspondence, 1926–1969* (Harcourt Brace Jonakovich, 1992).
43. See Diane F. Orentlicher, 'Settling Accounts: The Duty to Prosecute Human Rights Violations of a Prior Regime' (1991) 100 *Yale L. J.* 2537; Steven Ratner, Jason S. Abrams and James L. Bischoff, *Accountability for Human Rights Atrocities in International Law: Beyond the Nuremberg Legacy*, 3rd edn (Oxford University Press, 2009).

44. Also see Henry T. King Jr, 'The Legacy of Nuremberg' (2002) 34 *Case W. Res. J. Int'l L.* 335; and Christian Tomuschat, 'The legacy of Nuremberg' (2006) 4 *Journal of International Criminal Justice* 830.
45. See Makoto Usami, 'Retroactive justice: trials for human rights violations under a prior regime', in Burton Leiser and Tom Campbell (eds), *Human Rights in Philosophy and Practice* (Routledge, 2001); and Kirsten Sellars (ed.), *Trials for International Crimes in Asia* (Cambridge University Press, 2016).
46. See Aryeh Neier, *War Crimes: Brutality, genocide, terror, and the struggle for justice* (Crown Publishing Group, 1998).
47. See Cherif M. Bassiouni (ed.), *International Criminal Law, vol. 2: Multilateral and Bilateral Enforcement Mechanisms* (Brill, 2008); William Schabas, *An Introduction to the International Criminal Court* (Cambridge University Press, 2011); and Antonio Cassese et al., *Cassese's International Criminal Law* (Oxford University Press, 2013).
48. In terms of legal defence, arguing *ad hominem* is a legitimate strategy of using an interlocutor's concessions to show that the interlocutor is committed to a certain conclusion. The defensive *ad hominem* is an attack on an opponent's ethos. The circumstantial *ad hominem*, which attributes the position of one's opponent to self-interest or a dogmatic bias, raises legitimate suspicion about the credibility of the opponent's statements and arguments. See David Hitchcock, 'Is there an argumentum ad hominem fallacy?' in Hans V. Hansen and Robert C. Pinto (eds), *Reason Reclaimed: Essays in honor of J. Anthony Blair and Ralph H. Johnson* (Vale Press, 2007), pp. 187–99.
49. James Meernik, 'Victor's Justice or the Law? Judging and Punishing at the International Criminal Tribunal for the Former Yugoslavia' (2003) 47 *Journal of Conflict Resolution* 140; Victor Peskin, 'Beyond Victor's Justice? The Challenge of Prosecuting the Winners at the International Criminal Tribunals for the Former Yugoslavia and Rwanda' (2005) 4 *Journal of Human Rights* 213; Bill Wringe, 'Why punish war crimes? Victor's justice and expressive justifications of punishment' (2006) 25 *Law and Philosophy* 159; William A. Schabas, 'Victor's Justice: Selecting Situations at the International Criminal Court' (2009) 43 *J. Marshall L. Rev.* 535.
50. A similar problem emerges with public apologies for past atrocities. Since the 1990s, political leaders around the world have begun to apologize for, and seek reconciliation between the perpetrators and victims of, large-scale moral wrongs such as slavery, ethnic cleansing and official regimes of racial segregation. This politics of 'moral healing' and the emergence of an official regime of requesting forgiveness is at odds with full-fledged reconciliation concerning societal wrongs, unless it leads to concrete policies of amelioration, structural change, and implementation of restorative justice measures. In this context,

Isaacs's work is particularly relevant. In her *Moral Responsibility in Collective Context* she relates intentional collective action to collective moral responsibility, as distinct from collective guilt. She also traces the pedigree of individual responsibility for (and in) collective wrongs and links collective obligations with individual obligations. An interesting case in this regard is the matter of combatants discussed by Uwe Steinhoff in 'Rights, Liability and the Moral Equality of Combatants' (2012) 16 *Journal of Ethics* 339. According to the dominant position in the just war tradition from Augustine to Anscombe and beyond, there is no 'moral equality of combatants' for criminal justice purposes. In other words, combatants participating in a justified war may kill enemy combatants participating in an unjustified war. In the meantime, where combatants violate the rights of innocent people – known as collateral damage in humanitarian law – they are in fact liable to attack by the combatants even on the unjustified side for self-defence, indicating the fluidity of the concepts of liability, culpability and accountability, even during active warfare.

51. See Epicurus, *The Essential Epicurus: Letters, Principal Doctrines, Vatican Sayings, and Fragments* (Prometheus Books, 1993). This popular arrangement of fragments follows the outline set forth by C. Bailey's 1926 collection on the thinker. One of the major philosophers in the Hellenistic period (the three centuries following the death of Aristotle in 323 B.C.E.), Epicurus developed an unsparingly materialistic and empiricist epistemology, and is known for his hedonistic ethics. He rejected the existence of Platonic forms and an immaterial soul, declaring gods have no influence on our lives. In Anglo-American philosophical traditions, Epicurean thought re-emerged primarily in the context of moral responsibility and intentionality. See Phillip Mitsis, *Epicurus' Ethical Theory: The Pleasures of Invulnerability* (Cornell University Press, 1988).
52. Developing a core conception of moral responsibility, Epicurus poses the question of what human life without moral responsibility would be like. On the Epicurean legacy concerning contemporary debates on moral responsibility, see John Martin Fischer, *My Way: Essays on Moral Responsibility* (Oxford University Press, 2006). Fischer's work is particularly relevant in its emphasis on the connections between free will, freedom of action, and moral responsibility/accountability. This frame of reference ties together responsibility for actions and omissions with references to consequences.
53. Braham and van Hees's work is particularly significant for its examination of the structure of moral responsibility in relation to outcomes. A central feature of their analysis is a condition they term 'avoidance potential', indicating that moral responsibility implies a reasonable demand that an agent should have acted otherwise. On the issue of the allocation of moral responsibility to individuals in complex collective wrongdoings, also see Kenton Machina,

'Moral Responsibility – What is All the Fuss About?' (2007) 22 *Acta Analytica* 29; and Neil Levy and Michael McKenna, 'Recent Work on Free Will and Moral Responsibility' (2009) 4 *Philosophy Compass* 96.

54. Michael Bratman proposed a full-fledged theory of intention and treated intention as an essential element of plans for action. Bratman's work also explores the distinction between intended and expected effects of what one intends. These issues are critical for reaching a deeper understanding of collective responsibility. See Michael Bratman, *Intention, Plans, and Practical Reason* (University of Chicago Press, 1987).
55. Michael Bratman, *Shared Agency: A Planning Theory of Acting Together* (Oxford University Press, 2013).
56. For a debate on intergenerational collective responsibility, see Janna Thompson, 'Collective Responsibility for Historic Injustices' (2006) 30 *Midwest Studies in Philosophy* 154.
57. See Melvyn Freeman and Soumitra Pathare, *WHO resource book on mental health, human rights and jurisprudence* (World Health Organization, 2005); and Steven Fish, *Democracy Derailed in Russia: The failure of open politics* (Cambridge University Press, 2005).
58. For instance, the proxy wars in Iraq and Afghanistan have put front and centre the problem of dealing with non-uniformed combatants. They also led to questions concerning the legitimacy of resorting to martial violence under circumstances of quasi-occupation. The location of legal agency for attributing responsibility to right the wrongs committed after the fact, and who to turn to for that end, remain major issues, especially for the American military establishment. The specific problem of non-uniformed combatants and the general problem of justifying war are profoundly linked. War is but only one form of generalized collective violence. Collective violence poses a particular set of challenges to the application of moral and legal principles within the context of the traditional model of criminal responsibility. See Anna Stilz, 'Collective responsibility and the state' (2011) 19 *Journal of Political Philosophy* 190; and Christopher Kutz, 'The difference uniforms make: collective violence in criminal law and war' (2015) 33 *Philosophy & Public Affairs* 148.
59. This problem is discussed in detail in Avia Pasternak, 'The collective responsibility of democratic publics' (2011) 41 *Canadian Journal of Philosophy* 99. Also see Hanna F. Pitkin, *The Concept of Representation* (University of California Press, 1967).
60. See Yvonne Chiu, 'Liberal Lustration' (2011) 19 *Journal of Political Philosophy* 440. For a larger debate on war and justice, see Robert E. Williams and Dan Caldwell, '*Jus post bellum*: Just war theory and the principles of just peace' (2006) 7 *International Studies Perspectives* 309; Jens Meierhenrich, 'The ethics

of lustration' (2006) 20 *Ethics & International Affairs* 99; Darrel Mollendorf, 'Jus ex bello' (2008) 16 *Journal of Political Philosophy* 123; Mark Evans, 'Moral responsibilities and the conflicting demands of jus post bellum' (2009) 23 *Ethics & International Affairs* 147; Anatoly Levshin, '*Jus Contra Bellum* in the Modern States System: Observations on the Anomalous Origins of the Crime of Aggressive War' (2015) 10 *St Antony's International Review* 141.

61. For Held, the crux of the matter lies in the defining characteristics of a 'collectivity,' and how decisions that lead to harm are reached. She takes a strong position against 'methodological individualism', which I share full-heartedly. Also see Albert Flores and Deborah G. Johnson, 'Collective responsibility and professional roles' (1983) 93 *Ethics* 537. This is a key debate on the responsibilities of 'the peg in the cog', i.e. individuals working as part of large institutions and organizations and towards a cumulative end result. The authors reach the conclusion that collective responsibility cannot be attributed to individuals in such situations. Rather, specific individuals and offices that provide the overall design and goals of the organization and determine the distribution of duties should be held responsible for erroneous acts of such organized bodies. For a counter-argument, see W. H. Walsh, 'Pride, Shame and Responsibility' (1970) 20 *The Philosophical Quarterly* 1.
62. See Steven Sverdlik, 'Collective Responsibility' (1987) 51 *Philosophical Studies* 61. For him, moral blameworthiness requires the existence of bad intentions – or at least moral faultiness – on the part of those being held responsible. Otherwise, one cannot seek criminality. On this issue, also see Seumas Miller, 'Collective Responsibility' (2001) 15 *Public Affairs Quarterly* 65. Miller's emphasis is typical of the traditional criminal law approach to collective responsibility. He underlines joint actions, rather than omissions and complicity that cause grave harm. He also makes a clear distinction between retrospective and prospective responsibility, an issue best attended to in the context of debates on restorative justice.
63. See Angelo J. Corlett, *Responsibility and Punishment*, vol. 9. (Springer, 2009). For Corlett, collective intentionality is a required condition to ascertain collective liability and he argues that collective responsibility can only be ascertained if there was collective voluntariness and if a corporate moral agency for wrongdoing and harm can be identified.
64. Peter French's work on corporations is particularly useful in this context. See Peter A. French, 'The Corporation as a Moral Person' (1979) 16 *American Philosophical Quarterly* 207. Interestingly, this debate dates back to late 1970s, well before the post-Marxist critiques of international public law.
65. Also see Larry May, *The Morality of Groups* (University of Notre Dame Press, 1989).

66. Also see Margaret Gilbert, 'Modelling collective belief' (1987) 73 *Synthese* 185. According to both Margaret Gilbert and Michael Bratman, the key is joint commitment. In other words, group intentions exist when two or more persons constitute the plural subject of an intention to carry out a particular action. Also see David J. Velleman, 'What Happens When Someone Acts?' (1992) 101 *Mind* 461.
67. See Raimo Tuomela and Kaarlo Miller, 'We-intentions' (1988) 53 *Philosophical Studies* 367. Also see Raimo Tuomela, 'We-intentions revisited' (2005) 125 *Philosophical Studies* 327 and Raimo Tuomela, *The Philosophy of Sociality: The Shared Point of View* (Oxford University Press, 2007).
68. In his later treatise *Moral Limits of Criminal Law*, Feinberg focuses on the relationship between interests and wants. In particular, he focuses on hard cases for the application of the concept of harm. Examples of the 'hard cases' Feinberg uses are harm to character, vicarious harm, and prenatal and posthumous harm. Feinberg also discusses the relationship between harm and rights, the concept of a victim, and the distinctions of various quantitative dimensions of harm, consent and offence, including magnitude, probability, risk and the importance of harm for both the individual and the society at large. See Joel Feinberg, *The Moral Limits of Criminal Law* (Oxford University Press, 1984).
69. The main texts I refer to in this regard are again those pertaining to the Arendt–Jaspers correspondence. Also see Hannah Arendt, *German Guilt* (Jewish Frontier Association, 1945); and Karl Jaspers, *The Origin and Goal of History* (Routledge Revivals Series, Routledge, 2014).
70. See Carl Wellman, *A Theory of Rights: Persons under Laws, Institutions and Morals* (Rowman & Allanheld, 1985); Meir Dan-Cohen, *Rights, Persons, and Organizations: A Legal Theory for Bureaucratic Society* (University of California Press, 1986); and Allen Buchanan, 'Toward a Theory of the Ethics of Bureaucratic Organizations' (1996) 6 *Business Ethics Quarterly* 419. These essays articulate a crucial and yet neglected element pertaining to the general theory of ethics of bureaucratic organizations. The key to the approach developed here is the thesis that distinctive ethical principles must be applicable to bureaucratic organizations due to their aggregate power-holding status. This arises from the nature of bureaucratic organizations as complex webs of principal–agent relations that cannot be reduced to individual actions.
71. In his treatise *Doing and Deserving*, Feinberg covers the following notions that are most pertinent to the current debate on collective responsibility: supererogation and rules, problematic responsibility in law and morals, justice and personal desert, *sua culpa* and collective responsibility. Also see his *The Moral Limits of the Criminal Law* (Oxford University Press, 1984), which

is the first volume in a four-volume series entitled *The Moral Limits of the Criminal Law* addressing the question of what acts the state may rightly render as criminal. Here, Feinberg identifies four liberty-limiting or coercion-legitimizing principles, each of which is the subject of a separate volume. In the first volume, he looks at the principle of harm to others, which John Stuart Mill identified as the only liberty-limiting principle. The other principles that Feinberg considers in subsequent volumes are (1) the offence principle – it is necessary to prevent hurt or offence (as opposed to harm) to others; (2) legal paternalism – it is necessary to prevent harm to the actor herself; and (3) legal moralism – it is necessary to prevent immoral conduct whether or not it harms anyone. Feinberg rejects legal paternalism and legal moralism, maintaining that the harm principle and the offence principle exhaust morally relevant reasons for criminal prohibitions. Instead, he considers both the moral status of a failure to prevent harm and the problems related to assessing, comparing and imputing harms. These discussions are essential for developing a robust, legally applicable understanding of collective responsibility.

72. Justiciability is a key concept especially for constitutional and international law, due to the fact that it pertains to the determination of the limits posed upon legal issues over which a given court can exercise its judicial authority. It includes the legal concept of standing in order to determine if the party bringing a legal suit could establish whether an actual adversarial act or issue exists.
73. This is despite the fact that Christian teachings interpret Jesus' crucifixion as his vicarious punishment for the sins of all humankind.
74. See Victor Tadros, *The Ends of Harm: The Moral Foundations of Criminal Law* (Oxford University Press, 2011).
75. An interesting case on the issue of vicarious liability is that of *Lister v Hesley Hall* [2002] 1 AC 215. In this case, the House of Lords reformed the law on vicarious liability, in the context of a claim arising over the intentional infliction of harm, by introducing the 'close connection' test. The immediate catalyst was the desire to facilitate recovery of damages on the part of victims of child abuse. The precise form the revision assumed was derived from two Canadian Supreme Court cases: *Bazley v Curry* [1999] 174 DLR (4th) 45 and *Jacobi v Griffiths* [1999] 174 DLR (4th) 7. Compared with other common law practices, Canadian jurisprudence contains a detailed review of the policy factors underpinning the law of vicarious liability and expresses the view that the most significant of these is 'enterprise liability'. See Douglas Brodie, 'Enterprise Liability: Justifying Vicarious Liability' (2007) 27 *Oxford Journal of Legal Studies* 493. On the larger issue of permissibility to harm others and related legal liabilities, see Charlie Webb, 'What is Unjust Enrichment?' (2009) 29 *Oxford Journal of Legal Studies* 215; Victor Tadros, 'Duty and

Liability' (2012) 24 *Utilitas* 259; and Joanna Mary Firth and Jonathan Quong, 'Necessity, Moral Liability and Defensive Harm' (2012) 31 *Law and Philosophy* 673. The last two articles build upon Jeff McMahan's work on justified killing at times of war, setting out a number of conditions for a person to be liable to attack provided the attack is used to avert an objectively unjust threat. They are defined in the following terms: (1) the threat, if realized, will wrongfully harm another; (2) the person is responsible for creating the threat; (3) killing the person is necessary to avert the threat; and (4) killing the person is a proportionate response to the threat. See Jeff McMahan, *The Ethics of Killing: Problems at the Margins of Life* (Oxford University Press, 2002).

76. The non-identity problem emerged as an ethical debate concerning our obligations to future generations during the 1970s. It figured strongly in the works of Derek Parfit, Thomas Schwartz and Robert M. Adams. See Derek Parfit, Thomas Schwartz and Robert M. Adams (eds), *Reasons and Persons* (Oxford University Press, 1984); James Woodward, 'The non-identity problem' (1986) 96 *Ethics* 804; Doran Smolkin, 'The Non-Identity Problem and the Appeal to Future People's Rights' (1994) 32 *Southern Journal of Philosophy* 315; Derek Parfit and Samuel Scheffler, *On What Matters: Volume One* (Oxford University Press, 2011).

Chapter 5

1. The first-generation courts are the Nuremberg and Tokyo Tribunals, while the second-generation courts are the ICTY, ICTR and ICC. See the Project on International Courts and Tribunals at *http://www.pict-pcti.org/courts/hybrid.html* (accessed 25 May 2020).
2. Cesare Romano, André Nollkaemper and Jann K. Kleffner (eds), *Internationalized Criminal Courts and Tribunals: Sierra Leone, East Timor, Kosovo, and Cambodia* (Oxford University Press, 2004).
3. The Extraordinary Chambers in the Courts of Cambodia (ECCC) were established in 2004 through an agreement between the United Nations (UN) and the Cambodian government, as a means to address the crimes committed during the Khmer Rouge regime in Cambodia between 1975 and 1979. The ECCC encompasses both national and international elements in its structure, composition and jurisdiction. As with other hybrid courts, it was expected to allow for a higher degree of participation by national actors, and to be better placed to produce long-lasting effects. The value added by the participation by various national actors in the judicial proceedings is indeed the key feature of the ECCC, despite concerns raised about the judicial independence of the court. See Elizabeth Bruch, 'Hybrid Courts: Examining Hybridity through a Post-Colonial Lens' (2010) 28 *B. U. Int'l L. J.* 1.

4. The Extraordinary African Chambers (EAC) was created by the African Union (AU) and Senegal in 2012, specifically to try former Chadian president Hissène Habré and his officials for atrocities allegedly committed during his time in office between 1982 and 1990. Habré was accused of war crimes, crimes against humanity and torture. Some 40,000 surviving victims were directly represented in court and ninety-two witnesses and experts have recounted his fierce repression. The *Habré* trial represents the first trial by an African state of a former head of state of another African state. The EAC will also provide a valuable insight into what a regional approach to internationalized justice may look like. It is also important to note the consistency of the EAC Statute with the *nullum crimen sine lege* principle. See Sarah Williams, 'The Extraordinary African Chambers in the Senegalise Courts: An African Solution to an African Problem?' (2013) 15 *J. of Int. Crim. J.* 1139.
5. Etelle R. Higonnet, 'Restructuring hybrid courts: local empowerment and national criminal justice reform' (2005) 23 *Ariz. J. Int'l & Comp. L.* 347.
6. As an exception, see Jenia I. Turner, 'Transnational networks and international criminal justice' (2007) 105 *Michigan Law Review* 985. The theory of trans-governmental networks Turner uses describes how government officials make law and policy on issues of global concern by coordinating across borders, but without legal or official sanction. Banking, antitrust, environmental protection, and securities law are sample areas in this regard.
7. On how international human rights law 'works', see Kurt Mills and David Jason Karp (eds), *Human Rights Protection in Global Politics: Responsibilities of States and Non-State Actors* (Palgrave Macmillan, 2015); Alexandra Huneeus, 'Human Rights between Jurisprudence and Social Science' (2015) 28 *Leiden Journal of International Law* 255; William Armaline, Davita S. Glasberg and Bandana Purkayastha (eds), *The Human Rights Enterprise: Political Sociology, State Power, and Social Movements* (John Wiley & Sons, 2015); Courtney Hillebrecht, *Domestic Politics and International Human Rights Tribunals: The Problem of Compliance* (Cambridge University Press, 2014); Ryan Goodman and Derek Jinks, *Socializing States: Promoting Human Rights Through International Law* (Oxford University Press USA, 2013); Thomas Risse, Stephen C. Ropp and Kathryn Sikkink (eds), *The Persistent Power of Human Rights: From Commitment to Compliance* (Cambridge University Press, 2013).
8. Here, I rely heavily on the following sub-section of TWAIL scholarship: Luis Eslava, Michael Fakhri and Vasuki Nesiah (eds), *Bandung, Global History and International Law: Critical Pasts and Pending Futures* (Cambridge University Press, 2015); K. Mickelson, 'Taking stock of TWAIL histories' (2008) 10 *International Community Law Review* 355; M. Khosla, 'The TWAIL Discourse: The emergence of a new phase' (2007) 9 *International Community*

Law Review 291; Obiora Chinedu Okafor, 'Newness, imperialism, and international legal reform in our time: a TWAIL perspective' (2005) 43 *Osgoode Hall L. J.* 171.

9. See Antony Anghie, 'Colonialism and the Birth of International Institutions: Sovereignty, Economy, and the Mandate System of the League of Nations' (2002) 34 *NYU J. Int'l L. & Pol.* 513 at 517; Jose Manuel Barreto (ed.), *Human Rights from a Third World Perspective: Critique, History and International Law* (Cambridge Scholars Press, 2013), in particular his introductory essay, as well as Amy Maguire, 'Contemporary Anti-colonial Self-Determination Claims and the Decolonisation of International Law,' (2013) 22 *Griffith Law Review* 238, and Amy Maguire and Jeffrey Mcgee, 'A Universal Human Right to Shape Responses to a Global Problem? The Role of Self-Determination in Guiding the International Legal Response to Climate Change' (2017) 26 RECIEL 54. Maguire and Mcgee contribute to the existing debate on the relevance of human rights struggle in the Global South in the specific context of climate change and greenhouse gas emissions. They focus on the foundational principle of the self-determination of peoples as a collective human right, which has emerged in the context of movements of decolonization and emancipation of oppressed peoples. In their belief, self-determination might offer an alternative logic of duty on high-emitting States to the plight of populations who find their territories under threat from anthropogenic climate change.
10. Nicole Laliberté, 'Geographies of Human Rights: Mapping Responsibility' (2015) 9 *Geography Compass* 57.
11. Vijay Prashad, *The Poorer Nations: A Possible History of the Global South* (London: Verso, 2012).
12. The Andean Court of Justice, the Court of Justice of the Economic Community of West African States, the Caribbean Court of Justice, the Court of Justice and Arbitration of the Organization for the Harmonization of Business Laws in Africa, and the East African Community Court of Justice are some of the leading examples of non-European regional courts with a strong human rights-related track record of rulings.
13. For the text of the ICC indictment as well as the text of the April 2009 arrest warrant, please see the relevant documents at *http://www.icc-cpi.int/NR/exeres/0EF62173-05ED-403A-80C8-F15EE1D25BB3.htm* (accessed 25 May 2020). Specifically, the indictment indicates that the Sudanese President is suspected of being criminally responsible, as an indirect co-perpetrator, for intentionally directing attacks against a selected part of the civilian population of Darfur, Sudan, and murdering, exterminating, raping, torturing and forcibly

transferring large numbers of civilians, and pillaging their property. This was the first warrant of arrest issued for a sitting Head of State by the ICC.

14. Regarding the perception of the indictment, see the IPS poll results published in July 2009 at *http://ipsnews.net/news.asp?idnews=47678* (accessed 25 May 2020). The survey results indicated that the public in four majority Muslim and African nations, contrary to the positions of their governments, largely approved of the indictment of President al-Bashir by the International Criminal Court despite the fact that many fellow African and Muslim leaders have supported Bashir and cursed the indictment as politically motivated.
15. On this issue, see the manifesto of Doctors without Borders available at *http://doctorswithoutborders.org/publications/article.cfm?id=3516&cat=op-eds-articles* (accessed 25 May 2020). Their worry was directly related to the fact that with attacks on remaining aid workers increasing, the Sudanese president had declared that all international humanitarian aid organizations must leave the country in the foreseeable future, further endangering the delivery of food, water and medical care to millions of people in the war-scarred region. These expulsions are seen as a reprisal against groups suspected of being involved with the ICC investigations as well as against governments that support the indictment of President al-Bashir.
16. Elections were swiftly delayed in the aftermath of the ICC indictment. Under the 2005 peace deal to end years of war in the south, these elections were supposed to be held in 2009. The SPLM, former rebels from the south, were expected to field a candidate against President Omar al-Bashir. In 2010, there were six elections: national, presidential, and parliamentary, the south Sudanese presidency, state governors, the southern parliament and state assemblies. The polls were Sudan's first democratic elections in more than two decades. See BBC news at *http://news.bbc.co.uk/2/hi/7980032.stm* (accessed 25 May 2020)].
17. Al-Mahdi had been the head of the Umma party as well as the last democratically elected prime minister in 1986 before being toppled by a coup. He is also the spiritual leader of the powerful Ansar sect in the region. For his political profile, see his biography published by the Club of Madrid, an independent pro-democracy consortium at *http://www.clubmadrid.org/cmadrid/index.php?id=397* (accessed 25 May 2020).
18. For a sample of these arguments, see *http://africanarguments.org/2009/03/the-icc-sudan-and-the-crisis-of-human-rights/* (accessed 25 May 2020). African Arguments Online is a counterpart to the African Arguments book series, edited jointly by Alex de Waal and Richard Dowden, published by Zed Books in the UK and Palgrave Macmillan in the US.

19. For a detailed account of the jurisprudence of these hybrid courts, see the UN documents at *http://www.ohchr.org/Documents/Publications/HybridCourts.pdf* (accessed 25 May 2020).
20. The Rome Statute establishing the ICC contains a provision, Article 16, which allows the UN Security Council to pass a resolution (under its Chapter VII authority) to defer an ICC investigation or prosecution for a renewable period of twelve months. Article 16 states in full that 'No investigation or prosecution may be commenced or proceeded with under this Statute for a period of 12 months after the Security Council, in a resolution adopted under Chapter VII of the Charter of the United Nations, has requested the Court to that effect; that request may be renewed by the Council under the same conditions.' For a debate on the use of Article 16 of the Rome Statute in the Darfur context, see *http://www.hrw.org/en/news/2008/08/15/q-article-16* (accessed 25 May 2020).
21. See, for instance, Laura Dickinson, 'The Relationship Between Hybrid Courts and International Courts: The Case of Kosovo' (2003) 37 *New Eng. L. Rev.* 1059; as well as her 'Using Legal Process to Fight Terrorism: Detentions, Military Commissions, International Tribunals, and the Rule of Law' (2002) 75 *S. Cal. L. Rev.* 1407 and 'The Promise of Hybrid Courts' (2003) 97 *Am. J. Int'l L.* 295. Also see Abdul Tejan-Cole, 'The Complementary and Conflicting Relationship between the Special Court for Sierra Leone and the Truth and Reconciliation Commission' (2003) 6 *Yale Hum. Rts. & Dev. L. J.* 139; Suzanne Katzenstein, 'Hybrid Tribunals: Searching for Justice in East Timor' (2003) 16 *Harv. Hum. Rts. J.* 245; and Secretary-General, *The Rule of Law and Transitional Justice in Conflict and Post-conflict Societies*, UN Doc. S/2004/616 (23 Aug. 2004).
22. See the African Union report on the launch at *https://www.au.int/en/news-events/31469/press-conference-launch-african-union-campaign-restore-dignity-women-and* (accessed 25 May 2020).
23. For the full manuscript of Bineta Diop, see *http://www.peaceau.org/en/page/40-5676-static-bineta-diop* (accessed 25 May 2020).
24. Concerning the latest efforts for establishing a South Sudanese hybrid court, see *https://justiceinconflict.org/2017/02/28/the-hybrid-court-for-south-sudan-looking-for-a-way-forward-part-2/* (accessed 25 May 2020). South Sudan is a country in transition that is still struggling with the consequences of the fifty-year civil war as well as resurging internal ethnic conflict. Recent ethnic clashes in South Sudan are evidence that one of the main challenges for the newly independent country is the implementation of an accountability regime for organized political violence in the midst of more than sixty different ethnic groups.

25. These include key reports by the AU Commission of Inquiry Report at *http://www.peaceau.org/en/article/final-report-of-the-african-union-commission-of-inquiry-on-south-sudan* (accessed 25 May 2020), the Human Rights Watch Report on Sudan at *https://www.hrw.org/world-report/2017/country-chapters/sudan* [(accessed 25 May 2020), the United Nations Human Rights Council Report on Sudan at *http://www.ohchr.org/EN/HRBodies/HRC/CoHSouthSudan/Pages/Index.aspx* (accessed 25 January 2019) and Amnesty International Report on Sudan at *https://www.amnesty.org/en/countries/africa/sudan/report-sudan/* (accessed 25 May 2020),
26. For the full text of the Agreement signed on 17 August 2015, see *https://unmiss.unmissions.org/sites/default/files/final_proposed_compromise_agreement_for_south_sudan_conflict.pdf* (accessed 25 May 2020).
27. Also see the legal opinion expressed in the Office for Democratic Institutions and Human Rights document on the issue at *http://www.osce.org/odihr/elections/tunisia/247346?download=true* (accessed 25 May 2020).
28. This new article is to replace the 2008 Protocol on the Statute of the African Court of Justice and Human Rights, which had no immunity clause. For the immunity clause, see the relevant AU document and the full text of the article at *http://www.ijrcenter.org/2014/07/02/african-union-approves-immunity-for-heads-of-state-in-amendment-to-african-court-of-justice-and-human-rights-statute/* (accessed 25 May 2020).
29. See the ICTJ document on the AU's request for collective withdrawal at *https://www.ictj.org/news/au-withdrawal-icc-non-starter* (accessed 25 May 2020).
30. The treaty leading to the Rome Statute (2002) had 124 member states including 34 African states, which represents the largest regional bloc of member states. Since then, several African countries have expressed dissatisfaction with the Court and have accused it of bias. Gambia announced on 25 October 2016 that it would withdraw from the ICC, calling the Court an 'International Caucasian Court' for the persecution and humiliation of people of colour, especially Africans. Similarly, Burundi labelled the ICC as a 'Western tool to target African governments'. Uganda's president Yoweri Museveni called the ICC 'useless' and praised South Africa's decision to leave. Namibia is also reconsidering its membership. Additionally, the African Union earlier this year said it would consider a mass withdrawal from the Court – a proposal initiated by Kenyan president Uhuru Kenyatta, who had previously appeared at The Hague on allegations of crimes against humanity. Despite this, the Court also has remaining supporters in the region. At the African Union summit meeting in July 2016, the Democratic Republic of Congo, Ivory Coast, Nigeria, Senegal and Tunisia were among the countries that opposed

a Kenyan-led drive for a group walkout. As of December 2018, nine out of ten cases the Court was investigating were in African countries (Mali, Cote D'Ivoire, Central African Republic, Libya, Kenya, Sudan, Uganda, Democratic Republic of Congo). Georgia was the only country not in Africa facing an investigation. One example given of bias is the fact that The Gambia has pressured the ICC to try and punish the European Union for the deaths of thousands of African migrants trying to reach its shores, yet has been unsuccessful. See Jean-Baptiste Jeangène Vilmer, 'The African Union and the International Criminal Court: Counteracting the crisis' (2016) 92 *International Affairs* 1319.

31. See the American Bar Association's Report on South Sudan at *http://www.americanbar.org/content/dam/aba/directories/roli/sudan/aba_roli_sudan_assessment_final_report_0614.authcheckdam.pdf* (accessed 25 May 2020).
32. See Rosanna Lipscomb, 'Restructuring the ICC Framework to Advance Transitional Justice: A Search for a Permanent Solution in Sudan' (2006) *Columbia Law Review* 182.
33. Article 11 defines *jurisdiction ratione temporis* in the following terms: 'The Court has jurisdiction only with respect to crimes committed after the entry into force of this Statute, and, if a State becomes a Party to this Statute after its entry into force, the Court may exercise its jurisdiction only with respect to crimes committed after the entry into force of this Statute for that State, unless that State has made a declaration under article 12, paragraph 3.' For the full text of the treaty item, see *http://www.preventgenocide.org/law/icc/statute/part-a.htm* (accessed 25 May 2020).
34. On this issue, see Payam Akhavan, 'The International Criminal Court in Context: Mediating the Global and Local in the Age of Accountability' (2003) 97 *Am. J. of Int'l L.* 712.
35. See William W. Burke-White, 'Regionalization of International Criminal Law: A Preliminary Exploration' (2003) 38 *Tex. Int'l L. J.* 729 at 755–61; Thomas Buergenthal, 'Proliferation of International Courts and Tribunals: Is It Good or Bad?' (2001) 14 *Leiden J. Int'l L.* 267 at 272; Jonathan I. Charney, 'Is International Law Threatened by Multiple International Tribunals?' (1998) 271 *Recueil des Cours* 125.
36. Complementarity has been extolled as the pioneering way for the ICC to navigate the difficulties of state sovereignty when investigating and prosecuting international crimes. In Uganda, for instance, new laws, legal procedure and accountability for international crimes have been introduced over the past decade, all based on the complementarity principle, culminating in the trial of Thomas Kwoyelo. Meanwhile, while there has been a profusion of provisions to allow victims to participate, with protection measures and planned reparations, in practice very little has changed for them. There are dangers of

complementarity being proposed as the sole solution to protracted conflicts, in particular in the area of the realization of victims' rights. See Harmen van der Wilt, 'Complementary Jurisdiction (Article 46H)', in *The African Criminal Court* (TMC Asser Press, 2017), pp. 187–202.

37. For a full coverage of the crimes under consideration, see Richard Falk's report published in Le Monde diplomatique (March 2009) titled *Israel's war crimes: Calls for investigation into Gaza attacks*. For the full text, see *http://www.tni.org/detail_page.phtml?act_id=19322&username=guest@tni.org&password=9999&publish=Y&print_format=Y* (accessed 25 May 2020).
38. Here, I define accountability regimes in international law on par with Steven Ratner, Jason Abrams and J. Bischoff's definition in their work *Accountability for Human Rights Atrocities in International Law: Beyond The Nuremberg Legacy* (Oxford University Press, 2009), responding to the necessity of holding individuals *and* legal subjects accountable for gross human rights violations.
39. For an authoritative account of crimes against humanity from a historical perspective, see Larry May, *Crimes Against Humanity: A Normative Account* (Cambridge University Press, 2005).
40. On the issue of the use of the legal category of crimes against humanity in the context of transitional justice, see ICTJ, 'What is Transitional Justice?' *A Voice for Victims*, New York: International Center for Transitional Justice Annual Report 2004/2005, p. 1, and Naomi Roht-Arriaza and Javier Mariezcurrena (eds), *Transitional Justice in the Twenty-First Century: Beyond Truth versus Justice* (Cambridge University Press, 2006).
41. See Cherif Bassiouni, 'Chronology of efforts to establish an International Criminal Court' (2015) 86 *Revue internationale de droit pénal* 1163.
42. See David Pion-Berlin, 'The Pinochet Case and Human Rights Progress in Chile: Was Europe a Catalyst, Cause or Inconsequential?' (2004) 36 *Journal of Latin American Studies* 479; David Sugarman, 'From Unimaginable to Possible: Spain, Pinochet and the Judicialization of Power' (2002) 3 *J. of Spanish Cult. Stud.* 107; and A. Bianchi, 'Immunity versus human rights: the Pinochet case' (1999) 10 *European Journal of International Law* 237.
43. See John Dugard, 'Dealing With Crimes of a Past Regime. Is Amnesty Still an Option?' (1999) 12 *Leiden J. of Int'l L.* 1001.
44. See the *Haaretz* article, dated 31 October 2009 on the developments regarding the relations between Israel and Belgium on this issue. On 30 October 2009, the Belgian Supreme Court ruled that Defense Ministry director-general Amos Yaron could be prosecuted for his involvement in the Sabra and Shatila massacres in 1982 in Beirut, when he was commander of the IDF forces in the Lebanese capital at the time. The court also ruled that Prime Minister Ariel Sharon can be put on trial for his alleged involvement in the

affair, but only after he ceases to be prime minister, when he no longer has diplomatic immunity. Back in 2001, two separate claims against Sharon were brought under a 1993 Belgian law which allows war crimes and genocide to be tried in Belgium, even if the events took place elsewhere, and even if none of the victims were Belgian. The first case, charging Sharon with responsibility for the deaths, was lodged by a group of Palestinians, Lebanese, Moroccans and Belgians. The second suit for alleged crimes of crimes against humanity, genocide and war crimes was filed by twenty-three survivors of the massacres and five eyewitnesses. Initially, in 2002, the Belgian appeals court ruled on 26 June that the law was not applicable in Sharon's case because the accused was not on Belgian territory. However, the later verdict reversed that decision. Palestinian Authority Chairman Yasser Arafat was also in line for prosecution in Belgium, in the wake of complaints filed against him by Israeli terror victims. On 10 December 2008, a formal complaint was filed against Ehud Barak to the ICC, on suspicion of war crimes and crimes against humanity because of the siege of Gaza. For full details of both complaints, see *http://www.haaretz.com/hasen/pages/ShArt.jhtml?itemNo=262391&contrassID=2&subContrassID=1&sbSubContrassID=0&listSrc=Y* (accessed 25 May 2020).

45. The 1993 law, amended in 1999 and again in 2003, gives Belgian courts the authority to prosecute persons accused of genocide, crimes against humanity, or war crimes regardless of where the crimes took place or whether the suspect or the victims are Belgian. The new version of the 1993 law, however, grants immunity to serving heads of state or government, as well as ministers. It also acknowledges the pre-eminence of the ICC. Finally, the law creates a 'filter' against abusive lawsuits by granting the prosecutors' office the option of rejecting complaints if they are deemed unfounded or politically motivated. It is noteworthy that the Belgian law has served as a basis for complaints against a series of other foreign leaders, including Yasser Arafat. For a detailed analysis of the Belgian 'anti-atrocity' law, see the Human Rights Watch report at *http://thewe.cc/contents/more/archive2003/july/belgium_law_on_atrocities.pdf* (accessed 25 May 2020).

46. Proponents of universal jurisdiction argue that the principle is well established in international law and that a wide range of human rights offences are subject to universal jurisdiction. One such prominent group drafted the 'Princeton Principles on Universal Jurisdiction', which held that the following offences can be tried by any court in the world without regard to where the crime occurred or who committed it: piracy, slavery, war crimes, crimes against peace, crimes against humanity, genocide, and torture. Typically, legal specialists recognize five bases for jurisdiction under international criminal law. The two best-established jurisdictional bases concern the territoriality and nationality

principles, in which states have jurisdiction over crimes committed in their territory or by their nationals. Two other jurisdictional bases have received less consistent acceptance: passive personality, based on the nationality of the victim, and protective clause, based on the existence of serious threats to a state. The fifth jurisdictional base, the universality principle, refers to claims based only on the nature of the crime. For an all-encompassing debate on the fate of universal jurisdiction, see Antonia Cassesse, 'Is the Bell Tolling for Universality? A Plea for a Sensible Notion of Universal Jurisdiction' (2003) 1 *J. of Int'l Crim. Justice* 589. For the Princeton Principles document, see *http://lapa.princeton.edu/hosteddocs/unive_jur.pdf* (accessed 25 May 2020).

47. See the *Jurist* article on the issue at *http://www.jurist.org/paperchase/2017/01/belgium-court-orders-arrest-of-former-israel-top-official-for-war-crimes.php* (accessed 25 May 2020).
48. Canada became the first country to incorporate the obligations of the Rome Statute into its national laws when it adopted the Crimes against Humanity and War Crimes Act (CAHWCA) on 24 June 2000. To ensure that Canada can fully cooperate with ICC proceedings, the CAHWCA also amended existing Canadian laws like the Criminal Code, Extradition Act and Mutual Legal Assistance in Criminal Matters Act. For the full text of the Act, see *http://www.iccnow.org/documents/Canada.CrAgH.WcrEng.pdf* (accessed 25 May 2020). The first case under Canada's Crimes against Humanity and War Crimes Act (2000) opened at the main courthouse in Montreal on 26 March 2007. The defendant, Désiré Munyaneza, a Rwandan charged with genocide, faced seven charges in the indictment covering the period from 1 April 1994 to the end of July 1994, roughly corresponding to the 100 days of the genocide in Rwanda. Munyaneza, a Hutu, faced two counts of genocide, two counts of crimes against humanity and three counts of war crimes. For a case summary, see the International Criminal Database report at *http://www.internationalcrimesdatabase.org/Case/1176* (accessed 25 May 2020).
49. South Africa first withdrew from the ICC in 2016, and then reversed its withdrawal in March 2017. See the *New York Times* article (8 March 2017) on the issue at *https://www.nytimes.com/2017/03/08/world/africa/south-africa-icc-withdrawal.html?_r=0* (accessed 25 May 2020).
50. See Luc Reydams, *Universal Jurisdiction: International and Municipal Legal Perspectives* (Oxford University Press, 2003).
51. In 1960, Israeli agents kidnapped the Nazi official Adolf Eichmann in Argentina. They brought him to Jerusalem to be tried for crimes against humanity committed in Europe during the 1940s, before Israel achieved statehood. He was found guilty of crimes against humanity, war crimes and genocide and was hanged in 1962. Eichmann was charged under a 1950 Israeli law enacted to

punish Nazis and their collaborators. He was charged on fifteen counts. For a critical case history of the Eichmann trial, see Shoshana Felman, 'Theaters of Justice: Arendt in Jerusalem, the Eichmann Trial, and the Redefinition of Legal Meaning in the Wake of the Holocaust' (2001) 1 *Theoretical Inquiries in Law* 8.

52. Also see Laura Dickenson, 'The Promise of Hybrid Courts' (2003) 97 *Am. J. of Int'l L.* 295.
53. Regarding the arrest warrant, see Chanaka Wickremasinghe and Malcolm D. Evans, 'Case concerning the Arrest Warrant of 11 April 2000 (Democratic Republic of the Congo v. Belgium)' (2001) 50 *Int'l and Comp. Law Quarterly* 670.
54. See Stephen Ratner's work on transnational corporations, 'Corporations and Human Rights: A Theory of Legal Responsibility' (2001) 111 *Yale L. J.* 443.
55. See Christopher Mullins, David Kauzlarich and Dawn Rothe, 'The International Criminal Court and the Control of State Crime: Prospects and Problems' (2004) 12 *Crit. Crim.* 1205.
56. The question of the relationship between the international criminal court and the Security Council was only partially settled at the Rome Conference. Aspects of the power differences between Security Council members and lay members of the UN system in the application of international law remain the subject of a heated debate. For a critical account of this issue, see Louise Arbour, 'The Relationship between the ICC and the UN Security Council' (2014) 20 *Global Governance: A Review of Multilateralism and International Organizations* 195.
57. The ICC is structured in the following format. The Office of the Prosecutor is an independent organ of the court, and it decides whether there is a reasonable basis to investigate possible crimes. As already stated, cases are referred to this office either by a State Party or by the UN Security Council. The Pre-Trial Chamber has authority to issue an arrest warrant after considering submissions by the prosecutor. When a wanted person appears before the court, the Pre-Trial Chamber holds a hearing to confirm the charges that will be the basis of the trial. The Trial Chamber is where the actual hearings take place. If the charges are confirmed, the court assigns the case to the three-judge Trial Chamber responsible for conducting fair and expeditious proceedings. After the conclusion of testimony, the Trial Chamber issues its decision, acquitting or convicting the accused. If the person is convicted, the Trial Chamber issues a sentence of imprisonment and may also order reparations to victims. Finally, throughout the proceedings the parties can appeal decisions to an Appeal Chamber of five judges. The Trial Chamber's verdict or sentence may also be appealed by the prosecutor or by the accused.

58. On this issue, see the work of one of ICC's founders, Philippe Kirsch, in his and John T. Holmes's 'The Rome Conference on an International Criminal Court: The Negotiating Process' (1999) 93 *Am. J. Int'l L.* 2; his 'The International Criminal Court: Current Issues and Perspectives' (2001) 64 *L. and Contemp. Prob.* 3; and his 'The Role of the International Criminal Court in Enforcing International Criminal Law' (2007) 22 *Am. U. Int'l L. Rev.* 53.
59. According to Article 17, Section I, the Court shall determine that a case is inadmissible where: (a) the case is being investigated or prosecuted by a State which has jurisdiction over it, unless the State is unwilling or unable to genuinely carry out the investigation or prosecution; (b) the case has been investigated by a State which has jurisdiction over it and the State has decided not to prosecute the person concerned, unless the decision resulted from the unwillingness or inability of the State genuinely to prosecute; (c) the person concerned has already been tried for conduct which is the subject of the complaint, and a trial by the Court is not permitted under Article 20, paragraph 3; (d) the case is not of sufficient gravity to justify further action by the Court. The full text of the Statute can be accessed at *http://www.icc-cpi.int/legaltools/* (accessed 25 May 2020).
60. Part IX outlines principles of International Cooperation and Judicial Assistance. For full text of the Rome Statute Part IX, see *http://untreaty.un.org/cod/icc/statute/romefra.htm* (accessed 25 May 2020).
61. Meanwhile, whether a separate law should be adopted to provide for the required cooperation, or whether existing jurisprudence can be modified, depends entirely on the legal context of the State Party.
62. Here, International Human Rights Law (IHRL) is defined as a system of laws, domestic, regional and international, designed to promote human rights. States that ratify human rights treaties at least in principle commit themselves to enact domestic human rights jurisprudences. Human rights law is related to, but not the same as International Humanitarian Law or Refugee Law. In contrast, International Humanitarian Law (IHL) is defined as a set of rules that seek, for humanitarian reasons, to limit the effects of armed conflict. IHL's aim is to protect persons who did not or are no longer participating in the hostilities and to restrict or regulate the means and methods of warfare. IHRL and IHL are two distinct but complementary bodies of law. Both seek to protect the individual from arbitrary action and abuse. However, while IHRL is worded to protect the individual at all times, IHL only applies in situations of armed conflict. The ICC's mandate covers both areas due to the specific set of crimes it codified and, when applicable, adjudicates. However, it does not exhaustively cover either body of law since it deals with a specific

subset of crimes concerning crimes against humanity, genocide, crimes of aggression and war crimes.

63. For a detailed discussion of the domestication procedures of the Rome Statute and for a sample of implementation packages, see *http://www.iccnow.org/?mod=romeimplementation* (accessed 25 May 2020). The list of packages available for public review include those used by Uruguay, France, the Arab League, Commonwealth, Colombia, Bolivia, Kenya and Argentina as well as the ICC's own recommendations for implementation.
64. Article 79 is on the issue of Trust Fund, according to which a Trust Fund shall be established by decision of the Assembly of States Parties for the benefit of victims of crimes within the jurisdiction of the Court, and of the families of such victims. Paragraph 2 then states that the Court may order money and other property collected through fines or forfeiture to be transferred, by order of the Court, to the Trust Fund.
65. In addition, again in Article 77, it is stated that a fine could be issued under the criteria provided for in the Rules of Procedure and Evidence, or a forfeiture of proceeds, property and assets derived directly or indirectly from that crime could be confiscated, without prejudice to the rights of bona fide third parties.
66. See Mary Kimani, 'ICC and Africa: Pursuit of justice or Western plot? International indictments stir angry debate in Africa' (2009) 23 *Africa Renewal* 3; and Max du Plessis, *The International Criminal Court and Its Work in Africa: Confronting Myths* (ISS Paper 173, November 2008).
67. The Khmer Rouge seized power in Cambodia in 1975 and killed more than a million people during its four-year rule. It was only in March 2003 that the United Nations reached a draft agreement with the Cambodian government for the establishment of the Extraordinary Chambers in the Courts of Cambodia (ECCC) to try former Khmer Rouge leaders. The agreement took five years of negotiations and came into effect twenty-four years after Khmer Rouge were driven from power. The ECCC consists of both Cambodian and international judges and has exclusive jurisdiction over selected crimes committed by the Khmer Rouge regime between 1975 and 1979. However, only one person has been indicted due to interference from the government and resource issues, as well as responsible persons passing the age of seventy. For further details on the ECCC, see *https://www.un.org/ruleoflaw/thematic-areas/international-law-courts-tribunals/international-hybrid-criminal-courts-tribunals/* (accessed 25 May 2020).
68. See Mettraux, G., *International Crimes and the* ad hoc *Tribunals* (Oxford University Press, 2005).

69. For the actual text of the Malabo Protocol, see Amnesty International document *https://www.amnesty.org/download/Documents/AFR0130632016ENGLISH.PDF* (accessed 25 May 2020).
70. Concerning the promise of a new model of international criminal justice emerging from the African context, see Leigh Stewart, 'International Justice in Africa: Defining Authority and Localizing the Global' (2017) *iCourts Working Paper Series No. 86*, accessible at *http://dx.doi.org/10.2139/ssrn.2917110* (accessed 25 May 2020).
71. An important aspect of the debates on restorative justice is a critical analysis of how the main 'crime stakeholders' (victim, offender and the community at large) are represented within policy framework. The most recurrent normative representations of the victim, offender and community exhibit a range of typified features. In real cases, however, there is no 'ideal' victim or offender and communities are often implicit in mass crimes, pinpointing overlaps. Finally, the political and cultural contexts within which these representations have emerged influence both policy and laws pertaining to litigation. Here, restorative justice is understood to offer more than a critical reflection on the normative dimension of Western penal policies. See Daniel W. Van Ness and Karen Heetderks Strong, *Restoring Justice: An Introduction to Restorative Justice*, 5th edn (Routledge, 2014); and Gerry Johnstone, *Restorative Justice: Ideas, Values, Debates*, 2nd edn (Routledge, 2013).
72. See Kerry Clamp, 'Clearing the conceptual haze: restorative justice concepts in transitional settings' (2016) *Restorative Justice in Transitional Settings* 1; and Philip McCready, *Can restorative practices work in a Loyalist area?: A case study on restorative responses to community conflict of a Loyalist area in South Belfast* (dissertation, Ulster University, 2016).
73. The war in Northern Uganda between the Lord's Resistance Army (LRA) and Government of Uganda (GoU) forces dates back to 1986. In 2006, the Juba Peace Talks were held between the GoU and the LRA, mediated by Riek Machar, the Vice President of South Sudan. However, LRA leader Joseph Kony refused to sign the final peace agreement. Military campaigns by all parties to the conflict led to fierce attacks on civilian populations across Northern Uganda, which included raping, mutilating and abducting civilians, raiding villages, and looting and burning houses. The conflict has had disastrous economic, physical, social and psychological effects on the entire civilian population. Both during and after the conflict, women played important roles as combatants, in support roles in the military as well as the domestic sphere and in initiating community-led approaches to ending the violence. Nonetheless, transitional justice discussions in Uganda almost exclusively focus on male parties to the conflict. For a policy brief describing gender-based

violence, its occurrence and effects on local communities during and after the conflict in Northern Uganda, see Sylvia Pinia and Frederike Bubenzer, *Gender Justice and Reconciliation in Uganda* (Institute for Justice and Reconciliation, 2011).

74. For the full text of the government's declaration, see the Report by the Institute for War and Peace Reporting at *https://iwpr.net/global-voices/can-traditional-rituals-bring-justice-northern-uganda* (accessed 25 May 2020).
75. On Ugandan Peace Talks, see Ronald R. Atkinson, 'From Uganda to the Congo and Beyond: Pursuing the Lord's Resistance Army' (New York: International Peace Institute, December 2009) at *www.ipacademy.org/media/pdf/publications/e_pub_uganda_to_congo.pdf* (accessed 25 May 2020); Adam Branch, 'Uganda's civil war and the politics of ICC intervention' (2007) 21 *Ethics and International Affairs* 179; Mareike Schomerus, 'Small Arms Survey. The Lord's Resistance Army in Sudan: A History and Overview' (Geneva: Graduate Institute of International Studies, 2007); Moses Chrispus Okello, 'The false polarisation of peace and justice in Uganda', Expert paper for 'Workshop 2 – Justice in Situations of Ongoing Conflict', Conference organized by International Center for Transitional Justice (Nuremberg, Germany, June 2007), *www.peace-justice-conference.info/download/WS-2-Expert%20Paper-Okello.pdf* (accessed 25 May 2020).
76. Lucy Hovil and Joanna Quinn, 'Peace First, Justice Later: Traditional Justice in Northern Uganda', Refugee Law Project Working Paper No. 17 (Kampala: Refugee Law Project, 2005) at *www.refugeelawproject.org/working_papers.php* (accessed 25 May 2020).
77. See the report of International Crisis Group, *Northern Uganda: The road to peace, with or without Kony* (Africa Report No. 146, 10 December 2008).
78. See Franziska Boehme, '"We Chose Africa": South Africa and the Regional Politics of Cooperation with the International Criminal Court' (2016) 24 *International Journal of Transitional Justice*.
79. Congolese warlord Thomas Lubanga was found guilty of war crimes in recruiting and using child soldiers. The prosecutor, Luis Moreno-Ocampo, has vowed to seek the maximum sentence for Lubanga and called the conviction a victory for humanity. However, the case was twice delayed due to stays imposed by the judges in response to the office of the prosecutor's failure to disclose information to the defence. On 15 March 2020, Lubanga was released after serving the fourteen-year sentence. See the BBC News article (28 March 2012) on the issue at *http://www.bbc.com/news/world-africa-18779726* (accessed 25 May 2020).
80. In 2004, the Congolese government invited the ICC to investigate and prosecute war crimes that have occurred in the DRC since 1 July 2002. The ICC

has issued four arrest warrants concerning the conflict in the Ituri district of the DRC, for Thomas Lubanga Dyilo and the following suspects: Germain Katanga, alleged commander of the Force de Résistance Patriotique en Ituri (FRPI). The ICC charged Katanga with multiple counts of war crimes and crimes against humanity. Katanga has been in ICC custody since 2007. Mathieu Ngudjolo Chui, alleged former leader of the Front National Intégrationiste (FNI) and a colonel in the National Army of the DRC (FARDC) was charged with multiple counts of war crimes and crimes against humanity in Ituri. Ngudjolo was transferred to ICC custody in February 2008. Bosco Ntaganda, alleged former deputy chief of the general staff of the FPLC and alleged current chief of staff of the Congrès National pour la Défense du Peuple (CNDP) was subject to an arrest warrant on charges focusing on recruitment of child soldiers. In addition to the four ICC cases concerning the Ituri conflict in the DRC, the ICC has arrested another Congolese suspected war criminal: Jean-Pierre Bemba Gombo, leading Congolese opposition figure, president of the Mouvement de Libération du Congo (MLC), senator and former vice-president. Bemba was arrested in Belgium in May 2008 on an ICC arrest warrant charging him with war crimes committed in the Central African Republic in 2002–3. He was then transferred to ICC custody in The Hague in July 2008. See the special report by the International Justice Monitor at *https://www.ijmonitor.org/category/germain-katanga-and-mathieu-ngudjolo-chui/* (accessed 25 May 2020).

81. For the full text of the ICC Pre-Trial Chamber decision concerning the Case: *The Prosecutor v. Germain Katanga and Mathieu Ngudjolo Chui* Situation in the Democratic Republic of the Congo made in 2008, see *https://www.icc-cpi.int/Pages/record.aspx?docNo=ICC-01/04-01/07-717* (accessed 25 May 2020).
82. See Ben Okolo, 'African Renaissance, African Conflicts and the Regional Security Complex' (2010) 16 *The State of Africa 2010/11: Parameters and legacies of governance and issue areas* 103.
83. For details of these cases, see the documents published by ECCC at *https://www.eccc.gov.kh/en/case/topic/1?page=6* and *https://www.eccc.gov.kh/en/case/topic/1299* (accessed 25 May 2020).
84. For detailed information and case summaries, see Aaron Fichtelberg, 'Leading Cases of the Hybrid Courts', in *Hybrid Tribunals* (Springer New York, 2015), pp. 113–75.
85. See Cathy Caruth, *Unclaimed Experience: Trauma, narrative, and history* (JHU Press, 2016); Ross McGarry and Sandra Walklate, *Victims: Trauma, testimony and justice* (Routledge, 2015); and Dominick LaCapra, *Writing history, writing trauma* (JHU Press, 2014).

86. See Brianne McGonigle Leyh, 'Victim-Oriented Measures at International Criminal Institutions: Participation and its Pitfalls' (2012) 12 *International Criminal Law Review* 375.
87. The term 'therapeutic legalism' was coined by Duncan McCargo. See Duncan McCargo, 'Transitional Justice and Its Discontents' (2015) 26 *Journal of Democracy* 5.
88. For a detailed critique of the workings of the ICC and both its strengths and its failings in terms of upholding foundational principles of criminal justice, see Larry May and Shannon Fyfe, *International Criminal Tribunals: A Normative Defense* (Cambridge University Press, 2017).
89. See the lengthy tally of state behaviour provided in Nasser Zammit, *Human Rights and Responsibility* (Connaissances et savoirs, 2012).
90. See, for instance, the transcript of the group discussion titled 'Millennium 2000: Would an International Criminal Court Help or Hinder Pursuit of Global Justice', available online at *http://transcripts.cnn.com/TRANSCRIPTS/0001/02/bp.00.html* (accessed 25 May 2020).
91. The information on the trials and cases in the Court is available at ICC's official site, *http://www.icc-cpi.int/Menus/ICC/Situations+and+Cases/* (accessed 25 May 2020).
92. See Charles Call, 'Is Transitional Justice Really Just?' (2004) 11 *Brown Journal of World Affairs* 101.
93. Sentencing in international criminal law is an under-attended field. Based on the statutes and decisions of the International Tribunals for the former Yugoslavia (ICTY) and Rwanda (ICTR), one critical aspect of sentencing emerges as how judges assess the harm caused by the perpetration of international crimes. The aforementioned Tribunals' judges had great discretion in imposing sentences. This resulted in a lack of uniformity in sentencing decisions, both in sentence length and in methodology. There is indeed a need for in-depth conversations concerning the framework for evaluating the harm associated with the different kinds of crimes within the jurisdiction of the ICCTs as well as hybrid courts. The crimes within the jurisdiction of the ICC have two sets of elements: the chapeau, which confers international jurisdiction over the offence, and the enumerated acts, which resemble domestic crimes. Most hybrid courts consider only the harm associated with the enumerated act when imposing an appropriate sentence. However, it is critical that the courts also consider the chapeau elements in their harm determinations. These international criminal elements encode important information about the secondary harms caused by the offences. See Andrea Carcano, 'Sentencing and the gravity of the offence in international criminal law' (2002) 51 *Int. & Comp. Law Quarterly* 583; Allison Marston Danner, 'Constructing a hierarchy

of crimes in international criminal law sentencing' (2001) 87 *Virginia Law Review* 415; and William Schabas, 'Sentencing by international tribunals: a human rights approach' (1996) 7 *Duke J. Comp. & Int'l L.* 461.

94. See the original formulation of this opposition in Gabriel Joseph Starke, 'Monism and dualism in the theory of international law' (1936) 17 *Brit. Y. B. Int'l L.* 66. Also see Leslie C. Green, 'An International Criminal Code – Now' (1976) 3 *Dalhousie L. J.* 560.
95. Máximo Langer, 'Universal Jurisdiction is Not Disappearing: The Shift from "Global Enforcer" to "No Safe Haven" Universal Jurisdiction' (2015) 13 *J. of Int. Crim. J.* 245.
96. See Partha Chatterjee, 'Introduction: Postcolonial Legalism' (2014) 34 *Comparative Studies of South Asia, Africa and the Middle East* 224. This is a special issue that explores post-colonial practices of the law in four countries: India, Sri Lanka, Lebanon and South Africa. The key concern about the legal-constitutional framework of post-colonial politics is the question of social transformation induced by law rather than law's superior position as an abstract construct.
97. Nancy Combs, 'Seeking Inconsistency: Advancing Pluralism in International Criminal Sentencing' (2015) 41 *Yale J. Int'l L.* 387

Conclusion

1. See Gijsbert Jonkers, *The Textual Tradition of Plato's Timaeus and Critias* (Brill, 2016).
2. See Gerry Simpson, *Great Powers and Outlaw States: Unequal sovereigns in the international legal order*, vol. 32 (Cambridge University Press, 2004).
3. For a similar argument albeit with reference to the specific national context of India, see Shalini Randeria, 'The State Of Globalization: Legal Plurality, Overlapping Sovereignties and Ambiguous Alliances between Civil Society and the Cunning State in India' (2007) 24 *Theory, Culture & Society* 1.
4. A strict closure privileges existing authoritative legal practices, and thus assumes a protective stance vis-à-vis the *status quo* in international governance. See, for instance, Andrew Moravcsik, 'Taking Preferences Seriously: A Liberal Theory of International Politics' (1997) 51 *International Organization* 513; Richard Devetak and Richard Higgot, 'Justice Unbound? Globalization, States, and the Transformation of the Social Bond' (1999) 75 *International Affairs* 21; Taslim Elias, *The International Court of Justice and Some Contemporary Problems: Essays on International Law*, vol. 2 (Springer Science & Business Media, 2013); William A. Schabas, Gerry Simpson and Suzannah Linton, *For the Sake of Present and Future Generations: Essays on International Law, Crime and Justice in Honour of Roger Clark* (Brill Nijhoff, 2016).

5. On this issue, Steven Ratner's *The Thin Justice of International Law* offers a comprehensive interdisciplinary theory of international law's relationship with global justice. Ratner argues that the justice of legal norms that constitute our international legal order should be determined according to two criteria: the degree to which they causally bring about international and intra-state peace; and the degree to which they causally bring about a state of affairs in which basic human rights are respected. I disagree with Ratner's commitment to rule consequentialism, his treatment of the state system as a fixed attribute of our international legal order, and his particular embrace of a political conception of human rights. In his work, questions relating to international law's distribution of sovereignty – its origins, the episodic recalibrations to which it is subject, especially during and after times of war, and its distributional consequences remain outside the normative sphere of global justice. See Steven Ratner, *The Thin Justice of International Law: A Moral Reckoning of the Law of Nations* (Oxford University Press, 2015).
6. Here, the work of Nardin, Cox, Held, Murphy, Welch and Rosenau are representative of the origins of this debate. See Terry Nardin, *Law, Morality and the Relations of States* (Princeton University Press, 1983); James Rosenau and Ernst-Otto Czempiel (eds), *Governance Without Government: Order and Change in World Politics* (Cambridge University Press, 1992); David Welch, *Justice and the Genesis of War* (Cambridge University Press, 1993); James Rosenau, 'Governance in the Twenty-First Century' (1995) 1 *Global Governance* 13; David Held, *Democracy and the Global Order: From the Modern State to Cosmopolitan Democracy* (Stanford University Press, 1995); Daniele Archibugi and David Held (eds), *Cosmopolitan Democracy: An Agenda for a New World Order* (Polity Press, 1995); Robert Cox, 'An Alternative Approach to Multilateralism in the Twenty-First Century' (1997) 3 *Global Governance* 1; Craig Murphy, 'Global Governance: Poorly Done and Poorly Understood' (2000) 76 *International Affairs* 780. Also see Donatella Della Porta et al., *Global Justice Movement: Cross-national and transnational perspectives* (Routledge, 2015); and Satvinder Juss, *International Migration and Global Justice* (Routledge, 2016).
7. See Anthony Clark Arend and Robert J. Beck, *International Law and the Use of Force: Beyond the UN Charter Paradigm* (Routledge, 2014); and Upendra Baxi, 'Some Newly Emergent Geographies of Injustice: Boundaries and Borders in International Law' (2016) 23 *Indiana Journal of Global Legal Studies* 15. Baxi famously argues that the relationship between the boundaries and borders of international law and the production of geographies of injustice becomes devastatingly obvious when examined through the lens of colonial epistemologies. His work addresses the languages and logics of

'coloniality' and 'postcoloniality' under the complex and contradictory unity of neo-liberalism. Thus, it is both present- and future-oriented, rather than providing a chronology of injustices in international law. Baxi's interventions are essential in terms of deciphering the strong voices of discontent emanating from the Global South.

8. See the work of Andrew Guzman, in particular his 'International Organizations and the Frankenstein Problem' (2013) 24 *European Journal of International Law* 999.
9. In forced migration studies literature, this kind of accusation has been made widely against the UNHCR. See James Hollifield, Philip Martin and Pia Orrenius, *Controlling Immigration: A Global Perspective* (Stanford University Press, 2014).
10. The main reference to this debate is Immanuel Kant, 'Perpetual Peace: A Philosophical Sketch' in Hans Reiss (ed.), *Kant's Political Writings* (Cambridge University Press, 1992).
11. The two extremes of this argument are found in the work of Hedley Bull, 'The State's Positive Role in World Affairs' (1979) 108 *Daedelus* 111, and his *The Anarchical Society: A Study of Order in World Politics* (Macmillan, 1977); and John Rawls, *The Law of Peoples* (Harvard University Press, 1999).
12. For further debate, see the early work of Lawrence Finkelstein, 'What Is Global Governance?' (1995) 1 *Global Governance* 367; Martin Hewson and Timothy J. Sinclair (eds), *Approaches to Global Governance Theory* (SUNY Press, 1995); as well as John Ruggie, 'Global governance and "new governance theory": Lessons from business and human rights' (2014) 20 *Global Governance* 5–17; and Nico Krisch, 'The Decay of Consent: International Law in an Age of Global Public Goods' (2014) 108 *Am. J. Int'l L.* 1.
13. On the issue of substantive challenges to existing global governance structures via law, see Lawrence Gostin and Devi Sridhar, 'Global health and the law' (2014) 370 *New England Journal of Medicine* 1732; and Kenneth Gould, David N. Pellow and Allan Schnaiberg, *Treadmill of Production: Injustice and Unsustainability in the Global Economy* (Routledge, 2015).
14. As an exception, see Yves Dezalay and Bryant Garth (eds), *Lawyers and the Rule of Law in an Era of Globalization* (Routledge, 2011); and Yves Dezalay and Bryant Garth (eds), *Lawyers and the Construction of Transnational Justice* (Routledge, 2013).
15. Exemplary of this point of view, see Chris Brown, 'Review Article: Theories of International Justice' (2001) 27 *British Journal of Political Science* 371; and Antonio Franceschet, 'Theorizing state civil disobedience in international politics' (2015) 11 *Journal of International Political Theory* 239. Franceschet argues that by introducing a broader conception of resistance and proposing

two interdependent types of power, namely *constituent* power and *destituent* power, we would have a more accurate understanding of state criminality overall.

16. See, for instance, the articulation of a similar ideal (though in a different context) in Robert O'Brien, Anne Marie Goetz, Jan Aart Scholte and Marc Williams (eds), *Contesting Global Governance: Multilateral Economic Institutions and Global Social Movements* (Cambridge University Press, 2000).
17. See Karen Alter, *The New Terrain of International Law: Courts, politics, rights* (Princeton University Press, 2014); Charles De Visscher, *Theory and Reality in Public International Law* (Princeton University Press, 2015); and Eyal Benvenisti and Sarah M. H. Nouwen, 'Leaving Legacies Open-Ended: An Invitation for an Inclusive Debate on International Criminal Justice' (2016) 110 *Am. J. Int'l L.* 205.
18. See Michael James Grenfell, *Pierre Bourdieu: Key concepts* (Routledge, 2014); and Pierre Bourdieu, *Outline of a Theory of Practice*, vol. 16 (Cambridge University Press, 1977).
19. For a discontented critical analysis of academia, see Pierre Bourdieu, *Homo Academicus* (Stanford University Press, 1988); and Pierre Bourdieu, Franck Poupeau and Thierry Discepolo, *Political Interventions: Social science and political action* (Verso Books, 2008).
20. Antony Anghie and B. S. Chimni, 'Third World Approaches to International Law and Individual Responsibility in Internal Conflicts' (2003) 2 *Chinese J. Int'l L.* 77.

Bibliography

Abbott, K., 'International Relations Theory, International Law, and the Regime Governing Atrocities in Internal Conflicts' (1999) 93 *Am. J.Int'l L.* 361.

Accatino, D. and C. Collins, 'Truth, Evidence, Truth: The Deployment of Testimony, Archives and Technical Data in Domestic Human Rights Trials' (2016) 8 *Journal of Human Rights Practice* 81.

Adorno, T., *Can One Live after Auschwitz?: A Philosophical Reader*, ed. R. Tiedemann, trans. R. Livingstone et al. (Stanford University Press, 2003).

Akhavan, P., 'The International Criminal Court in Context: Mediating the Global and Local in the Age of Accountability' (2003) 97 *Am. J. of Int'l L.* 712.

Akhavan, P., 'Reconciling Crimes Against Humanity with the Laws of War Human Rights, Armed Conflict, and the Limits of Progressive Jurisprudence' (2008) 6 *J. of Int. Crim. J.* 21.

Alford, R., 'Misusing International Sources to Interpret the Constitution' (2004) 98 *Am. J. of Int'l L.* 57.

Alter, K., *Establishing the Supremacy of European Law: The Making of an International Rule of Law in Europe* (Oxford University Press, 2001).

Alter, K., *The New Terrain of International Law: Courts, politics, rights* (Princeton University Press, 2014).

Amin, S., *Capitalism in the Age of Globalization: The Management of Contemporary Society* (ZED Books, 2014).

Anderson, B., *Imagined Communities: Reflections on the origin and spread of nationalism* (Verso Books, 2006).

Anghie, A., 'Colonialism and the Birth of International Institutions: Sovereignty, Economy, and the Mandate System of the League of Nations' (2002) 34 *NYU J.Int'l L. & Pol.* 513.

Anghie, A., 'Imperialism and International Legal Theory', in A. Orford and F. Hoffmann (eds), *The Oxford Handbook of the Theory of International Law* (Oxford University Press, 2015).

Anghie, A., *Imperialism, Sovereignty and the Making of International Law*, Cambridge Studies in International and Comparative Law, vol. 37 (Cambridge University Press, 2007).

Anghie, A., 'International Law and the Pre-History of Globalisation' (2015) 33 *Sing. L. Rev.* 3.

Anghie, A., 'TWAIL: Past and Future' (2008) 10 *Int'l Comm. L. Rev.* 479.

Anghie, A. and B. S. Chimni, 'Third World Approaches to International Law and Individual Responsibility in Internal Conflicts' (2003) 2 *Chinese J. Int'l L.* 77.

Anghie, A. et al., *The Third World and International Order: Law, Politics, and Globalization* (Martinus Nijhoff, 2003).

Arato, A., 'The Bush Tribunals and the Specter of Dictatorship' (2002) 9 *Constellations* 457.

Arbour, L., 'The Relationship between the ICC and the UN Security Council' (2014) 20 *Global Governance: A Review of Multilateralism and International Organizations* 195.

Archer, S., D. Drache and P. Zumbansen (eds), *The Daunting Enterprise of the Law: Essays in Honour of Harry Arthurs* (McGill-Queen's University Press, 2017).

Archibugi, D. and D. Held (eds), *Cosmopolitan Democracy: An Agenda for a New World Order* (Polity Press, 1995).

Arend, A. C. and R. J. Beck, *International Law and the Use of Force: Beyond the UN Charter Paradigm* (Routledge, 2014).

Arendt, H., *Eichmann in Jerusalem* (Penguin, 1963).

Arendt, H., 'Eichmann in Jerusalem: An exchange of letters between Gershom Scholem and Hannah Arendt' (1964) 22 *Encounter* 51.

Arendt, H., *German Guilt* (Jewish Frontier Association, 1945).

Arendt, H., *Hannah Arendt/Karl Jaspers Correspondence, 1926–1969* (Harcourt Brace Jonakovich, 1992).

Arendt, H., 'Personal responsibility under dictatorship', in *Responsibility and Judgment* (Schocken Books, 2003), pp. 17–48.

Arendt, H., *Responsibility and Judgment* (Schocken Books, 2003).

Arendt, H., *The Human Condition* (University of Chicago Press, 2013).

Arendt, H., *The Origins of Totalitarianism* (Meridian Books, 1962).

Arendt, H. and R. Beiner, *Lectures on Kant's Political Philosophy* (University of Chicago Press, 1989).

Armaline, W., Davita S. Glasberg and Bandana Purkayastha (eds), *The Human Rights Enterprise: Political Sociology, State Power, and Social Movements* (John Wiley & Sons, 2015).

Arrighi, G., 'Hegemony unravelling – 2' (2005) 33 *New Left Review* 83.

Arrighi, G., 'Lineages of empire' (2002) 10 *Historical Materialism* 3.

Arrighi, G., 'Spatial fixes, switching crises, and accumulation by dispossession' (2006) *Global social change: Historical and comparative perspectives* 201.

Arrighi, G., *The Long Twentieth Century: Money, Power, and the Origins of our Times* (Verso, 1994).

Atkinson, R. R., 'From Uganda to the Congo and Beyond: Pursuing the Lord's Resistance Army' (New York: International Peace Institute, December 2009).

Badar, M., 'From the Nuremberg Charter to the Rome Statute: Defining the elements of crimes against humanity' (2004) 5 *San Diego Int'l L. J.* 73.

Badaru, O. A., 'Examining the Utility of Third World Approaches to International Law for International Human Rights Law' (2008) 10 *Int'l Comm. L. Rev.* 379.

Barak, G. (ed.) *Crimes by the Capitalist State: An introduction to state criminality* (SUNY Press, 1991).

Barreto, J. M. (ed.), *Human Rights from a Third World Perspective: Critique, History and International Law* (Cambridge Scholars Press, 2013).

Bassiouni, C., 'Chronology of efforts to establish an International Criminal Court' (2015) 86 *Revue internationale de droit pénal* 1163.

Bassiouni, C., *Crimes against Humanity: Historical Evolution and Contemporary Application* (Cambridge University Press, 2011).

Bassiouni, C., 'Crimes Against Humanity: The Case for a Specialized Convention' (2010) 9 *Wash. U. Global Stud. L. Rev.* 575.

Bassiouni, C., 'International crimes: jus cogens and obligatio erga omnes' (1996) 59 *Law & Contemp. Probs.* 63.

Bassiouni, C., *The Legislative History of the International Criminal Court* (Transnational Publishers, 2005).

Bassiouni, C. (ed.), *International Criminal Law, vol. 2: Multilateral and Bilateral Enforcement Mechanisms* (Brill, 2008).

Bates, S., 'The Responsibility of Random Collections' (1971) 81 *Ethics* 343.

Baxi, U., 'Some Newly Emergent Geographies of Injustice: Boundaries and Borders in International Law' (2016) 23 *Indiana Journal of Global Legal Studies* 15.

Baxter, H., 'Autopoiesis and the Relative Autonomy of Law' (1997) 19 *Cardozo L. Rev.* 1987.

Bayat, A., 'From Dangerous Classes' to Quiet Rebels' Politics of the Urban Subaltern in the Global South' (2000) 15 *International Sociology* 533.

Bazyler, M. J. and F. M. Tuerkheimer, *Forgotten Trials of the Holocaust* (NYU Press, 2015).

Bederman, D. and C. Keitner, *International Law Frameworks*, 4th edn (West Academic, 2016).

Beigbeder, Y., *International Justice against Impunity: Progress and new challenges* (Martinus Nijhoff Publishers, 2005).

Beiner, R., 'Rereading Hannah Arendt's Kant Lectures' (1997) 23 *Philosophy and Social Criticism* 21.

Benhabib, S., 'Arendt's Eichmann in Jerusalem', in Dana Richard Villa (ed.), *The Cambridge Companion to Hannah Arendt* (Cambridge University Press, 2000), pp. 65–85.

Benhabib, S., 'On the Alleged Conflict between Democracy and International Law' (2005) 19 *Ethics and International Affairs* 85.

Benhabib, S. (ed.), *Politics in Dark Times: Encounters with Hannah Arendt* (Cambridge University Press, 2010).

Benvenisti, E., 'Reclaiming Democracy: The Strategic Uses of Foreign and International Law by National Courts' (2008) 102 *Am. J. Int'l L.* 241.

Benvenisti, E. and G. W. Downs, 'The empire's new clothes: Political economy and the fragmentation of international law' (2007) 60 *Stanford Law Review* 595.

Benvenisti, E. and G. W. Downs, 'The premises, assumptions, and implications of Van Gend en Loos: Viewed from the perspectives of democracy and legitimacy of international institutions' (2014) 25 *European Journal of International Law* 85.

Benvenisti, E. and S. M. H. Nouwen, 'Leaving Legacies Open-Ended: An Invitation for an Inclusive Debate on International Criminal Justice' (2016) 110 *Am. J. Int'l L.* 205.

Berger, M., 'After the Third World? History, destiny and the fate of Third Worldism' (2004) 25 *Third World Quarterly* 9.

Berkowitz, R., J. Katz and T. Keenan (eds), *Thinking in Dark Times: Hannah Arendt on Ethics and Politics* (Fordham University Press, 2010).

Berkowitz, R. and M. Yar, 'From Actor to Spectator: Hannah Arendt's Two Theories of Judgment' (2010) 26 *Philosophy and Social Criticism* 1.

Berman, P. S., 'A Pluralist Approach to International Law' (2007) 32 *Yale J. Int'l L.* 301.

Berman, P. S., 'From international law to law and globalization' (2004) 43 *Colum. J. Transnat'l L.* 485.

Berman, P. S., 'Global legal pluralism' (2006) 80 *Cal.L. Rev.* 1155.

Bernstein, P., 'Derrida: The aporia of forgiveness?' (2006) 13 *Constellations* 394.

Bianchi, A., 'Immunity versus human rights: The Pinochet case' (1999) 10 *European Journal of International Law* 237.

Bianchi, A. (ed.), *Non-State Actors and International Law* (Routledge, 2017).

Billig, M., *Banal Nationalism* (Sage, 1995).

Birmingham, P., 'Holes of Oblivion: The Banality of Radical Evil' (2003) 18 *Hypatia* 80.

Bo, M., 'The Situation in Libya and the ICC's Understanding of Complementarity in the Context of UNSC-Referred Cases' (2014) 25/3–4 *Criminal Law Forum*.

Boehme, F., '"We Chose Africa": South Africa and the Regional Politics of Cooperation with the International Criminal Court' (2016) 24 *International Journal of Transitional Justice*.

Boot, M., *Genocide, Crimes Against Humanity, War Crimes: Nullum crimen sine lege and the subject matter jurisdiction of the International Criminal Court*, vol. 12 (Intersentia, 2002).

Booth, K. and T. Erskine (eds), *International Relations Theory Today* (John Wiley & Sons, 2016).

Bordin, L. F., 'Reflections of Customary International Law: The Authority of Codification Conventions and ILC Draft Articles in International Law' (2014) 63 *Int. & Comp. Law Quarterly* 535.

Bourdieu, P., *Homo Academicus* (Stanford University Press, 1988).

Bourdieu, P., *Outline of a Theory of Practice*, vol. 16 (Cambridge University Press, 1977).

Bourdieu, P., F. Poupeau and T. Discepolo, *Political Interventions: Social science and political action* (Verso Books, 2008).

Bowring, B., *The Degradation of the International Legal Order?: The rehabilitation of law and the possibility of politics* (Routledge, 2008).

Braham, M. and M. van Hees, 'An Anatomy of Moral Responsibility' (2012) 121 *Mind* 601.

Branch, A., 'Uganda's civil war and the politics of ICC intervention' (2007) 21 *Ethics and International Affairs* 179.

Bratman, M., *Faces of Intention: Selected essays on intention and agency* (Cambridge University Press, 1999).

Bratman, M., *Intention, Plans, and Practical Reason* (University of Chicago Press, 1987).

Bratman, M., *Shared Agency: A Planning Theory of Acting Together* (Oxford University Press, 2013).

Breuilly, J., *Nationalism and the State* (Manchester University Press, 1993).

Brodie, D., 'Enterprise Liability: Justifying Vicarious Liability' (2007) 27 *Oxford Journal of Legal Studies* 493.

Brown, C., 'Review Article: Theories of International Justice' (2001) 27 *British Journal of Political Science* 371.

Bruch, E., 'Hybrid Courts: Examining Hybridity through a Post-Colonial Lens' (2010) 28 *B. U. Int'l L. J.* 1.

Buchanan, A., *Justice, Legitimacy, and Self-Determination: Moral Foundations for International Law* (Oxford University Press on Demand, 2007).

Buchanan, A., 'Toward a Theory of the Ethics of Bureaucratic Organizations' (1996) 6 *Business Ethics Quarterly* 419.

Buchanan, R., 'Legitimating Global Trade Governance: Constitutional and Legal Pluralist Approaches' (2006) 57 *Northern Ireland Legal Quarterly* 1.

Buchanan, R., 'Reconceptualizing Law and Politics in the Transnational: Constitutional and Legal Pluralist Approaches' (2008) 4 *Comparative Research in Law and Political Economy.*

Buchanan, R., 'Writing Resistance into International Law' (2008) 4 *International Community Law Review* 445.

Buchanan, R. and S. Pahuja, 'Legal Imperialism: Empire's Invisible Hand', in *Empire's New Clothes* (Routledge, 2004), pp. 73–95.

Buchanan, R. and L. G. Trubek, 'Resistances and possibilities: A critical and practical look at public interest lawyering' (1992) 19 *New York University Review of Law and Social Change* 687.

Buck-Morss, S., *The Origin of Negative Dialectics; Theodor W. Adorno, Walter Benjamin and the Frankfurt Institute* (Free Press, 1977).

Buergenthal, T., 'Proliferation of International Courts and Tribunals: Is It Good or Bad?' (2001) 14 *Leiden J. Int'l L.* 267.

Bull, H., *The Anarchical Society: A Study of Order in World Politics* (Macmillan, 1977).

Bull, H., 'The State's Positive Role in World Affairs' (1979) 108 *Daedelus* 111.

Burke-White, W., 'A Community of Courts: Toward a system of international criminal law enforcement' (2002) 24 *Mich. J. Int'l L.* 1.

Burke-White, W., 'International Legal Pluralism' (2003) 25 *Mich. J. Int'l L.* 963.

Burke-White, W., 'Regionalization of International Criminal Law Enforcement: A Preliminary Exploration' (2003) 38 *Tex. Int'l L.J.* 729.

Burrows, N., 'Nemo Me Impune Lacessit: The Scottish Right of Access to the European Courts' (2002) 8 *Eur. Pub. L.* 45.

Bustelo, M., *Whose New World Order: What role for the United Nations?* (Wm Gaunt & Sons, 1991).

Byers, M., *International Law and the Arctic* (Cambridge University Press, 2013).

Calder, T., 'Shared Responsibility, Global Structural Injustice and Restitution' (2009) 36 *Social Theory and Practice* 263.

Call, C., 'Is Transitional Justice Really Just?' (2004) 11 *Brown Journal of World Affairs* 101.

Canefe, N., 'Management of Irregular Migration: Syrians in Turkey as Paradigm Shifters for Forced Migration Studies' (2016) 54 *New Perspectives on Turkey* 9.

Canefe, N., 'Post-Colonial State and Violence: Rethinking the Middle East and North Africa outside the Blindfold of Area Studies' (2015) 45 *Refugee Watch* 7.

Canefe, N. (ed.), *Transitional Justice and Forced Migration: Critical Perspectives from the Global South* (Cambridge University Press, 2019).

Carcano, A., 'Sentencing and the gravity of the offence in international criminal law' (2002) 51 *Int. & Comp. Law Quarterly* 583.

Card, C., *The Atrocity Paradigm: A theory of evil* (Oxford University Press, 2002).

Carty, A., *Philosophy of International Law* (Edinburgh University Press, 2007).

Caruth, C., *Unclaimed Experience: Trauma, narrative, and history* (JHU Press, 2016).

Cassese, A., 'Is the Bell Tolling for Universality? A Plea for a Sensible Notion of Universal Jurisdiction' (2003) *1 J. of Int'l Crim. Justice* 589.

Cassese, A., *Self-Determination of Peoples: A legal reappraisal*, No. 12 (Cambridge University Press, 1995).

Cassese, A., 'The Nicaragua and Tadić tests revisited in light of the ICJ judgment on genocide in Bosnia' (2007) 18 *European Journal of International Law* 649.

Cassese, A. et al., *Cassese's International Criminal Law* (Oxford University Press, 2013).

Cavanagh, E., 'Prescription and Empire from Justinian to Grotius' (2017) 60 *The Historical Journal* 273.

Charney, J., 'Is International Law Threatened by Multiple International Tribunals?' (1998) 271 *Recueil des Cours* 125.

Charney, J., 'The impact on the international legal system of the growth of international courts and tribunals' (1998) 31 *NYU J. Int'l L. & Pol.* 697.

Charney, J., 'Universal International Law' (1983) 87 *Am. J. of Int'l L.* 529.

Chatterjee, P., 'Introduction: Postcolonial Legalism' (2014) 34 *Comparative Studies of South Asia, Africa and the Middle East* 224.

Chayes, A. and A. Handler Chayes, *The New Sovereignty* (Harvard University Press, 1998).

Cheah, P. and J. Culler, *Grounds of Comparison: Around the work of Benedict Anderson* (Routledge, 2013).

Chesterman, S., I. Johnstone and D. M. Malone, *Law and Practice of the United Nations: Documents and Commentary* (Oxford University Press, 2016).

Chimni, B. S., 'International institutions today: An imperial global state in the making' (2004) 15 *European Journal of International Law* 1.

Chimni, B. S., 'The world of TWAIL: Introduction to the special issue' (2011).

Chimni, B. S., 'Third World approaches to international law: A manifesto' (2006) 8 *Int'l Comm. L. Rev.* 3.

Chiu, Y., 'Liberal Lustration' (2011) 19 *Journal of Political Philosophy* 440.

Cichowski, R. A., *The European Court and Civil Society: Litigation, Mobilization and Governance* (Cambridge University Press, 2007).

Clamp, K., 'Clearing the conceptual haze: restorative justice concepts in transitional settings' (2016) *Restorative Justice in Transitional Settings* 1.

Clarke, K. M. and S. Koulen, 'The Legal Politics of the Article 16 Decision: The International Criminal Court, the UN Security Council and Ontologies of a Contemporary Compromise' (2014) 7 *African Journal of Legal Studies* 297.

Coburn, B., *Autonomy and Liberalism* (Routledge, 2010).

Cohen, J., 'Whose sovereignty? Empire versus international law' (2004) 18 *Ethics & International Affairs* 1.

Collins, C., K. Hite and A. Joignant (eds), *The Politics of Memory in Chile: From Pinochet to Bachelet* (Lynne Rienner Publishers, 2013).

Combs, N., 'Seeking Inconsistency: Advancing Pluralism in International Criminal Sentencing' (2015) 41 *Yale J. Int'l L.* 387.

Conant, L., *Justice Contained: Law and Politics in the European Union* (Cornell University Press, 2002).

Conklin, W., 'The peremptory norms of the international community' (2012) 23 *European Journal of International Law* 837.

Connell, R., *Southern Theory: The global dynamics of knowledge in social science* (Polity Press, 2007).

Cooper, D. E., 'Collective responsibility' (1968) 43 *Philosophy* 258.

Coplin, W., 'International law and assumptions about the state system' (1965) 17 *World Politics* 615.

Copp, D., 'What Collectives Are: Agency, Individualism and Legal Theory' (1984) 23 *Dialogue* 249.

Cordonier Segger, M. and Judge CG Weeramantry (eds), *Sustainable Development Principles in the Decisions of International Courts and Tribunals: 1992–2012* (Routledge, 2017).

Corlett, A. J., *Collective Responsibility* (John Wiley & Sons, 2001).

Corlett, A. J., *Responsibility and Punishment*, vol. 9 (Springer, 2009).

Cover, R. M., 'Nomos and Narrative' (1983) 97 *Harv. L. Rev.* 4.

Cox, R., 'An Alternative Approach to Multilateralism in the Twenty-First Century' (1997) 3 *Global Governance* 1.

Croce, M. and M. Goldoni, 'A Sense of Self-Suspicion: Global Legal Pluralism and the Claim to Legal Authority' (2015) 8 *Ethics & Global Politics* 1.

Crowe, J., 'The limits of legal pluralism' (2015) 24 *Griffith Law Review* 314.

Cryer, R. et al., *An Introduction to International Criminal Law and Procedure* (Cambridge University Press, 2014).

Cryer, R., *Prosecuting International Crimes: Selectivity and the International Criminal Law Regime* (Cambridge University Press, 2005).

d'Aspremont, J., *Epistemic Forces in International Law* (Edward Elgar Publishing, 2015).

Damgaard, C., *Individual Criminal Responsibility for Core International Crimes: Selected Pertinent Issues* (Springer, 2008).

Dan-Cohen, M., *Rights, Persons, and Organizations: A Legal Theory for Bureaucratic Society* (University of California Press, 1986).

Danner, A. M., 'Constructing a hierarchy of crimes in international criminal law sentencing' (2001) 87 *Virginia Law Review* 415.

Davies, M., *Law Unlimited* (Routledge, 2017).

Davies, M., 'The Ethos of Legal Pluralism' (2005) 27 *Sydney Law Review* 317.

Degryse, A., '*Sensus Communis* as a Foundation for Men as Political Beings: Arendt's Reading of Kant's Critique of Judgment' (2011) 37 *Philosophy and Social Criticism* 345.

de Sousa Santos, B., *Toward a New Legal Common Sense: Law, globalization, and emancipation* (Cambridge University Press, 2002).

de Sousa Santos, B. and C. A. Rodríguez-Garavito (eds), *Law and Globalization from Below: Towards a Cosmopolitan Legality* (Cambridge University Press, 2005).

De Visscher, C., *Theory and Reality in Public International Law* (Princeton University Press, 2015).

Deitelhoff, N., 'The Discursive Process of Legalization: Charting Islands of Persuasion in the ICC Case' (2009) 63 *International Organization* 33.

Della Porta, D. et al., *Global Justice Movement: Cross-national and transnational perspectives* (Routledge, 2015).

Delmas-Marty, M., *Ordering Pluralism: A Conceptual Framework for Understanding the Transnational Legal World* (Bloomsbury Publishing, 2009).

den Heijer, M. and H. van der Wilt (eds), *Netherlands Yearbook of International Law 2015: Jus Cogens: Quo Vadis?*, vol. 46 (Springer, 2016).

Derrida, J., *On Cosmopolitanism and Forgiveness* (Psychology Press, 2001).

Devetak, R. and R. Higgot, 'Justice Unbound? Globalization, States, and the Transformation of the Social Bond' (1999) 75 *International Affairs* 21.

Dezalay, Y. and B. Garth (eds), *Lawyers and the Construction of Transnational Justice* (Routledge, 2013).

Dezalay, Y. and B. Garth (eds), *Lawyers and the Rule of Law in an Era of Globalization* (Routledge, 2011).

Dickinson, L., 'The Promise of Hybrid Courts' (2003) 97 *Am. J. Int'l L.* 295.

Dickinson, L., 'The Relationship between Hybrid Courts and International Courts: The Case of Kosovo' (2003) 37 *New Eng. L. Rev.* 1059.

Dickinson, L., 'Using Legal Process to Fight Terrorism: Detentions, Military Commissions, International Tribunals, and the Rule of Law' (2002) 75 *S. Cal. L. Rev.* 1407.

Diehl, P. F., C. Ku and D. Zamora, 'The Dynamics of International Law: The Interaction of Normative and Operating Systems' (2003) 57 *Int'l Org.* 43.

Downie, R. S., 'Collective responsibility' (1969) 44 *Philosophy* 66.

du Plessis, M., *The International Criminal Court and Its Work in Africa: Confronting Myths* (ISS Paper 173, November 2008).

Dubois, D., 'The Authority of Peremptory Norms in International Law: State Consent or Natural Law?' (2009) 78 *Nordic Journal of International Law* 133.

Dugard, J., 'Dealing With Crimes of a Past Regime. Is Amnesty Still an Option?' (1999) 12 *Leiden J. of Int'l L.* 1001.

Dunoff, J., S. Ratner and D. Wippman, *International Law: Norms, Actors, Process* (Wolters Kluwer, 2015).

Dworkin, R., *Law's Empire* (Harvard University Press, 1986).

Dyzenhaus, D., 'Legal theory in the collapse of Weimar: contemporary lessons?' (1997) 91 *American Political Science Review* 121.

Dyzenhaus, D., 'The Genealogy of Legal Positivism' (2004) 24 *Oxford Journal of Legal Studies* 39.

Eberhard, C., 'Towards an Intercultural Legal Theory' (2001) 10 *Social & Legal Studies* 171.

Ebling, T. J., 'History, Violence, and Legitimacy in Uganda: An Anthropological Analysis of Post-Colonial Politics and ICC Intervention' (2015) 7 *Journal of Collegiate Anthropology* 20.

Eisenstadt, S. N., 'Multiple Modernities' (2002) 129 *Daedalus* 1.

Elias, O. A. and C. L. Lim, *The Paradox of Consensualism in International Law* (Kluwer Law International, 1998).

Elias, T., *The International Court of Justice and Some Contemporary Problems: Essays on International Law*, vol. 2 (Springer Science & Business Media, 2013).

Ellis, M. S., 'The international criminal court and its implication for domestic law and national capacity building' (2002) 15 *Fla. J. Int'l L.* 215.

Engle Merry, S., 'Legal pluralism' (1988) 22 *Law & Society Review* 869.

Epicurus, *The Essential Epicurus: Letters, Principal Doctrines, Vatican Sayings, and Fragments* (Prometheus Books, 1993).

Escobar, A., 'Thinking-feeling with the Earth: Territorial Struggles and the Ontological Dimension of the Epistemologies of the South' (2016) 11 *AIBR. Revista de Antropología Iberoamericana* 11.

Eslava, L., M. Fakhri and V. Nesiah (eds), *Bandung, Global History and International Law: Critical Pasts and Pending Futures* (Cambridge University Press, 2015).

Eslava, L. and S. Pahuja, 'Between resistance and reform: TWAIL and the universality of international law' (2011) 3 *Trade L. & Dev.* 103.

Evans, M., 'Moral responsibilities and the conflicting demands of jus post bellum' (2009) 23 *Ethics & International Affairs* 147.

Evans, T., 'International Human Rights Law as Power/Knowledge' (2005) 27 *Human Rights Quarterly* 1046.

Falk, R., 'Israel's war crimes: Calls for investigation into Gaza attacks', *Le Monde Diplomatique* (March 2009).

Feinberg, J., 'Collective responsibility' (1968) 65 *Journal of Philosophy* 674.

Feinberg, J., *Doing and Deserving: Essays in the Theory of Responsibility* (Princeton University Press, 1970).

Feinberg, J., *The Moral Limits of Criminal Law* (Oxford University Press, 1984).

Felman, S., 'Theaters of Justice: Arendt in Jerusalem, the Eichmann Trial, and the Redefinition of Legal Meaning in the Wake of the Holocaust' (2001) 1 *Theoretical Inquiries in Law* 8.

Ferencz, B., 'A Nuremberg Legacy: The Crime of Aggression' (2016) 15 *Wash. U. Global Stud. L. Rev.* 555.

Fichtelberg, A., 'Leading Cases of the Hybrid Courts', in *Hybrid Tribunals* (Springer New York, 2015), pp. 113–75.

Fidler, D. P., 'Revolt Against or From Within the West?: TWAIL, the Developing World, and the Future Direction of International Law' (2003) 2 *Chinese J. Int'l L.* 29.

Fierke, K. and K. Erik Jorgensen, *Constructing International Relations: The next generation* (Routledge, 2015).

Fine, R., 'Crimes against Humanity: Hannah Arendt and the Nuremberg Debates' (2000) 3 *European Journal of Social Theory* 293.

Finkelstein, L., 'What Is Global Governance?' (1995) 1 *Global Governance* 367.

Firth, J. M. and J. Quong, 'Necessity, Moral Liability and Defensive Harm' (2012) 31 *Law and Philosophy* 673.

Fischer, J. M., *My Way: Essays on Moral Responsibility* (Oxford University Press, 2006).

Fischer, J. M. and M. Ravizza, *Responsibility and Control: A Theory of Moral Responsibility* (Cambridge University Press, 2000).

Fischer-Lescano, A. and G. Teubner, 'Regime-Collisions: The Vain Search for Legal Unity in the Fragmentation of Global Law' (2004) 25 *Mich. J. .Int'l L.* 999.

Fish, S., *Democracy Derailed in Russia: The failure of open politics* (Cambridge University Press, 2005).

Fletcher, G., *Basic Concepts of Criminal Law* (Oxford University Press, 1998).

Flores, A. and D. G. Johnson, 'Collective responsibility and professional roles' (1983) 93 *Ethics* 537.

Fogelson, S., 'The Nuremberg Legacy: An Unfulfilled Promise' (1989) 63 *S. Cal. L. Rev.* 833.

Formosa, P., 'Thinking, Conscience and Acting in the Face of Mass Evil', in Andrew Schaap, Danielle Celermajer and Vrasidas Karalis (eds), *Power, Judgment and Political Evil: In Conversation with Arendt* (Ashgate, 2010).

Formosa, P., 'Thinking, Willing, Judging' (2009) 4 *Crossroads* 53.

Franceschet, A., 'Theorizing state civil disobedience in international politics' (2015) 11 *Journal of International Political Theory* 239.

Frankfurt, H. G., 'Alternate possibilities and moral responsibility' (1969) 23 *Journal of Philosophy* 829.

Fraser, N., *Scales of Justice: Reimagining Political Space in a Globalizing World* (Columbia University Press, 2009).

Freeman, M. and S. Pathare, *WHO resource book on mental health, human rights and jurisprudence* (World Health Organization, 2005).

French, P. A., 'The Corporation as a Moral Person' (1979) 16 *American Philosophical Quarterly* 207.

Futamura, M., *War Crimes Tribunals and Transitional Justice: The Tokyo trial and the Nuremberg legacy* (Routledge, 2007).

Galán, A. and D. Patterson, 'The limits of normative legal pluralism: Review of Paul Schiff Berman, *Global Legal Pluralism: A Jurisprudence of Law beyond Borders*' (2013) 11 *International Journal of Constitutional Law* 783.

Gandesha, S., 'Writing and Judging: Adorno, Arendt and the Chiasmus of Natural History' (2004) 30 *Philosophy and Social Criticism* 445.

Gassama, I., 'Dealing with the world as it is: Reimagining collective international responsibility' (2013) 12 *Wash. U. Global Stud. L. Rev.* 695.

Gassama, I., 'The Incoherence and Functional Incompetence of International Law: Toward a New Paradigm of Human Relationship' (2013) 37 *Fordham Int'l L. J.* 53.

Gathii, T. J., 'Alternative and Critical: The Contribution of Research and Scholarship on Developing Countries to International Legal Theory' (2000) 41 *Harv. Int'l L. J.* 263.

Gathii, T. J., 'TWAIL: A brief history of its origins, its decentralized network, and a tentative bibliography' (2011) 3 *Trade L. & Dev.* 26.

Gellner, E. and J. Breuilly, *Nations and Nationalism* (Cornell University Press, 2008).

Gilbert, M., 'Collective guilt and collective guilt feelings' (2002) 6 *Journal of Ethics* 115.

Gilbert, M., *Joint Commitment: How we make the social world* (Oxford University Press, 2015).

Gilbert, M., *Living Together: Rationality, sociality, and obligation* (Rowman & Littlefield Publishers, 1996).

Gilbert, M., 'Modelling collective belief' (1987) 73 *Synthese* 185.

Gilbert, M., *On Social Facts* (Princeton University Press, 1992).

Gilbert, M., 'Shared Intention and Personal Intentions' (2009) 144 *Philosophical Studies* 167.

Gilbert, M., *Sociality and Responsibility: New Essays in Plural Subject Theory* (Rowman & Littlefield Publishers, 2000).

Gill, S. (ed.), *Globalization, Democratization and Multilateralism* (Springer, 2016).

Gill, S., *Power and Resistance in the New World Order: Fully Revised and Updated* (Springer, 2008).

Gill, S. and A. C. Cutler (eds), *New Constitutionalism and World Order* (Cambridge University Press, 2014).

Gill, S. and David Law, 'Global hegemony and the structural power of capital' (1993) 26 *Cambridge Studies in International Relations* 93.

Goldman, A., 'An Antinomy of Political Judgment: Kant, Arendt and the Role of Purposiveness in Reflective Judgment' (2010) 43 *Continental Philosophy Review* 331.

Goldsmith, J. and S. D. Krasner, 'The limits of idealism' (2003) 132 *Daedalus* 47.

Goldsmith, J. and E. A. Posner, *The Limits of International Law* (Oxford University Press, 2005).

Goodale, M. and S. Engle Merry (eds), *The Practice of Human Rights: Tracking Law Between the Global and the Local* (Cambridge University Press, 2007).

Goodman, C. and D. Jinks, *Socializing States: Promoting Human Rights Through International Law* (Oxford University Press USA, 2013).

Gordon, S., 'Indigenous Rights in Modern International Law from a Critical Third World Perspective' (2007) 31 *Am. Ind. L. R.* 401.

Gostin, L. and D. Sridhar, 'Global health and the law' (2014) 370 *New England Journal of Medicine* 1732.

Gott, V. L., 'The National Socialist theory of international law' (1938) 32 *Am. J. Int'l L.* 704.

Gould, K., D. N. Pellow and A. Schnaiberg, *Treadmill of Production: Injustice and Unsustainability in the Global Economy* (Routledge, 2015).

Gould, W. and Michael Barkun, *International Law and the Social Sciences* (Princeton University Press, 2015).

Grabowski, A., 'The Missing Link in the Hart–Dworkin Debate' (2016) 36 *Oxford Journal of Legal Studies* 476.

Green, L. C., 'An International Criminal Code – Now' (1976) 3 *Dalhousie L. J.* 560.

Greenfeld, L., *Nationalism: Five roads to modernity* (Harvard University Press, 1993).

Grenfell, M. J., *Pierre Bourdieu: Key concepts* (Routledge, 2014).

Griffiths, J., 'What is Legal Pluralism?' (1986) 24 *Journal of Legal Pluralism and Unofficial Law* 1.

Gur-Arye, M. and A. Harel, 'Taking Internationalism Seriously: Why International Criminal Law Matters', in Jens David Ohlin (ed.), *Oxford Handbook of International Criminal Law*, Hebrew University of Jerusalem Legal Research Paper No. 16-21 (2017).

Gutto, S., 'Created and Limited by Politics: A view of the ICC from Africa' (2003) 12 *African Security Studies* 127.

Guzman, A., 'International Organizations and the Frankenstein Problem' (2013) 24 *European Journal of International Law* 999.

Guzman, A. and J. Hsiang, 'Some Ways that Theories on Customary International Law Fail: A Reply to László Blutman' (2014) 25 *European Journal of International Law* 553.

Hafner, G., 'Pros and Cons Ensuing from Fragmentation of International Law' (2003) 25 *Mich. J. Int'l L.* 849.

Hahn, H., 'The Global Consequences of Participatory Responsibility' (2008) 5 *Journal of Global Ethics* 43.

Hammer, L., *A Foucauldian Approach to International Law: Descriptive thoughts for normative issues* (Routledge 2007).

Hannum, H., *Autonomy, Sovereignty, and Self-Determination: The accommodation of conflicting rights* (University of Pennsylvania Press, 2011).

Harbin, A. and J. Lewelyn, 'Restorative Justice in Transitions: The Problem of "The Community" and Collective Responsibility', in Kerry Clamp (ed.), *Restorative Justice in Transitional Settings* (Routledge, 2016), pp. 133–51.

Hart, H. L. A., 'Positivism and the Separation of Law and Morals' (1958) 71 *Harvard Law Review* 593–629.

Hart, H. L. A., *The Concept of Law* (Oxford University Press, Clarendon Law Series [1961] 2012).

Hart, H. L. A., 'The New Challenge to Legal Positivism (1979)' (2016) 36 *Oxford Journal of Legal Studies* 459–75 [the reprint of the original lecture delivered in 1979].

Hathaway, O., 'The Continuing Influence of the New Haven School' (2007) 32 *Yale J. Int'l L.* 553.

Hazan, P., 'Measuring the impact of punishment and forgiveness: a framework for evaluating transitional justice' (2006) 88 *International Review of the Red Cross* 19.

Held, D., *Democracy and the Global Order: From the Modern State to Cosmopolitan Democracy* (Stanford University Press, 1995).

Held, V., 'Can a random collection of individuals be morally responsible?' (1970) 67 *Journal of Philosophy* 471.

Heller, K. J., 'The Shadow Side of Complementarity: The Effect of Article 17 of the Rome Statute on National Due Process' (2006) 17 *Criminal Law Forum* 255.

Herzog, A., 'Reporting and Storytelling: Eichmann in Jerusalem as Political Testimony' (2002) 68 *Thesis Eleven* 83.

Hess, K. M., 'Because They Can: The Basis for the Moral Obligations of Collectives' (2014) 38 *Midwest Studies in Philosophy* 203.

Hewson, M. and T. J. Sinclair (eds), *Approaches to Global Governance Theory* (SUNY Press, 1995).

Higonnet, E., 'Restructuring hybrid courts: local empowerment and national criminal justice reform' (2005) 23 *Ariz. J. Int'l & Comp. L.* 347.

Hillebrecht, C., *Domestic Politics and International Human Rights Tribunals: The Problem of Compliance* (Cambridge University Press, 2014).

Hitchcock, D., 'Is there an argumentum ad hominem fallacy?', in Hans V. Hansen and Robert C. Pinto (eds), *Reason Reclaimed: Essays in honor of J. Anthony Blair and Ralph H. Johnson* (Vale Press, 2007), pp. 187–99.

Hobsbawm, E., *Age of Capital: 1848–1875* (Hachette UK, 2010).

Hobsbawm, E., *Nations and Nationalism since 1780: Programme, myth, reality* (Cambridge University Press, 2012).

Hobsbawm, E., *The Age of Extremes: A history of the world, 1914–1991* (Pantheon Books, 1995).

Hollifield, J., P. Martin and P. Orrenius, *Controlling Immigration: A Global Perspective* (Stanford University Press, 2014).

Holmes, P., 'The politics of law and the laws of politics: The political paradoxes of transnational constitutionalism' (2014) 21/2 *Indiana Journal of Global Legal Studies* 553.

Hongju Koh, H., 'Transnational Legal Process' (1996) 75 *Neb. L. Rev.* 181.

Hooker, M. B., *Legal Pluralism: An introduction to colonial and neo-colonial laws* (Clarendon Press, 1975).

Hovil, L. and Quinn, J., 'Peace First, Justice Later: Traditional Justice in Northern Uganda', Refugee Law Project Working Paper No. 17 (Kampala: Refugee Law Project, 2005).

Huneeus, A., 'Human Rights between Jurisprudence and Social Science' (2015) 28 *Leiden Journal of International Law* 255.

Isaacs, T., *Moral Responsibility in Collective Contexts* (Oxford University Press, 2011).

Isiksel, T., 'Global legal pluralism as fact and norm' (2013) 2 *Global Constitutionalism* 160.

Jacobi v Griffiths [1999] 174 DLR (4th) 7.

Jain, A. G., 'Universal civil jurisdiction in international law' (2015) 55 *Indian Journal of International Law* 209.

Jankélévitch, V., *L'imprescriptible. Pardonner? Dans l'honneur et la dignité* (Le Seuil, 2015).

Jaspers, K., *Die Geistige Situation der Zeit* (Berlin: de Gruyter). Translated as *Man in the Modern Age*, trans. E. Paul and C. Paul (Routledge, 1933).

Jaspers, K., *Die Schuldfrage* (Heidelberg: Schneider). Translated as *The Question of German Guilt*, trans. E. B. Ashton (The Dial Press, 1947).

Jaspers, K., *Existenzphilosophie* (Berlin: de Gruyter). Translated as *Philosophy of Existence*, trans. R. F. Grabau (University of Pennsylvania Press, 1971).

Jaspers, K., *Nietzsche: Einführung in das Verständnis seines Philosophierens* (Berlin: de Gruyter). Translated as *Nietzsche: An Introduction to his Philosophical*

Activity, trans. C. F. Wallraff and F. J. Schmitz (University of Arizona Press, 1965).

Jaspers, K., *The Origin and Goal of History* (Routledge Revivals Series, Routledge, 2014).

Jaspers, K., *The Question of German Guilt* (Fordham University Press, 2009).

Jaspers, K., *Vernunft und Existenz* (Groningen: Wolters). Translated as, *Reason and Existenz*, trans. W. Earle (Noonday Press, 1955).

Jeangène Vilmer, J., 'The African Union and the International Criminal Court: Counteracting the crisis' (2016) 92 *International Affairs* 1319.

Jessup, P., *Transnational Law* (Yale University Press, 1956).

Johnstone, G., *Restorative Justice: Ideas, Values, Debates*, 2nd edn (Routledge, 2013).

Jonkers, G., *The Textual Tradition of Plato's Timaeus and Critias* (Brill, 2016).

Jørgensen, N., *The Responsibility of States for International Crimes* (Oxford University Press, 2000).

Juss, S., *International Migration and Global Justice* (Routledge, 2016).

Kaczorowska-Ireland, A., *Public International Law* (Routledge, 2015).

Kaldor, M., 'Civil society and accountability' (2003) 4 *Journal of Human Development* 5.

Kaldor, M., *Global Civil Society: An Answer to War* (John Wiley & Sons, 2003).

Kant, I., *Grounding for the Metaphysics of Morals*, in I. Kant, *Ethical Philosophy*, trans. James W. Ellington (Hackett Publishing, [1785] 1983).

Kant, I., *Metaphysical Elements of Justice*, ed. John Ladd (Hackett, [1797] 1999).

Kant, I., 'Perpetual Peace: A Philosophical Sketch', in Hans Reiss (ed.), *Kant's Political Writings* (Cambridge University Press, 1992).

Katzenstein, S., 'Hybrid Tribunals: Searching for Justice in East Timor' (2003) 16 *Harv. Hum. Rts. J.* 245.

Kaul, H.-P., 'The Nuremberg Legacy and the International Criminal Court – Lecture in Honor of Whitney R. Harris, Former Nuremberg Prosecutor' (2013) 12 *Wash. U. Global Stud. L. Rev.* 637.

Kelly, J. T., 'The moral foundations of international criminal law' (2010) 9 *Journal of Human Rights* 502.

Kennedy, D., *A World of Struggle: How power, law, and expertise shape global political economy* (Princeton University Press, 2016).

Kennedy, D., 'The disciplines of international law and policy' (1999) 12/1 *Leiden Journal of International Law* 9–133.

Keohane, R., 'International Relations and International Law: Two Optics' (1997) 38 *Harv. Int'l L. J.* 487.

Keohane, R., *Power and Governance in a Partially Globalized World* (Routledge, 2002).
Keohane, R., 'Reciprocity in international relations' (1986) 40 *International Organization* 1.
Khosla, M., 'The TWAIL Discourse: The emergence of a new phase' (2007) 9 *International Community Law Review* 291.
Kimani, M., 'ICC and Africa: Pursuit of justice or Western plot? International indictments stir angry debate in Africa' (2009) 23 *Africa Renewal* 3.
Kindred, H. et al., *International law, chiefly as interpreted and applied in Canada* (Emond Montgomery Publications, 2014).
King Jr, H. T., 'The Legacy of Nuremberg' (2002) 34 *Case W. Res. J. Int'l L.* 335.
Kingsbury, B., 'Sovereignty and inequality' (1998) 9 *European Journal of International Law* 599.
Kingsbury, B., N. Krisch and R. B. Stewart, 'The emergence of global administrative law' (2005) 68 *L. and Contemp. Prob.* 15.
Kirsch, P., 'The International Criminal Court: Current Issues and Perspectives' (2001) 64 *L. and Contemp. Prob.* 3.
Kirsch, P., 'The Role of the International Criminal Court in Enforcing International Criminal Law' (2007) 22 *Am. U. Int'l L. Rev.* 53.
Kirsch, P. and John T. Holmes, 'The Rome Conference on an International Criminal Court: The Negotiating Process' (1999) 93 *Am. J. Int'l L.* 2.
Kleffner, J., 'The impact of complementarity on national implementation of substantive international criminal law' (2003) 1 *Journal of International Criminal Justice* 86.
Kleinhans, M. and R. MacDonald, 'What is a Critical Legal Pluralism?' (1997) 12 *Canadian Journal of Law and Society* 25.
Knoops, G., *An Introduction to the Law of International Criminal Tribunals: A Comparative Study* (Martinus Nijhoff Publishers, 2014).
Knop, K., *Diversity and Self-Determination in International Law*, vol. 20 (Cambridge University Press, 2002).
Kolb, R., *Peremptory International Law – Jus Cogens: A General Inventory* (Bloomsbury Publishing, 2015).
Koller, D., 'The End of Geography: The Changing Nature of the International System and the Challenge to International Law: A Reply to Daniel Bethlehem' (2014) 25 *European Journal of International Law* 25.
Koskenniemi, M., *From Apology to Utopia: The structure of international legal argument* (Cambridge University Press, 2006).
Koskenniemi, M., 'International law and hegemony: a reconfiguration' (2004) 17 *Cambridge Review of International Affairs* 197.

Koskenniemi, M., 'The Fate of Public International Law: Between Technique and Politics' (2007) 70 *Mod. L. R.* 1.

Koskenniemi, M., *The Gentle Civilizer of Nations: The rise and fall of international law 1870–1960*, vol. 14 (Cambridge University Press, 2001).

Koskenniemi, M., '"The Lady Doth Protest Too Much": Kosovo, and the Turn to Ethics in International Law' (2002) 65 *Mod. L. R.* 159.

Koskenniemi, M., 'What is international law for?' (2003) 89 *International Law* 110.

Koskenniemi, M. and P. Leino, 'Fragmentation of international law? Postmodern anxieties' (2002) 15 *Leiden Journal of International Law* 553.

Koven Levit, J., 'A Bottom-up Approach to International Lawmaking: The Tale of Three Trade Finance Instruments' (2005) 30 *Yale J. Int'l L.* 125.

Koven Levit, J., 'Bottom-up International Lawmaking: Reflections on the New Haven School of International Law' (2007) 32 *Yale J. Int'l L.* 393.

Krasner, S., 'Compromising Westphalia' (1995) 20 *International Security* 115.

Krasner, S., 'The Hole in the Whole: Sovereignty, shared sovereignty, and international law' (2003) 25 *Mich. J. Int'l L.* 1075.

Kreß, C., 'Major Post-Westphalian Shifts and Some Important Neo-Westphalian Hesitations in the State Practice on the International Law on the Use of Force' (2014) 1/1 *Journal of the Use of Force and International Law* 1154.

Krisch, N., 'International law in times of hegemony: unequal power and the shaping of the international legal order' (2005) 16 *European Journal of International Law* 369.

Krisch, N., 'The Decay of Consent: International Law in an Age of Global Public Goods' (2014) 108 *Am. J. Int'l L.* 1.

Kristeva, J., *Hannah Arendt*, vol. 1 (Columbia University Press, 2001).

Krueger, A., 'Conference Report: The Battle for International Law in the Decolonization Era' (2016) 49 *VRÜ Verfassung und Recht in Übersee* 80.

Künkler, M. and Y. Sezgin, 'The Unification of Law and the Postcolonial State: The Limits of State Monism in India and Indonesia' (2016) 60 *American Behavioral Scientist* 987.

Kutz, C., 'The difference uniforms make: collective violence in criminal law and war' (2015) 33 *Philosophy & Public Affairs* 148.

Kutz, C., *Complicity: Ethics and Law for a Collective Age* (Cambridge University Press, 2007).

LaCapra, D., *Writing History, Writing Trauma* (JHU Press, 2014).

Laliberté, N., 'Geographies of Human Rights: Mapping Responsibility' (2015) 9 *Geography Compass* 57.

Landauer, C., 'The Ever-Ending Geography of International Law: The Changing Nature of the International System and the Challenge to International Law: A Reply to Daniel Bethlehem' (2014) 25 *European Journal of International Law* 31-34.

Lang, A., *World Trade Law after Neoliberalism: Reimagining the Global EconomicOorder* (Oxford University Press, 2011).

Lang, A. F., *Punishment, Justice and International Relations: Ethics and Order after the Cold War* (Routledge, 2009).

Langer, M., 'Universal Jurisdiction is Not Disappearing: The Shift from "Global Enforcer" to "No Safe Haven" Universal Jurisdiction' (2015) 13 *J. of Int. Crim. J.* 245.

Langford, M., *Global Justice, State Duties: The extraterritorial scope of economic, social, and cultural rights in international law* (Cambridge University Press, 2013).

Lauterpacht, H., 'The Grotian Tradition in International Law' (1946) 23 *British Yearbook of International Law* 1.

Laverick, W., *Global Injustice and Crime Control* (Routledge, 2016).

Lawson, B., 'Individual Complicity in Collective Wrongdoing' (2013) 16 *Ethical Theory and Moral Practice* 227.

Leathley, C., 'An institutional hierarchy to combat the fragmentation of international law: Has the ILC missed an opportunity?' (2007) 40 *NYU J. Int'l L. & Pol.* 259.

Levit, J. K., 'Bottom-Up International Lawmaking: Reflections on the New Haven School of International Law' (2007) 32 *Yale J. Int'l L.* 393.

Levshin, A., '*Jus Contra Bellum* in the Modern States System: Observations on the Anomalous Origins of the Crime of Aggressive War' (2015) 10 *St Antony's International Review* 141.

Levy, D. and N. Sznaider, 'Forgive and not forget: Reconciliation between forgiveness and resentment', in *Taking Wrongs Seriously: Apologies and Reconciliation* (Stanford University Press, 2006), pp. 83–100.

Levy, N. and M. McKenna, 'Recent Work on Free Will and Moral Responsibility' (2009) 4 *Philosophy Compass* 96.

Levy, T. J., 'National and statist responsibility' (2008) 11 *Critical Review of International Social and Political Philosophy* 485.

Lewis, H. D., 'Collective responsibility' (1948) 23 *Philosophy* 3.

Leyh, B. M., 'Victim-Oriented Measures at International Criminal Institutions: Participation and its Pitfalls' (2012) 12 *International Criminal Law Review* 375.

Lippert-Rasmussen, K., 'Responsible nations: Miller on national responsibility' (2009) 2 *Ethics & Global Politics* 21.

Lippman, M., 'They Shoot Lawyers Don't They: Law in the Third Reich and the Global Threat to the Independence of the Judiciary' (1992) 23 *Cal. W. Int'l L. J.* 257.

Lipscomb, R., 'Restructuring the ICC Framework to Advance Transitional Justice: A Search for a Permanent Solution in Sudan' (2006) *Columbia Law Review* 182.

Loewenstein, K., 'Law in the Third Reich' (1936) 45 *Yale L. J.* 716.

Luban, D., 'A theory of crimes against humanity' (2004) 29 *Yale J. Int'l L.* 85.

Luban, D., 'State Criminality and the Ambition of International Criminal Law', in T. Isaacs and R. Vernon (eds), *Accountability for Collective Wrongdoing* (Cambridge University Press, 2011), pp. 61–91.

MacCormick, N., R. S. Summers and A. L. Goodhart (eds), *Interpreting Precedents: A Comparative Study* (Routledge, 2016).

Macdonald, R., 'Metaphors of multiplicity: civil society, regimes and legal pluralism' (1998) 15 *Ariz. J. Int'l & Comp. L.* 69.

Machina, K., 'Moral Responsibility – What is All the Fuss About?' (2007) 22 *Acta Analytica* 29.

MacInnis, L., 'Two Concepts of Monism: Axiomatic and Asymptotic' (2015) 77 *The Review of Politics* 603.

Mack, E. and C. Westbrook, 'Does Customary International Law Obligate States to Extradite or Prosecute Individuals Accused of Committing Crimes against Humanity' (2015) 24 *Minn. J. Int'l L.* 73.

Maguire, A., 'Contemporary Anti-colonial Self-Determination Claims and the Decolonisation of International Law' (2013) 22 *Griffith Law Review* 238.

Maguire, A. and J. Mcgee, 'A Universal Human Right to Shape Responses to a Global Problem? The Role of Self-Determination in Guiding the International Legal Response to Climate Change' (2017) 26 RECIEL 54.

Majeed Khan, M. and A. Majeed Khan Marwat, 'International Criminal Court (ICC): An Analysis of Its Successes and Failures and Challenges Faced by the ICC Tribunals for War Crimes' (2016) 11 *Dialogue* 243.

Mandel, M., *How America Gets Away with Murder: Illegal Wars, Collateral Damage and Crimes Against Humanity* (Pluto Press, 2004).

Matas, D., 'Prosecuting Crimes against Humanity: The Lessons of World War I' (1989) 13 *Fordham Int'l L. J.* 86.

Maxwell, L., 'Towards an Agonistic Understanding of Law: Law and Politics in Hannah Arendt's Eichmann in Jerusalem' (2010) 11 *Contemporary Political Theory* 88.

May, L., 'Complicity: Ethics and Law for a Collective Age' (2002) 111 *Philosophical Review* 483.

May, L., *Crimes Against Humanity: A Normative Account* (Cambridge University Press, 2005).

May, L., *Genocide: A Normative Account* (Cambridge University Press, 2010).

May, L., *Sharing Responsibility* (University of Chicago Press, 1992).

May, L., *The Morality of Groups* (University of Notre Dame Press, 1989).

May, L. and S. Fyfe, *International Criminal Tribunals: A Normative Defense* (Cambridge University Press, 2017).

May, L. and S. Hoffman (eds), *Collective Responsibility: Five decades of debate in theoretical and applied ethics* (Rowman & Littlefield Publishers, 1992).

McAuliffe deGuzman, M., 'The road from Rome: the developing law of crimes against humanity' (2000) 22 *Human Rights Quarterly* 335.

McCargo, D., 'Transitional Justice and Its Discontents' (2015) 26 *Journal of Democracy* 5.

McCready, P., 'Can restorative practices work in a Loyalist area?: A case study on restorative responses to community conflict of a Loyalist area in South Belfast' (dissertation, Ulster University, 2016).

McDougal, M. S., H. D. Lasswell and W. M. Reisman, 'The World Constitutive Process of Authoritative Decision' (1967) 19 *Journal of Legal Education* 403.

McDougal, M. S., H. D. Lasswell and W. M. Reisman, 'Theories about international law: prologue to a configurative jurisprudence' (1967) 8 *Va. J. Int'l L.* 188.

McDougal, M. S. and W. M. Reisman, 'The Prescribing Function in World Constitutive Process: How International Law is Made' (1980) 6 *Yale Studies of World Public Order* 249.

McGarry, R. and S. Walklate, *Victims: Trauma, testimony and justice* (Routledge, 2015).

McGary, H., 'Morality and collective liability' (1986) 20 *Journal of Value Inquiry* 157.

McMahan, J., *The Ethics of Killing: Problems at the Margins of Life* (Oxford University Press, 2002).

McVeigh, R., 'Hate and the State: Northern Ireland, Sectarian Violence and "Perpetrator-less Crime"', in A. Haynes et al. (eds), *Critical Perspectives on Hate Crime* (Palgrave Macmillan, 2017).

Meernik, J., 'Victor's Justice or the Law? Judging and Punishing at the International Criminal Tribunal for the Former Yugoslavia' (2003) 47 *Journal of Conflict Resolution* 140.

Meierhenrich, J., 'The ethics of lustration' (2006) 20 *Ethics & International Affairs* 99.

Melissaris, E., *Ubiquitous Law: Legal theory and the space for legal pluralism* (Routledge, 2016).

Meron, T., 'The Martens Clause, principles of humanity, and dictates of public conscience' (2000) 94 *Am. J. Int'l L.* 78.

Merry, S. E., 'Legal pluralism' (1988) 22 *Law & Society Review* 869.

Mettraux, G., *International Crimes and the* ad hoc *Tribunals* (Oxford University Press, 2005).

Michaels, R., 'The re-state-ment of non-state law: the state, choice of law, and the challenge from global legal pluralism' (2005) 51 *Wayne L. Rev.* 1209.

Michaels, R., 'The true lex mercatoria: law beyond the state' (2007) 14 *Indiana Journal of Global Legal Studies* 447.

Michelman, F., 'Reasonable Umbrage: Race and Constitutional Antidiscrimination Law in the United States and South Africa' (2004) 117 *Harv. L. R.* 1378.

Mickelson, K., 'Rhetoric and Rage: Third World Voices in International Legal Discourse' (1998) 16/2 *Wisconsin International Law Journal* 353.

Mickelson, K., 'Taking stock of TWAIL histories' (2008) 10 *International Community Law Review* 355.

Mill, John Stuart, *On Liberty*, David Spitz (ed.) (Norton, [1859] 1975).

Miller, D., 'Collective responsibility and international inequality in the law of peoples', in *Rawls's Law of Peoples: A Realistic Utopia?* (2006), pp. 191–205.

Miller, D., 'National responsibility and global justice' (2008) 11 *Critical Review of International Social and Political Philosophy* 383.

Miller, S., 'Collective Responsibility' (2001) 15 *Public Affairs Quarterly* 65.

Mills, K. and D. J. Karp (eds), *Human Rights Protection in Global Politics: Responsibilities of States and Non-State Actors* (Palgrave Macmillan, 2015).

Mitsis, P., *Epicurus' Ethical Theory: The Pleasures of Invulnerability* (Cornell University Press, 1988).

Mollendorf, D., 'Jus ex bello' (2008) 16 *Journal of Political Philosophy* 123.

Moore, M., 'Global justice, climate change and Miller's theory of responsibility' (2008) 11 *Critical Review of International Social and Political Philosophy* 501.

Moravcsik, A., 'Taking Preferences Seriously: A Liberal Theory of International Politics' (1997) 51 *International Organization* 513.

Moreno-Lax V. and P. Gragl, 'Introduction: Beyond Monism, Dualism, Pluralism. The Quest for a (Fully-Fledged) Theoretical Framework: Co-Implication, Embeddedness, and Interdependency between Public International Law and EU Law' (2016) 35 *Yearbook of European Law* 455.

Moreno-Ocampo, L., 16 June 2003, Ceremony for the Solemn Undertaking of the Chief Prosecutor, quoted in ICC Office of the Prosecutor, Informal Expert Paper (2003).

Morgenthau, H., *Politics among Nations* (Alfred Kopf, 1948).

Mouffe, C., 'Democratic citizenship and the political community', in *Dimensions of Radical Democracy: Pluralism, Citizenship, Community* (Verso, 1992), pp. 225–39.

Mullins, C., D. Kauzlarich and Dawn Rothe, 'The International Criminal Court and the Control of State Crime: Prospects and Problems' (2004) 12 *Crit. Crim.* 1205.

Murphy, C., 'Global Governance: Poorly Done and Poorly Understood' (2000) 76 *International Affairs* 780.

Murray, C. and A. O'Donoghue, 'A path already travelled in domestic orders? From fragmentation to constitutionalisation in the global legal order' (2017) *International Journal of Law in Context* 1.

Mutua, M. and A. Anghie, 'What is TWAIL?' (2000) 94 *Proceedings of the Annual Meeting (American Society of International Law)* 31.

Mutua, W. M., 'Savages, Victims, and Saviors: The Metaphor of Human Rights' (2001) 42 *Harvard International Law Journal* 201.

Nagel, T., 'The Problem of Global Justice' (2005) 33 *Philosophy and Public Affairs* 113.

Nardin, T., *Law, Morality and the Relations of States* (Princeton University Press, 1983).

Narveson, J., 'Collective responsibility' (2002) 6 *Journal of Ethics* 179.

Nedelsky, J., 'Communities of Judgment and Human Rights' (2000) 1 *Theoretical Inquiries in Law* 245.

Nedelsky, J., *Law's Relations: A relational theory of self, autonomy, and law* (Oxford University Press USA, 2011).

Nedelsky, J., 'Reconceiving Autonomy: Sources, Thoughts, and Possibilities' (1989) 1 *Yale Journal of Law and Feminism* 7.

Neier, A., *War Crimes: Brutality, genocide, terror, and the struggle for justice* (Crown Publishing Group,1998).

Neiman, S., *Evil in Modern Thought: An alternative history of philosophy* (Princeton University Press, 2015).

Neuman, G. L., 'Human Rights and Constitutional Rights: Harmony and Dissonance' (2003) 55 *Stanford L. Rev.* 1863.

Neuman, G. L., 'The Uses of International Law in Constitutional Interpretation' (2004) 98 *Am. J. Int'l L.* 82.

Newman, D., 'The Rome Statute, Some Reservations Concerning Amnesties, and a Distributive Problem' (2004) 20 *Am. U. Int'l L. Rev.* 293.

Ngugi, J., 'Making new wine for old wineskins: can the reform of international law emancipate the Third World in the age of globalization' (2002) 8 *UC Davis J. Int'l L. & Pol'y* 73.

Noortmann, M., A. Reinisch and C. Ryngaert (eds), *Non-State Actors in International Law* (Bloomsbury Publishing, 2015).

Nooruddin, I. and A. L. Payton, 'Dynamics of influence in international politics: The ICC, BIAs, and economic sanctions' (2010) 47 *Journal of Peace Research* 711.

O'Brien, R., A. M. Goetz, J. A. Scholte and M. Williams (eds), *Contesting Global Governance: Multilateral Economic Institutions and Global Social Movements* (Cambridge University Press, 2000).

Odumosu, I., 'Challenges for the (Present/) Future of Third World Approaches to International Law' (2008) 10 *Int'l Comm. L. Rev.* 467.

Ohlin, J. D. (ed.), *Oxford Handbook of International Criminal Law*, Hebrew University of Jerusalem Legal Research Paper No. 16-21 (2017).

Okafor, O. C., 'Critical Third World Approaches to International Law (TWAIL): Theory, Methodology, or Both?' (2008) 10 *Int'l Comm. L. Rev.* 371.

Okafor, O. C., 'After Martyrdom: International Law, Sub-State Groups, and the Construction of Legitimate Statehood in Africa' (2000) 41 *Harv. Int'l L. J.* 503.

Okafor, O. C., 'Is There a Legitimacy Deficit in International Legal Scholarship and Practice?' (1997) 13 *International Insights* 91.

Okafor, O. C., 'Newness, imperialism, and international legal reform in our time: a TWAIL perspective' (2005) 43 *Osgoode Hall L. J.* 171.

Okello, M. C., 'The false polarisation of peace and justice in Uganda', Expert paper for 'Workshop 2 – Justice in Situations of Ongoing Conflict', organized by International Center for Transitional Justice.

Okolo, B., 'African Renaissance, African Conflicts and the Regional Security Complex' (2010) 16 *The State of Africa 2010/11: Parameters and legacies of governance and issue areas* 103.

Oksanen, M., 'Species Extinction and Collective Responsibility' (2007) in *The Proceedings of the Twenty-First World Congress of Philosophy* (vol. 3 at pp. 179–83).

Okumu, W., 'Humanitarian international NGOs and African conflicts' (2003) 10 *International Peacekeeping* 120.

Oppenheim, L. and H. Lauterpacht, *International Law: A Treatise* (Longmans Green, 1952).

Orentlicher, D. F., 'Politics by Other Means: The Law of the International Criminal Court' (1999) 32 *Cornell Int'l L. J.* 489.

Orentlicher, D. F., 'Settling Accounts: The Duty to Prosecute Human Rights Violations of a Prior Regime' (1991) 100 *Yale L. J.* 2537.

Orford, A. et al., *The Oxford Handbook of the Theory of International Law* (Oxford University Press, 2016).

Osiel, M., *Mass Atrocity, Ordinary Evil and Hannah Arendt: Criminal consciousness in Argentina's dirty war* (Yale University Press, 2001).

Osiel, M., *Obeying Orders: Atrocity, military discipline and the law of war* (Routledge, 2017).

O'Sullivan, A., *Universal Jurisdiction in International Criminal Law: The Debate and the Battle for Hegemony* (Routledge, 2017).

Ozsu, U., *Formalizing Displacement: International law and population transfers* (Oxford University Press, 2015).

Pablo, H., 'The politics of law and the laws of politics: The political paradoxes of transnational constitutionalism' (2014) 21/2 *Indiana Journal of Global Legal Studies* 553–83.

Parekh, S., *Hannah Arendt and the Challenge of Modernity: A Phenomenology of Human Rights* (Routledge, 2018).

Parfit, D. and S. Scheffler, *On What Matters: Volume One* (Oxford University Press, 2011).

Parfit, D., T. Schwartz and R. M. Adams (eds), *Reasons and Persons* (Oxford University Press, 1984).

Pasternak, A., 'The collective responsibility of democratic publics' (2011) 41 *Canadian Journal of Philosophy* 99.

Paterson, R. K., 'Resolving Material Culture Disputes: Human Rights, Property Rights and Crimes against Humanity' (2006) 14 *Willamette Journal of International Law and Dispute Resolution* 161.

Patterson, D., 'Cosmopolitanism and Global Legal Regimes' (2015) 67 *Rutgers U. L. Rev.* 7.

Pereboom, D., *Living without Free Will* (Cambridge University Press, 2006).

Peskin, V., 'Beyond Victor's Justice? The Challenge of Prosecuting the Winners at the International Criminal Tribunals for the Former Yugoslavia and Rwanda' (2005) 4 *Journal of Human Rights* 213.

Petersson, B., 'Co-responsibility and Causal Involvement' (2013) 41 *Philosophia* 847.

Pierik, R., 'Collective responsibility and national responsibility' (2008) 11 *Critical Review of International Social and Political Philosophy* 465.

Pinia, S. and F. Bubenzer, *Gender Justice and Reconciliation in Uganda* (Institute for Justice and Reconciliation 2011).

Pion-Berlin, D., 'The Pinochet Case and Human Rights Progress in Chile: Was Europe a Catalyst, Cause or Inconsequential?' (2004) 36 *Journal of Latin American Studies* 479.

Pitkin, Hannah, F., *The Concept of Representation* (University of California Press, 1967).

Prashad, V., *The Poorer Nations: A Possible History of the Global South* (London: Verso, 2012).

Preece, J. J., 'Minority rights in Europe: from Westphalia to Helsinki' (1997) 23 *Review of International Studies* 75.

Preece, J. J., *National minorities and the European nation-states system* (Oxford University Press, 1998).

Přibáň, J., 'Asking the Sovereignty Question in Global Legal Pluralism: From "Weak" Jurisprudence to "Strong" Socio-Legal Theories of Constitutional Power Operations' (2015) 28 *Ratio Juris* 31.

Provost, R. (ed.), *State Responsibility in International Law* (Routledge, 2017).

Radi, Y., 'In Defence of "Generalism" in International Legal Scholarship and Practice' (2014) 27 *Leiden Journal of International Law* 303.

Raimondo, F., *General Principles of Law in the Decisions of International Criminal Courts and Tribunals* (Brill, 2008).

Rajagopal, B., 'Counter-hegemonic international law: rethinking human rights and development as a Third World strategy' (2006) 27 *Third World Quarterly* 767.

Rajagopal, B., 'From Resistance to Renewal: The Third World, Social Movements, and the Expansion of International Institutions' (2000) 41 *Harv. Int'l L. J.* 529.

Rajagopal, B., *International Law from Below: Development, Social Movements and Third World Resistance* (Cambridge University Press, 2003).

Rajagopal, B., 'International Law and Its Discontents: Rethinking the Global South' (2012) 106th American Society of International Law Proceedings, March 2012.

Rajagopal, B., 'The role of law in counter-hegemonic globalization and global legal pluralism: lessons from the Narmada Valley struggle in India' (2005) 18 *Leiden Journal of International Law* 345.

Randeria, S., 'Entangled Histories of Uneven Modernities: Civil Society, Caste Solidarities and Legal Pluralism in Post-Colonial India', in Y. Elkana et al. (eds), *Unraveling Ties: From Social Cohesion to New Practices of Connectedness* (Campus Verlag: 2002), pp. 284–311.

Randeria, S., 'The State of Globalization: Legal Plurality, Overlapping Sovereignties and Ambiguous Alliances between Civil Society and the Cunning State in India' (2007) 24 *Theory, Culture & Society* 1.

Rao, P. S., 'Multiple International Judicial Forums: A Reflection of the Growing Strength of International Law or Its Fragmentation' (2003) 25 *Mich. J. Int'l L.* 929.

Ratner, S., 'Corporations and Human Rights: A Theory of Legal Responsibility' (2001) 111 *Yale L. J.* 443.

Ratner, S., *The Thin Justice of International Law: A Moral Reckoning of the Law of Nations* (Oxford University Press, 2015).

Ratner, S., J. S. Abrams and J. L. Bischoff, *Accountability for Human Rights Atrocities in International Law: Beyond the Nuremberg Legacy*, 3rd edn (Oxford University Press, 2009).

Raustiala, K. and A. M. Slaughter, 'International law, international relations and compliance', in W. Carlsnaes, T. Risse and B. Simmons (eds), *Handbook of International Relations* (Sage, 2002).

Rawls, J., *The Law of Peoples* (Harvard University Press, 1999).

Raz, J., *The Morality of Freedom* (Clarendon 1986).

Raznik, L., 'Collective Responsibility and Duties to Respond' (2001) 27 *Social Theory and Practice* 455.

Reeves, C., 'Exploding the Limits of Law: Judgment and Freedom in Arendt and Adorno' (2009) 15 *Res Publica* 137.

Rehbein, B., *Critical Theory After the Rise of the Global South: Kaleidoscopic Dialectic*, vol. 5 (Routledge, 2015).

Reisman, M., 'Theory about Law: Jurisprudence for a Free Society' (1999) 108 *Yale L. J.* 935.

Report, *Crimes against Humanity and War Crimes are the Reason behind the Forced Migration in Darayya: Siege, Chemical Weapons, Barrel Bombs, and International Silence.*

Report of International Crisis Group, *Northern Uganda: The road to peace, with or without Kony*, Africa Report No. 146, 10 December 2008.

Reydams, L., *Universal Jurisdiction: International and Municipal Legal Perspectives* (Oxford University Press, 2003).

Reynolds, J. and S. Xavier, '"The Dark Corners of the World", TWAIL and International Criminal Justice' (2016) 14 *Journal of International Criminal Justice* 959.

Ricoeur, P., 'The Plurality of Sources of Law' (1994) 7 *Ratio Juris* 272.

Risse, T., Stephen C. Ropp and K. Sikkink (eds), *The Persistent Power of Human Rights: From Commitment to Compliance* (Cambridge University Press, 2013).

Robertson, G., *Crimes Against Humanity: The struggle for global justice* (The New Press, 2013).

Robinson, D., 'Defining "Crimes Against Humanity" at the Rome Conference' (1999) 93 *Am. J. Int'l L.* 43.

Robinson, D. et al., 'Amicus Brief of Professors Robinson, De Guzman, Jalloh and Cryer on Crimes against Humanity (Cases 003 and 004)' (2016).

Robinson, J., *And the Crooked Shall Be Made Straight: The Eichmann Trial, the Jewish Catastrophe, and Hannah Arendt's Narrative* (MacMillan, 1965).

Rogat, Y., 'The Judge as Spectator' (1964) 31 *University of Chicago Law Review* 213.

Roht-Arriaza, N. and J. Mariezcurrena (eds), *Transitional Justice in the Twenty-First Century: Beyond Truth versus Justice* (Cambridge University Press, 2006).

Romano, C., A. Nollkaemper and J. K. Kleffner (eds), *Internationalized Criminal Courts and Tribunals: Sierra Leone, East Timor, Kosovo, and Cambodia* (Oxford University Press, 2004).

Rosenau, J., 'Governance in the Twenty-First Century' (1995) 1 *Global Governance* 13.

Rosenau, J. and E. Czempiel (eds), *Governance without Government: Order and Change in World Politics* (Cambridge University Press, 1992).

Rosenbaum, T., 'Essay: the romance of Nuremberg and the tease of moral justice' (2005) 27 *Cardozo L. Rev.* 1731.

Rosenthal, J., *Ethics and International Relations* (Routledge, 2017).

Rothe, D. L., *State Criminality: The crime of all crimes* (Lexington Books, 2009).

Ruggie, J., 'Global governance and "new governance theory": Lessons from business and human rights' (2014) 20 *Global Governance* 5.

Rupert, M., *Ideologies of Globalization: Contending visions of a new world order* (Routledge, 2012).

Ryngaert, C., *Jurisdiction in International Law*, 2nd edn (Oxford University Press, 2015).

Sadat, L. N., 'Codifying the "Laws of Humanity" and the "Dictates of the Public Conscience": Towards a New Global Treaty on Crimes Against Humanity', in M. Bergsmo and S. Tianying (eds), *On the Proposed Crimes Against Humanity Convention* (Torkel Opsahl Academic EPublisher 2014), pp. 17–46.

Saffa Abdulai, E., 'The Standoff between ICC and African Leaders Debate Revisited', in The Foundation for Law, Justice and Society (ed.), *Oxford Transitional Justice Research: Debating International Justice in Africa* (2010).

Saner, H., 'Karl Jaspers', *Encyclopaedia Britannica.*

Scanlon, T., *What We Owe to Each Other* (Belknap Press/Harvard University Press, 1998).

Schabas, W., *An Introduction to the International Criminal Court* (Cambridge University Press, 2011).

Schabas, W., 'Sentencing by international tribunals: a human rights approach' (1996) 7 *Duke J. Comp. & Int'l L.* 461.

Schabas, W., 'State Policy as an Element of International Crimes' (2008) 98 *Journal of Criminal Law and Criminology* 959.

Schabas, W., *The International Criminal Court: A Commentary on the Rome Statute* (Oxford University Press, 2017).

Schabas, W., 'Victor's Justice: Selecting Situations at the International Criminal Court' (2009) 43 *J. Marshall L. Rev.* 535.

Schabas, W., G. Simpson and S. Linton, *For the Sake of Present and Future Generations: Essays on International Law, Crime and Justice in Honour of Roger Clark* (Brill Nijhoff, 2016).

Schiff, J., 'Confronting Political Responsibility: The Problem of Acknowledgement' (2008) 23 *Hypatia* 99.

Schlütte, B., *Theory and Practice of the ICJ and the International ad hoc Tribunals for Rwanda and Yugloslavia* (Martinus Nijhoff, 2010).

Schnapper, D., *La communauté des citoyens* (Gallimard, 2003).

Schomerus, M., 'Small Arms Survey. The Lord's Resistance Army in Sudan: A History and Overview' (Geneva: Graduate Institute of International Studies, 2007).

Scott, S. D., *Law after Modernity* (Bloomsbury Publishing, 2013).

Sellars, K. (ed.), *Trials for International Crimes in Asia* (Cambridge University Press, 2016).

Seneca, *Melancholy*.

Seymour, D., 'From Auschwitz to Jerusalem to Gaza: Ethics for the Want of Law' (2011) 6 *Journal of Global Ethics* 205.

Shaffer, G., 'International Law and Global Public Goods in a Legal Pluralist World' (2012) 23 *European Journal of International Law* 669.
Shaffer, G., 'The New Empirical Turn in International Law Scholarship' (2014) 108 *Am. Soc'y Int'l L. Proc.* 369.
Shelton, D., 'International law and "relative normativity"' (2006) 2 *International Law* 159.
Shivji, I., 'Constructing a New Rights Regime: Promises, Problems and Prospects' (1999) 8 *Soc. & Legal Studies* 243.
Silcock Downie, R., 'Collective responsibility' (1969) 44 *Philosophy* 66.
Simbeye, Y., *Immunity and International Criminal Law* (Routledge, 2017).
Simpson, G., *Great Powers and Outlaw States: Unequal sovereigns in the international legal order*, vol. 32 (Cambridge University Press, 2004).
Simpson, G., *Law, War and Crime: War crimes, trials and the reinvention of international law* (Polity, 2007).
Simpson, G., 'The sentimental life of international law' (2015) 3 *London Review of International Law* 3.
Simpson, G., 'The situation on the international legal theory front: the power of rules and the rule of power' (2000) 11 *European Journal of International Law* 439.
Sinclair, I. McTaggart, *The Vienna Convention on the Law of Treaties*, 2nd edn (Manchester University Press, 1984).
Singer, M. and A. B. Wildavsky, *The Real World Order: Zones of peace, zones of turmoil* (Chatham House Pub., 1996).
Sivakumaran, S., 'The influence of teaching of publicists on the development of international law' (2017) 66 *Int. & Comp. Law Quarterly* 1.
Slaughter, A., *A New World Order* (Princeton University Press, 2009).
Slaughter, A., 'International Law in a World of Liberal States' (1995) 6 *European Journal of International Law* 1.
Slaughter, A., 'Judicial Globalization' (2000) 40 *Virginia Journal of International Law* 1103.
Slaughter, A. and W. Burke-White, 'An international constitutional moment' (2002) 43 *Harv. Int'l L. J.* 1.
Slaughter, A. and S. R. Ratner, 'Appraising the methods of international law: A prospectus for readers' (1999) 93 *Am. J. Int'l L.* 291.
Slaughter, A., A. S. Tulumello and S. Wood, 'International law and international relations theory: A new generation of interdisciplinary scholarship' (1998) *Am. J. Int'l L.* 367.
Smiley, M., 'From Moral Agency to Collective Wrongs: Rethinking Collective Moral Responsibility' (2010) 1 *Journal of Law and Policy* 171.

Smith, A., *Nationalism and Modernism* (Routledge, 2013).

Smith, A., *Nations and Nationalism in a Global Era* (John Wiley & Sons, 2013).

Smolkin, D., 'The Non-Identity Problem and the Appeal to Future People's Rights' (1994) 32 *Southern Journal of Philosophy* 315.

Stahn, C., 'Complementarity, amnesties and alternative forms of justice: some interpretative guidelines for the International Criminal Court' (2005) 3 *Journal of International Criminal Justice* 695.

Stark, B. (ed.), *International Law and its Discontents: Confronting Crises* (Cambridge University Press, 2015).

Starke, G. J., 'Monism and dualism in the theory of international law' (1936) 17 *Brit. Y. B. Int'l L.* 66.

Steinhoff, U., 'Rights, Liability and the Moral Equality of Combatants' (2012) 16 *Journal of Ethics* 339.

Stewart, L., 'International Justice in Africa: Defining Authority and Localizing the Global' (2017) *iCourts Working Paper Series No. 86*.

Stilz, A., 'Collective responsibility and the state' (2011) 19 *Journal of Political Philosophy* 190.

Sugarman, D., 'From Unimaginable to Possible: Spain, Pinochet and the Judicialization of Power' (2002) 3 *J. of Spanish Cult. Stud.* 107.

Sungi, S., 'Is it pragmatism or an injustice to victims? The use of plea bargaining in the International Criminal Court' (2015) 7 *Journal of Theoretical & Philosophical Criminology* 21.

Sverdlik, S., 'Collective Responsibility' (1987) 51 *Philosophical Studies* 61.

Tadros, V., 'Duty and Liability' (2012) 24 *Utilitas* 259.

Tadros, V., *The Ends of Harm: The Moral Foundations of Criminal Law* (Oxford University Press, 2011).

Tamanaha, B., 'A Non-Essentialist Version of Legal Pluralism' (2000) 27 *Journal of Law & Society* 296.

Tamanaha, B., 'The folly of the "social scientific" concept of legal pluralism' (1993) 20 *Journal of Law and Society* 192.

Tanaka, Y., Tim McCormack and Gerry Simpson (eds), *Beyond Victor's Justice? The Tokyo War Crimes Trial Revisited* (Martinus Nifhoff, 2010).

Tannsjo, T., 'The Myth of Innocence: On Collective Responsibility and Collective Punishment' (2007) 36 *Philosophical Papers* 295.

Taylor, D., 'Hannah Arendt on Judgment: Thinking for Politics' (2002) 10 *International Journal of Philosophical Studies* 151.

Tejan-Cole, A., 'The Complementary and Conflicting Relationship Between the Special Court for Sierra Leone and the Truth and Reconciliation Commission' (2003) 6 *Yale Hum. Rts. & Dev. L. J.* 139.

Teubner, G., *Constitutional Fragments: Societal constitutionalism and globalization* (Oxford University Press, 2012).

Teubner, G., '"Global Bukowina": Legal Pluralism in the World Society', in Gunther Teubner (ed.), *Global Law without a State* (Dartmouth Publishing, 1997).

Teubner, G. (ed.), *Global Law without a State* (Dartmouth Publishing, 1997).

Teubner, G., *Law as an Autopoietic System* (Blackwell Publishers, 1993).

Teubner, G., 'Societal Constitutionalism: Alternatives to State-Centered Constitutional Theory?', in Joerges, Sand and Teubner (eds), *Transnational Governance and Constitutionalism* (Hart, 2004).

Teubner, G., 'Substantive and reflexive elements in modern law' (1983) *Law and Society Review* 239.

Teubner, G., 'The Anonymous Matrix: Human Rights Violation by "Private" Transnational Actors' (2006) 69 *Mod. L. R.* 327.

Teubner, G., 'The King's Many Bodies: The Self-Deconstruction of Law's Hierarchy' (1997) 31 *Law & Soc. R.* 76.

Teubner, G., 'The two faces of Janus: Rethinking legal pluralism' (1991) 13 *Cardozo L. Rev.* 1443.

Therborn, G., 'Entangled Modernities' (2003) 6 *European Journal of Social Theory* 293.

Thompson, J., 'Collective Responsibility for Historic Injustices' (2006) 30 *Midwest Studies in Philosophy* 154.

Thuo Gathii, J., 'TWAIL: a brief history of its origins, its decentralized network, and a tentative bibliography' (2011) 3 *Trade L. & Dev.* 26.

Tinnevelt, R., 'Collective Responsibility, National Peoples and the International Order' (2009) 2 *Netherlands Journal of Legal Philosophy* 147.

Tomuschat, C., 'The legacy of Nuremberg' (2006) 4 *Journal of International Criminal Justice* 830.

Toufayan, M., 'When British Justice (in African Colonies) Points Two Ways: On Dualism, Hybridity, and the Genealogy of Juridical Negritude in Taslim Olawale Elias', in *African Legal Theory and Contemporary Problems* (Springer Netherlands, 2014), pp. 31–70.

Trubek, D., Y. Dezalay, R. Buchanan and John R. Davis, 'Global Restructuring and the Law: Studies of the Internationalization of Legal Fields and the Creation of Transnational Arenas' (1993) 44 *Case W. Res. L. Rev.* 407.

Trubek, D., J. Mosher and J. S. Rothstein, 'Transnationalism in the Regulation of Labor Relations' (2000) 25 *Law & Social Inquiry* 1187.

Trubek, D. and L. G. Trubek, 'Hard and Soft Law in the Construction of Social Europe: The Role of the Open Method of Co-ordination' (2005) 11 *European Law Journal* 343.

Tully, J., *Strange Multiplicity: Constitutionalism in an age of diversity* (Cambridge University Press, 1995).

Tuomela, R., *The Philosophy of Sociality: The Shared Point of View* (Oxford University Press, 2007).

Tuomela, R., 'We-intentions revisited' (2005) 125 *Philosophical Studies* 327.

Tuomela, R. and K. Miller, 'We-intentions' (1988) 53 *Philosophical Studies* 367.

Turley, J., 'Dualistic Values in the Age of International Legisprudence' (1993) 44 *Hastings Law Journal* 185.

Turner, J. I., 'Transnational networks and international criminal justice' (2007) 105 *Michigan Law Review* 985.

Tyner, D., 'Internationalization of War Crimes Prosecutions: Correcting the International Criminal Tribunal for the Former Yugoslavia's Folly in Tadic' (2006) 18 *Fla. J. Int'l L.* 843.

Unger, R. M., *The Critical Legal Studies Movement: Another Time, a Greater Task* (Verso Books, 2015).

Usami, M., 'Retroactive justice: trials for human rights violations under a prior regime', in Burton Leiser and Tom Campbell (eds), *Human Rights in Philosophy and Practice* (Routledge, 2001).

Vagts, D. F., 'Hegemonic International Law' (2001) 95 *Am. J. Int'l L.* 843.

Vagts, D. F., 'International Law in the Third Reich' (1990) 84 *Am. J. Int'l L.* 661.

van der Wilt, H., 'Complementary Jurisdiction (Article 46H)', in *The African Criminal Court* (TMC Asser Press, 2017).

Van Ness, D. W. and K. Heetderks Strong, *Restoring Justice: An Introduction to Restorative Justice*, 5th edn (Routledge, 2014).

van Sliedregt, E. and S. Vasiliev (eds), *Pluralism in International Criminal Law* (Oxford University Press, 2014).

Vasiliev, S., 'On Trajectories and Destinations of International Criminal Law Scholarship' (2015) 28 *Leiden Journal of International Law* 701.

Velleman, D. J., 'What Happens When Someone Acts?' (1992) 101 *Mind* 461.

Vernon, R., 'What is a Crime against Humanity?' (2002) 10 *Journal of Political Philosophy* 242.

Villa, D., 'From the Critique of Identity to Plurality of Politics: Reconsidering Adorno and Arendt', in Lars Rensmann and Samir Gandesha (eds), *Arendt and Adorno: Political and Philosophical Investigations* (Stanford University Press, 2012).

Villiger, M. E., *Commentary on the 1969 Vienna Convention on the Law of Treaties* (Brill, 2009).

Villiger, M. E., *Customary international law and treaties: a study of their interactions and interrelations, with special consideration of the 1969 Vienna Convention on the Law of Treaties* vol. 7 (Brill Publishers,1985).

Voeten, E., 'Competition and Complementarity between Global and Regional Human Rights Institutions' (2017) 8 *Global Policy* 119.

von Benda-Beckmann, F., 'Who's afraid of legal pluralism?' (2002) 34 *Journal of Legal Pluralism and Unofficial Law* 37.

von Benda-Beckmann, F. and K. von Benda-Beckmann, *Mobile People, Mobile Law: Expanding legal relations in a contracting world* (Routledge, 2017).

Wai, R., 'In the Name of the International: The Supreme Court of Canada and the Internationalist Transformation of Canadian Private International Law' (2001) 39 *Canadian Yearbook of International Law* 117.

Wald, P., 'Genocide and crimes against humanity' (2007) 6 *Wash. U. Global Stud. L. Rev.* 621.

Walkinshaw, R., 'The Nuremberg and Tokyo trials: another step toward international justice' (1949) 35 *American Bar Association Journal* 299.

Wallace, J. R., *Responsibility and the Moral Sentiments* (Harvard University Press, 1984).

Wallach, D., 'The Irrationality of Universal Civil Jurisdiction' (2014) 46 *Geo. J. Int'l L.* 803.

Wallerstein, I., *Modern World-System in the Longue Durée* (Routledge, 2015).

Wallerstein, I., *The modern world-system I: Capitalist agriculture and the origins of the European world-economy in the sixteenth century, with a new prologue* (University of California Press, 2011).

Walsh, W. H., 'Pride, Shame and Responsibility' (1970) 20 *The Philosophical Quarterly* 1.

Webb, C., 'What is Unjust Enrichment?' (2009) 29 *Oxford Journal of Legal Studies* 215.

Weeramantry, C., *Universalising International Law*, vol. 48 (Martinus Nijhoff Publishers, 2014).

Wehberg, H., 'Pacta sunt servanda' (1959) 53 *Am. J. of Int'l L.* 775.

Weiss, T. (ed.), *The United Nations and changing world politics* (Westview Press, 2016).

Weissner, S., 'Law as a Means to a Public Order of Human Dignity: The Jurisprudence of Michael Reisman' (2009) 34 *Yale J. Int'l L.* 525.

Welch, D., *Justice and the Genesis of War* (Cambridge University Press, 1993).

Wellens, K., 'Diversity in secondary rules and the unity of international law: some reflections on current trends' (1994) 25 *Netherlands Yearbook of International Law* 3.

Wellens, K., 'Fragmentation of International Law and Establishing an Accountability Regime for International Organizations: The Role of the Judiciary in Closing the Gap' (2003) 25 *Mich. J. Int'l L.* 1160.

Wellens, K., *Negotiations in the Case Law of the International Court of Justice: A Functional Analysis* (Routledge, 2016).

Wellman, C., *A Theory of Rights: Persons under Laws, Institutions and Morals* (Rowman & Allanheld, 1985).

Werle, G., *Principles of International Criminal Law* (Oxford University Press, 2005).

Werle, G. and F. Jessberger, *Principles of International Criminal Law* (Oxford University Press, 2014).

Wickremasinghe, C. and M. D. Evans, 'Case concerning the Arrest Warrant of 11 April 2000 (Democratic Republic of the Congo v. Belgium)' (2001) 50 *Int'l and Comp. Law Quarterly* 670.

Williams, G., 'No Participation without Implication: Understanding the Wrongs We Do Together' (2002) 8 *Res Publica* 201.

Williams, R. E. and D. Caldwell, '*Jus post bellum*: Just war theory and the principles of just peace' (2006) 7 *International Studies Perspectives* 309.

Williams, S., 'The Extraordinary African Chambers in the Senegalise Courts: An African Solution to an African Problem?' (2013) 15 *J. of Int. Crim. J.* 1139.

Wojcikiewicz Almeida, P. and J. Sorel (eds), *Latin America and the International Court of Justice: Contributions to International Law* (Routledge, 2016).

Wolfe, R., 'Flaws in the Nuremberg Legacy: An Impediment to International War Crimes Tribunals' Prosecution of Crimes against Humanity' (1998) 12 *Holocaust and Genocide Studies* 434.

Woodward, J., 'The non-identity problem' (1986) 96 *Ethics* 804.

Wringe, B., 'Why punish war crimes? Victor's justice and expressive justifications of punishment' (2006) 25 *Law and Philosophy* 159.

Xavier, S., 'False Universalism of Global Governance Theories: Global Constitutionalism, Global Administrative Law, International Criminal Institutions & the Global South' (dissertation, Osgoode Hall Law School Toronto, Ontario, 2015).

Yablonka, H., 'The development of Holocaust consciousness in Israel: The Nuremberg, kapos, Kastner, and Eichmann trials' (2003) 8 *Israel Studies* 1.

Young, M. I., 'Responsibility and Global Justice: A Social Connection Model' (2006) 23 *Social Philosophy and Policy* 102.

Young, M. I., *Responsibility for Justice* (Oxford University Press, 2011).

Zacher, M., H. N. Brehm and J. Savelsberg, 'NGOs, IOs, and the ICC: Diagnosing and Framing Darfur' (2014) 29 *Sociological Forum* 1.

Zammit, N., *Human Rights and Responsibility* (Connaissances et savoirs, 2012).

Ziemele, I., *Reservations to Human Rights Treaties and the Vienna Convention Regime: Conflict, Harmony or Reconciliation* (Springer, 2013).

Zoller, D., 'Moral Responsibility for Distant Collective Harms' (2015) 18 *Ethical Theory and Moral Practice* 995.

Zumbansen, P., 'Defining the space of transnational law: legal theory, global governance, and legal pluralism' (2012) 21 *Transnat'l L. & Contemp. Probs.* 305.

Zumbansen, P., 'Law after the welfare state: Formalism, functionalism, and the ironic turn of reflexive law' (2008) 56 *American Journal of Comparative Law* 769.

Zumbansen, P., 'The law of society: governance through contract' (2007) 14 *Indiana Journal of Global Legal Studies* 191.

Zumbansen, P., 'Transnational Law', in *The Encyclopedia of Comparative Law* (Edward Elgar 2006), pp. 738–54.

Zumbansen, P., 'Transnational legal pluralism' (2010) 1 *Transnational Legal Theory* 141.

Legal Documents

1. Mary Kimani, *Pursuit of Justice or Western Plot*? Online: UN Africal Renewal, *https://www.un.org/africarenewal/magazine/october-2009/*
2. *Charter*, Online: Doctors Without Borders, *https://www.doctorswithoutborders.org/who-we-are/principles/charter*
3. *Sudan elections put back to 2010*, Online: BBC News, *http://news.bbc.co.uk/2/hi/7980032.stm*
4. *Al-Mahdi, Sadig*, Online: World Leadership Alliance: Club Madrid, *http://www.clubmadrid.org/miembro/sadig-al-mahdi/*
5. *The ICC, Sudan, and the Crisis of Human Rights*, Online: African Arguments Online, *https://africanarguments.org/2009/03/05/the-icc-sudan-and-the-crisis-of-human-rights/*
6. *Rule-of-Law Tools for Post-Conflict States: Maximizing the Legacy of Hybrid Courts*, Online: Office of the United Nations High Commissioner for Human Rights, *https://www.ohchr.org/Documents/Publications/HybridCourts.pdf*

7. *Article 16: Questions and Answers*, Online: Human Rights Watch: The Rome Statute in the Darfur Context, *https://www.hrw.org/news/2008/08/15/article-16*
8. *Nuremberg Trial Proceedings Vol. 1: Charter of the Nuremberg Military Tribunal*, Online: Yale Law School: Lillian Goldman Law Library, *https://avalon.law.yale.edu/imt/imtconst.asp*
9. UN General Assembly, *Statute of the International Court of Justice*, Can TS 7 (1945), Art. 38 para. 1
10. *Extraordinary Chambers in the Courts of Cambodia*, Online: *https://www.eccc.gov.kh/en*
11. *Millennium 2000: Would an International Criminal Court Help or Hinder Pursuit of Global Justice*, Online: CNN Transcripts, *http://transcripts.cnn.com/TRANSCRIPTS/0001/02/bp.00.html*
12. Online: International Criminal Court: Situations and Cases, *https://www.icc-cpi.int/Pages/Main.aspx*
13. *DR Congo warlord Thomas Lubanga sentenced to 14 years*, Online: BBC News, *https://www.bbc.com/news/world-africa-18779726*
14. *Germain Katanga & Mathieu Ngudjolo Chui*, Online: International Justice Monitor: *https://www.ijmonitor.org/category/germain-katanga-and-mathieu-ngudjolo-chui/*
15. *The Prosecutor v. Germain Katanga and Matieu Ngudjolo Chiu: Decision on the confirmation of charges*, Online: International Criminal Court (ICC), *https://www.icc-cpi.int/Pages/record.aspx?docNo=ICC-01/04-01/07-717*
16. Julius Ocen, *Can Traditional Rituals Bring Justice to Northern Uganda?* Online: the Institute for War and Peace Reporting (IWPR), *https://iwpr.net/global-voices/can-traditional-rituals-bring-justice-northern-uganda*
17. UN General Assembly, *Rome Statute of the International Criminal Court (last amended 2010)*, 17 July 1998, Art. 17, para. 1, online: *https://www.icc-cpi.int/nr/rdonlyres/ea9aeff7-5752-4f84-be94-0a655eb30e16/0/rome_statute_english.pdf*
18. UN General Assembly, *Rome Statute of the International Criminal Court (last amended 2010)*, 17 July 1998 Part X, online: *https://www.icc-cpi.int/nr/rdonlyres/ea9aeff7-5752-4f84-be94-0a655eb30e16/0/rome_statute_english.pdf*
19. *International and Hybrid Criminal Courts and Tribunals*, Online: United Nations and the Rule of Law, *https://www.un.org/ruleoflaw/thematic-areas/international-law-courts-tribunals/international-hybrid-criminal-courts-tribunals/*

20. Princeton Project on Universal Jurisdiction, *The Princeton Principles on Universal Jurisdiction* (Princeton University Press, 2001)
21. Ruben Sindahl, *Belgium court orders arrest of former Israel top official for war crimes*, Online: Jurist, *https://www.jurist.org/news/2017/01/belgium-court-orders-arrest-of-former-israel-top-official-for-war-crimes/*
22. *Crimes Against Humanity and War Crimes Act*, SC 2000, c. 24.
23. *Her Majesty the Queen v. Désiré Munyaneza*, Superior Court, Criminal Division, No. 500-73-002500-052, 22 May 2009.
24. Norimitsu Onishi, *South Africa Reverses Withdrawal from International Criminal Court*, Online: *The New York Times*, *https://www.nytimes.com/2017/03/08/world/africa/south-africa-icc-withdrawal.html?_r=0*
25. *Charter of the United Nations*, c. VII
26. Law on the Establishment of the Extraordinary Chambers in the Courts of Cambodia for the Prosecution of Crimes Committed During the Period of Democratic Kampuchea, NS/RKM/1004/006 (2004), Art. 5
27. Nuon Chea (ECCC-002/14-08-2006), Provisional Detention Order, 19 September 2007, para. 5
28. *The Hague Conventions on the Laws and Customs of War on Land* (1899), Preamble.
29. *Prosecutor v Dusko Tadic (Judgment)*, IT-94-1-A, International Criminal Tribunal for the former Yugoslavia (ICTY), 15 July 1999
30. *Prosecutor v. Dusko Tadic (Appeal Judgment)*, IT-94-1-A, International Criminal Tribunal for the former Yugoslavia (ICTY),15 July 1999
31. *Malabo Protocol: Legal and Institutional Implications of the Merged and Expanded African Court* (London, UK: Amnesty International Ltd, 2016), Online: *https://www.amnesty.org/download/Documents/AFR0130632016ENGLISH.PDF*
32. *Press Conference to Launch the African Union Campaign to Restore the Dignity of Women and for Accountability in South Sudan (#4WomenofSouthSudan)*, Online: African Union, *https://au.int/en/newsevents/31469/press-conference-launch-african-union-campaign-restore-dignity-women-and*
33. *Bineta Diop, Special Envoy on Women, Peace, and Security*, Online: African Union, Peace and Security Dept., *http://www.peaceau.org/en/page/40-5676-static-bineta-diop*
34. Mark Kersten, *The Hybrid Court for South Sudan? Looking for a Way Forward (Part 2)*, Online: Justice in Conflict, *https://justiceinconflict.org/2017/02/28/the-hybrid-court-for-south-sudan-looking-for-a-way-forward-part-2/*

35. *Final Report of the African Commission of Inquiry on South Sudan* (Addis Ababa, Ethiopia: 15 October 2004), Online: *http://www.peaceau.org/en/article/final-report-of-the-african-union-commission-of-inquiry-on-south-sudan*
36. *Commission on Human Rights in South Sudan*, Online: United Nations Human Rights Council: Independent Investigations, *https://www.ohchr.org/EN/HRBodies/HRC/CoHSouthSudan/Pages/Index.aspx*
37. *Sudan: Events of 2016*, Online: Human Rights Watch: World Report 2017, *https://www.hrw.org/world-report/2017/country-chapters/sudan*
38. *Agreement on the Resolution of the Conflict in the Republic of South Sudan* (Addis Ababa, Ethiopia: Intergovernmental Authority on Development, 2015), Online: *https://unmiss.unmissions.org/sites/default/files/final_proposed_compromise_agreement_for_south_sudan_conflict.pdf*
39. *African Union Approves Immunity for Government Officials in Amendment to African Court of Justice and Human Rights Statute*, Online: International Justice Resource Center, *https://ijrcenter.org/2014/07/02/african-union-approves-immunity-for-heads-of-state-in-amendment-to-african-court-of-justice-and-human-rights-statute/*
40. *AU Strategy for Collective Withdrawal from the ICC a Non-Starter*, Online: International Center for Transitional Justice (ICTJ), *https://www.ictj.org/news/au-withdrawal-icc-non-starter*
41. 'Assessment of Justice, Accountability and Reconciliation Measures in South Sudan: Final Report and Recommendations' (Washington, DC: American Bar Association, 2014), Online: *http://www.americanbar.org/content/dam/aba/directories/roli/sudan/aba_roli_sudan_assessment_final_report_0614.authcheckdam.pdf*
42. UN General Assembly, *Rome Statute of the International Criminal Court (last amended 2010)*, 17 July 1998, Preamble
43. *Law No. 64: Nazi and Nazi Collaborators (Punishment) Law, 1950*, Online: International Committee of the Red Cross, *https://ihl-databases.icrc.org/applic/ihl/ihl-nat.nsf/0/9D6164171FA43DE7C12575AE0034A437*
44. *The Eichmann Trial – Proceedings: The 15 Charges*, Online: Remember.org, *http://remember.org/eichmann/charges*
45. 'What is Transitional Justice?' in *A Voice for Victims* (New York: International Center for Transitional Justice Annual Report 2004/2005), p. 1
46. Corrigendum of the Decision Pursuant to Article 15 of the Rome Statute on the Authorization of an Investigation into the Situation in the Republic of Kenya, ICC-01/09-19-Corr, para. 89

47. 'Charter of the International Military Tribunal (IMT)', in Agreement for the Prosecution and Punishment of the Major War Criminals of the European Axis (London Agreement), 8 August 1945, 58 Stat. 1544, E.A.S. No. 472, 82 U.N.T.S. 280, Art. 6(c)
48. *Trial of the Major War Criminals before the International Military Tribunal: Nuremberg 14 November 1945 – 1 October 1946* (Nuremberg, Germany: International Military Tribunal, 1947) at 171
49. *Cases By Name*, Online: International Criminal Database (ICD), *http://www.internationalcrimesdatabase.org/Cases/ByName*
50. *Nuremberg Trials Final Report Appendix D: Control Council Law No. 10*, Online: Yale Law School, *http://avalon.law.yale.edu/imt/imt10.asp*
51. *Draft Code of Crimes against the Peace and Security of Mankind with Commentaries* (1996), Online: *http://legal.un.org/ilc/texts/instruments/english/commentaries/7_4_1996.pdf*
52. *Commentary on the Rome Statute, Art. 5*, Online: Case Matrix Network, *https://www.casematrixnetwork.org/cmn-knowledge-hub/icc-commentary-clicc/commentary-rome-statute/commentary-rome-statute-part-2-articles-5-10/*
53. Yoriko Otomo, 'The Decision Not to Prosecute the Emperor' in Yuki Tanaka, Tim McCormack and Gerry Simpson (eds), *Beyond Victor's Justice? The Tokyo War Crimes Trial Revisited* (Leiden: Martinus Nijhoff Publishers, 2010), p. 63
54. UN General Assembly, *Rome Statute of the International Criminal Court (last amended 2010)*, 17 July 1998, Art. 7
55. UN General Assembly, *Rome Statute of the International Criminal Court (last amended 2010)*, 17 July 1998, Art. 7(2)(a)
56. *R v Pinochet* [1998] UKHL 41, [2000] AC 61, Judgment, Online: *https://publications.parliament.uk/pa/ld199899/ldjudgmt/jd990115/pino01.htm*
57. General Assembly resolution 377 (V), *Uniting for Peace*, A/RES/377 (3 December 1950), available from *https://unispal.un.org/DPA/DPR/unispal.nsf/0/55C2B84DA9E0052B05256554005726C6*
58. United Nations, General Assembly, *The Rule of Law and Transitional Justice in Conflict and Post-conflict Societies*, S/2004/616 (23 August 2004)
59. *Chambers*, Online: The United Nations International Criminal Tribunal for the Former Yugoslavia, *https://www.icty.org/en/about/chambers*
60. *Vienna Convention on the Law of Treaties*, 1969, United Nations, Treaty Series, Vol. 1155 at p. 331
61. *Statute of the International Tribunal for Rwanda*, 2007

62. *Statute of the International Criminal Court*, UN Doc. A/CONF.183/9 (1998), Art. 1 and Art. 17
63. Project on International Courts and Tribunals (PICT), Online: WorldLII, *http://www.pict-pcti.org/courts/hybrid.html*
64. *International Law Commission's Draft Code on Crimes Against the Peace and Security of Mankind*, ILC 1996, art. 18
65. *The Charter and Judgment of the Nürnberg Tribunal – History and Analysis: Memorandum*, Online: United Nations Digital Library, *https://digital library.un.org/record/160809?ln=en*
66. Moses Crispus, 'The False Polarization of Peace and Justice in Uganda' (Nuremberg: 2007)
67. *Draft Code of Crimes against the Peace and Security of Mankind with Commentaries, 1996*, Online: UN Legal Department, *https://legal.un.org/ilc/texts/instruments/english/commentaries/7_4_1996.pdf*
68. Guido Acquavia, *Forced Displacement and International Crimes*, online: *https://www.refworld.org/pdfid/4e09a5622.pdf*
69. *The Law on the Establishment of the Extraordinary Chambers in the Courts of Cambodia (ECCC)*, 2004, art. 5
70. *The Statute of the International Criminal Tribunal for Rwanda (ICTR)*, UNSC 1994, art. 3.
71. *Bazley v Curry* [1999] SCR 534 [*Bazley*]
72. *Lister v Hesley Hall Ltd* [2001] UKHL 22 [*Lister*]

Human Rights Watch report at *http://thewe.cc/contents/more/archive2003/july/belgium_law_on_atrocities.pdf* (accessed 25 May 2020)

http://sn4hr.org/wpcontent/pdf/english/Crimes_against_humanity_forced_displacement_for_Daraya_en.pdf (accessed 25 May 2020)

Haaretz article, dated 31 October 2009, http://www.haaretz.com/hasen/pages/ShArt.jhtml?itemNo=262391&contrassID=2&subContrassID=1&sbSub ContrassID=0&listSrc=Y (accessed 25 May 2020)

Index

J

K

S

T